NICHOLAS D. KRISTOF

AND SHERYL WUDUNN

CHINA WAKES

Nicholas D. Kristof grew up on a sheep and cherry farm near Yamhill, Oregon, and began his reporting career as a high school sophomore covering agriculture for the county semiweekly newspaper. He graduated from Harvard College in three years, Phi Beta Kappa, then studied law at Oxford University on a Rhodes Scholarship. After graduating with first class honors, he studied Arabic for a year in Cairo and joined *The New York Times* in 1984 as an economics reporter. He was Los Angeles financial correspondent for *The Times* before becoming Hong Kong bureau chief in 1986 and Beijing bureau chief in 1988.

Sheryl WuDunn, a third-generation Chinese-American who grew up in New York City, graduated with honors from Cornell University and worked as an international loan officer for Bankers Trust Company for three years. She then went to Harvard Business School, where she earned her M.B.A., and to Princeton University, where she earned a master's of public administration in international affairs. Her interests switched to journalism, and she worked for several major newspapers before joining *The New York Times* as a correspondent in Beijing.

Kristof and WuDunn were married in 1988 and have two sons: Gregory, born in 1992, and Geoffrey, born in May 1994. Kristof and WuDunn won the Pulitzer Prize for their coverage of the 1989 Tiananmen protests in China, becoming the first married couple ever to win a Pulitzer for journalism. Their China coverage also won them the George Polk Award for foreign reporting. They are now correspondents in Tokyo for *The New York Times*.

CHINA WAKES

THE STRUGGLE FOR THE SOUL OF A RISING POWER

When China wakes, it will shake the world.
—Attributed to Napoleon Bonaparte

NICHOLAS D. KRISTOF

AND SHERYL WUDUNN

VINTAGE BOOKS
A DIVISION OF RANDOM HOUSE, INC. NEW YORK

For Our Parents, Ladis and Jane Kristof
and David and Alice WuDunn,
and for Sirena WuDunn (1962–1983)

FIRST VINTAGE BOOKS EDITION, AUGUST 1995

Copyright © 1994 by Nicholas D. Kristof and Sheryl WuDunn
Maps copyright © 1994 by Anita Karl and Jim Kemp

Portions of this work were originally published in different form in *Foreign Affairs* and *The New York Times Magazine*.

The Library of Congress has cataloged the Times Books edition as follows:
Kristof, Nicholas D.
China wakes : the struggle for the soul of a rising power / Nicholas D. Kristof and
Sheryl WuDunn.
p. cm.
Includes index.
ISBN 0-8129-2252-2 (alk. paper)
1. China—Economic conditions—1976– 2. China—Social conditions—1976–
3. China—Politics and government—1976–
I. WuDunn, Sheryl. II. Title.
HC427.92.K75 1994
306'.0951—dc20 94-10609
Vintage ISBN: 0-679-76393-7

Chinese calligraphy by Chingan Tang

Manufactured in the United States of America
1 0

AUTHORS' NOTE

Our foremost concern in writing this book has been to protect our Chinese friends and acquaintances. Too many Chinese are already languishing in jail because foreigners were insufficiently careful, and we have no desire to add to the prison crowding problem.

Consequently, we have changed the names of some Chinese sources. Whenever we give a one-word name—such as Hongjun, who spied on us—it is a pseudonym. When we give a full name— such as Lin Hanxiong, the government minister who could not control his libido—it is a real one.

As will become clear, Nick wrote Chapter 1 and the subsequent odd-numbered chapters, while Sheryl wrote Chapter 2 and the other even-numbered ones (except for the last chapter, which we wrote together). As our two lives have been independent yet intertwined, it seemed best to write in the same way.

CONTENTS

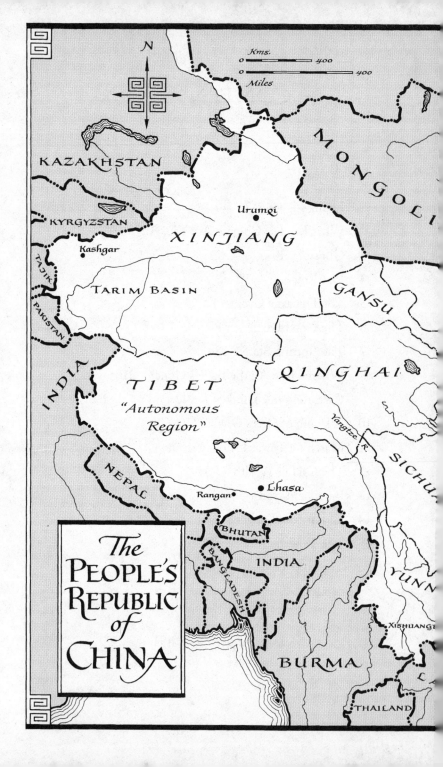

CHINA WAKES

NICHOLAS D. KRISTOF

紀思道

飛鴿

FLYING
PIGEON

Be sure to prevent any contact between the barbarians and the population.

—Emperor Qianlong, October 11, 1793,
ordering the authorities to keep foreign
visitors from talking to Chinese

1

ang Chigang, an illiterate peasant who early in life was a beggar, wonders what is in store for his
eat-grandson. [Photo by Nicholas D. Kristof.]

What do you say to a crumpled young woman after she has seen her brother beaten to death with iron pipes?

"Did he die right there?" I asked. "On the floor?"

Tang Rimei sniffed and nodded. Twenty-three years old, she is tall and thin, with a mouth that naturally perks upward at the sides, as if it were made to smile. But now, as she recounts what happened to her in the southern Chinese city of Shenzhen, she sniffs as if she is about to burst into tears. In her brief career as a dissident, whistle-blower, prisoner, and fugitive, she took on the Chinese state and won—but at the price of her brother's life. A handful of potbellied British businessmen were relaxing across from us in the Dragon Bar in Hong Kong, their ties loosened and their curiosity aroused. They heard me speaking Chinese to a teary young woman, who would have been attractive if her eyes hadn't been so puffy, and they whispered to one another that a romance must be breaking up.

"So what happened when you called the police?" I was resolved to press on. I cocked my pen and prepared to scribble her answer in my notebook.

"I phoned the police station and shouted at them that some thugs had come to murder me," Tang said softly in a numbed voice. "But they said, 'Oh, we know about this. It's not our affair.' The police station was only three minutes away, but no one came. And while I was pleading with them, the telephone operator cut off the phone line. The Boss had connections at the telephone office. By that time, the thugs had smashed open the door."

Tang paused to steady herself, and I pushed the cup of coffee in front of her. She hadn't taken even a sip, and she didn't touch it now.

"My big brother tried to protect me, so they hit him with their iron bars. I was screaming, 'Help! Help!' They hit me a little bit, but because my big brother was protecting me they mostly hit him. Then some people came by, and they got scared and ran away.

"My big brother was bloody and lying on the floor. He was still breathing, but he had no reactions. I was pleading for people to help. Finally, after fifty minutes, the police came and took my big brother to the hospital. By that time, he had stopped breathing. He was dead."

It was time for me to ask a question, but for a long moment I simply sat there, tensed, my fingers clamped around the pen, as I struggled to contain my feelings. So much in China followed the principle *leigong da doufu,* "the God of Thunder smashes the tofu." In other words, the powerful crush the weak. Sheryl and I saw so much tofu crushed while we were in China . . .

But more of that later. I'm getting ahead of my story.

The first thing I ever did in China was illegal, and it's been a tussle with the authorities ever since.

It was a dazzling morning in July 1983, the sun rising over the wheat fields and bare brown hills on either side of the train carrying me from Mongolia. I was a freshly minted lawyer, just graduated from university in England and now traveling (the long way) back to my home in Oregon. Under the rules then prevailing for tourists in China, I was not allowed to get off the train until I reached Beijing. But the first stop was Datong, a city famous for its 1,500-year-old carved Buddhas, some as high as a four-story building. The train chugged to a halt in the station, and a load of Chinese passengers got off. It seemed a pity to miss such a sight.

"So?" I asked my traveling companion, Tim McCourt. "What would happen if we got off? Do you think they'd ever catch us?"

We peeked through the train windows. Crowds of Chinese were milling on the platform, running this way and that, occasionally into one another, lugging cardboard boxes and burlap sacks and a few antique suitcases. It looked terribly alluring.

"They'll probably never know," Tim said thoughtfully.

We grabbed our backpacks and slinked to the west end of the train car, away from the hulking attendant guarding the door at the east end. When he was looking away, we leaped off the train and hurried down the platform in the other direction, as nonchalantly as is possible when you're dwarfed by a huge blue backpack. We raced through the exit and only stopped to catch our breath a few minutes later, in the huge plaza outside the train station. Our trans-Siberian train was pulling out of the station, and no policemen were running after us. We had escaped without getting caught!

I looked around to see if anyone had noticed us. They had.

Several hundred Chinese peasants and workers were gathered in the huge square, mostly sitting on the concrete to wait for trains, surrounded by hillocks of burlap sacks and plastic suitcases. Almost everyone was wearing a Mao suit and sandals, and on the adjacent streets there were no cars—just a few buses and a stream of identical black, single-speed bicycles. Every person in sight was staring at us. Most were poking each other and pointing at our backpacks with expressions of amazement, yanking back children who were scrambling toward us.

I felt like Alice in Wonderland. I had stepped off the train, made a brief dash, and ended up in an entirely different world. Not only were there no other Westerners around but there were no Cokes, no *Newsweek*s, no English letters, no sign that the West even existed. The people were chattering about us, and their tonal roller coaster sounded as if it belonged to another planet. I had backpacked through Africa, India, and the Middle East, but never before had I felt quite such a sense of landing in a different universe.

That evening Tim and I wandered into a little restaurant and were shown a chalkboard filled with gibberish. The waitress pointed impatiently to it and launched a soliloquy of what sounded like monosyllabic screeches. We decided that the chalkboard was a menu, but we had no idea what was what. We tried clucking like a chicken, to order sweet and sour chicken, but the waiters didn't understand; apparently even chicken noises were different in China. So we randomly ordered three dishes and sat at a sagging old table beside a group of drunken young men. Soon our dishes came out: a bowl of bamboo shoots, a bottle of sorghum liquor, and a plate of something that I am convinced was mealworms.

That experience of backpacking around China for three weeks cured me of any long-lasting affection for the Middle Kingdom—or so I thought. Life beyond the Bamboo Curtain was fascinating, exotic, and redolent of smells and sights and sounds I had never encountered before, but it was not for me. I went off to study Arabic in Cairo and then joined *The New York Times* as an economics writer in 1984. A year later, *The Times* posted me in Los Angeles to write about business, and there I met someone who professed to love to hear my China horror stories. We were set up by a mutual friend, Eileen, who told me in advance all about her: "She's gorgeous, dark haired, very smart, and she's just graduated from Harvard Business

School. She's worked for *The Miami Herald,* and this summer she's working for *The Wall Street Journal.* . . ." But when I met Sheryl I had to stifle a laugh: The one thing that Eileen hadn't said was the most obvious—that Sheryl is a Chinese-American. Eileen was so concerned with not being racist that she studiously ignored Sheryl's race.

China was the last thing on my mind then. My interests (other than Sheryl) were Africa, Europe, and the Middle East. Aside from my trip through China, I had had hardly any exposure to the country or anything related to it. I grew up on a sheep and cherry farm four miles from the town of Yamhill, Oregon, population 640, where my parents still live, but there were no Asian kids in the local high school. At Harvard College, I studied government, but my Asian interests were limited to excursions with friends to a bar called the Hong Kong. At Oxford University, I nominally studied law while devoting a good bit of time to reading about and visiting Eastern Europe, Africa, and India. China seemed too remote and forbidding, shrouded by a complex language and by names that all sounded the same.

So although I thought Sheryl was terrific, there was a problem in our relationship: I wanted to become a foreign correspondent in a place like Egypt or the Ivory Coast, whereas Sheryl wanted to go to Asia. In a non-Cartesian proof that there is a God, the foreign editor of *The New York Times* out of the blue proposed in the fall of 1986 that the newspaper make me Hong Kong bureau chief. A few weeks later I was ensconced in the plush Mandarin Hotel next to the Hong Kong Harbor. I had begun my career as a China watcher.

Sheryl came out to Hong Kong the next summer to work for Reuters and then the *South China Morning Post.* We traveled together around Guangdong Province in southern China, and in our visits we could feel the excitement as the region shed its old form, the way a caterpillar turns into a butterfly. That fall of 1987, Guangdong already had one of the most dynamic economies in the world. Among those leading that charge was Liu Shuji, the Communist Party secretary in the bustling town of Dongguan, where toy and shoe factories sprouted from the rice paddies. When we met him, Liu was still wearing a Mao jacket, but his main job was to promote foreign investment. He laughed about his past as a leader of Mao's Red Guards, and he said that now his favorite economist was Milton Friedman.

It was an exhilarating environment, and I was delighted when the *Times*'s foreign editor called up and asked if I wanted to be the next Beijing bureau chief. So in December 1987, *The Times* sent me to Taiwan to study Chinese full-time, in preparation for Beijing. A few weeks later, Sheryl and I took a vacation in Indonesia and hiked up to the lip of Mt. Bromo, an active volcano. As smoke belched out I asked her to marry me. The ground trembled, but it may just have been the volcano.

We were married in October 1988 and started our lives together in China a few weeks later. It was our honeymoon. That was the most open time in Communist Chinese history, a great time to be a reporter in Beijing. We soon met a pudgy, sloppily dressed Chinese reporter named Zhang Weiguo, and we began seeing him regularly. A lawyer by training, Zhang was the senior journalist in Beijing for the *World Economic Herald,* the most daring newspaper in the country. Its cluttered offices, right behind the Forbidden City, were a campaign headquarters for political and economic reform.

Whenever we dropped by to see Zhang Weiguo and the other journalists there, we stumbled across some eminent professor or official chatting about change or dropping off a manuscript. Someone would pour us a cup of lukewarm tea, and we would end up spending hours talking about policy and power struggles in Zhongnanhai, the red-walled leadership compound less than a mile away.

We felt welcome in China, and we relished the chance to burrow into Chinese society and *bao jiaozi,* or make dumplings, with our friends in their cramped kitchens. We went native: We spoke more Chinese than English, we listened to Chinese music, we watched Chinese films. We felt a growing excitement at the change sweeping across the nation, a deepening affection for the country itself.

Then, seven months after we arrived, during the predawn hours of June 4, 1989, I stood at the north end of Tiananmen Square and watched China go mad. For several hours that night I looked on as the People's Liberation Army fired on pro-democracy demonstrators—and on me. I wasn't hit, but some around me were. I saw the bodies crumple. I watched the blood pour out. I ran the three miles back home, filed the story that would be bannered across *The New York Times* front page a few hours later, and in the morning I lay down on my bed to sleep. Instead, I found myself fighting back tears. The tears were for a seventeen-year-old acquaintance who was killed, machine-gunned while riding his bicycle to work. They were for the crippled bodies and bleeding corpses of young students and workers. They were for the kids I had seen burned up in a bus on Tiananmen Square. And they were for China.

Almost overnight, China had changed—in my mind and in the minds of most Americans. Before it had been an exhilarating land of pandas and peasants, steeped in history as well as in hope for better times. Now it was a bloodstained dungeon.

In the next few months, the authorities arrested tens of thousands of people, among them many of our friends. The *World Economic Herald* was closed down, its Beijing compound left empty and deserted. Zhang Weiguo disappeared into the bowels of the prison system for the next twenty months, without a trial, without any reliable word on his fate. Sheryl and I agonized over whether we were to blame for his arrest. We remembered a couple of phone calls with Zhang in which we had asked him about Politburo meetings. In retrospect we realized that it had been incredibly stupid for us to discuss such things on a phone that was almost certainly bugged—probably at his end as well as ours. We knew that many of the prisoners were tortured, that common criminals were frequently ordered to beat up and humiliate political prisoners. In Yingshan Prison in Guangxi Province, a convict was locked up for two years in a solitary confinement cell that was never cleaned. He died there, and officials weren't sure what had killed him. One possibility was that he froze to death, for he had no blankets. The other possibility was that he died from the gases produced by the fermentation of the fourteen-inch pile of his own excrement. We wondered whether Zhang Weiguo was enduring conditions like that, and whether he would ever come out.

As the hard-liners reasserted their power, tired old Marxist slogans returned, and the newspapers published attacks on private enterprises. The authorities harassed us, denounced us, and almost expelled us from the country. They made us *chuan xiao xie,* or wear tight shoes, to let us feel the pinch, to remind us who was in charge. Even the suave Foreign Ministry officials sometimes seemed barely house-trained. When our son Gregory was born in Hong Kong in March 1992, at a time when Prime Minister Li Peng was furious with me for an article I had written about him, the Foreign Ministry

refused to give Gregory a visa. We finally obtained a three-month
tourist visa for him through a cooperative travel agent, but then the
Foreign Ministry refused to give Gregory a residence permit. Only
after the foreign press wrote a few stories about the bullying of our
baby did the Foreign Ministry relent.

At times like that, we felt China was like Brezhnev's Soviet Union—
or like Gorbachev's, in the sense that it seemed to be hastening
toward collapse. China was surviving on repression rather than legitimacy, run by a few old men who were steadily alienating themselves
even from Communist Party members. Many of our Chinese intellectual friends insisted that China was rotting away, and there were
many times when we believed it. Yet as the 1990s progressed, we
came to realize that there was another side to China as well. Some
900 million of China's 1.2 billion inhabitants are peasants, and I
never got very far when I tried to discuss human rights or democracy
with them. It became clear that if Sheryl and I focused just on the
way the regime bullied and tortured its critics, we would be missing
a major dimension of the story.

I thought about this in particular after receiving permission in
1990 to attend a conference in a Tibetan area of Qinghai Province in
the west of China. Qinghai had previously refused to allow me to
visit—government permission was necessary any time a reporter
traveled in China outside Beijing—so the conference was a rare
opportunity to visit a Tibetan area. Naturally, I spent very little time
at the conference itself, instead hiking through the mountains, talking to Tibetans. It was a spectacular setting, with snowcapped peaks
presiding over a vast plateau of grain speckled with little villages.
Occasional horse carts passed me on the winding dirt paths I was
hiking on, and everyone waved a startled greeting. "Uncle, are you
Chinese?" asked a little Tibetan girl who had never seen a foreigner
before.

Only one Tibetan I talked to, a young man of twenty-four, was
strongly anti-Chinese. He paced up and down the dirt floor of his
mud-brick home as his wife nursed their eighteen-month-old baby.
The baby took a break from the meal and played a bit on the floor
with a piece of string before complaining and whining. This time the
grandmother picked up the baby and put him to her withered breast.

This puzzled me, for I didn't see how the grandmother could possibly have any milk. But then I realized that in such a poor area parents have no pacifiers; when a baby cries they use a natural alternative: the nipple of whatever woman is nearest.

The baby's father was venting his yearning for Tibetan independence, gushing forth with his respect for the Dalai Lama, his frustration at not being able to speak freely, his fury at the government for interfering with the monasteries. He reverentially showed me a dusty photo of a Buddhist lama who had been the senior religious figure in the area—until he was tortured to death in the 1960s.

Most of the Tibetans I talked to were more like Wenchangtai, a young peasant whom I met along a dry creek one morning. He invited me into his home for a breakfast of oily dough sticks, so I sat on a wooden stool at the rickety table next to him and his wife. The floor and walls were made of mud, with a couple of posters—taken from old calendars—for decoration. It quickly turned out that Wenchangtai supported the government.

"We get along pretty well with the Chinese," he said. Then he offered proof: His wife, a short, sturdy woman with red cheeks who listened quietly to our conversation, was not a Tibetan but a Chinese. Wenchangtai was happy with his life and particularly proud of his new blue motorcycle, the first in the neighborhood. The motorcycle stood gleaming in his courtyard, and he agreed to give me a lift down the road. As I bounced over the ruts I began to feel better about China.

The next evening, I hiked through the windswept wheat fields toward a small village of about twenty mud-brick homes, tucked into the side of a jutting mountain. It was late evening, and the golden prairies glowed in the amber light of the fading sun, with snowy mountain peaks shining in the distance. I was in a great mood, for I relished the opportunity to roam freely among the peasants and talk to them without an escort. I squatted in the fields and conversed with peasants who had not yet heard that the earth revolves around the sun, and I sat around their mud huts and joked about the children's curiosity about my big nose.

I didn't think I was being followed. It was true that when I had sneaked out of town, two middle-aged men in Mao suits had ambled 200 yards behind me. But when I cut across the wheat fields just outside of town, the two men stayed on the winding dirt road and then disappeared from sight. The only people visible were six Tibetans, one big family, busy harvesting the grain, and they merrily waved back and shouted greetings in heavily accented Mandarin. Other sounds carried across the fields from faraway homes: the throaty barking of a mastiff, the restless *baaaa*s of a herd of sheep being driven home from pasture, and the *clackety-clack* of a horse cart bouncing on the ruts somewhere over the hill.

When I reached the village, I felt it could have belonged to the fifteenth century almost as easily as to the twentieth. Most of the homes were made of packed mud, a couple of rooms with a sheep shed or horse stable attached. The homes were surrounded by small courtyards set off by high mud walls, and dogs growled ferociously from the courtyards as I passed by on the outside. I walked along the dirt paths between the compounds, searching for an open door or someone to talk to. Laughter and conversation wafted over the walls, but nobody was outside—except an old Tibetan woman who stopped in horror when she saw me, then whirled around and hobbled away. Finally, on a hillside behind the village, I came across a three-bedroom house still under construction. In local terms it was a mansion, for it was made of concrete, not mud, with a mosaic of green tiles for decoration. The main gate of the courtyard was black wrought iron, made into bars eight feet high, and it was opened to reveal a half dozen workmen completing the building's interior.

"*Qing jin!*" called out a roly-poly man who seemed to be the boss. "Come in! Have you eaten yet?"

He looked to be in his midthirties, a squat man with ragged whiskers and a deep, leathery tan from a lifetime working on the mountains. The wrinkles under his eyes danced as he introduced himself as Ma Musha, and he wore a white lace skullcap that identified him as a Muslim. Ma explained that he was building a new house, replacing his old mud-brick home, and he could not have been more proud. "There'll be lights on the ceiling there," he said, pointing in the living room. "Real electric lights. And heating! Electric heating! No more burning cow chips. A toilet, too. Inside, you know, one that flushes."

Ma gestured, flipping the handle on an imaginary toilet, and delightedly imitated the sound of the water swishing away. The home was still crude in many ways: an ugly concrete floor, no bath or shower, no telephone, and the certain prospect of repeated electrical failures. But it was a palace compared with the hut in which Ma used to live, and it had established him as a big man in the village.

"Yo! It is pretty nice, isn't it!" he said, acknowledging a compliment. "It's only the third concrete house in the village, and I figure it's the best. Of course, next summer, there'll be a bunch more folks knocking down the huts and building concrete homes, so I suppose this'll be outclassed before long as well."

Ma said he was a chauffeur, one of the most lucrative jobs available in rural areas, and he pointed to an ancient brown Shanghai-brand sedan a hundred feet away. He also farmed a bit of land with his family, growing wheat and barley. I asked what local people thought of the government.

"The government's terrific!" Ma stated with a grin, and he seemed to mean what he said. "Ever since 1978 and the reforms, the Communist Party has just been letting us do our own thing, letting us get rich. Look at this new house! Why, in the past I could never have dreamed of getting such a place. Everybody's getting much richer and building better houses. I tell you, we owe the party a big thank-you."

A few minutes later, Ma abruptly turned and waved to someone at the gate. "Come on over," he called out. "Let me introduce you to an American."

I turned and saw the two men who had been behind me earlier. Now they were skulking outside the gate, intensely embarrassed at being invited in.

"Come on over here," Ma called. "What are you waiting for?" And he marched over to the gate to greet them.

"You'll never guess who this is," he told the two men excitedly. "An American! He's a reporter from *The New York Times*. Big newspaper! He's come to talk to folks around here."

"Hmph, hmph," one of the tails said sulkily. "We know who he is."

"These guys are my friends," Ma said, oblivious to their discomfort. "They work for the police."

I often thought of that little episode later, for it captured the two overwhelming forces that are reshaping China today. These two forces dominated our five years in Beijing. Each is of historic proportions and seemingly unstoppable, yet at least on the surface they appear incompatible and competing. I frequently puzzled over how to make sense of them.

The first of these forces is China's instinctive repressiveness, coupled with all the signs that this is an illegitimate, collapsing dynasty. There are parallels between the regime today and the declining days of the Qing, the Ming, and all the other dynasties. The Communist emperors are clinging to an outdated ideology, and they are steadily losing the hearts and minds of their citizens. The police surveillance underscores the regime's repressiveness even to well-meaning people like Ma. A week after returning to Beijing, I learned from a well-connected friend that the authorities had punished Wenchangtai, the young man who supported the government. The police had found out from neighbors that he had given me a ride, and they hauled him in for interrogation and fined him. They also confiscated his motorcycle.

I seethed when I heard that. It was the kind of harsh capriciousness typical of the Eastern European regimes as they alienated their people and rode the alienation to oblivion. Certainly many of our Chinese friends regard the repression as the last spasm of a dying dynasty, the death rattle of Chinese Communism as it proceeds in the direction of Soviet Communism. Four decades ago, Mao Zedong said, "The Soviet Union's today is China's tomorrow." At times like that, I believed it.

On the other hand, Ma Musha's newfound prosperity reflects an ongoing "second revolution," one whose significance dwarfs that of the first revolution by the Communists in 1949. Westerners understand the repression, but many do not yet grasp the implications of this economic and social revolution. We severely mislead ourselves if we see only the first China and not the second. In the long run, the explosion of wealth in China may prove to be the most important trend in the world during this age. Perhaps no question will be so important to humanity in the coming decades as whether China can sustain its present revolution.

If China can hold its course, it will produce the greatest economic miracle in recorded history. Never before has such a large proportion of humanity risen from poverty so rapidly. Studies that measure the size of an economy in terms of purchasing power indicate that China's economy is already the third largest in the world, after those of the United States and Japan. At present rates the Chinese economy may surpass America's within a few decades to become the biggest in the world. Just as the West failed to appreciate the strength of the Japanese economic challenge until the 1980s, we have not yet awoken to the potential strength of the Chinese economic challenge.

Unlike Japan, a purely economic rival, China can be destabilizing in many areas at once. The World Bank estimates that its population in the year 2025 will be 1.6 billion—and still rising—while the United States's is forecast to be 307 million and Japan's is projected to be 128 million and shrinking. For starters, the industrialization of such a huge population as China's will create unparalleled pressures on the global environment. Imagine a China where most people have cars, air conditioners, and refrigerators. Already China is the fastest-growing producer of greenhouse gases, and continued rapid economic growth will add to the problem of global warming, possibly raising the level of the seas and even inundating densely populated regions like the Bangladesh delta. China's industrialization will raise energy prices around the world and create pollution problems, such as acid rain, that will affect distant countries.

There is also a strategic element to this takeoff. China, which already has by far the world's largest army, is using its economic boom to finance a far-reaching military buildup that could destabilize all of Asia. China, after all, has disagreements about its sea or land boundaries with nine of its neighbors, has fought with four of them in the last half century, and appears to claim as its own the entire South China Sea—including major international shipping channels that carry Middle Eastern oil to Japan. China is becoming a regional superpower, dominant throughout Asia, and it may even be trying to acquire bases from Burma in the Indian Ocean. It will take time for the Chinese military to familiarize itself with the new tanks, destroyers, submarines, fighters, and bombers that it is acquiring, but sometime after the year 2000 the world may wake up and marvel at China's emergence as a major military power.

The West, in short, has not yet begun to consider the consequences of China as a modern nation: Imagine another Japan, but with a dozen times as many people—plus nuclear weapons.

For much of the last 4,000 years of human civilization, China has been more important, advanced, and sophisticated a place than Europe or America. It is only since the year 1500 that the West has unmistakably pulled ahead. No one knows whether China can sustain its present pace of economic growth, but it is a reasonable possibility. In a century or two the world's leading historians may well look back and decide that the crucial trend at the close of the twentieth century was the rise of China. They will be especially likely to think so if they have names like Wu instead of names like Smith.

We spent our five years in Beijing trying to reconcile these two faces of China. Is China plunging downward, on the trajectory of the Soviet Union? Or is it soaring upward, simultaneously shedding repression and accumulating wealth, on the path of Taiwan and South Korea? Should we be portraying China as the evil empire, a disintegrating dynasty, the last bastion of Communism? Or as an awakening giant, one that is raising the living standards of its citizens more quickly than any other major country in the world? If China is a bankrupt regime, why is a baby born today in Shanghai expected to live 76 years, 2.2 years more than an infant born in New York City? Why is that baby less likely to die in its first year of life if it lives in Shanghai rather than New York? And why is it more likely to learn to read if it grows up in Shanghai instead of New York City?

China is confusing because it marks the intersection of two of the most important trends of the final decades of the twentieth century: the collapse of Communism and the rise of East Asia as an industrial powerhouse. The juxtaposition of these trends is one of the most vexing aspects of reporting from Beijing. During our years in the Chinese capital, we constantly debated whether we should be writing more about people like Professor Peng Yuzhang or about people like Ye Hongcheng.

Professor Peng, retired and in his seventies, is a distinguished scholar from Hunan University, full of fire and drive. He joined in the hunger strikes and demonstrations during the 1989 Tiananmen protests and afterward was imprisoned in the No. 1 Jail in the central Chinese city of Changsha. The Hunanese are famous for personalities as peppery as their food, and many of China's great revolutionaries—including Mao Zedong—came from Hunan. Professor Peng is just as rebellious, and he used to shout regularly from his cell: "I demand to be released!" and "Why are you holding me?"

The guards responded in their own way. They fastened him to a shackle board: a piece of wood the size of a door, with cuffs at each corner to secure the victim's hands and feet. A hole in the lower end of the board allows the prisoner to excrete his waste. The other convicts heard Professor Peng's cries. "Let me out!" he shrieked. "I need to take a bath!" Or he would sing a children's song, his voice rising to a crescendo with the final line "Stand firm and never waver!"

This lasted twenty-four hours a day for three months. A fellow prisoner and acquaintance of ours, Tang Boqiao, saw Professor Peng as the old man was being carried back from an interrogation session. Tang later described what he saw: "All shriveled and dried up, he was barely conscious and was being carried out on a warden's back. I began to say, 'Professor Peng, you've suffered so much,' but my voice became choked with sobs and I couldn't go on. Somehow he managed to smile at me."

Professor Peng then disappeared from the jail and reportedly was committed to an insane asylum. None of his friends or family members were allowed to visit him, but a recent report says that he was released in about 1993 and is now allowed to live quietly at home, presumably under the continuing scrutiny of the authorities.

Cases like Professor Peng's left me feeling as if my mouth were coated with some disgusting ash from the Chinese air itself. But for every case like his, there are dozens like that of the cheery Ye Hongcheng. I met Ye, a forty-two-year-old peasant, on her farm near the southern Chinese city of Dongguan. Liu Shuji, the local Communist Party secretary and fan of Milton Friedman, introduced us. Ye is a tiny woman with a round, weathered face and hair that was neatly fluffed up for my visit. She was wearing a white blouse, buttoned to the top, and a stern blue-gray jacket that for some reason she thought was stylish.

For most of her life, she had toiled as her ancestors had done: wading in rice paddies under the sun, struggling to harvest enough simply to get through the winter. Then, in the 1980s, the local authorities gave Ye and her husband a thirty-year lease on what had been wasteland. The fields were no good for rice or most crops, but Ye started to raise chickens and rabbits and sell them on the market. Then she added fishponds and planted orchards.

"We just planted lychees this year; they'll begin to produce in three years, and the crop'll get bigger each year after that," Ye said. The local officials let her keep the income, which exceeded $50,000 a year, and she reinvested it. Now she and her husband have leased forty acres of land, a huge area in China, and have sixty laborers working on the property. Of course, the economic boom has its underside as well, and the growing income disparities between Ye and her laborers are an example of it. Yet in visiting people like Ye, I couldn't help feeling heartened—almost giddy—because of the new opportunities they exemplified. For her part, Ye has bought a refrigerator for the first time and plans to buy a washing machine soon. The only thing she won't get is a television.

"We don't need a TV in the house," she protested. "We don't have any time to watch TV. I'm too busy reading agricultural journals."

So which is the real China? The village of Ye Hongcheng or the prison of Professor Peng? How do we judge a regime that battles leprosy and dissent with equal vigor? Is there some formula of moral equivalency that allows us to balance the regime's accomplishments against its brutality? Those are some of the questions we struggled with as we probed life around us in China.

Most oppressive governments have the good sense to try to show their better side to foreign reporters. China's regime, by contrast, has the worst public relations sense of any major government in the world. It went out of its way to remind us almost every day of its inanity and repressiveness. Our Foreign Ministry liaison, Zhao Xingmin, a fifty-year-old Shanghainese with a personality like a fingernail on a chalkboard, used to summon me regularly to be scolded about my stories or Sheryl's.

"You have lashed out with personal abuse at Prime Minister Li Peng," Zhao warned me in a typical session in May 1992. "This is by no means tolerable. Your articles are fabricated with ulterior motives."

"Well, Old Zhao," I replied, using the most unctuous Chinese I could muster, "if there's any error, we would certainly like to publish a correction. What exactly was the mistake?"

"You must pay attention to your conduct," Zhao continued, looking a bit like a Red Guard at a struggle session. "Or you will bear full responsibility for all the consequences."

"Well, even if you can't find any mistakes in my articles, perhaps you think the tone is unfair. If so, we would welcome a letter to the editor."

Zhao looked as if he were about to explode. The Chinese note taker, a young man who apparently had had insufficient ideological training, buried himself in his notebook and seemed to stifle a giggle.

"You must not abuse the goodwill of the Chinese people!" Zhao roared. "This is not pre-1949 China. We value our sovereignty! If anyone wants to harm our sovereignty or independence, then we will never allow it."

The criticisms wore us down, and it would have been much grimmer if Chinese acquaintances had not given us so much support. I remember being particularly shocked on June 23, 1989, when the *People's Daily* denounced me by name. "This *New York Times* reporter, named Kristof, has in his reports boldly made false assumptions, played games with numbers, and spread new lies," the Communist Party newspaper declared. "Responsible people point out that this correspondent is writing not news reports but fiction." That evening, the television network news repeated the item, and I began to wonder how I could function with the news media attacking me. I felt a new empathy with the pro-democracy "hoodlums" whom the government was excoriating each evening on the news.

The next day, I was eating lunch in a restaurant in the center of town when several waitresses came over to my table. One spoke for the group. "Are you the one they mentioned on the television news last night?" she asked. "The reporter who lies?"

"Yes," I answered defensively, putting down my chopsticks. "But . . ."

"Never mind," she interrupted, and they all beamed. "There's no need to pay your bill. We'll take care of it. We're all hoodlums here."

State Security tried on several occasions to set me up, perhaps to have an excuse to expel us, so Sheryl and I resolved that we would never accept a package or document from anyone we didn't completely trust. We became concerned about being framed after getting some strange phone calls. At a time when even our close friends were worried about meeting us, Chinese whom we didn't know would breezily call up and offer to meet us and give us "important information" or documents. We dryly told the callers to mail any information to us. None ever arrived.

The most amusing setup call came one day from someone who seemed to have watched too many American movies.

"Hello," said a woman's voice, speaking in Chinese, and she asked for Ji Sidao, which is my name in Chinese.* "How are you? Do you want to get together? We could chat a bit. Do you want to sleep with me?"

Like most optimists about China, after the Tiananmen crackdown we felt betrayed. And, like most, we lost much of our confidence in the future of the Middle Kingdom. But what had really happened was that we had misjudged China in the first place. We thought that China had changed, had become more humane as it opened up to the West, had adopted Western attitudes as it donned Western clothes. We were proven wrong, and we were angry at China for not changing. I felt that sense of betrayal, like bile, almost every day for several years. I feel it every time I think of our friendship with Hongjun.

Bespectacled, with a round face and balding pate that balances precariously on a thin frame, Hongjun lost his job after the Tiananmen crackdown. He wears a perpetually humble expression, and he often worried about the risks of meeting with us. We used to meet for dinner at a Cantonese restaurant in the twenty-nine-story Citic Building, and as waitresses swished by with trays of food, he offered nuggets of information and insights into the thinking of the leadership.

---

*I was given my Chinese name, Ji Sidao 紀思道, by a scholar in Hong Kong. He chose it largely because in Cantonese, spoken in Hong Kong, it is pronounced "kay see do"—which is supposed to bear a vague correspondence to Kristof. But in Mandarin it is pronounced "gee suh dow," which doesn't sound even remotely like Kristof. My surname, Ji, means "discipline" and is a Chinese family name. The next two characters mean "thought" and "path," so the name means "the man named Ji who takes the path of thoughtfulness."

Sheryl's grandfather chose her Chinese name, Wu Jiefang 伍潔芳. The Wu is the family name, but it is a different character than that of most Chinese people named Wu. The common surname Wu is pronounced in a rising tone; Sheryl's is pronounced first in a falling tone and then a rising tone. Her last two characters mean "clean" and "fragrant," which is the kind of feminine name that old Chinese traditionally gave their granddaughters.

Gregory follows my English surname but Sheryl's Chinese surname. So he's Gregory Kristof but Wu Kairui 伍凱瑞. That means approximately "victorious and lucky Wu."

What I liked most about Hongjun was that he never lost his sense of fairness. He was an enthusiastic reformer, but he always tried to understand why the hard-liners did what they did. He often revealed a profound ambivalence, almost desperation.

"I know that I'm unusual," Hongjun told me one autumn evening, as we were about to part on the street after dinner. "Most people don't get hurt by the government, because they don't care about politics. Money—that's all most people think about. Money!"

He kicked his foot in the dust contemptuously. "And they're living better lives, and I'm sure that one day they'll live freer lives as well. Bit by bit, the party'll loosen up. It has to. Look at South Korea, look at Taiwan, look at the Philippines. Democracy will come, but it'll come slowly, much more slowly than we would like.

"Democracy has never really worked smoothly in Asia—even Japan isn't really a democracy, and it had MacArthur's help. In Asia we don't have any experience in it, so we've got to be patient. Most Chinese still want a strongman to ensure order. We intellectuals are the only people here who ever really think about democracy."

There was a long pause, and I asked him what his own plans were. He shrugged.

"I've been a Communist Party member for a decade," he said, his voice inflected with despair. "I believed in the party, and I worked for the country. And now look what has happened! I've lost my job. I've got no work unit, not even prospects for a job."

He waved his hands to his sides, and I heard the bitterness seep into his voice. "The party always hurts those who most try to help it."

My heart went out to him. Normally Sheryl and I never discussed one Chinese friend with another, for fear of the word getting out that we were in touch with someone. But, moved by Hongjun's little speech, I asked him if there was any word about a mutual friend who was now in prison.

"He's still inside, but there's no news," Hongjun replied. "Did you know him?"

"Oh, a bit," I replied.

"He was a classmate of mine, a friend at university," Hongjun reminisced. "Did you know that? Did you used to meet with him before his arrest?"

"Well, we knew him a little bit," I said edgily.

"But did you have regular contact with him?" Hongjun seemed very interested, and that bothered me.

"Not too much," I lied.

Hongjun kept bringing the conversation back to our friend, and I just as obstinately deflected the topic. Our friend had not yet been charged with a crime, and if the authorities knew of our contacts with him they could sentence him to a decade in prison for leaking state secrets.

A week later, another friend asked me to go out for a walk.

"You know Hongjun, don't you?" she asked. "Well, you should know that he's not for real. He's a spy for State Security, and you should never, ever trust him with any information. He's been a spy for a long time, and now he's interested in you and Sheryl. He's been asking about a book he thinks you're writing, and about how you're writing it. He wants to know if you're writing it on the hard drive of the computer, or on floppy disks. If you are writing a book, you might want to be very, very careful with it."

I was speechless. I hadn't told Hongjun about a book. But State Security undoubtedly had heard telephone taps of conversations with a literary agent we talked to once in a while. We checked with friends and were soon able to confirm as best we could that Hongjun was a career spy. He had never even been a formal member of his previous reformist "work unit"—State Security had simply posted him there because it gave him a great cover.

Yet our Chinese friends also said that as far as they could tell, Hongjun was a genuine reformer and believer in democracy, and did not blindly obey State Security. They suggested that he probably fed some bits of information to his bosses but withheld other bits. "You shouldn't think that someone is all bad just because he belongs to State Security," said one mutual acquaintance. "He still has his autonomy, he still controls himself. You can do good or bad in any job."

The uncertainty was maddening. Hongjun continued to regard us as friends, and we continued to enjoy his company and respect his insights. In 1992 he asked me to write a letter of recommendation for him to win a fellowship at an American university. At first I simply wrote a lukewarm letter explaining how I knew Hongjun, but after mailing it I decided that that was not enough. On my next trip to Hong Kong, where I knew the phone was not tapped, I called the head of the fellowship program. I told him that I wasn't certain but that I suspected Hongjun might be a State Security employee. The phone call probably killed Hongjun's chances of winning the fellowship.

I avoided Hongjun for some months after that, partly because I felt he was being dishonest with me and partly because I was ashamed of being dishonest with him. When we finally did meet for lunch, he helped me with a couple of stories. Once more, I found him eminently decent and likable, and I subsequently learned that he had left State Security. Even as I write this, I'm thinking of what Hongjun will feel as he reads it. He will immediately recognize himself. And then he will know that I knew that he was spying on me, and he will also know that I killed his chances of studying in America. It will be very awkward when we next meet.

Our relationship with Hongjun taught us to mistrust everybody, to worry constantly about getting friends in trouble. We feared being followed to a rendezvous, being overheard at a dinner table, having our notebooks or address books taken, causing a friend to be imprisoned. For several years after the 1989 crackdown, Sheryl and I never spent a waking hour in China in which such a fear didn't flutter by at least once. We had invested our souls in China. Reporters are supposed to be dispassionate, but we were never dispassionate about China; we loved some things about it and hated others. It was not just the backdrop to our lives; it was our lives.

Our feelings of betrayal were multiplied as the authorities fortified the system of apartheid instituted to separate us from ordinary Chinese. Of course, the government's anxiety about keeping foreigners at a distance is nothing new. In 1793, one of China's greatest emperors, Qianlong, personally directed secret efforts to keep a delegation of British visitors from talking to any local people. The authorities went so far as to arrest a Chinese man named Guo who had learned a bit of English from the trade that his dead father had conducted with Europeans. Guo had the misfortune to live near the route that the British were expected to take on their way out of China, and the authorities worried that the British might stop in his city, stumble across him, and engage him in conversation. Unlikely, perhaps, but the emperor himself took charge of the case, declaring of Guo, "Let him be brought to Beijing, taking care that his path does not cross the embassy's." I often thought of Qianlong's instructions about keeping barbarians from having any contact with the Chinese, and I wondered if the order had ever been revoked.

The updated, post-Tiananmen version of this policy was *neijin, waisong*, meaning "tranquillity on the surface and repression on the inside." As foreign correspondents, we were supposed to see only the tranquillity, without talking to ordinary Chinese and taking the measure of the repression. So correspondents were forced to live and work in one of four diplomatic compounds scattered around Beijing. Our compound, Jianguomenwai, is a ten-acre cluster of a dozen gray high-rises, surrounded by an iron fence topped with barbed wire. The apartments come equipped with some modern facilities: a network of video cameras inside and outside the compound, and a telephone tapping and taping system to record our phone calls.

One cool clear day in January 1990, I drove off to find Gao Xin, a dissident who had just been released from prison. A friend had given me the address, but I didn't know if Gao wanted to talk, and we were fearful that a visit might bring him trouble. So I was particularly careful in driving there, and I kept watching my rearview mirror. When I found the address on Dongzhimenwai Avenue and pulled into the bicycle lane, a tan Toyota three cars behind pulled in as well. Probably just a coincidence, I thought, but to be sure I pulled back onto the road and went around the corner and stopped. A moment later, the tan Toyota turned around the corner and stopped as well, a hundred yards back. I aborted the trip, and we never did meet Gao Xin.

For the next few years, there were periods when for months we were tailed constantly, every day, every time we left the compound. They even followed me when I went jogging—except that they used a motorcycle or bicycle. I'm normally a pretty tolerant person, but I hated those tails. On rainy days, I used to catch myself hoping that the motorcyclists would slip on the wet pavement and fall beneath the wheels of a truck.

Duan Jin, a dour, prune-faced Foreign Ministry spokesman, solemnly denied at a briefing that foreign correspondents were ever tailed. It might have been more convincing if I hadn't been tailed by three different vehicles while driving to that very briefing. The tailing at least gave us an insight into the bland willingness of officials like Duan to lie, as well as into the extraordinary resources that the regime devotes to surveillance. Almost nothing can be done during the lunch hour in China, or in the evening, but State Security mustered teams of agents at a moment's notice to tail us even during rainstorms in the middle of the night. Agents with walkie-talkies are stationed along the major roads to monitor the cars that go by. Video cameras are mounted at scores of intersections so that a vehicle's movements can be followed for miles on monitors in a control room. One indication of the scale of government security operations came with the official disclosure that more than 600,000 people were involved in security work when the Asian Games were held in the capital in 1990.

The problem with the surveillance is not, of course, just that it robs us of our privacy. We got used to the idea that our bedroom was bugged. We didn't protest when the Foreign Ministry ordered the tax bureau to give us trouble, when State Security burglarized our office, when police stole our car license plates, when the post office confiscated our mail, when agents scraped the paint off three sides of our car so that they could recognize it more easily. The real problem was the risk to our friends, acquaintances, and sources. In at least eighteen cases since China launched its open-door policy in 1978, Chinese have gone to prison or labor camp for terms of up to life imprisonment because they helped foreign correspondents.

Working as journalists in this kind of situation is a grim, alienating, and topsy-turvy experience, packed with ethical dilemmas. We constantly weighed dangers, not to ourselves but to our Chinese acquaintances. If there is a one percent chance that a visit to a friend will get him in trouble, do I take the risk to confirm a story? Is it worth it for a front-page story? For a short inside story? For any story? Hongjun, who befriended us and also spied on us, once said something over dinner that I think came from his heart, not from his job. I had asked him to confirm something, and there was a long pause. Then Hongjun looked morosely across the table at me. "You probably know that there are two famous brands of bicycle in China," he began. "There's the Flying Pigeon bicycle, and there's Forever brand. Well, you must never forget one thing. You foreign correspondents are all Flying Pigeons, here today and gone tomorrow. And we Chinese, we're Forever."

Sheryl and I weren't the only reporters embittered by the harassment. It would be hard to find a regime that tried harder than China to ruin its own image for the outside world. The authorities not only shadowed, denounced, and threatened foreign reporters but occasionally beat us up. The worst case involved Todd Carrel, the forty-one-year-old ABC television correspondent in Beijing. A fluent Chinese speaker with a Chinese-American wife, Todd was in Tiananmen Square on June 3, 1992, the third anniversary of the massacre. Suddenly a Chinese dissident tried to unfurl a protest banner, and Todd and a handful of other reporters ran over to photograph the man being dragged off. Todd had a little video camera that he was shooting with, and this apparently enraged the police. They began beating and punching Todd and the other reporters, using their fists and bandannas wrapped around either stones or lead. The journalists were tossed into an army jeep, and the beating continued as they were driven to a police station. Several hours later the police released the journalists but confiscated the videotape.

Todd ached from his bruises, but he didn't think he had been severely injured. As time went on, however, he found the pain got worse. A month after the beating, he could no longer work and had to fly back to the United States for medical treatment. Soon he couldn't walk, stand, or sit, his vision deteriorated, and he was in constant pain. Doctors found he had injuries to his spine and to soft tissues throughout his body. His brain couldn't drain fluid.

A couple of years later, Todd still walks with a limp. He is in pain and unable to sit for more than twenty minutes at a time. What was most intriguing was what three traditional Chinese doctors told him: that the goons who beat him up knew just what they were doing, that the blows were intended to cause severe internal injuries without leaving obvious marks. What a tidy image for how the regime tries to do things!

Naturally, Sheryl and I spent our time rooting for economic takeoff as the force to prevail in the Middle Kingdom. In some ways, we hoped that all of China could resemble the bustling southern city of Shenzhen. The most open and prosperous city in China, Shenzhen sprouts high-rises, as an old saying goes, like bamboo shoots after a spring rain. In Shenzhen, on the border with Hong Kong, families watch Hong Kong television and the Communist Party is almost irrelevant. Optimists often portray Shenzhen as China's model for the twenty-first century. But in Shenzhen, as in other parts of China, the sparkling high-rises and karaoke bars and satellite dishes can be deceptive. As the Chinese sometimes say when foreign business executives gush about the boom in their country: *lu fen dan, biaomian guang*—on the outside, even donkey droppings gleam.

Shenzhen is where Tang Rimei saw her brother beaten to death. The entire city is constructed of an alloy of hope and brutality, the same alloy that characterizes much of China in the 1990s. It is this paradox that so troubles me about Tang's story.

A native of northeastern China, Tang Rimei was the daughter of a revolutionary soldier who was an early believer in Communism. She was the kind of youngster on whom the party had put its hopes. But she became a leader of the Tiananmen democracy movement at her university and, fearful of being arrested, fled to Shenzhen. Ordinary Chinese are not allowed to go to Shenzhen without permission—it is a "special economic zone" surrounded by a "second border"—but Tang paid a ten-dollar bribe to get inside. She worked in Shenzhen for two months, enjoying a high salary, before returning to her university to scout out the situation.

"The Public Security Bureau wanted to arrest me, but my teachers protected me," she recalled. "They said that they would punish me administratively within the university, so that there was no need to arrest me. That meant I was able to stay in the university and graduate in 1990. But the problem was that I was studying building materials engineering, in preparation for a career designing fighter planes. The military didn't want someone with my background, so I couldn't get a job. That was when I decided to go back down to Shenzhen. I paid 800 yuan* to bribe a policeman to get a Shenzhen ID card—it was the only way—and I got a job at a trading company called the Yellow River Corporation."

The head of the Yellow River Corporation, a sixty-four-year-old man named M. C. Wang, hired Tang because she could write Chinese

---

*Eight hundred yuan is equivalent to a bit less than $100 at today's exchange rate of about 8.7 yuan to the dollar. Throughout this book, where we give a figure in dollars, we have converted at the official rate unless the context indicates otherwise. Since we moved to China in 1988, however, the official exchange rate has gone from 3.7 to the dollar to 8.7 to the dollar—partly because of greater inflation in China than in the United States and partly because of the authorities' decision to move their currency closer to a realistic market rate. The market rate may reach 10 yuan to the dollar before long, and that will make conversions easy: Just drop a zero.

well and knew a little English. It was a useful background for the task
he had in mind for her: forging documents.

Yellow River, with sixty employees, was nominally a branch of a
state-owned company. But in effect it had been hijacked by Boss
Wang and a few other employees as a personal moneymaking venture. The secret to their success was to win protection by building
connections—*guanxi*—with local police and Communist Party officials. Boss Wang spent huge amounts on "gifts" for Shenzhen officials, and he took them on expense-paid vacations around China. He
even treated them to fancy call girls, winning the officials' friendship
and obtaining something to hold over them.

Boss Wang asked Tang to draft a false contract for the sale of televisions so that he could approach the banks to get a phony bridge
loan. "He knew about the political problems in my background, so
he thought I would obediently write the fake contract," Tang said.
"He's also very close to the police in Shenzhen, and he said that if I
didn't obey, he would get them to come and take me away."

Tang did not go along with the corruption, however. Instead, she
reported Boss Wang to the Communist Party secretary of Yellow
River's parent company, and she complained to the public prosecutor
in Shenzhen. Both simply passed on her complaints to Boss Wang.
He was livid. Boss Wang kicked her out of the company apartment
in which she was living and hoodlums came to threaten her. The
police began to interrogate her about her past pro-democracy activities. One policeman told her, "Nobody dares to mess with Boss
Wang. You're the only one who wants to cause trouble."

At this point, Tang raised the ante. She put up several posters in
front of the city government offices, accusing the Yellow River Corporation of corruption and calling on the authorities to investigate.
She also sent letters to officials all over China denouncing the graft.

An older Yellow River official, a soft-spoken, graying man named
Yang Zhenguo, took pity on Tang. Yang is physically a big man, but
I found him so deferential and timid that he seemed much smaller
than his bulk; apparently this is the legacy of the time he spent in a
prison camp from 1968 to 1978 for "counterrevolutionary" offenses.
His main crime then was being a freethinking intellectual and the
son of a landlord.

Yang let Tang stay in his company apartment, but Boss Wang
quickly found out and tried to evict both of them. They refused to

move out, so Boss Wang cut off their electricity and water. He also fired Yang and arranged for Yang's sister—employed at a different company in Shenzhen—to be dismissed as well.

Tang's older brother, Tang Richeng, a tall, strong man studying at a sports institute in Dalian, heard about what was happening and came down to Shenzhen to protect his sister. Some young toughs came around a few times to tell him to go home, but he refused. That was where things stood on June 29, 1991, when Han Deji, a Yellow River manager, showed up at Tang's door with a gang of nine hoodlums, "businessmen" whom he employed. Tang and her brother were the only ones at home, and they were horrified when the gang began to smash the iron door to the apartment and yelled that they were going to kill her.

Three days after the murder, the police detained the hoodlums who had beaten Tang's brother to death, and later the authorities also detained Han Deji. Tang demanded that the police also arrest Boss Wang, and she began churning out letters to officials all over China, describing what had happened. The next month gangs twice attacked her apartment again, but they could not break in and eventually ran away when other people showed up. Tang continued to write protest posters and plaster them all over Shenzhen; she also gave interviews to Hong Kong reporters. That so infuriated the government that it detained her.

"The police took me into custody and told me that I was attacking the Communist Party," she said. "The police kept me in a cell and wouldn't give me food, wouldn't let me use the toilet. And even after they released me, they sent people to tail me everywhere I went. My letters were seized. I was desperate."

In November 1991, she and Yang fled to Hong Kong, where I interviewed them. Several months later, four of the thugs went on trial, along with Han Deji, the Yellow River manager. An agreement appeared to have been reached that the matter would end there, but then Han unexpectedly confessed to the killing in open court and claimed that Boss Wang had planned the whole operation. The court suspended the trial indefinitely.

Meanwhile, Boss Wang no longer shows up at work but still gets his paychecks, according to a Yellow River manager named Sha, whom I reached by telephone. Sha took issue with Tang's account, saying that the Yellow River Corporation had merely been trying to evict her from the apartment. Then, he said, a fight broke out and her brother was killed in the melee. "The incident has been exaggerated," Sha said. "It was all a misunderstanding."

Tang seemed in slightly better spirits when we finished our last interview. She smiled a bit as we shook hands and said good-bye, and she held her head up as she walked away. Perhaps it had helped her to talk about it. But I felt worse.

Her odyssey reminded me that China is always more complex than it seems. Tang Rimei's tragedy occurred in the city that is supposed to symbolize the economic takeoff, the future of China. Shenzhen is widely seen as the triumph of the market over Communist dogma. The thought that this might be China's best hope was most disquieting.

That evening, after I paid for our drinks—leaving a tip tucked beside Tang Rimei's untouched cup of cold coffee—I walked heavily back to my hotel room. I thought of Tang Rimei and her uncertain future in Hong Kong, which is due to return to Chinese control at midnight on June 30, 1997. The United States and other Western countries refuse to give Tang a visa, so perhaps Boss Wang and his cronies will come looking for her in a few years. I worried about her.

How nice it would be, I thought as I rode up in the elevator, to report from a country where I could hide behind a screen of dispassionate objectivity. How nice it would be not to care about the nation I wrote about.

SHERYL WUDUNN

伍潔芳

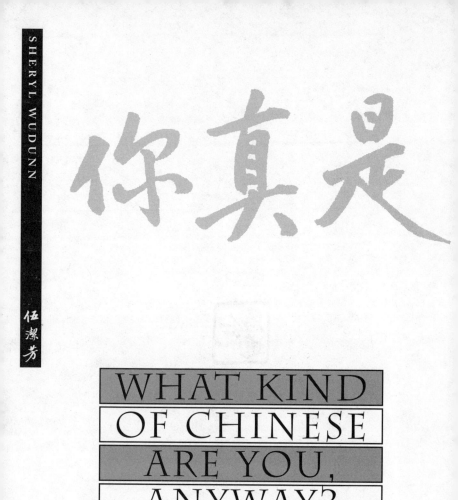

你真是

WHAT KIND
OF CHINESE
ARE YOU,
ANYWAY?

*The most outstanding characteristic of Eastern civilization is to
know contentment, whereas that of Western civilization is not to
know contentment.*

—Hu Shih, Chinese scholar and diplomat, 1891–1962

2

中國人？

In her first visit to the land of her ancestors, Sheryl meets the children of Shun Shui village, Guangdong Province. [Photo by Nicholas D. Kristof.]

Gangli was as slim as she was powerful. Even her red cashmere sweater seemed to hang nobly on her body like an imperial robe, and I scurried behind her with anticipation. The daughter of one of China's most powerful leaders, she was escorting me to a private party and led me through a mazelike room of drab metal desks, all arranged in perfect rows, all spaced at even intervals. It was a fairly new office, but somehow it had that air of state-run simplicity—the cheap, dull lamps, the straw-swept colorless floors, the beige plastic telephones. Everywhere, I saw neat piles of papers, marred by Chinese scribbles or bearing the *mimi, jimi,* or *juemi* stamps of secret documents. I craned my neck to get a peek at the papers, but she was walking too fast. We turned a corner into a small hallway. She grabbed the knob of a brown door, turned it, and pushed, and we entered a flood of darkness.

It was a large room, brightened intermittently by a spinning strobe flashing rays of light upon seventy people who were gathered in clumps, all keyed up to sing around the karaoke video and bop on the dance floor. A dozen male guests, in dark suits, shiny shoes, and loosened red ties, were laughing boisterously around the corner bar. A dozen beautiful female assistants and secretaries, dressed in black and glitter and balancing awkwardly on high heels, stood by a row of foldable steel chairs. I immediately felt a bit out of place in my low heels and wool suit.

The young women had been summoned to serve as dance partners for high-ranking male cadres. One of those officials, Construction Minister Lin Hanxiong, wasn't satisfied with the secretaries. Instead, he fixed his eyes on me. I am a Chinese-American, born in New York. But Minister Lin, a big, hearty, sixty-one-year-old in the reformist camp, apparently assumed that I was a local. The president of the Chinese company holding the party approached me and explained in a low voice that Minister Lin would like to meet me. I was delighted to meet a cabinet member, so I went over, and the president introduced me.

"This is Wu Jiefang," he said, using my Chinese name. I had been reporting from China for less than two years, and I felt a stab of excitement at the prospect of cultivating a cabinet minister as a source. In Chinese society, the leaders live virtually in the clouds, dashing back and forth through the crowds behind the tenebrous, tinted windows of their Mercedes-Benzes, and they are very leery of foreign journalists. Dancing with one is not an everyday opportunity.

So Minister Lin led me out to the darkened dance floor. As we sauntered over to an empty spot, I was dying to ask him about power struggles and ministerial gossip. I had a brief vision of writing illuminating stories attributed to a "Chinese cabinet member." Still, I couldn't very well blurt out: Is Deng Xiaoping still kicking? Do you eat giant shrimps every night? What does the latest Politburo document say?

Minister Lin solved my mental puzzle by thrusting another kind of problem at me. He promptly wrapped his arms around me and hugged me tightly, pulling me against him until we were chest to chest. I felt as if I were being tugged relentlessly into the mouth of an octopus. I put my arms in front of me and gently but firmly nudged him away. He hugged tighter. I pushed harder, and our bodies became locked together. What do you do when a Chinese cabinet minister tries to molest you? I wasn't sure. We circled awkwardly around the room like this for a few minutes, and I gave up the idea of cultivating him as a source.

"Do you know who I am?" I asked in Chinese, a bright idea having come to me. "I'm an American!" He twitched slightly in shock. Then I added quickly, "And I'm a reporter for *The New York Times!*"

Minister Lin's hands instantly relaxed, leaving me a bit of wiggle room as he digested this startling thought. I began asking some questions about whether he had ever been to the United States, but he just nodded blandly, waiting for the song to end. He did not ask me for the next dance.

Being groped by Minister Lin was not one of my most pleasant moments in China, but in some respects it was among my most insightful. I realized that most Chinese women at the party would have had to put up with Minister Lin's squeezing, and perhaps with other requests as well. So this, I began to think, is really what is meant by *buji daiyu,* minister-level treatment. The term embraced more than just the use of Mercedes-Benzes. It also included the right to molest young women.

I was surprised by what had happened, yet in some strange way I also found it a bit gratifying: My Chinese looks were a ticket to view the real side of China. I doubt Minister Lin would have tried the same thing if I had looked Caucasian, like Nick. The faces of foreigners create a sense of distance for the Chinese, putting them instantly on their best behavior, giving them a chance to stage a performance, and often preventing foreigners from understanding directly the problems faced by ordinary Chinese. It's one thing to understand intellectually that ministers enjoy tremendous power; it's another to have Minister Lin enveloping you in his beefy arms.

As soon as my plane landed in Beijing in 1988, I made a pact with myself: I would learn to be as Chinese as the Chinese. So, in an effort to blend in, I spent a good part of my first year in Beijing trying to disguise myself as a native. I discarded my heels for black flats, put away my Italian leather jacket for a rough wool one purchased in a state-owned store, and got my hair cut in a short bob, like thousands of other Chinese women. I could roam the streets, chatting to ordinary people about the hassles they faced, about their dreams and frustrations. During our first few years in Beijing, when the political atmosphere was grim, Chinese friends would often prefer to see me alone, without Nick, because I could slip into their buildings without being noticed. On the streets in certain cities, I could also purchase *Cankao Xiaoxi*, or *Reference News*, a confidential newspaper available to ordinary Chinese but forbidden to foreigners.

I was excited to move to China precisely because I knew I would blend in. When I was growing up on the Upper West Side of Manhattan, speaking English at home, my friends and neighbors and schoolmates were overwhelmingly white Americans. Like many third-generation Chinese-Americans growing up in the United States, I was the only Chinese in my class at school. To be sure, my family celebrated Chinese New Year and went on outings with other Chinese-American families. My brother and sisters and I, like all my dozens of cousins, were raised amid hopes we would marry other Chinese. In adolescence, however, being different was sometimes a source more of embarrassment than of pride, and I found myself looking for ways to assimilate.

It was only after I arrived at Cornell University that I began to take the slightest interest in China, and, even then, it played second fiddle to a love of European literature. As an undergraduate, I started dabbling in the Chinese language and later visited Asia with my family. Then I took a job as a lending officer at Bankers Trust, where I worked with Taiwan bankers and corporate officials, and gradually my perception of China broadened. By my late twenties I was thinking that someday I might work in Asia. So I was delighted when Nick and I moved to Beijing and I had the chance to meet my distant cousins: all one billion of them. I wondered what the welcome would be like.

On my third day in Beijing, I decided to take a stroll down the Avenue of Eternal Peace, the main drag near our residential compound. It was a wonderfully breezy afternoon in November, and I was in such good spirits that the scent of burning coal in the air made me think of a charcoal barbecue rather than pollution. Men and women strolled leisurely down the broad street, and their colorless outfits and the blacks and grays of the plain, squat buildings seemed to suggest elegant simplicity rather than lack of progress. For my part, I had not yet relegated to the closet my black leather jacket, the kind with big shoulders and plenty of pleats, that I had just purchased during my honeymoon in Rome, and I wore it with self-assurance. Then I passed a group of young men, also wearing leather jackets, but thick, crude ones that looked like rawhide. One looked at me and smiled, so I smiled back, thinking this was a nice, friendly city. Then one of them snapped, *jiayangguizi,* or "fake foreign devil."

I felt crushed and deflated. Maybe we weren't one big happy family after all. Nominally, China may not be a class society, but I soon discovered that in reality many Chinese people are very class—and race—conscious. Foreigners, particularly blacks or other Asians, are often considered a notch below Chinese, even though they are envied for their wealth and higher standard of living. They were derisively referred to as "foreign devils" or, in the case of Westerners, "big noses." Overseas Chinese, like myself, often inspire jealousy, and that jealousy sometimes takes the form of resentment.

But simply because I wasn't considered a real foreign devil, just a *jiayangguizi,* I could mingle in the local world more easily and make my way into people's homes and hearts. I often became a "compatriot." When Nick and I wanted to visit Mao's old home in Zhongnanhai, the special compound where the highest leaders live and work, a Chinese Foreign Ministry official, Li Zhaoxing, now the ambassador to the United Nations, told me that I could go since I was an overseas Chinese. But Nick would not be allowed to go. The discrimination was obvious.

It was a dual existence. I felt myself constantly shifting between two profiles: one of an overseas Chinese who was returning to her homeland, finally feeling "at home," blending in with the multitudes of look-alikes with straight black hair and black almond eyes. The other was of an American hacking through the brush of an unknown Chinese forest, often losing her way down twisting paths that were dead ends or circles. I may have looked like the Chinese walking beside me on the street, but the society was alien. People also seemed puzzled about how to relate to me. I looked Chinese, and so they expected me to understand their feelings and sentiments. But since I was raised in America, they wondered if I was really American. Moreover, to them, *The New York Times* was an exceptionally "American" institution. One Chinese friend never gave up his suspicions that *The Times* was part of the American government.

What I found ironic was that this awkward duality was exactly the state I had found myself in when I was in the United States. I was born with a Chinese name, Ng Git-fong (or Wu Jiefang in Mandarin), but I go by my American name. I studied Mandarin at college and in Taiwan, but I never learned the Taishan dialect of my ancestors; I learned kung fu but spent more time on aerobics; I can use chopsticks, but I like to eat with a fork; I feel American, but I also feel Chinese. In New York, I had spent much of my life trying to be American, playing by American rules, learning the ins and outs of American society. In China, I found myself trying to be Chinese, playing by Chinese rules, and learning how to operate in Chinese society. Yet in neither place did I entirely fit in the mainstream. So, perhaps inevitably, my five years in China were not just a search for the "Real China" but also a search for an identity.

That meant finding my roots. In China, where you come from, where your family comes from, is a critical part of your character. In America, when you first meet someone you might want to find out about his family, his interests, his background. In China, you want to know his *laojia*, his "ancestral home," where his family came from. Ask an American where his family comes from and he might say, "We're Irish," or "Italian." Ask what village he is from, and he would probably shrug his shoulders. A Chinese-American in China finds out very early on that she had better know exactly where her family is from.

Scattered across the rice paddies and vegetable plots, along the roads and rivers of a region called Taishan in Guangdong Province, are hundreds of small villages that formed the most vivid memories of the Chinese pioneers who left for America in the nineteenth and early twentieth centuries. My grandfathers were among them, both desperate peasants escaping from a land that at the time was growing increasingly poor. They went to America with dreams pieced together from tales of foreign missionaries, but powerful enough to carry them through the pain and hardships of beginning a new life 10,000 miles from home.

My grandparents died in America, never having entirely adjusted to a funny land where people have hairy faces and a language so crude that it does not even have tones. My parents and their sisters and brothers didn't seem to care much about Taishan, about searching for their roots. We entirely lost touch. In 1982, my sisters Sirena and Sondra went with a group of Chinese-Americans on a government-sponsored trip to China and tried to find our *laojia*. But the government could not arrange it, and my sisters had to give up. Then in 1987, my boyfriend, Nick, insisted that I go to Taishan and try once more. "It'd be fascinating to go back!" he said. "You should find out where your family comes from."

"But there'll just be a bunch of poor peasants there," I retorted. "I don't know them and don't feel any ties to them. Why should I go back?"

Still, something was kicking at me inside, and it said: You'll have to face the motherland at some point in your life. So, with a mixture of curiosity, fascination, and trepidation, I resolved to go.

Taishan, I knew, would be an impoverished land of mud huts and barefoot peasants, and I thought I should look modest, too. So I put on an old button-down shirt and blue jeans, took off my earrings, and pulled out a pair of black shoes that should have gone into the garbage. Nick and I were going with Hilda, a Hong Kong Chinese educated at Dartmouth College, who was quietly horrified at having to go into China. There would probably be no place to do laundry, she thought, so she packed a few bags of disposable underwear.

On a chilly day in November, Hilda, Nick, and I set out by ferry
to Macao, crossed the border into China, then took a five-hour
evening taxi ride through the crowded, earthen roads of the southern
part of Guangdong Province. We had to wait an hour and a half in
the dark, at the foot of a drawbridge, while the two halves of the
bridge opened to make way for a boat passing in the night. It seemed
as though everyone else was as surprised and annoyed as we were,
and we had interesting company: pigs in a trailer, drivers carting
tanks of oil, construction workers piled in the back of a pickup truck,
and vehicles carrying all sorts of metal containers filled with iron
rods, piping, and steel reinforcements. The road was rough and in
places the car tires dipped in the dirt, and our taxi driver honked her
horn at every bend. But it was obvious that this skimpy path was the
lifeline for the region.

We finally arrived in Taishan, where we stayed in a spacious but
sparsely furnished guest house that was surrounded by a simple tree
garden and a small pond. Early the next day, we embarked in a
dented, scratched van for a long, bumpy ride down a dirt path. We
ended up in Shun Shui, Smooth Waters, a village of about a hundred
people who all belonged to my family clan of Wu—or Ng, as it is
pronounced in the Taishanese dialect. We walked down a muddied
path to the center of the village, a cluster of crumbled-brick, gray and
clay-colored houses that faced a vast sweep of rice paddies. Behind
the brick houses, narrow footpaths led up an incline to more shabby
old abodes, but everyone seemed to have abandoned those homes. As
we sauntered on, a curious parade formed behind us: squawking
chickens, chattering children, a slim pig, and a farmer pulling a
wagon. Finally we stood in the middle of Shun Shui, surrounded by
a huddle of sunburned Chinese peasants whose bewildered stares
made me believe we were the local event of the year.

I towered over them, seeming gigantic at five feet five inches,
feeling almost embarrassed by the nutrition in my upbringing.
Most of the villagers we met were elderly men and women, too old
to do field work. They were tiny people, raised for decades on just
rice and vegetables. Their grandchildren and great-grandchildren
hid between their legs, turning away shyly when I smiled at them.
The children, too, were awfully little, I thought. Taishan was one of
the wealthier parts of China, and I feared what the rest of the
country must be like. I felt a race apart from them. And it seemed

awkward asking them if they knew my grandfather, about as awk-ward as if I'd asked the same question of strangers on the streets of Cairo.

The villagers showed no hint of this strangeness and chattered away in Taishanese, struggling to recall the man who had left the vil-lage sixty to seventy years earlier. I thought of Grandpa, my dad's father, whose home this village had been. He died in 1963, when he was seventy-two years old, and the only thing I remembered as a four-year-old was that he towered over me, like my father. Thin and white haired, he seemed a wise old sage, and I was always nervous around him. I met him only a few times, and we couldn't communi-cate because he spoke little English.

"Ng Hok-yik. Ng Hok-yik. That was his Chinese name," my father had said, passing on a few details about my grandfather. Before that, I had known him only by his American name, William Dunn. When he arrived in the United States, immigration officers asked his name, and he replied with his nickname, Ng Dan-sook. The immigration officers didn't know what to do with the Ng, but the Dan caught their attention. They anglicized that to Dunn, and he was Mr. Dunn for the next few decades. Late in his life, he grew tired of being a Chinese with an Irish surname. So he took the Man-darin pronunciation of his Chinese surname and added it to the Dunn. That's why I'm a WuDunn.

I told the villagers my grandfather's Chinese name, and the older ones lit up. "That's my lineage," shouted Wong Yu-gap, a short, angular woman whose thick, bronzed face reflected decades of farm-ing. Wong, a bright-eyed, talkative fifty-six-year-old woman, stepped forward and said proudly that she was married to my second cousin.

Then Wong Yu-gap and three white-haired women spoke a bit about my grandfather, and Wong announced, "He had two wives." My smile vanished, and a chill raced through my body. I had never heard this. Had we been discussing the wrong man?

"His first wife didn't bear him a son," one old woman said, her head tilted up toward me but her mind transporting her back to life in this village sixty-five years earlier. "She had two daughters, but he never got the son he wanted. So he came back from the United States, came back to the village, with his first wife. Your grandfather left his first wife here and then married another woman, your grand-mother. He left his first wife here and took his second wife back to

America. His first wife lived here for the rest of her life and died in the 1960s."

Grandpa had abandoned his first wife to marry Grandma? I suddenly felt limp, but the village women just kept waving their leathery hands, nodding their heads with their salt-and-pepper hair, cackling in a babble I couldn't understand, as though what Grandpa had done was perfectly natural. Of course, I was their guest, and they wouldn't criticize my family in front of me, but my sense was that they didn't see anything strange about this. The practice was common in those days. Chinese society was cruel to women, as it was to impoverished peasants, and that was the way life was. I was about to ask them about this topic when I noticed that Wong Yu-gap had slipped away. A moment later, she appeared at my side with an object wrapped in paper.

"Look, here's your grandfather's chop," Nick said, handing over a large old wooden seal that had three characters inscribed on it: Ng Hok-yik. In China, chops are regarded essentially as signatures, used on all documents. I clasped the chop, overcome with emotions. Just then, someone tapped me on the shoulder and I found myself being introduced to a stocky old man in a faded blue shirt. He was shorter than I by a head, and his eyes looked dull and empty.

"This is your second cousin, Ng Ping-lam," the Taishanese interpreter explained. I looked at my cousin. He was a sixty-three-year-old unshaven peasant, gnarled and weather-beaten.

"He's too old," I said coldly. He smiled rather shyly. I was embarrassed. This man was so different from me; he was not exactly the kind of distinguished scholar I could have welcomed as a relative. Later, when I asked him to write down his name and address, he couldn't. I felt myself looking down on him, though of course he couldn't help the fact that his grandfather hadn't migrated to America. He and his wife tried to explain that it was possible for a man more than twice my age to be my cousin. His grandfather was Grandpa's older brother, and his grandfather and father had had children while still young. Grandpa had been middle-aged when he had Dad. My skepticism began to fade.

"Do you want to see your grandfather's house?" asked Wong Yu-gap, the wife of my cousin. We followed her as she weaved in and around the abandoned yellow and gray houses. Finally, she stopped short in the middle of an alleyway and pointed to an old stone-and-brick house, desolate and aged by years of heat, humidity, and rain. We walked into the bare-walled rooms covered only with decades of dust. On one side of the room where we stood was a brown chest we couldn't open, but beside it was a box filled with old, yellowed papers. I sifted through the piles of documents, surprised to find some of them written in English. I grabbed a decaying sheet that read "Fire insurance . . . Mandarin Restaurant, Springfield, Massachusetts."

My grandfather had settled in New Jersey and New York, where my father grew up. These papers—bond certificates, operating licenses, letters of incorporation—must have belonged to someone else, I thought. I felt crushed. Just then, Nick called out, "Look here! This insurance document has your grandfather's name on it." I glanced at the delicate document and at the name printed on it: Wm. W. Dunn. This was the confirmation I'd been looking for.

Later I found out that my grandfather initially had gone to Massachusetts, where he had operated the Mandarin Restaurant. The documents were his, apparently brought back to the village when he returned to marry again. He had left his first wife and daughters there, but one of the daughters from that marriage made her way to America much later.

I cringed at my grandfather's cruelty but felt immense relief that this was indeed my grandfather the villagers were talking about, whose papers I was rummaging through. I picked up a brown document that read:

Identification of Eng Hen Tun, minor son of Eng Fon Mon, Merchant and member of the firm of Messieurs Helps Tuck Lung & Co., #30 Lafayette St., Newark, N.J.

I make this affidavit in order to prove my status as a merchant, and thus enable my son Eng Hen Tun, age 18, whose photograph is attached hereto, to enter the United States where I will undertake his care and support. . . .

"Who is Eng Hen-tun?" I asked, but no one seemed to know. Later I found out that these were the false identity papers that my grandfather had purchased to come to America. Without these faded documents, he would have remained in the village, and his progeny—me, or some different version of me—would be wading in the rice paddies.

I took a closer look at the old man who was my second cousin. His story could be multiplied a million times in China. A Chinese Everyman. He had started in the rice paddies and then moved on to work in a biscuit factory. He had fathered five sons, who followed in his footsteps. A grin betrayed missing teeth, and his toes stuck out beyond the edges of his sandals. But for the grace of God, I thought . . .

Later, I would often reflect on this visit when Chinese friends asked me for help getting to America, and it added to my tangled feelings about identity. I felt on the one hand that I should help them, because, after all, I was a beneficiary of one man's risky journey abroad on false papers. I also felt that somehow my contribution would help repay a debt to all those who had helped my grandfather emigrate. On the other hand, I didn't want to use connections, *guanxi,* to help someone obtain a visa to the United States. And the fact that in my own circle of friends I encountered dozens of Chinese who wanted to flee made me sad for China. Chinese people had been trying for 150 years to leave China, and that seemed to me one of the nation's great shames. Nothing had changed since Grandpa's time. China was still a place to escape from. I wanted to feel patriotic about China, proud of my ancestral homeland. But I also felt tremendous relief that Grandpa had fled.

As I stood beside my second cousin in Shun Shui, I felt an abyss between us that cut deeper than our bloodline. As I watched him and his wife and his sons, I rested a hand on my smooth black leather bag, which all of a sudden seemed to boast of opulence. I had gone to private schools on the East Coast and taken jazz dance and French lessons. My cousin had dropped out of school before he learned to write. I had grown up shopping in Bloomingdale's and eating bagels. He had never even been to the provincial capital of Guangzhou. And now I carried $150—or four months' worth of his salary—in my wallet. When I departed, I left half of my money with Ng Lap-ting, the village chief: "Use it toward buying a television for the village," I urged. And I left the other half with my relatives, stuffing it hurriedly into my second cousin's hand.

I wasn't the only one leaving piles of cash behind in China. Like my grandfather, millions of Chinese had forsaken their homeland from the seventeenth century on, fleeing poverty and seeking a better life. This diaspora embraces more than 50 million ethnic Chinese, now living in Taiwan, Hong Kong, Singapore, Indonesia, Malaysia—and, of course, the Upper West Side of Manhattan. While Chinese in China remained mired in poverty, those abroad became successful traders and often did better than the local people. That's why—at least until the Deng era—Chinese always seemed far more dynamic when you encountered them in Jakarta or Singapore than when you visited Shanghai. Chinese ethnic minorities play a hugely disproportionate role in the business communities of Thailand, Indonesia, the Philippines, and Chinese dominate such dynamos as Taiwan, Hong Kong, and Singapore.

It has always struck me as odd that many nationalities should thrive abroad while seeming listless at home. India is a laggard, yet Indians dominate the Fijian economy. Tamils are far more impressive abroad in Sri Lanka than at home in Tamil Nadu. Perhaps it has to do in part with the immigrant mentality lighting a fire under people in their new homes. Perhaps they are bound at home by the burdens of caste and culture, finding themselves free only when they are far away. And perhaps it is self-selection: The risk takers are those who flee their homelands to work on plantations in Fiji, to work in construction in Sri Lanka—or to open a Mandarin Restaurant in Massachusetts.

In any case, the overseas Chinese have been a godsend for China. Beginning in the 1970s, they shuffled in through the door when other foreigners demurred; they traveled by rickety car and rackety bus through the rice paddies to see their *laojia* and to invest in local factories; they brought in radios and cameras and, over banquets of stir-fried pig stomach and sea urchin, told about life in the world beyond; they offered investment, expertise, modern manufacturing techniques, and a great desire to do business with their homeland. Today, they run all over China, their arms overflowing with gifts and *hong bao*—red envelopes containing money—for their relatives. They have become role models for the Chinese.

The Chinese diaspora is one reason China has been a great deal more successful than the European alumni of the Communist Bloc. How many overseas Bulgarian businessmen are there abroad to set up factories in their hometowns? No other country has had remotely as much support from compatriots as China. Some three-fourths of foreign investment in China has come from ethnic Chinese abroad, mostly in Hong Kong and Taiwan. The biggest single foreign investor in China is a Thai Chinese who runs an agribusiness empire. As labor costs soared in Southeast Asia, many overseas Chinese businessmen moved their entire assembly lines or their back offices into their ancestral hometowns in China.

The overseas Chinese brought other baggage with them as well. They lugged their Scandinavian furniture, their Persian carpets, their long-haired cats, their love of Western books and newspapers, and a large basket of Western values. They even brought their American husbands! Maybe it wasn't such a pity after all that the poor or the persecuted fled China, for they always seemed to return—often as foreign citizens—to the motherland, whether to tour, to live, to invest, or to die. And how intoxicating it was for many local Chinese to see this, and how puzzling! Were these overseas Chinese really Chinese? Or were they foreigners in Chinese skins? Or some weird hybrid? But the Chinese liked what they saw. For a time the top pop singer in China was Fei Xiang, the blue-eyed, six-foot-tall son of a Taiwan woman and an American father. Anything foreign had cachet. Companies began changing their names to sound foreign, as if they were translated from English, even if they weren't. Chinese began spelling their names in the Taiwan and Hong Kong way, like Chang instead of Zhang and Chow instead of Zhao. People gave themselves English names (sometimes with disastrous results, as when Miss Chow named herself Kitty). And these newly styled Chinese began asking their government for more. As the economy soared and the confidence of economists and intellectuals rose in the late 1980s, there was a strange sense, a wistful hope, that China was transforming into a new country, one more like the overseas Chinese communities abroad.

But it was going to be a battle, a tug-of-war for the soul of the new China. The revolutionary generation was not amenable to sweeping change, and to them this new orientation was tantamount to abandoning the nation's pride. The growing dependence on the West was too much for many of the old cadres, whose fathers and forefathers had spent their lives fighting off the foreigners. China's emperors, from Qianlong to Mao, had struggled to keep China an economic island unto itself, shunning Western help and advice.

"Our Celestial Empire possesses all things in prolific abundance," Emperor Qianlong declared to Lord Macartney in 1793, explaining

China's refusal to trade with the West. Ever since, Chinese have agonized over the merits of contact with the West. Some of them, like Mao, boasted of self-reliance, and those who took up his mantle wanted to believe that China could advance on its own, with limited foreign assistance. They were embarrassed, humiliated, by their country's mood. They disparagingly called it *chongyang meiwai*—worshiping the West and fawning on foreigners.

I wasn't the only one with an identity crisis: China was in the midst of one, too. Would it be traditional or Western? Would it maintain strict controls on society or be bold enough to liberalize? Would it allow people to speak out more openly, perhaps even to criticize the emperor and his retinue? These questions bubbled in the atmosphere during the months before the Tiananmen Square democracy movement. The government's unequivocal answer came soon enough.

The first two dead bodies I ever saw were both Chinese. One was that of my grandfather in America. The other was that of a stranger in China, and he was wrapped in a red cloth and nestled in a bed of ice on a table.

A thin crowd of students hovered around the grim display, their heads bowed and their eyes closed in silence, while the dozen pallbearers prepared themselves, clenching their fists and swallowing their sorrows, before they carried their friend to the crematorium. Next to the body I noticed a white "A01" license plate, the code for a high-ranking military vehicle and now, for the students, a spoil of war.

"I want to take revenge," a twenty-two-year-old student told me, his voice choking and his eyes beginning to tear beneath his wire-rim glasses. "It will be blood for blood."

It was June 5, 1989, a day after Chinese soldiers had taken their tanks and machine guns and fired on students and workers around Tiananmen Square. The sounds of gunshots seemed to echo against the dank walls. They echoed, too, in my memory, as I recalled the terrible news of an acquaintance who had been killed by a bullet in his back—on a small street on his way to work five miles from the Square. Here, in this large, vacant hall, a poor student had become a martyr for the movement.

The air was damp and heavy with the smell of death, and the floor was splotched with pools of water where ice had melted. The body, along with four others, had been carried by workers on the previous morning from Tiananmen Square to a small alley in the western part of the city. From there, the bodies were transported by car to the dark, empty front hall at the University of Politics and Law, where the last one now remained and where I stood.

I stared at the table in front of me, focusing on the blood-colored sheet that revealed the contours of the stiff yet serene body. I had never associated China with death. When I was growing up, China was always a place in my dreams, a land grand and glorious, a nation destined for great achievements. Across the ocean, over a rainbow, it was where my ancestors came from once long, long ago. Actually, China was a state of mind, not a place. I always imagined that the Chinese people could produce magic, like the Chinese acrobats who traveled across America and somersaulted through human hoops, like the kung fu artist who could break bricks with his head, like the Chinese laundryman down the street who put his kids through college and bought several country homes in Florida, like the guy at college who sat in the back of the room and never spoke but ended up the first in his class. And so, when I came to China, that was the prism I was hoping to peer into.

But that's not exactly what I found. All of a sudden in the post-Tiananmen period, China was about oppression and death; it was a society in chains.

The manacles fascinated me, for they were so distinctively Chinese. They reminded me of China's inventiveness in developing instruments of oppression. There was, for example, the cangue: a long, flat board in which prisoners used to be locked up in the Qing dynasty. It had a space for the prisoner's head and each of his arms, so it was a bit like the stocks except that the prisoner carried it around with him. Because the cangue was long and wide, and because the prisoner's hands could not reach his face, he had to depend on others to feed him. Otherwise, he starved to death. Then there were other Chinese innovations, like death by a thousand cuts. And one of the eeriest Chinese characters, *yi*, which fortunately has fallen into disuse, is made by combining the characters for knife and nose. It means cutting off a convict's nose. That was one of the Zhou dynasty's "five punishments"—the others were tattooing, cutting off the feet, castration, and execution.

In the 1990s as well, the manacles are peculiarly Chinese. I had hoped that what would be most distinctive about China would be Peking opera, or else the mountain-and-river watercolor scrolls, or perhaps the intellectual ferment among scholars in the tradition of Confucius and Mencius. Instead, perhaps the most distinctive feature of China today is the social controls that it employs. The Communist Party relies upon an ingenious "iron triangle": the residence permit, which limits where you live; the secret personnel file, which records your sins and political reliability; and the work unit, which supervises every aspect of your life. This triangle controls your life.

The *hukou,* or residence permit, is a little booklet that declares where you live and lists the members of your family. You are supposed to have a Beijing *hukou* before you can move to Beijing, or a Xian *hukou* before you are allowed to move to Xian. The problem is that the government does not easily give out a *hukou.* It is virtually impossible for a peasant to get a *hukou* for a big city, and it is difficult for a resident of one city to get a *hukou* for another city. Every year at college graduation time, girlfriends and boyfriends must tearfully part at campuses around the country. If the man is from Beijing and the woman from a county town in Henan Province, then the man can almost certainly get permission to move to Henan. But it would be very difficult for the woman to get a *hukou* for Beijing. If she went to Beijing anyway, without a *hukou,* it would be difficult to get a good job. And if they were to have a child, it would have the same Henan *hukou* as the mother. That means it would not be allowed to enter a Beijing school, at least not without paying a substantial bribe.

The *dangan,* or secret personnel file, hangs over every Chinese as well. All urban Chinese have two *dangan,* one kept by the local police station and the other at the work unit, neither of which they are allowed to see. The *dangan* looks like a manila envelope, and there is a special postal system for transferring them around the country. If you make a serious political mistake, your leaders put a note in your *dangan,* and it will haunt you in the future whenever you try to change your job, go abroad, or get a promotion.

The linchpin of the iron triangle is the *danwei,* or work unit, which provides housing, medical care, and political indoctrination.

Its permission is necessary to marry, to have a baby, to go abroad, to change apartments. To be sure, economic and social change are generally corroding the iron triangle, and more and more people are able to slip off the manacles. The *danwei* is no longer as important as it once was, and some Chinese in the 1990s manage to get by without one. But for the great majority of urban citizens, the controls remain in place. And the *danwei* is the most important simply because it determines where and how you live.

There are rules about who can get a two- or three-bedroom apartment, about how long you wait before you are assigned a place, and about where your place will be. For many people, it is the bane of their lives, for there is a chronic shortage of housing, and kids always squeeze in with their parents, wives with their in-laws, grandsons with their grandpas and grandmas. The managing editor of a large Communist newspaper once told me, "You would think I spend most of my time evaluating stories. You know what I really spend almost all of my time on? Trying to find apartments for my employees. Reporters call me at midnight to discuss their housing problems. The system's a mess."

At many work units, you are allowed to get housing only if you get married, and even then it sometimes depends on your connections with the bosses. Most people cope, and as long as you aren't politically inclined, you can live your life within the birdcage, without constantly running into the bars. But it isn't always like that, especially for intellectuals.

Huali, a young Chinese teacher who had just graduated with a master's degree, was assigned to work in a research institute teaching English. He was assigned housing, a room about six by nine feet, big enough to fit a bed for him and his wife, a desk, and a few boxes of books. Their clothes were stuffed into boxes underneath the bed, and their kitchen utensils and tiny wok were stashed in a corner. The paint was chipped, and the lighting consisted of one forty-watt bulb that Huali hunched next to at night to do his translations. Outside, in the dark cement hallway, they shared kitchen space and a bathroom with a dozen neighbors. The building had no shower or bathtub, so he and his wife were obliged to shower once a week at work.

Soon after Huali settled in, his *danwei* discovered he was a political troublemaker, a die-hard democracy activist who had a penchant for saying what was on his mind. The *danwei* assigned the teachers a certain number of classes, depending upon how "successful" they were. As the years progressed, Huali was given fewer and fewer classes to teach, and his career prospects quickly dwindled. Soon he wasn't teaching at all. His bosses changed, but they all knew about Huali even before they met him. That was because the authorities inserted notes in his *dangan,* explaining that he was a reactionary element who should not be trusted. The real frustration came when his work unit wouldn't let him go overseas to study; but wouldn't let him teach at home either.

"What can I do?" he asked me one afternoon. "They know I want to go, and they know that I have nothing to do here. Why do they keep me there? It's a form of punishment. I might as well be in a prison; instead, they just hang me on a wall the way you might hang a picture on the wall. And there are hundreds of people just like me just hanging on the walls with nothing to do. We're twiddling our thumbs. What a waste of human talent! I can't leave my work unit, because then I'll have no place to live, and my wife's work unit won't give her a room because it knows that we have this one."

The system also created real idiosyncrasies. Peilin, another friend of mine, was senior enough to be assigned a three-room apartment for himself, his wife, and their eleven-year-old daughter. He was living in a two-room apartment, and his work unit, a newspaper, had limited space and didn't have exactly what he was entitled to. So they offered him a deal: He could keep the two rooms he was living in and they would give him a third room—in a building eight miles away from his apartment.

The *danwei* kept its claws on you in other ways, too. One of our friends in Beijing was a banker named Chaolan, a woman in her late twenties. She was entitled to have a baby, and it was certain that she could get permission to have one if she wanted to. But she and her husband planned to wait a couple more years. Then she became pregnant by mistake and decided to go through with the pregnancy. Her work unit, however, told her that she would have to get an abortion first, then apply for a "pregnancy permission slip." A permission slip could not be issued for an existing pregnancy. But Chaolan had already had one abortion, and she and her husband wanted this child. Chaolan finally lied and said that she was not pregnant after all. A bribe convinced the officials that this was true, and they gave her a pregnancy permission slip. Six months later, she gave birth to a son.

The officials ignored the speed with which she had apparently conceived and given birth.

Imagine discovering that you have some distant relatives. You travel 10,000 miles to visit them, find that they live in a run-down home, spit on the floor, abuse their children, and then curse you for having visited without helping them beat their kids. That's how I sometimes felt in China. Much of the harassment came from the government. Sometimes I felt it particularly because I was working as a reporter, sometimes because I looked Chinese, sometimes because I was both.

During the spring of 1993, I was visiting the southern province of Hainan, an island that felt like a happy-go-lucky, economic merry-go-round, a place that resembled Hong Kong more than it resembled the rest of China. I fit in reasonably well, and I was still amused by the way I'd been taken for a local Chinese the previous night. I'd been interviewing hookers at a bar cum brothel when one of them walked up and asked if I was the new girl. Now, however, I was with my official escort, for I had just stepped out of the main government building following an interview with provincial officials. We were waiting for our car to pull up and take me back to the hotel when I noticed a group of peasants sitting on the lawn in a protest. I was curious to find out what they were angry about and walked up to them and started asking questions. They spoke a local dialect that I didn't understand, but I thought I should at least capture the moment on film. I took a few shots with my Nikon camera, then wandered over to a group of bystanders and asked them what was going on. A local man, rather big and stocky, seemed to speak some Mandarin, so I asked him.

"I don't know what they're doing here," he said. Then he noticed my camera. "Were you taking pictures?"

"Just one or two," I blurted out, without thinking. Only then did I realize it was the wrong thing to say. He sauntered over to me.

"May I see your camera? How many pictures did you take?"

"Do you know what they're doing?" I asked, ignoring his question. "By the way, I see people up there taking pictures, too."

"Give me your camera!" He grabbed for my camera. I turned away. He and another man surrounded me and started pulling the strap of my camera. They were clearly security goons, and they jerked me back and forth, grabbing my arms, yanking me around. I fell to the ground, trying to protect my camera, and began to scream. My escort had run over and was yelling at the men that I was an American journalist. They didn't believe her, because I looked Chinese, and continued to pull at me. They demanded to see her identification. She pulled out her government ID card, showing that she was in the Provincial Foreign Affairs Office. The security men didn't pay much attention, for they were afraid that pictures of the protest might appear in the newspapers. They took me back inside the government building, and there were intensive and furious negotiations between the police and the Foreign Affairs Office. In the end the police confiscated my negatives.

Being mistaken for a local person was alternately infuriating and satisfying. The compound in which Nick and I were forced to live had three entrances that were guarded, around the clock and even on holidays, by People's Armed Police stationed there to "protect" us. Chinese are not allowed in except with a pass or when escorted by a foreigner, and they often stopped me when I tried to enter. They allowed me in only when I produced evidence that I was a foreigner. At various times, the guards knocked Chinese-Americans to the ground when they tried to enter, and there were periodic confrontations with Japanese and others whom the guards mistook for local Chinese. One time, the Taiwanese wife of an American diplomat was bicycling into the compound when a guard, trying to stop her, pushed her down. The American Embassy protested, and the harassment lightened up for a few weeks.

I found the guards incredibly annoying, and one day I complained to Baiyan, a Chinese artist who had spent some time in the United States.

"Doesn't it get you so angry the way the police bark instructions at you?" I asked him.

"Oh no, not at all." Baiyan chuckled. "I'm used to it. All policemen are like that. It doesn't bother me at all."

"Do you ever talk back to them? At least to ask them to be more polite?"

"Definitely not. That would only anger them, and then who knows what kind of trouble that would bring you. No, the best thing is just to be silent, smile, and obey their instructions. Then they can't do anything to you."

Since the government didn't want foreigners to see how China treated its own people, it had mixed attitudes toward Chinese-American journalists like me. Those attitudes also reflected its ambivalent feelings toward foreigners, feelings that have hovered about for centuries. China wants foreign partners but not foreign ideas. It chants the slogans of the third world but is embarrassed by its own poverty and failures, striving to conceal Chinese reality and replace it with a new smiley face that foreigners constantly try to pry off. The extent to which the government sometimes goes to disguise the real lives of its people is material for a tragic comedy of the absurd. Comic because its methods are hilarious, tragic because time and effort go into hiding problems rather than solving them.

When China was preparing to host the 1990 Asian Games, a mini-Olympiad, it worried about how Beijing would appear to all the foreign athletes as they drove about town. China wanted to show that it was wealthy enough to join the ranks of the established Asian powers, and the ability to host the Asian Games symbolized this coming of age. Nick and I often drove down Stadium Road on the way to our health club, and it was a typical wide street lined with run-down residential *pingfang,* or single-story houses. Generally, each compound had been built for a single family in the 1920s but now housed half a dozen families, all crammed into tiny rooms, all getting on one another's nerves. The walls of the buildings were crumbling with age, their red paint fading from the sunlight. Layers of black and gray dust had burned their colors into the rooftops, and every now and then a shingle fell off and was not replaced. If you peeked into one of the narrow alley entrances, you saw an old woman cooking dinner, a housewife hanging up her family's laundry to dry, a graybeard repairing a stool, or a peddler hawking tofu.

A few months before the games began, we noticed construction along the side of Stadium Road. Weeks later the construction began to take shape, and we noticed a flat cement wall, like a stage set, forming along the edge of the old *pingfang* along the road. We couldn't imagine why they were building a wall. More weeks passed, and the wall was painted gray, with white lines to make it look as if it were made of bricks. The houses were now completely hidden, and from the street the set resembled the brick wall of a large, stately residence, hinting of neatness, newness, and cleanliness inside. There was even a fake sloping rooftop that jutted out from the fake wall.

The entrances to the buildings were smartly painted mock-ups, cheap versions of Potemkin villages. When we drove by, we were amazed at how it appeared as though an entire block of buildings had just been constructed. But those of us who lived in the area knew that nothing really had changed, that the smoke puffing from the coal-burning stoves would soon blacken the shiny gray paint and the white-and-black entrances would soon turn ashen. *Lu fen dan, biao-mian guang:* it's shiny on the outside, just like donkey droppings.

The wall was a fine symbol of the way China operates: The government puts on a facade, and foreigners may be fooled, but residents are not. The *xiao shimin,* or the little city people, were indignant at the deceit. "Why can't they use the money to build real new buildings?" asked an angry young Beijing worker as we passed by the wall. "How can they waste money on building a fake wall when so many people in Beijing don't have housing? They're afraid to let the world know how poor China is, but it'll only get poorer if they continue this way."

Often I felt that the most useful perspective for reporting was that of a psychologist, treating China as if it were a neurotic on my couch, as if I were listening sympathetically to its dreams and delusions, gradually identifying its multiple personalities. There were two main ones: One was the proud, intolerant bully with a sadistic streak. The other was the dazzlingly successful economic entrepreneur, determined to change his ways and impress the world. They jostled back and forth, one sometimes dominant, at other times the two coexisting in peace or even cooperating.

But the shoving among the personalities produced a strange organism, an alternately depressing and exhilarating blend of authoritarianism and free markets. The metamorphosis now under way is loosening the iron triangle of controls and provoking all kinds of tensions within Chinese society. I'm not the only one at a crossroads of cultures. China today faces the turmoil that rapid modernization always brings: the urbanization, the changes in job patterns, the rise of individuality, the replacement of the extended family with the nuclear family, the fraying of traditional morality. And at the same time, it faces a crisis of faith, the end of Communist ideology and the search for something to take its place. It is also remotely conceivable that it may face a crisis of territorial loss, if Tibet or even Xinjiang goes its own way.

Just as painful, China will probably have to come to terms with its past, to learn its real history and sift through its real heritage. How should it view Confucius, who has inspired intellectuals for the past twenty-five centuries? Confucius never emphasized the individual but rather the individual's obligation to fit into the larger scheme of things, and that has had a profound influence on the Chinese nation. When Western artists were producing masterpieces like the *Mona Lisa* or *The Night Watch,* Chinese artists were painting magnificent scrolls in which the humans were just specks, like a tiny monk observing a huge waterfall. How will China accommodate the monk's aspirations and ambitions today?

While China comes to terms with its heritage, I'm coming to terms with my own. The past is inescapable. We go forward while looking in our rearview mirrors.

Riding back in the car down the pebble-strewn roads from my grandfather's village of Shun Shui, I felt a mixture of joy and unease. It was wonderful to have found relatives, but I had also glimpsed a darker side of my family's past.

"That's terrible, what your grandfather did, taking his first wife back from America and dumping her here," Nick said. I bridled, resenting his comment. It was common in those days for men to have several wives, several concubines, and my father used to say that Grandpa sent money back to the village. Besides, how could I judge a man in those times by today's standards? And if Grandpa hadn't abandoned her, would I be here today? Sure, I wondered how Grandpa's first wife had felt, especially when he brought his second wife back to the village for a visit before returning to America. Probably she was bitter. But was I to be responsible for Grandpa's actions?

We rode in silence over the bumpy paths that took us past scores of construction sites, passing bicycle riders balancing giant baskets of vegetables or pigs on their back wheels. I wondered what my life would have been like if I had been born in Shun Shui. Everything in the village seemed so alien to me. I felt the thrill of finding my relatives, and a twinge of embarrassment that they were illiterate peasants. Somehow I felt, as I drove away, more American than ever. I knew I could never grow accustomed to Chinese peasant society. And I wasn't sure I could become a Real Chinese. I was as American as I was Chinese.

A test of that came soon after. My parents had been delighted in the mid-1980s when I was going out with another Chinese-American, a fellow Harvard Business School student with an instinctive feel for making money. Then we split up, to the horror of both our families, and I began dating Nick. The problem was that, however obliging Nick might be, there was one thing he couldn't do: He couldn't become Chinese. While it was Nick who had urged me to go to Taishan in the first place, after my visit I wondered how my feelings for him fit in with my own identity. Was I selling out part of my Chinese soul by falling in love with a Caucasian? Perhaps so, but I couldn't help it. A couple of months later, when Nick proposed, I didn't hesitate.

NICHOLAS D. KRISTOF

紀思道

GHOSTS

Those who use the past to criticize the present should be put to death, together with their relatives.

—Li Si, Chinese prime minister in the third century B.C.

3

魂

ick and Sheryl covering protests in Tiananmen Square, May 1989. [Collection of the authors.]

The Holy City of Chinese Communism is Yanan, the yellow-dust hamlet in north-central China where Mao and his guerrillas lived in caves and plotted their revolution. The party portrays it as a utopia, where the titans of the Long March strolled among the peasants, lived simply, and shared their rice bowls with their neighbors. One of the Communists in Yanan was an earnest writer named Wang Shiwei. A smooth-cheeked young man with neatly parted hair, he had the same high forehead as Mao, and he was full of the same revolutionary fervor. Nobody believed more in Marxism than Wang Shiwei, who had visited the Soviet Union and translated Marxist works into Chinese.

Unfortunately, in 1942, at the age of thirty-six, Wang got carried away with his idealism and wrote several articles in the Communist press calling for more egalitarianism. At that time in Yanan, the Communist leadership divided everyone into five categories, depending on their level in the party, and those in the best category ate meat while those in the worst ate cabbage. Wang complained about this and criticized the party's tendency to drift into a hierarchy and bureaucracy. Wang Shiwei also called for democratic elections within the party, and he encouraged people to speak more openly.

"Are there some things," he asked, "that we don't dare say to our leaders?"

If there were, it turned out there was good reason for the reticence. Mao turned on the gentle Wang and denounced him as a Kuomintang spy. Hauled before public meetings to be vilified, Wang refused to confess. So, as the witch-hunt continued, his friends and associates were summoned to attack him. By the sixth consecutive day of meetings, his colleagues were reporting that he had once had contact with Trotskyites and that he had made horrifying statements such as "Stalin's personality isn't lovable." Several months later, the leadership expelled Wang from the party and lumped him with four others as an "antiparty clique." The party accused him of having been a Trotskyite for the previous thirteen years and of trying to be a "counterrevolutionary mole within the party."

For a man like Wang Shiwei, who had risked his life to advance the revolution, this was agony. In tears, he complained that he had never been a Trotskyite. He begged to be allowed to retain his party membership. He pleaded to be given merely a six-month suspension.

Instead, the party locked him up and declared him a "counterrevolutionary enemy agent." For five years, the party jailed Wang in a cave and refused to allow him visitors. He spent his days making matchboxes. Then, in 1947, when the Communists evacuated Yanan, they decided that they could not take him along. They either shot Wang or, one researcher tells me, chopped off his head.

I was shocked when I learned about Wang Shiwei. Like many Americans and Chinese, I thought that the Communists in the 1940s were the good guys, the idealistic patriots fighting the corrupt and brutal Kuomintang. Nearly everything I had read suggested that the Communist Party had started off right and then gone astray in the late 1950s.

My sympathies for the Communist Revolution arose partly because of my travels around Africa, Asia, and Latin America— where a redistribution of land often seemed rather a good idea—and partly because of my readings about China before and after "Liberation" in 1949. The Communists had begun with a devastated country, where few people could read, where inflation was so high that prices sometimes rose daily, where landlords were free to rape their tenants' daughters, where rickshaw boys froze in the streets during the winter, where pimps sometimes blinded young girls because it was thought that this improved their tactile senses and made them better prostitutes. The Communists took this wreck of a nation and transformed it. They halted the inflation, divided up the land, ended opium addiction and prostitution, banned child marriages, campaigned to raise the status of women, and breathed new hope into the people. The Chinese scholar Zhu Xi had proposed back in the twelfth century that a universal public education system be established, but it wasn't until the 1950s that many peasant children had an opportunity to go to school. For many poor peasants, the 1949 revolution really was a liberation.

So I held the conventional liberal view that the Communist Revolution itself was not such a bad thing for China, even if the Communists later went terribly astray. That also was the view of many of our Chinese friends in 1988, when Sheryl and I arrived in Beijing. I was pretty sure that if I had been a Chinese living in the 1940s, I would have been an enthusiastic Communist.

Then bit by bit, over the next few years, I was forced to reexamine China's history. Gradually, tortuously, I found myself questioning my early faith that the party had started off right. My Chinese friends were going through this same mental journey, this demythification of Communist history. Fundamentally, we were all coming to grips with the ghosts of people like Wang Shiwei. Their ghosts are haunting the regime today, eating away at the Mandate of Heaven— the source of legitimacy for any Chinese dynasty.

History has always been a puppet of the rulers in China, a method for building legitimacy rather than a subject for scholarly analysis. The Communists, like the emperors before them, have gone to great lengths to create their own history and mythology. The party has a "central leading group for party history work," headed by the former president of the country, Yang Shangkun, as well as a central party history research center. For decades, the Communist Party controlled its past, whiting out characters like Wang Shiwei. The problem is that now the party is finally losing control over history.

When we wanted a historical perspective, Sheryl and I often sought out an octogenarian named Luhui. A former senior official, Luhui lived in a huge and comfortable apartment that was his reward for a lifetime of supporting the Communist Party. In earlier days, he had frequented the leaders' clubhouse near Zhongnanhai and even played bridge with Deng Xiaoping. Now he is feeble and can't get around very well, so on a free afternoon we would bring some Cantonese steaks—his favorite dish—and his maid would set the meal out on the dining room table. When she had disappeared into the kitchen, Sheryl and I would talk with Luhui and his wife. I figured that, given his background, I could count on him to give me a glowing review of Communist China's history.

"Some young people think the party has done as much harm to China as good," I once began, delicately. "What do you think?"

"Good?" he said, pausing over a juicy chunk of steak cradled between his chopsticks. "But what good has the party done? I can't think of anything. It's been a disaster for more than forty years."

"Surely it's not that bad," I protested, taken aback to hear such a distinguished revolutionary express a counterrevolutionary thought. "In the 1950s, at least, the party did some good."

Luhui looked at me as if I were crazy. "Good? Where? It's been a catastrophe. There hasn't been a single good thing that has come out of Communism."

"What about women? You've got to admit women are better off today."

Luhui paused for a moment. He seemed to think it was a novel idea that the Communist Party might have done any good at all. Finally, he said dismissively, "Well, okay, the status of women improved a little bit, maybe. But that's the only bit of good the party's ever done. And look at all the disasters."

Bit by bit, these disasters are emerging in the public consciousness. When I arrived in China, I didn't appreciate the degree to which long-ago events could destabilize today's China. In the West, where events can be openly debated and written about, we already know in general about the sins of our past. We know that we slaughtered Native Americans, that we relied upon slavery to help build our economy, that President Kennedy regularly cheated on his wife. Our ghosts have been exorcised, our heroes pulled down a notch. The American political system is still seen as legitimate, because it is reasonably democratic and because we cannot see any clear alternative.

In China, on the other hand, the Communist system is undemocratic, and many Chinese see attractive alternatives. So the political system's legitimacy, such as it is, rests on its economic performance and on its history. The problem is that whenever a Chinese historian pries open a closet, a skeleton falls out. Someday, when all the closets start popping open, China's mythology will collapse and society will face a huge trauma: the way you'd feel if your parents suddenly turned out to be ogres who molested your siblings and killed the neighbors. In the Soviet Union of the 1980s, this kind of discovery of history undermined the state and helped provoke the collapse of Communism. In the end it may prove nearly as grave a challenge in China.

Still, whenever I contemplated the demons of China's past, I thought of Chen Longqing and was slightly reassured. Chen, our office assistant for a time, was sent by the government to spy on us. A loyal Communist Party member, Chen was in his fifties, short and balding, a bit pudgy, with a frightful Zhejiang accent when he spoke Mandarin. We tried to buy Chen's support with overtime payments and bonuses, but he refused to take money unless it went through the

Diplomatic Service Bureau (which took 80 percent for itself). At first we doubted his faith, because just about every other Communist we knew was a hypocrite, but as we came to know his background we decided that his loyalty was genuine.

Chen grew up in a small village in Zhejiang Province, where his family had no land and life was a bitter ordeal of survival. He managed to attend primary school, where he displayed his brilliance and was the best boy in the school. But when junior high began, his parents forbade him to go. "We don't have the money for tuition, and anyway, we need you to work in the fields," his father told him. The boy was devastated and spent the next two weeks at home, crying every day, all day.

Finally his mother took pity on him, pulled out the tuition money from the family savings, and gave it to him. He returned to school, again soared to the top of the roster, and was soon the most literate person in his village. Even though he was still a boy, during "Liberation" in 1949 he was honored with the job of keeping the records of the property taken from the landlords and given to the peasants—no one else could write so well. Later on, as the Communists opened up the universities, Chen got a chance to earn a college degree in Beijing. He became a diplomat, and later an assistant to foreign journalists, trusted to spy on them. It was the kind of mobility that no one could have imagined in the days of his youth, and he felt an enormous gratitude to the party for giving such opportunities to a poor peasant. Chen may be disturbed when revelations about party history emerge, but he—and many others like him who benefited from the revolution—will not find their faith fundamentally shaken. He will keep spying for the party.

For those of Chen's generation, especially peasants who gained land, the Communist Party's early achievements weigh heavily. The party showed its patriotism by fighting the Japanese and other imperialists, in the way that Tito proved his nationalism by fighting the Germans in Yugoslavia. The party shored up its Mandate of Heaven with land reform and the social revolution it launched in 1949.

Unlike the Russian Bolsheviks, who lost the constituent assembly elections in 1917–18 and had to maintain power by force, Mao Zedong almost certainly could have won a free election. Probably nowhere in the world did a Communist Party come to power with such popular support as in China.

Yet for Chinese young people today (and half the population is under twenty-five) the disenchantment is such that many now negate the Communist Party's genuine early achievements. In part, this evolution in attitudes is the result of new historical writings, particularly by Dai Qing, revealing that the party was pretty brutal even before it took power. The more people dug, the more they realized that there may never have been a golden age.

Zhou Enlai, for example, is regarded by many Chinese as the most decent Communist leader they ever had. What they don't know is what he did to the family of Gu Shunzhang, his security chief. In 1931, when the party was still underground, Gu was arrested at a golf course in Shanghai by the Nationalist government. Perhaps under torture, he revealed the names of other Communist Party members. In all, some 800 Communists were arrested, a huge setback for the party. Zhou felt that it was essential that any other Communist who was captured should think twice before spilling what he knew. So he ordered a massacre of Gu's entire family, including his wife, three children, and all his in-laws. Altogether, perhaps as many as thirty of Gu's relatives were killed.

Even the Communists' finest hour, the 1950s, began with a bloodbath. In a secret speech in 1957, Mao described the killings that took place during the campaign to eliminate counterrevolutionaries in 1950, 1951, and 1952: "Basically there were no errors; that group of people should have been killed. In all, how many were killed? Seven hundred thousand were killed, [and] after that time probably more than 70,000 more may have been killed. But less than 80,000. Since last year, we basically have not killed people; only a small number of people have been killed."

Mao's tone was defensive, so if anything he probably underestimated the fatalities. In addition, he did not include the huge number of landlords beaten to death in the countryside in 1949 and earlier. A broader estimate of the number of people killed during the birth pangs of the People's Republic comes from Luo Ruiqing, a former minister of public security. He reportedly estimated that 4 million people had been executed from 1948 through 1955. And that was in Mao's benevolent period.

That bloodletting was supplemented by the loss of hundreds of thousands of Chinese soldiers in the Korean War from 1950 to 1953. There are no reliable figures, but estimates of the Chinese dead range from 500,000 to 1 million—probably more than the number of Koreans who died. In contrast, fewer than 34,000 Americans died in that war. This conflict also served to turn Beijing decisively against the West, and within China the security forces began persecuting anyone with connections to the United States.

The killing in China subsided by the mid-1950s, but the mass political campaigns continued. In 1955, Hu Feng, one of China's great writers, was denounced, humiliated, and imprisoned for urging artistic freedom. The Anti-Rightist Campaign in 1957 led the authorities to denounce as rightists 552,877 of China's smartest, boldest patriots, men and women who had dared to respond to Mao's invitation to "let a hundred flowers bloom, let a hundred schools of thought contend." Tens of thousands of these "rightists" died in prison camps, often of starvation, over the next decade. In the end, the rightist label was removed, in many cases posthumously, from all but ninety-six of these half million victims.

Then, in 1958, came Mao's disastrous Great Leap Forward, designed to allow China to catch up with the West. Instead, it provoked the worst famine in world history. In many villages, life had never been so tough, even under the landlords. Peasants lived, if they survived at all, by eating leaves, bark, and grass. Parents sometimes had to choose which of their children to feed; they did not have enough to feed them all. In the hamlet of Tuqiao in Anhui Province, where some survived by eating the flesh of human corpses, an old peasant named Wang Chigang told me that one-fifth of the people in his village had died in that famine.

Demographic evidence suggests that across China about 30 million people died in the aftermath of the Great Leap Forward. Thirty million! Never before had so many people died in one country for any reason, whether because of war or natural disaster. Even Stalin killed only about 10 million of his subjects by famine or execution. The Chinese Communist famine was roughly three times as bad as the previous worst famine in world history, one occurring in northern China in the late 1870s. Mao managed to kill almost 5 percent of his subjects, a figure equivalent to the entire population today of the state of California.

The turmoil of the 1950s seemed a bit remote to me until I met Harold Xu. A thin, bespectacled man with graying hair, Harold is reserved and a bit nervous-looking. Maybe that's what happens when you spend most of your adult life in prison and disgrace. Sheryl met Harold and brought him into my office one day when I had just come back from a trip. I was busy with the mound of messages that had accumulated during my absence, and at first I was irritated by the intrusion. Then, as he related his life's story, I forgot about everything else and listened spellbound.

Born in Shanghai in 1936, the son of a businessman who made a small fortune speculating on currencies, Harold learned his perfect English at Catholic schools in Shanghai's foreign enclaves. The family lived in a comfortable four-story house, and Harold's father thought about fleeing China at the time of the Communist Revolution. But, after exploring the possibility of moving to Hong Kong, he decided to stay.

The Communist Party in those days impressed the Xu family, for although Harold had distant relatives who served in the Nationalist government and army, the Communist Party did not harm him or his parents. The party simply arranged for Harold's father to become a university professor, ending his career as a speculator, and it allowed him to retain his large house. Harold himself was given a place at the Foreign Languages Institute in Beijing and then, upon graduation, a post in the Foreign Service. At the age of seventeen, Harold became China's youngest diplomat.

He was working as a liaison to English-speaking embassies when, in 1955, Zhou Enlai was looking for a new English interpreter. The choice came down to Harold or the somewhat older Ji Chaozhu, later undersecretary general of the United Nations, and in the end Harold was picked. It was an extraordinary honor, for Zhou Enlai was both foreign minister and prime minister. Yet Harold shone at his job and was soon also interpreting for foreign ambassadors when they met Chairman Mao. A natural diplomat, with a brilliant mind and an amiable personality, Harold was on a trajectory that could have taken him to the top of the ministry. He was a real star, much more so than another young diplomat at the time, Qian Qichen, who is now foreign minister and deputy prime minister.

Then, in late 1956, Harold was assigned to make preparations for a forthcoming visit to India by Zhou Enlai. The Indian ambassador and his wife asked Harold, with whom they were friendly, about Zhou's color and food preferences. Zhou was going to stay at the presidential house in New Delhi, and Indian officials wanted to make his visit as comfortable as possible.

"I asked for approval to release this information about Zhou Enlai's preferences, and my leaders said no," Harold remembered. "But I decided on my own to release it."

So he told the Indians that Zhou liked meatballs and seemed fond of purple. Why did Harold, then twenty, violate instructions?

"Out of vanity," he recalled. "The Indian ambassador knew I was a rising star. I was embarrassed to say that I didn't know Zhou Enlai's color preference. It was very simple. I just wanted to show off."

Harold then set off for India to make preparations for the visit. Like the other diplomats, he was given a dollar a day as spending money while abroad, but this was paid only after he returned to China. However, Harold was put in charge of the money for tips in India, and he used some of this as an advance so that he could make a few purchases: two shirts, several pairs of socks, and two decks of playing cards. Someone in the group—perhaps even Harold's roommate, Han Xu, who would go on to serve as the Chinese ambassador to Washington in the late 1980s—noticed the purchases and reported him. As soon as Harold returned to Beijing, he was summoned to the home of the head of the Protocol Division for a "serious discussion."

"I told the chief everything," Harold recalled. Pressed to confess any other wrongdoing, Harold told how he had violated orders and disclosed Zhou Enlai's color and food preferences. He also confessed that he had once accepted a gift of a cigarette case from the wife of the Indian ambassador.

"This was followed by internal meetings and self-criticism sessions. I think they thought I showed a bourgeois tendency even before the trip, because I was one of the first officers to wear Western suits. . . . I also liked to socialize with foreign diplomats; and my colleagues thought that was too much. They thought you should keep a stern face on every occasion when you represent the PRC. And once I played bridge with some diplomats, and then after that the Norwegian chargé started to send me bridge clippings once a week from some newspaper. This was all criticized as a so-called informal relationship with foreign diplomats.

"So they suspended me."

Then, on April 28, 1957, Harold was summoned to the Foreign Ministry once more. His boss told him that the ministry had decided to refer the matter to the courts. Harold naively thought that was fine; perhaps the courts would clear him. Then the police walked into the room and handcuffed Harold. They led him out to a jeep—mercifully, not too many people were around to see the humiliation—and then to the Paoju jail, a crumbling old prison in the alleys just inside the City Wall. Harold suddenly realized how serious the situation was. He thought of his mother. He was her only child, and he knew she would be shattered, so he begged the prosecutors not to inform her. They were noncommittal.

"The prosecutor told me that they would give me two years in prison, just to teach me a lesson. The Foreign Ministry would send me books in English, so that during those two years I would not forget my English. They said it was education."

Unfortunately for Harold, Mao launched the Anti-Rightist Campaign before the trial could be held. Sentences became much longer, and when Harold had his day in court, at the end of 1957, he was sentenced to a ten-year term. The crimes were revealing state secrets (Zhou Enlai's preferences) and misappropriation of state funds (the advance to buy shirts). Soon there was no longer talk of supplying Harold with English books, or of the Foreign Ministry's taking him back. Harold was to be crushed as an example. What saved his psyche perhaps was simply his optimism—a naive, silly, unfounded optimism that was nonetheless enormously comforting. "When I heard the sentence, ten years, one thought came into my head: I'll be thirty-two years old when I get out, and that's still young. That's okay."

Harold was sent with other felons to a prison camp on Xingkai Lake, in Manchuria, near the border with the Soviet Union. The prisoners worked on a farm, planting wheat and rice, under the scrutiny of unarmed guards. The camp was in the middle of the wilderness, so there was no place to run even if a prisoner wanted to escape. Harold and the others worked eight or nine hours a day, with one day off every two weeks, and life was tough but bearable. The Communist Party then still had its ideals about rehabilitation, and it wanted to reform people like Harold rather than make enemies of them. A guard once explained that the prison tried to avoid having anyone die in custody, because that would turn the prisoner's family against the government.

Food was short, but no more so than in poor villages in China. A typical ration was a bowl of corn soup and seven and a half *wotou*—

cornmeal buns—a day. "The soup cheated the stomach—you felt kind of full for a little while, at least," Harold recalled. "Not for very long, though."

The nationwide famine from 1958 to 1961 made everything tougher. Because of a shortage of corn and wheat, the kitchens began mixing ground elm leaves into the flour. There wasn't any nutrition in the leaves, but at least they added bulk, so that a meal didn't seem so pitiful. In 1961 hundreds of new prisoners arrived, many of them already weak and sick, and almost all died of hunger and related illness. "They had a way of testing you," Harold told us. "They would use a finger to poke you in the leg. If the skin remained depressed and didn't jump out again, then you were in trouble. You had dropsy. Then you were transferred to another camp. Some of the people in my brigade were transferred to the other camp, but I never found out what happened to them afterward. I don't know whether they died."

Harold survived without difficulty because, as a cadre, he was given the crucial responsibility of looking after his brigade's food supply. This meant that he could eat what he needed.

In 1962, Harold was transferred back to prisons nearer to Beijing because of worsening Sino-Soviet relations. The Chinese feared that if the Soviets crossed the border and captured him, he could tell them state secrets. So he worked at a prison elevator factory and then at a brick factory until his sentence expired in 1967. All this time, Harold still fundamentally believed in the Communist Party, in the revolution. He had been treated harshly, but it was, after all, in the name of fighting corruption.

It was not his own experience but the Cultural Revolution that shattered Harold's illusions. Mao launched the Great Proletarian Cultural Revolution in 1966 to destroy the party's incipient bureaucratism and restore its revolutionary nature. "Bombard the headquarters," Mao advised, and millions of Red Guards took him at his word. Young people attacked their teachers, forcing them to kneel on glass and confess their errors. Children denounced their parents, and young cadres tortured and humiliated their leaders. For a time, cars were instructed to go forward at red lights and to stop at green, because red was a revolutionary color signifying action. That plan was dropped when not enough drivers got the message and pileups occurred at major intersections.

The chaos reached the highest levels of government, with Red Guards arresting and tormenting even President Liu Shaoqi. Liu died of pneumonia, unkempt and denied medical care, in a prison cell in 1969. Hundreds of thousands of lesser figures also died in the Cultural Revolution from abuse or, more commonly, in armed battles between factions. The army intervened to restore a bit of order, but only by mowing people down with machine guns.

Paradoxically, the prison walls protected Harold. After the expiration of his sentence, he applied to go back to Shanghai, but his request was denied. Instead, he was not really released but simply assigned a job and a room in the prison brick factory where he had worked during his sentence. This was a common arrangement in China, in part because it allowed the authorities to keep an eye on ex-convicts and in part because most normal factories did not want former criminals. In this case, the arrangement was a godsend. The Red Guards in the county seat near the prison wanted to "struggle against" the prisoners and ex-prisoners, and they tried to break into the jail to do so. But the administrators refused to let the Red Guards in, and the walls were too solid for them to break in.

Elsewhere, however, the Red Guards raided offices and published many secret documents, usually in attempts to discredit one leader or another. Often they did not even know what the documents were. But people copied them down from the wall posters, or picked up copies of newsletters in which documents were reproduced, and brought them back to the prison. Harold read them in horror. He recalled, "I was shocked. The classified information that was published during the Cultural Revolution showed the Chinese people how totalitarian, how cruel, how inhuman the regime was. None of us had known. But then everything came out."

Finally in 1969, Harold, shorn of his illusions, was sent to Gucheng, a village in Hebei Province in northern China, where he worked with the peasants in fields of corn, wheat, and sweet potatoes. Gucheng was also a refuge, for the peasants didn't care about politics, and Harold spent the next decade in the village. Only in 1979 was he allowed to return to Beijing and become an English teacher. Harold's English was rusty, after twenty-two years of disuse, but the need for English teachers was so great that he got a job and a transfer of his *hukou,* or residence permit.

There was a long pause when we reached the end of his story. I sat in silence, looking at him, contemplating what he had been through. Then I suddenly thought of his mother, the doting woman who had placed all her hopes on his career. I asked Harold if the prosecutors had informed his mother of his arrest. They had, he said.

"So," I said, "she must have been very upset."

He was silent for a moment. "She killed herself," he said slowly.

She was fifty-five years old when she ended her life in 1957, shortly after his arrest, by jumping from a third-floor balcony. The family knew that she was in despair, and Harold's cousin—then twelve years old—had been assigned to keep an eye on her. He wasn't quick enough.

"Mother knew that her husband had a concubine, so she placed all her hopes on me. With my arrest, her last hopes were gone.

"I got the news in prison. My father wrote a letter to tell me."

Sheryl and I met Harold often during our time in Beijing. We talked easily about China, its problems and its hopes, and we generally held similar views. I often wondered what would have happened if Harold had not made the trip to India, or if the shirts had not been spotted in his suitcase. Would Harold now be foreign minister? Would he be on the evening news each day, thundering against American interference in China's "internal affairs"? Would the Foreign Ministry still harass me and threaten me with expulsion?

I tend to think that someone as decent and brilliant as Harold would make a difference, but only a modest one. As foreign minister, Harold would have to voice hard-line views that he disagreed with, and he would have to lie and spout indignation that he did not feel. Acquaintances of various senior officials, including a couple of foreign ministers, described them as secretly civilized. Friends described Li Zhaoxing, the Foreign Ministry's former spokesman, now ambassador to the United Nations, as a closet reformer who had quietly intervened to rescue one of his junior officers from imprisonment after Tiananmen. Yet at a microphone, Li could come across as a graceless xenophobe. I couldn't help thinking that reformers like him were the prisoners, and that it was Harold who had been freed. Harold, at least, had never had his tongue plucked out; he had never undergone an ideological lobotomy.

Yet in all fairness to the government, what happened to Harold at least had some basis—even if it was viciously and inanely out of proportion. Harold had violated rules and misused public funds. His downfall was not simply the result of some leader's jealousy or venality but rather of the government's systematized brutality and overzealousness in trying to maintain discipline.

Communist Party principles disappeared, however, in the Cultural Revolution. That decade of chaos undermined the party's legitimacy more than anything else, and it is impossible to exaggerate the savagery that went on. In 1992 I obtained a trove of secret Communist Party documents attesting to large-scale cannibalism during the Cultural Revolution in the Guangxi region of southern China. The documents were given to me by Zheng Yi, a Chinese writer and dissident who had conducted a lengthy investigation into the cannibalism. At first I was skeptical, but the more I read the documents, and the more I talked to Chinese, the more I became convinced that the documents were genuine. They were printed on letterhead and stamped with official seals, listing just how many copies of each were printed—thirty-nine of one, eighteen of another, and so on.

The documents suggest that at least 137 people, and probably hundreds more, were eaten in the towns and villages of Guangxi Province in the late 1960s. In most cases, many people shared a corpse, so the cannibals may have numbered in the thousands. While this apparently was one of the largest episodes of cannibalism anywhere in the world in the last century or more, it is different from most other cases in that those who ate the flesh were not motivated by hunger or by psychopathic illness.

Instead, the compulsion was ideological: The cannibalism took place in public, often organized by Communist Party officials, and people indulged communally to prove their revolutionary ardor. The first person to strip meat from the body of one school principal was the former girlfriend of the man's son; she wanted to show she had no sympathy for him and was just as "red" as anybody else. At some high schools, students butchered and roasted their teachers and principals in the school courtyard and feasted on the meat to celebrate a triumph over "counterrevolutionaries." Government-run cafeterias are said to have displayed corpses dangling on meat hooks and to have served human flesh to government employees.

The documents I saw were prepared by the local authorities in the 1980s and are critical of the atrocities that they describe. The following comes from a single page in an account about the Cultural Revolution in Guizhou Province:

A mass meeting for dictatorship was held at Shangsi Junior High School, and twelve people, including cadres, were publicly killed. The livers were ripped out of some of the bodies and taken back to the cafeteria of the county government. Some of the county and commune officials participated.

Also in Shangsi County, in Siyang Commune, the Army Affairs Director went to Hexing Village. He and his partners killed Deng Yanxiong and ripped out his liver and boiled and ate it. He encouraged everybody to eat human liver, saying that this would make them braver. The next day, he arranged the killing of four more people and ripped out their livers, and distributed them to two or three production teams to show "collective dictatorship."

Bodies were humiliated and destroyed, so that while the killing was awful, what came next was even worse. Take the case of three women: Lu Yu, of Siyang Commune; Huang Shaoping, a teacher at Guangjiang River Elementary School; Chen Guolian, of Hepu County's Shikang Township. After they were beaten to death, sticks were poked into their vaginas and their corpses were left naked along the roadside.

In Pubei County's Beitong Commune, ten hoodlums from the Boxue Work Team tied up Liu Zhengjian and carried him off to the hillside along with his seventeen-year-old daughter. They beat him to death and then gang-raped his daughter. Then they beat the daughter to death with clubs and ripped out her liver and cut off her breasts and vagina.

In Dongxing County's Naqin Commune, in the Nabo Work Team, they wanted to execute Zhang Yueye, but he was still alive after being shot. So the director of the Office Against Speculation forced a detonator inside Zhang's nasal cavity. With the explosion, Zhang's blood and flesh flew in the air.

In the fighting in Qinzhou County, a broadcaster from a minor faction, Lu Jiezhen, was captured and stabbed to death. The assailants pulled off her pants, and forced a huge firecracker into her vagina. They lit it and exploded it.

Most of those killed, as elsewhere in China, were former land-lords or intellectuals or their descendants. Others had quarreled with someone powerful, or were made to suffer for the supposed sins of their parents or spouses. One woman was forced to identify and denounce the mutilated corpse of her husband, who had been killed, stripped of his flesh, and mostly eaten. As punishment for having loved a "counterrevolutionary," she was then forced to sleep with his severed head beside her.

Some of those involved in the cannibalism in Guangxi received minor punishments after the Cultural Revolution ended. Wuxuan County expelled ninety-one people from the party for having eaten human flesh, and it demoted or cut the wages of thirty-nine nonparty members, but no one, apparently, faced criminal prosecution. A female deputy head of Wuxuan County, who liked to eat the genitals of men, was dismissed from her post and expelled from the party. She moved away from the county, and her whereabouts are not known.

In 1980, the central government tried the "Gang of Four," who had helped rule the nation in that period, for killings and other crimes during the Cultural Revolution. But other criminal prosecu-tions were extremely rare, and at the local levels in China it was nor-mal for people literally to get away with murder. "For the children of the victims, the worst thing is that the murderers were never seri-ously punished," Zheng Yi said. "They say that every day on the streets, they see the people who killed and ate their parents."

Why go into these horrors at such length? Because they are just the ones we know about, the ones that were documented. As the country loosens, many more such horrors may emerge into the pub-lic eye to challenge the legitimacy of the regime. Someday, historians will have a field day in China.

Somehow the party kept getting away with it, because it controlled history. The huge famine in the late 1950s and early 1960s was named "the three years of natural disasters," so it seems that the blame lay with flooding and drought rather than Mao's mistakes. China has never acknowledged the scale of the death toll, so most Chinese have no idea that the famine was the worst in history. Indeed, since the famine is almost never mentioned in the books or the press, some younger Chinese do not even know very clearly that it happened.

The government has distorted the language in other ways as well. The Korean War is called "the war to resist America and help Korea." The Vietnam War is called "the war to resist America and help Vietnam." The 1949 revolution is called "Liberation." The leadership of China during the Cultural Revolution is called the "Gang of Four," as if those four people were the culprits and not Mao himself. The authorities applied the term *counterrevolutionary rioting* to the 1989 Tiananmen student movement.

This manipulation of the language was moderately successful. I initially resisted using these loaded expressions when I spoke Chinese, but I found that without them I sometimes couldn't communicate. If I asked a peasant what he did before the 1949 revolution, he usually looked puzzled and asked what that revolution was all about. Only when I asked him what he did before Liberation did he understand. So, grudgingly, I was sometimes forced to use the term *Liberation,* and it has a subtle psychological effect. If you say it a hundred times, you get used to the idea that it was something good.

Fang Lizhi, the great astrophysicist and dissident, a pudgy man with a laugh like a freight train, has written of the Communist "technique of forgetting history." By this he meant the party's success in erasing unflattering episodes from its past. He recalled his own befuddlement when the Communist Party viciously turned on him during the Anti-Rightist Campaign of 1957; he had not thought that such a thing could happen. Older intellectuals laughed at his naiveté; they remembered the 1942 "rectification" in Yanan in which Wang Shiwei and other writers were persecuted. During the Cultural Revolution, it was Professor Fang's turn to laugh at the naiveté of the Red Guards when Mao turned on them and sent them to the countryside. And in 1989 it was the turn of the former Red Guards, some of them now plucking the odd gray hair from their scalps, to smile sadly and knowingly at the university students who were so surprised when the army turned its machine guns on them.

Yet as Professor Fang has noted, the government is finally losing its ability to rewrite history. In 1982, the Communist Party issued a directive banning further works about the Cultural Revolution, yet new books and articles on the subject trickle out nonetheless. They slip in from Taiwan and Hong Kong, and they are also published domestically because of cracks in the Communists' monitoring process.

In 1993 a landmark book, *The Catastrophes of Chinese Leftism*, came out; it delved enthusiastically into the Communist Party's dirty laundry. The book, published under a pen name, even described cases such as Wang Shiwei's that took place before the party took power. It discussed the 1958–1961 famine, the Anti-Rightist Campaign, and numerous other episodes that the Communists had tried to expunge from the record. The book caused a sensation, and even though it was promptly banned it was sold widely by private booksellers.

So the "technique of forgetting history" is no longer very effective. In "the struggle of memory against forgetting," to use Milan Kundera's phrase, memory is winning. This is particularly true of the period after the authorities crushed the Tiananmen democracy movement in 1989. In the past, repression and torture were applied secretly; this time, the party obligingly carried out its slaughter in front of foreign television cameras.

For us, the first inkling of that great spasm of China came when the phone jangled in the early afternoon of April 15, 1989. It was Fei Xiaodong, an exuberant young journalist at the *World Economic Herald*, a colleague of Zhang Weiguo. "Did you hear?" Fei asked as soon as I picked up the receiver. "Hu Yaobang has died." Hu Yaobang, the former Communist Party leader, had been ousted at the beginning of 1987 by hard-liners. A rather ineffectual leader when in power, prone to impetuous suggestions—such as the advice that Chinese abandon chopsticks and switch to knife and fork—he was transformed by his dismissal into a hero for all intellectuals. Now he was becoming a martyr as well.

A thin, lithe figure, barely five feet, three inches tall, Hu had suffered a heart attack a week earlier—embarrassingly, forty minutes into a Politburo meeting. The doctor ordered him to spend a week in bed, but Hu was impatient. He was also tired of bedpans. So in the early morning of April 15, he rose from his bed and stepped toward the bathroom. It was too much for him. He suffered a seizure, collapsed, and died.

Fei's voice bubbled with excitement over the phone line as he told me about Hu Yaobang's death. "I hear there may be something happening at Beijing University this evening," he said. "You might want to drop by and see if there are any posters."

And of course there were: Wall after wall of posters mourned Hu Yaobang, portraying him as a great democrat, calling for more democracy, and even taking pokes at Deng Xiaoping. A couple of posters bluntly declared: "The wrong man died." We walked among the students for most of the evening, talking to them, tapping their souls, measuring their irritation. Sheryl spoke at length with Wang Dan, a short, ever-serious history student, owlish in his spectacles, who was to become the leader of the Tiananmen movement, the most wanted student in China.

"This could be a turning point," he said. Yet that night, neither he nor anybody else expected that the movement would take off in quite the way it did.

Deng Xiaoping later charged that the democracy movement was a conspiracy by a small number of counterrevolutionaries who used the students for their own purposes. In a sense, he was right. From the beginning, students like Wang Dan were advised, guided—and, yes, used—by various graduate students, professors, businessmen, and officials. A steering committee of about two dozen people, many of them in their thirties or forties, met each day to help plan the protests and offer instructions. In addition, these "advisers" gave tens of thousands of dollars to the students, as well as access to printing presses, cars, and meeting rooms.

Yet the students were also using these advisers, precisely to get the cars and printing presses. As in any human situation, everybody was using everybody else—or, to put it more charitably, everybody was contributing something. The advisers stayed in the background mostly because they knew the risks of involvement; they feared the movement would end the way it did. They were people like Zheng Yi, the writer; Wan Runnan, a computer company manager; Wang Juntao, a journalist; and Chen Ziming, a social scientist and entre-preneur. In short, they were people who had no hidden agenda but simply sought a more democratic and open China. Many of them were party members who sought to save the party rather than extin-guish it. They were Gorbachevs, not Yeltsins.

The student movement was also caught up in a power struggle within the leadership of the Communist Party. Zhao Ziyang, the party leader, who was already under attack from hard-liners before the movement began, was temperamentally inclined to sympathize with the students. Zhao rode in his Mercedes-Benz 500 limousine around Tiananmen Square, looking through the tinted glass at the students, who could not see who was inside. He stood on top of the Great Hall of the People and used a pair of binoculars to peer down at the students. He knew that they, like him, were reformers, and he wondered whether he dared use the unrest in the power struggle.

Meanwhile, the hard-liners used the protests to press their campaign to dismiss Zhao. The Beijing Communist Party apparatus, run by two notorious hard-liners, prepared a report for Deng Xiaoping that emphasized the most extreme of the student slogans—such as those calling for the ouster or even death of Deng himself. When Zhao left for a previously scheduled trip to North Korea on April 23, the hard-liners swung into action. The Politburo Standing Committee—presided over by Prime Minister Li Peng, Zhao's main rival—met the next day and resolved that the party had to act firmly to halt the demonstrations. On April 25, two black Mercedes-Benz limousines wound their way through the streets north of the Forbidden City until they pulled into a narrow lane marked with a stern Do Not Enter sign. A team of elite bodyguards opened the steel gate and admitted Prime Minister Li and President Yang Shangkun into the home of Deng Xiaoping.

Deng was in a grim mood, thanks in part to the report from the Beijing party committee. As aides scribbled his comments, he warned that other Communist countries that had tolerated protests—he cited Poland—had experienced economic collapse. He praised the authorities in the Soviet Republic of Georgia for their firm measures against unrest, in a reference to a recent Georgian army attack that had killed at least nineteen protesters. "We do not fear spilling blood," Deng said, "and we do not fear the international reaction."

Deng's comments may seem brutal to us, but we should understand that he feared for his country as much as he feared for his power base. Deng grew up in an era when China was torn apart by warlords and foreign invaders, and he had lived through famines, civil war, and attacks by marauding Red Guards in the Cultural Revolution. By some accounts, his own father was beheaded by bandits in 1941, at a time when there was no government to establish order. All this bred in him a primal fear of chaos. To him, the pro-democracy protesters were no better than the equally idealistic Red Guards two decades earlier who had attacked his family, crippling his son and driving his brother to suicide.

On Deng's orders, an editorial condemning the protest was prepared for the *People's Daily*. When a draft was rushed to his home that evening, he crossed out each use of *xuechao* (student movement) and substituted *dongluan* (turmoil), the same pejorative term used to describe the Cultural Revolution.

When the *People's Daily* arrived the next morning, the editorial was splashed across the top of the front page. "This is a planned conspiracy, a riot, whose real nature is fundamentally to negate the leadership of the Chinese Communist Party and to negate the socialist system," it declared. "Comrades of the whole party and people of the whole nation must see clearly that China will be in agony if this turmoil is not ended."

The protests could no longer be regarded as a lark; any students who pressed ahead would risk their careers, their freedom, and perhaps their lives. Wang Dan and other student leaders called for a march to Tiananmen Square the next day, but it seemed unlikely to succeed. At nearby Qinghua University, considered the MIT of China, the student leaders announced that they would not join in. Tens of thousands of armed police were trucked into the capital that evening to take up positions near the universities. That night, those students at Beijing University who planned to protest wrote out their wills. They half-expected to be clubbed to death in the streets.

As I drove to Beijing University early on the morning of April 27, I saw police lining the streets, preparing blockades to halt the demonstrators. There seemed little hope. The democracy movement appeared to be over.

Then a bit before 9:00 A.M. a band of students marched out the main gate of the university, waving banners and chanting pro-democracy slogans. French-language students waved a banner reading, "*Vive la liberté!*" Other students prepared a large black banner aimed at workers: "You work but you get nothing; your life is bitter." They were a puny, defenseless force, symbolized by the scrawny Wang Dan trying to lead them.

Yet over the next hour or so a miracle occurred. When the demonstrators reached the first line of troops, the police did not use their clubs, and after ten minutes of jostling, the students pushed their way through. Crowds of workers and young people along the way joined the students, and at the next blockade they pushed their way through again.

What had happened was this: While Deng had ordered that the demonstration be crushed, he had not bothered with the details. They were left to lower officials, particularly Qiao Shi, the head of the security forces. Qiao, a careful man whose daughter was studying medicine in Texas, didn't want to offend Deng and didn't want to be blamed for killing students. So, after a night-long discussion with lower officials, he ordered the police to block the students but not to beat them or shoot them. As it turned out, a show of force was not enough.

Even the heavens sided with the students, for the sun came out and presided over a gorgeous spring day, with the trees and parks sprouting a rich, deep green and the city itself exhaling cheer and warmth and hope. Crowds of students from other universities joined the marchers, and so did parents, teachers, workers, and passersby. Soon the highway was swarming with hundreds of thousands of bobbing heads, so that as far as I could see there were nothing but protesters. Even the bridges and the trees brimmed with bystanders hoping to get a good look. Shop owners rushed out to give free drinks to the marchers and old ladies tossed snacks down to the students from their balconies. As the marchers approached, workers left their factories and offices to join the throng. Some half a million people took part as the students marched for fourteen hours to Tiananmen Square and back. At the square, where several truckloads of troops were surrounded by workers, the students had to be called in to rescue the police. And when the students returned to the university late at night, white-haired professors were at the gate, waiting for them, embracing them, crying for them, hailing them as heroes.

That evening Sheryl and I drove to the *People's Daily* compound, parked several hundred yards away, and took advantage of the dusk to slip in the back entrance. I wound my way through the buildings into the dormitory and found the room of my friend Dalei and his wife. Normally taciturn and restrained, Dalei seemed ready to hug me; I had never seen him so exuberant. "This was unbelievable today," he said, beaming. "It was the first time in Chinese history that the ordinary people won a great victory. The date will live in history. Until now, people were always afraid of the emperors, always willing to be slapped around. That'll never happen again. You mark my words—it's probably the most important day in the last few hundred years. It's the beginning of a revolution."

It was one of the most exhilarating days of my life, and not just because it was also my thirtieth birthday.

Zhao Ziyang returned from North Korea a few days later and immediately began trying to use the protests to bolster his own position. "The just demands of the students must be met," he declared in a speech, and his top aide, Bao Tong, ordered the newspapers and television stations to report the comment prominently. Zhao and his supporters also instructed the news media to begin reporting on the protests, and the result was a wave of news coverage that gave new impetus to the democracy movement. The public, sensing the split in the leadership, backed the students with even more boldness.

In mid-May, Mikhail Gorbachev arrived in Beijing for a summit intended to normalize relations after the three-decade Sino-Soviet split. Gorbachev was treated as a hero by the protesting students, who admired his attempts to make the Soviet system more humane and tolerant. The students had now gone on a hunger strike, and this turned out to be a brilliant strategic move that won enormous sympathy from ordinary workers. The students conducted their hunger strike in Tiananmen Square, and they regularly fainted and had to be rushed to the hospital to be revived. Ambulance sirens blared all over the capital, pricking people's hearts, as medics evacuated those who had lost consciousness. As soon as they recovered a bit, the students plucked the IV tubes from their arms and demanded to be returned to Tiananmen Square to resume their fast.

"Our hearts bleed when we hear the sound of ambulances," a gray-haired schoolteacher told Sheryl between sobs. The teacher was standing alongside the Avenue of Eternal Peace, watching the ambulances race by with students who had fainted, and she was crying into her handkerchief. "They are no longer children. They are the hope of China." The teacher, one of about a million people on the streets of Beijing to support the students, saw a group of students passing around a cardboard box to raise money, and she pulled out her faded purse and contributed twenty yuan, a week's wages. "I want to thank them," she said. "They represent our hearts. They represent our hopes."

Perhaps the students might have won if Zhao Ziyang had not made a lunge for power. He told Gorbachev—in a comment broad-

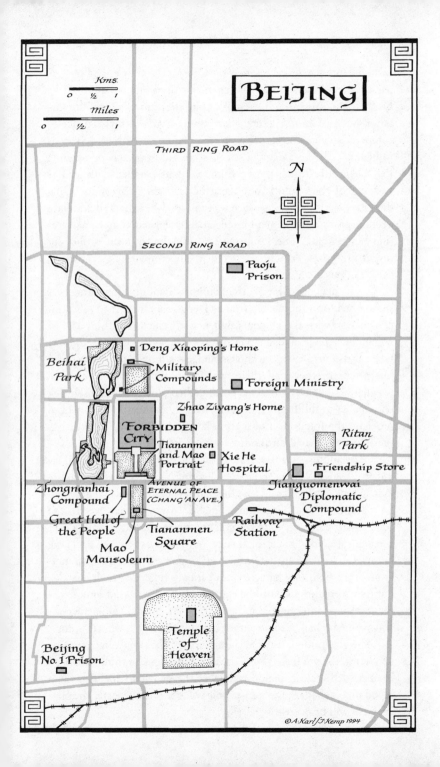

cast on Chinese television—that the Central Committee had secretly passed a resolution requiring that major decisions be approved by Deng. Zhao presented his remark as a reflection of Deng's importance, but all Chinese knew what he was trying to say: "I'd like to compromise with the students, but my hands are tied; Old Deng is to blame." The next day the streets were full of posters demanding that Deng give up all power. Some workers paraded with a huge painting of the empress dowager, the last real ruler of the Qing dynasty, except that Deng's face was painted where hers should have been. A group of prominent intellectuals circulated an open declaration that stated, "The Qing dynasty has already been extinct for seventy-six years. Yet China still has an emperor without a crown, an aged, fatuous dictator."

On the next day, May 17, the Politburo Standing Committee was summoned to the home of a furious Deng Xiaoping. Zhao called for conciliation with the students, but nobody sided with him against Deng. The other octogenarian elders—the so-called eight immortals—also demanded a crackdown, and, even though they were nominally retired, they had their way. Zhao then wrote a letter of resignation, but Deng rejected it, and Zhao proclaimed himself sick and unable to fulfill his duties. On May 19, a meeting was held to proclaim the imposition of martial law, and Zhao was supposed to preside; instead he didn't bother to show up.

Sheryl and I were at the *World Economic Herald* that evening, talking to Zhang Weiguo about the slugging match in the Politburo. Zhang took a call and said that the martial law announcement would be made shortly at Tiananmen Square, so we headed over to the square with him. Li Peng's voice, taut with anger, was booming over the loudspeakers. "The capital is in a critical situation," he declared, but he was so nervous that he kept making mistakes in his pronunciation of the Chinese characters. Our friends hooted at each mistake, but they were furious with the content of the martial law announcement. We ran into one of our best Chinese friends, Danping, a general's son who had become a university professor. He was steaming.

"The government is crazy," he shouted, as Li Peng's voice continued to reverberate through the square. "How does he think he can go against such a clear demonstration of the people's will? The more blood that is shed, the angrier people will get, and the faster the government will be overthrown."

Danping had told us a few months earlier that he didn't want to join the dissident movement. "We can accomplish a lot more if we work for change within the system, in the legal code, in the economy," he had said then. But after martial law he stood with his students on Tiananmen Square, openly defying the Communist Party. "How can I sit in the university, preparing research articles, when my students are risking their lives?" he asked. "If they're willing to take these risks, then I'll stand up, too. And if the tanks roll over them, the tanks will first have to roll over me."

Zhao Ziyang now found himself confined to his home in Zhongnanhai. His nine bodyguards were changed, and the new ones responded not to his instructions but to those from the Politburo. Some 200,000 troops from all over China camped around Beijing, but they were not immediately an ominous sight. Their commanders knew that the party was split, so the troops remained at their stations, suffering the indignity of lectures from the public, of pleas not to crush the students. The students let the air out of the tires of their trucks and sometimes took their spark plugs. The soldiers sat, immobile and expressionless, in the backs of the trucks. Most were eighteen-year-old peasants who had never before been in Beijing. They were terrified.

Hundreds of thousands of people were still manning roadblocks throughout the capital, lying down in front of tanks to keep them from moving. One evening Sheryl dropped by the *People's Daily* to see how Dalei and his wife were doing and to find out what was happening at the newspaper. Dalei was just finishing dressing down his younger brother, a university student who wanted to go out and spend the night in Tiananmen Square to keep the troops at bay.

"Don't you dare go out tonight," Dalei scolded, his voice shaking. "Mom spent her whole life raising us. The government, those troops, if they come out, they'll have no mercy." His brother sank into a chair and nodded submissively. A few minutes later he wandered off.

"So, Dalei, what do you think is going to happen?" Sheryl asked.

"I don't know, but I'm worried," he said. "I'm afraid there's going to be blood on the streets."

"What are you doing tonight?" Sheryl asked.

"I'm going out to Tiananmen Square," Dalei said. "I've got to go out and support the students. If they're willing to stand up for democracy, then the rest of us have to stand with them."

In the predawn hours of Saturday, June 3, citizens stopped an unmarked bus that was carrying machine guns and ammunition to the troops, and they confiscated the weapons. Hard-liners used the seizure to charge that "counterrevolutionaries" were stealing weapons and preparing to attack the party. That evening, the order was given by the martial law enforcement office to all the army commanders to use their guns if necessary. The biggest historical mystery of recent years is who gave the order to shoot, which apparently was never written down.

Deng Xiaoping's children have told friends that their father didn't give the order and didn't know about it ahead of time, although he supported it after the fact. Chen Yun, the octogenarian patron of the hard-liners and at the time the most powerful person after Deng, has also spread the word that he was not involved in the decision to open fire. My guess is that Deng gave the basic instructions, along the lines that "resolute measures must be taken to end the turmoil" and that "this chaos must end immediately." I suspect that it was Yang Shangkun, then the president and vice chairman of the Central Military Commission, who implemented Deng's order by commanding the troops to load their guns and make their way to Tiananmen Square that evening, firing if necessary.

To encourage the troops to move more quickly, the generals made a game of it: The Twenty-seventh and Thirty-eighth armies were pitted against each other, in a race, with all honor going to the first army to reach Tiananmen Square. "Comrades!" one army officer declared to his troops as they were about to set off, "the present circumstances are extremely dangerous, and the student movement in the capital has already degenerated into turmoil and counterrevolutionary rebellion. . . . We must enter Tiananmen and occupy Tiananmen Square! We must protect the party, we must protect the government, we must protect the capital!" Similar exhortations were taking place all over Beijing, as the officers and political commissars prepared the troops to fire on the "hoodlums." In the mission command center in the Great Hall of the People, the generals moved pins on a map to keep track of the troops, radioing instructions for them to move faster.

Sheryl and I were at our computers, frantically writing stories on the evening of June 3. Then, at 11:38 P.M., an "URGENT" clattered over our AP machine: "Chinese troops opened fire on crowds as tens of thousands of people swarmed into Beijing streets to block their advance." Sheryl started calling hospitals and fielding the stream of phone calls as I rushed to Tiananmen Square. Students had set up antitank barricades, making cars useless, so I rode my single-speed black Phoenix bicycle, pedaling frantically down the Avenue of Eternal Peace.

It was a crazy ride. Gunfire rattled continuously ahead, and crowds were streaming along, running toward me and away from the shooting. Hunched over the handlebars, careering around the antitank blockades, I mused at the absurdity of a profession that obliges one to rush in the direction that everyone else is running away from. Soon I was at Tiananmen Square, on the front line. I parked my bike on the north end of the square, about 500 feet from the lines of green-uniformed troops. Two armored personnel carriers were burning, where workers had ignited them with Molotov cocktails, and the acrid smoke burned my eyes. A few minutes later, the troops began shooting. At first I wondered if they were firing blanks, but then some people fell to the ground, wounded or dead, and I joined the panicky flight, sprinting along the avenue away from the troops, abandoning my bicycle.

For the next two hours, the troops slowly advanced on the crowd, firing each time. The people retreated each time, but they were so furious that they then rallied and began throwing rocks in the direction of the soldiers. None of the rocks landed near the troops, but each time the soldiers fired again, and more people fell to the ground. After the crowd had retreated, the rickshaw drivers—mostly peasants or uneducated workers—slowly pedaled their rickshaws into the no-man's-land, bravely facing down the soldiers, to pick up the dead and wounded. Then the rickshaws came back, the drivers pedaling frantically, tears running silently down their cheeks.

Frustrated by their inability to attack the soldiers, the protesters commandeered a bus. Inside, about a dozen young people, some armed with Molotov cocktails or iron bars, stood in the aisle, waving out the window to the cheering crowd. The driver was a young man, perhaps twenty years old, short, frightened, and determined. He could not drive very well, but he slowly accelerated and wound the bus around the barricades toward the troops. He was moving at perhaps fifteen miles an hour, and the bus had gone no more than half the distance when the troops opened fire. The windows popped out as thousands of rounds pulverized the bus, yet for a few moments it kept moving—perhaps the young man had fallen on the gas pedal. Then it slowly ground to a halt. I watched in silence, terrified of being hit but too riveted by the scene to run, scarcely daring to breathe. For ten seconds afterward there was no movement on the bus; then, finally, one solitary teenager jumped out the back exit and ran to safety. Everyone else onboard apparently had been shot.

A few minutes later, another group of young people took off on the same kind of suicide mission. Their bus did not even get as far as the first one. The troops opened fire, it ground to a halt, and then it burst into flames. This time, nobody got out.

The Chinese in the crowd were hysterical with grief and rage, and the notebook clutched in my palm was stained through with the sweat of my fear. The protesters grabbed at me, pulling me this way and that. They wanted me to see the bleeding bodies as they were carted by rickshaw to the hospitals. They knew that the gunfire would be followed by an enforced silence, that they would be unable to describe what had happened except in the safety of their own homes, and that they would have to depend on foreigners to spread the word.

"Tell the world!" a twenty-year-old art student with shaggy hair shouted at me. Nearly incoherent with fury, he gripped my shoulder and screamed, "You've got to tell the world what is happening, because otherwise all this counts for nothing. So tell the world!"

One of those out on the street was Yuejin, a thirty-one-year-old engineer with seven patents to his name. He had spent the morning walking the streets with his wife, and they had seen the troops chatting amiably with local residents. She had returned home at 11:00 A.M. to look after their four-year-old child, and he went home at midnight, after the shooting started.

"I've got to go out again," he said immediately, as he scribbled a note with his name, address, and phone number. He put the paper into his pocket, just in case something happened to him. His wife pleaded with him to stay inside, but he was determined.

"There's violence out there, and the students are poor and weak," he told her. "I've got to go and help them."

The woman waited inside, listening to the gunfire. At 3:00 A.M. the telephone rang.

"*Wei?*" she answered, saying hello in Chinese.

"*Wei?* This is the Xie He Hospital." The nurse pronounced her husband's name and asked if this was his home. The woman's world was shattering.

"He's been shot in the stomach," the nurse said. "He needs emergency surgery. His condition isn't very good."

At about that time, when the crowd had been driven away near the Beijing Hotel, I ran a mile to that very hospital. It was a bloody mess, with hundreds of injured lying on the floors, and it was impossible to find several of my friends who were doctors there. But I saw the bullet holes in the ambulances, and the drivers spoke of the troops firing on them as they tried to pick up the wounded. From the hospital, I ran the three miles back home, my senses overwhelmed, every element of my being furious with China.

Sheryl and the editors were getting frantic, for I still hadn't returned as the deadline approached, and they feared I'd been shot. In fact, there was a simpler explanation: I had forgotten that it was a Saturday night, and thus that there were early deadlines for the Sunday paper. After bursting inside the door, and embracing Sheryl for a long, desperate hug to drive away the demons, I pounded out my story on the computer keyboard. Our stories filled most of the front page the next morning, under a six-column banner headline, but I was never so sad to lead the paper, never so depressed, never so bitter about the city in which I lived.

A few hours later, Sheryl and I drove by back lanes to the Xie He Hospital. Police were guarding the entrances, but a sympathetic workman asked if we were journalists.

"Then come with me," he said, and he led us into a neighboring building and through an underground tunnel into the hospital itself. It was a nightmare. Hundreds of gunshot victims filled every bed and lined the corridors, groaning, shouting deliriously, as their parents and wives and husbands cried over them. One of the victims was a Chinese exchange student who had just returned triumphantly from his studies in Japan. As he was coming home from the airport, he crossed the Avenue of Eternal Peace—and was shot in the back. "He'll be paralyzed for life," a tired doctor told us, shaking his head bleakly, but speaking too low for the man's wife to hear.

Yuejin, the engineer with seven patents, was still alive—barely— after seven hours of emergency surgery. His thirty-year-old wife was sitting on a bench outside the intensive care unit, crying quietly, her eyes puffed and red.

"He was convinced that by staying in the Communist Party he was in a better position to contribute to the reforms," she told Sheryl. "At the time, he said that such a party could never hurt the people. But he was wrong.

"So many party members think the way he does. They're all deluded."

Our friends were picked up by the police, one by one, and disappeared into the prison system: Zhang Weiguo, Wang Dan, and several others. At the *People's Daily*, Dalei and many other reporters were forced to confess their errors and write self-criticisms. They were barred from writing any articles.

There is some dispute about how many people were killed on June 4. After tabulating hospital totals, obtained from friendly doctors around the city, Sheryl and I stick with our original estimate that 400 to 800 people were killed and several thousand injured. That is lower than most other estimates at that time, for even the State Department initially suggested that about 3,000 had been killed. But most of the higher estimates have been scaled back, partly because it is now clear that there was no huge massacre of students within Tiananmen Square itself. Instead, most of the killing was in the western part of Beijing and in the streets around the square.

Four hundred or 800 deaths may seem a modest number compared with initial student claims that thousands or tens of thousands were slaughtered. But even 400 is far more than the number of students killed altogether in other such protests over the last century in China. On June 4, the Communist Party revealed itself to the public at home and abroad. It suffered a catastrophic setback in its program of manipulating history, of covering up its brutality. The government tried very hard to coin the phrase *counterrevolutionary rebellion* to describe the Tiananmen movement, but the term never really caught on among the general public. The regime was forced to accept the neutral linguistic ground of "the June 4 incident," and that is how it is now known in Chinese.

Those killings may have marked the beginning of the last chapter of Communist rule in China. Students are revered in China, for they embody education and responsibility, and the one certain rule in Chinese history is that no one can kill them with impunity. Not even a red emperor.

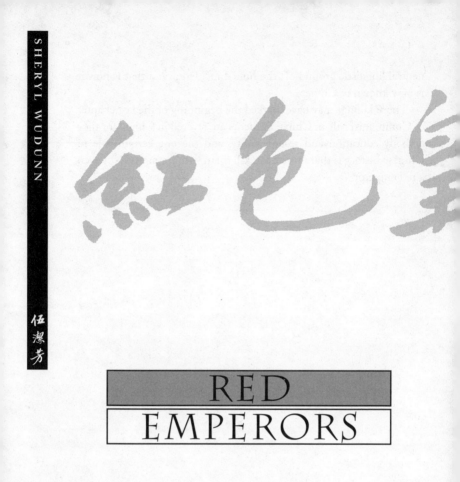

SHERYL WUDUNN

紅色皇

伍潔芳

RED
EMPERORS

Before the revolution, we were slaves. And now we are the slaves
of former slaves.

—Lu Xun, early-twentieth-century writer,
referring to the 1911 revolution

4

eng Xiaoping shaking hands with General Secretary Jiang Zemin in 1992. Flanking them are
'an Li, then head of the National People's Congress, and Deng's daughter, Deng Rong. [Photo by
nhua.]

China's leaders wanted to host the Summer Olympics in the year 2000, and they planned to let nothing get in their way.

At least two dissidents who opposed Beijing's Olympic bid were hustled into insane asylums. And the authorities stepped up their campaign as the International Olympic Committee prepared for an inspection tour of Beijing beginning on March 7, 1993. The government closed down factories so black fumes wouldn't mar the skies. It shut off electricity in some neighborhoods that the committee would not visit, even turning off traffic lights there, to ensure an adequate supply at sports facilities. Every taxi in the city was ordered to buy a "Beijing 2000" bumper sticker. Schoolchildren had to wear their yellow safety caps, even at schools miles from any place on the visitors' itinerary. The homeless were shipped out of town, and the entire city underwent a face-lift.

So the parents of Wang Chaoru, a forty-one-year-old retarded man, weren't surprised when a knock came on their door two days before the delegation was to arrive. Their home, on an alley in the southern part of Beijing, was a tiny room filled with the smell and smoke of burning coal and occupied mostly by a big bed where the parents slept. Three feet away was a smaller cot for Wang. By the window, there was an old wooden desk where the family kept two metal hot-water thermoses, the day's newspapers, and a small, old television. A plain calendar hung on the wall, next to a steel-rimmed, white-faced clock. The paint on the ceiling was sooty and chipping, and brown-paper boxes were stacked on a dark wooden shelf along the wall above the big bed. It was a simple home, typical for a small working-class family in Beijing.

Sure enough, at the door was Zhang Guiying, the graying woman who is deputy head of the Neighborhood Committee, accompanied by a boorish policeman. The Olympic delegation was unlikely to approach that neighborhood, and it would certainly never go by their alley, but the authorities considered Wang an embarrassment because of his mental disability, and perhaps they feared that he would stray to a major street and gawk as the Olympic inspectors whizzed by in their Mercedes-Benzes. Wang was only mildly retarded; he could speak simple sentences and find his way around the neighborhood. He could light the stove, cook simple meals, and help his parents clean up the house. But he couldn't write down his address, and he might gape and point and come across as an oaf, thus harming Beijing's Olympic prospects. A long shot, perhaps, but nothing was to be left to chance.

The policeman wanted to take Wang away, but the retarded man began shrieking his protests. So the policeman and Zhang left.

The next morning, Zhang returned—this time with two policemen. They had no arrest warrant, no detention warrant, and they didn't suggest that Wang had broken any law or endangered anybody. They didn't give any reason for wanting to take him away, but they insisted that he had to leave with them.

"I don't want to go!" Wang cried out in fear. "Mama! Papa!" He raced to the corner of the big bed, shielding his head with his arms. His parents knew that it would be futile to resist, so they watched helplessly as the two policemen dragged away their terrified son.

Wang had reason to be frightened. A year earlier, as part of their efforts to beautify Beijing in preparation for the annual session of the National People's Congress, the police had taken him to a sanatorium on the outskirts of Beijing and beaten him to a pulp. A few days later, they drove him to the Temple of Heaven, where they deposited him in a wounded clump at the front gate. It took Wang two hours of walking to find his way home.

There's a law in China that protects the mentally retarded and assures them of the same rights as everyone else. There are also laws that forbid the police from beating people up, as well as laws that strictly limit the ways police can detain suspected criminals. Of course, there are other laws protecting freedom of speech and freedom of religion. There's even a constitutional right to take a rest during the day.

So why did the police drag away Wang Chaoru? I doubt that there was any formal decision by the Communist Party to clear the streets of handicapped and retarded people before the Olympic delegation came to Beijing. But like other developing countries, China is not kind to disabled citizens. There are no special ramps at building entrances or street corners, and the handicapped are rarely given the chance to take meaningful jobs.

In this instance, some local boss probably decided that retarded people in the neighborhood were an eyesore, an embarrassment.

What is clear is that Wang and his parents were the victims of a society run by what the Chinese call *renzhi*, rule by individuals, as opposed to *fazhi*, the rule of law. *Renzhi* pervades the nation and displays itself in both innocuous and insidious ways. But as I sat and talked with Wang's parents, as I heard his father, Wang Shanqin, relate the full story, choking back his tears, I realized that, at its worst, the system was absolutely inhumane. It was a thugocracy.

Renzhi, unfortunately, means rule by not just one thug but a hierarchy of thugs. The nation's emperor has the ultimate say, but power trickles down. Each lower official acts like a prince on his own turf, from the ministry to the department to the section to the team, from the factory manager to the production manager to the workshop director. The petty autocrats are often the worst, as well as the most difficult to escape. In many villages, the local chief rules even more absolutely than Deng Xiaoping, for he decides who can marry, who can get good land, who can get water for irrigation, who can be buried where. He is almost as powerful as God, but not so remote.

Renzhi is not a Communist Party innovation; it goes back 4,000 years to the dawn of Chinese civilization. It may have had its advantages in earlier eras, for a single strongman could make crucial decisions about irrigation and could force people to work on the dikes. Such leadership, in turn, promoted agriculture in the Yellow River valley and helped nurture the rise of the Chinese nation. But an industrial society and market economy needs laws. One of China's biggest challenges in the years ahead will be to build a *fazhi*, a system of laws, so that democracy and a market economy can take firmer root. Otherwise, tomorrow's democrats may simply turn into the following day's autocrats.

One of the characteristics of *renzhi* is that it doesn't make any sense. It means government by whim. Sometimes that means rule by superstition, as when Mao chose an official named Wan Li as his minister of railways. Wan's name sounds like "ten thousand miles," and Mao thought it an auspicious name for a minister of railways. Government by caprice becomes even more unpredictable when it is mixed up with government by *guanxi*, with everybody trying to take advantage of relationships to nullify the rules that do exist. Wang

Chaoru's family had no *guanxi,* no relatives or friends in high places who could protect them. There were other disabled people in Wang's neighborhood, but their families had a bit more standing. Wang paid the price for his lack of *guanxi.*

As the Olympic delegation toured Beijing's sports facilities on March 7, 1993, Wang's parents waited anxiously. There was no word about their son. On the following evening, a policeman appeared at their door and told them they should go early the next morning to visit their son.

"Is he dead?" Wang Shanqin, the sixty-eight-year-old father, quizzed the policeman.

"I . . . I . . . don't know. He's sick. Just be ready tomorrow morning."

As dawn's first light illuminated the narrow alley the next day, Wang's mother, An Yulian, ran out and bought a cake and six eggs. "They said he was sick," she told me later. "I had to bring something for my poor boy."

A police car came to pick them up, but the police officer said that only one of the parents could go. The parents, now desperate with worry, imagining their son beaten bloody, perhaps even in a coma, insisted that they both go. The police backed down and drove them out to Fangshan, a hospital closely associated with the Public Security Bureau. The parents were accompanied by the head of the local police station, a section chief at the station, and a representative from the city police.

When they arrived, the police took the parents into an office that was bare except for several chairs and a table.

"The person has died," an officer informed them, matter-of-factly. "We have inspected the body."

Wang Shanqin and An Yulian were devastated. They felt responsible for their son, who had depended on them. He had pleaded with them to let him stay, yet they had allowed the police to take him away.

"W-w-why did he die?" Wang asked, his trepidation in the presence of authority fused with fury.

"We don't know."

"We want to see the body," he demanded. The officer led them down a long corridor and then into another building. They were taken to a morgue to look at the corpse of their son.

I was sitting in the parents' home, transfixed by their story, a lump in my throat. "What did your son look like?" I asked softly. "What was his face like?"

"There was blood all over his head," the father recalled, speaking slowly and hesitantly, like a man fighting with himself, negotiating between his desire to tell the world and the pain of remembering. "His hair was all red with blood. His lips were cut up, and his eyes— they were pierced, as if they had burst open and then swollen shut."

"What did his body look like?" I pressed.

"His face was yellow."

"And his body?" I asked again, meekly.

"His whole body was dry and stiff. In his back, there was a big hole. Someone must have stuck a police baton into his back, boring it into the flesh. And his behind was all bruised.

"Then they wanted us all to eat lunch. We couldn't eat a thing. All of them were slurping up the food, laughing and joking around. My wife and I just sat there, stunned, horrified. Oh, my son!"

Wang Shanqin and An Yulian were driven back home and told to bring other relatives as witnesses the next day. When Wang and the relatives appeared at the local police station, the police drove the group in a bus to the hospital.

"The doctor wouldn't say anything," Wang told me later. "He said he couldn't issue a death certificate, and he wouldn't say why. But you know, he expressed his regrets to me."

"When did your son actually die?" I asked, gingerly.

"The police said that my son had died on the night of the sixth." That was just hours before the Olympic delegation arrived. "They said he went mad and died on the streets. That's impossible! When they said that, I yelled at the policemen. They were just too inhumane. How could they hate my son so much?

"The back of my son's legs," he continued, as he rubbed his hands underneath his kneecaps, "had these huge bumps, these swellings. I told them I wanted to sue, and you know what they said? 'You'll never win.'

"On the day we cremated him, they gave me a bag with 5,000 yuan in it. They didn't say what the money was for." They didn't need to. It was hush money, and also an apology of sorts. It was as close to an admission of a mistake as the authorities ever offered.

Had I found out about Wang Chaoru's case while I was still reporting for *The Times*, the resulting story might have helped skewer China's chances to host the Olympics. The incident was tailor-made for front pages around the world. It was too stunning, too macabre, too revolting—nobody could even have imagined that the authorities were so twisted that they would beat to death a mentally retarded man because he didn't fit in with the Olympic image. It was the kind of thing that the Nazis might have done before their 1936 Berlin Olympiad, but not even China's worst critics could have expected this from a country whose slogan in the Olympic bidding was "A More Open China Welcomes the 2000 Olympics."

In fact, one of my friends tried to tell me about Wang's killing shortly after it happened. But of course he couldn't explain over the phone what had happened, or even indicate that he wanted to talk to me about a potential story. He simply called up and asked if we could get together, and I thought he was suggesting a social call and told him I was very busy. So I missed the story until months later.

As it was, Beijing missed getting the Olympiad by two votes, forty-five to forty-three, with Sydney winning. So even from the twisted perspective of those who thought he might harm the Olympic bid, Wang Chaoru was sacrificed for nothing.

The case of Wang Chaoru haunted me. I wondered what kind of monsters would kill him. Searching for clues about his death, I went to Strawmaker's Alley and found a small sign marked No. 16. I walked in through the open doorway.

"Hello, is anyone home? Is Grandma Zhang around?" I called out as I tiptoed into the courtyard complex. It was a run-down compound of one-story brick apartments opening on a tiny brick courtyard. No one responded.

"Grandma Zhang?" I called out again. "Grandma Zhang? Are you here?"

I heard a stirring in the room by the door, and an old woman called out, "Here, here, are you looking for Neighborhood Committee Director Zhang? Here, here. Come in."

I opened the screen door onto a living room. It was twice the size of Wang Chaoru's home, with a large bed and two sofas against the walls. Opposite the larger sofa was a big table with a thermos tucked under the sill of a ramshackle window, and the autumn breeze rattled the loose glass in its dry wooden frame. On the wall by the window hung a collection of photographs, including one of a woman as a Red Guard during the Cultural Revolution. I wondered if it was of Grandma Zhang herself or of her daughter.

Grandma Zhang had been napping on the sofa, but she quickly roused herself and stretched. She was rumpled and a bit bent, her hair dyed in a feeble attempt to look younger. She was a slightly stout woman in a gray-blue Mao jacket, her shirts and sweater sticking out at the wrists and the waist. Although she appeared frumpy, her eyes were quick and alert, looking at me with curiosity and a bit of annoyance at the disruption. I looked back, searching for some kind of guilt. Or evil. This was Zhang Guiying, the deputy director of the Neighborhood Committee, the woman who had twice brought the police to take Wang Chaoru away.

"Who are you?" she asked, suspiciously. "Where are you from?"

"Hi, Grandma Zhang," I said, using the common honorific for an old woman. "I've come to discuss some business with you. I have a friend to introduce to you."

I went and called Nick, who was waiting outside. He was my protection, just in case the police wanted to drag me away in the same way that they had dragged off Wang. They might easily beat up a Chinese-American, but that was less likely for a Caucasian.

"This friend is from the United States, and we have something to discuss with you," I said in as sweet a voice as I could muster.

"Who are you?" she asked, tossing her head.

"We're writers, Grandma," I said. "We've come here to talk about something that occurred in March, just before the International Olympic Committee came to Beijing on March 7 and 8 for an investigation. We know that before the committee came, everyone wanted to clean up the streets and make the place look pretty for the outside world."

"Have you made arrangements with the Neighborhood Committee to come here?" Grandma shot back. She was the deputy head of it, so she knew we hadn't.

"Grandma, China's Olympic bid is over," I replied soothingly. "So now we want to look into this matter. You know—the matter that you were involved in. We understand that as part of an effort to clean up for the Olympics, you led two policemen to the family of a retarded man. They took him away and beat him to death. We'd like to hear your side of the story."

I had no sooner finished talking than Grandma started coughing. "There's no such matter as this. This never happened. Where did you hear this?"

"Grandma, we know this happened. Everyone in the neighborhood saw you lead the two policemen to the house, everyone knows what happened. Many people have told us this."

"You can't just come to my home. You have to go talk to the Neighborhood Committee. Have you talked to them yet?"

"Grandma, we don't want to talk to them. We want to talk to you."

"I can't answer any of your questions," she said nervously, and she got up and walked over to her desk, poured a glass of hot water from her thermos, and took a swig. She swished it around in her mouth, walked toward the door and opened it, then spat out the water in the courtyard. She took another swig and spat. She cleared her throat. She seemed to be thinking furiously, and finally she opened the door for us to go. "You must get out of here and go to the Neighborhood Committee."

"Grandma, look, we know that as part of the Olympic cleanup this retarded man was taken away. We know that you led the two policemen to the family's house. We just want to hear your side of it."

"I, I can't answer these questions. I know nothing. It wasn't me. You have to talk to the Neighborhood Committee."

"You mean, you weren't involved in this?"

"No, no. Not me. You have to speak to the Neighborhood Committee."

"Who on the Neighborhood Committee should we talk to? Aren't you the head of the Neighborhood Committee?"

"You have to go to the office. You can talk to anyone there."

We left. She was clearly rattled and confused, and she wasn't going to say anything. This little old lady with glasses and short, permed hair had decided she would make her neighborhood safe for the Olympic delegation. So she called the police and told them to cart away the retarded man on the block. The saddest thing about her was that she wasn't scary-looking; she wasn't menacing.

She was absolutely ordinary.

Grandma Zhang is her street's tyrant, a woman who can literally get away with murder. Above her is the tyrant of the Chongwenmen District. Higher still is the tyrant of Beijing, Chen Xitong, a brash man with a taste for limousines and tennis games. And above them all is the emperor.

I once asked Luhui, our octogenarian friend, whether he thought China operated as an imperial system, whether it had an emperor.

"China is definitely run by emperors," he said. "Isn't it clear who the emperor of China is? Who else could it be but Deng?"

In newspaper articles, we didn't know quite how to refer to Deng Xiaoping, since his most significant formal title in the 1990s was honorary chairman of the China Bridge Association, a reflection of his favorite card game. We couldn't very well write: "Deng Xiaoping, the Honorary Chairman of the China Bridge Association, called today for sweeping economic changes in coastal areas." So instead we used expressions like "senior leader" and "paramount leader." But the best way to understand his role is simply to see him as emperor.

The man who really controls the country is China's emperor— first Mao, and then Deng. Though barely five feet tall in his (white) socks, though barely able to walk or talk, Deng uttered guttural-sounding noises that were still passed around the country like the word of God.

Well, not quite God.

A senior official who in the 1980s worked in Deng's circle once told Nick and me that Mao was God to the Chinese, while Deng was simply an emperor. I suppose that's progress.

As might be expected in a system of *renzhi*, Deng Xiaoping's authority was personal. It didn't stem from any official post he has occupied; in fact, he never actually held the top position in either the Chinese government or the Communist Party. In the 1980s, when he first took ultimate power, he was simply deputy prime minister. To his credit, he never sought to be the party chairman, prime minister, or president. Instead, he wanted two things, power and popularity, and in the 1980s he achieved both to an incalculable degree.

For starters, Deng won a measure of approval from the ordinary people. He was regarded as talented and moderate—a lesser version of Zhou Enlai—and he was not associated with the Gang of Four or any of the horrors of the Cultural Revolution. Xiaoping (Deng's given name, meaning "little peace") is pronounced the same way as the Chinese for "little bottle." So in 1977 and 1978, when Deng was struggling back to power after the Cultural Revolution, many ordinary people showed their support for him by setting up glass bottles in public places.

Historians may conclude that, in the post–Cold War era, the most important man in the world was Deng Xiaoping. American presidents have their significance, of course, but the difference between a Clinton and a Bush—even a Clinton and a Reagan—is one of degree. The United States will continue to thrive no matter who is in office. But Deng Xiaoping seemed to be the glue that held together more than one-fifth of the world's population. Like Stalin or Brezhnev or Tito, he defined an era. And, as with their deaths, his passing would certainly start China on the course of far-reaching change. Brezhnev's death started the Soviet Union on the road to democracy and disintegration, and Tito's launched Yugoslavia on a course that ten years later would take it to civil war. As for Deng, he was the last of the revolutionary generation to lead China, and the last top party official with undisputed control over the army. His well-being was intimately related to that of 1.2 billion people, not counting the nervous neighbors, and anything could happen in the succession struggle after his death.

The paradox was that Deng Xiaoping was so powerful that he was often nearly invisible. I never met him, and neither did any of my colleagues. I never even saw him in person. By the end of our time in China, our only glimpse of him had been his annual or semiannual appearances on television, hobbling along and greeting political leaders. Most of the time you couldn't even hear his voice; the television announcer drowned him out.

Frustrated by the difficulty of getting to know something about the emperor, I arranged in 1991 to visit his birthplace and childhood home. I thought that much of the worldview that shaped his policies—the political repression, the economic liberalization—had been formed during the era of revolution and chaos in which he grew up. Perhaps a visit to his home village of Paifang would help me understand him better as a leader. His home, however, was in an area of Sichuan Province closed to foreigners. I applied to the Foreign Ministry for a permit to go to Deng's village, and the authorities obliged.

With Jan Wong, the correspondent of the Toronto *Globe and Mail*, I embarked on my own pilgrimage to understand the emperor.

We landed in the provincial capital, Chengdu, where we were met by two Sichuan officials, and they accompanied us on the plane and train journey to Deng's home county. After two days of traveling, Jan and I found ourselves in a minivan, inching up a slender hill that overlooks an expansive farming community. By the time we got to the top, I felt almost dizzy from looping through the fields of rice and corn and mud and from the smell of the Chinese roses craning toward the road in front of the Deng house. Nowhere else in China have I ever seen flowers on peasant land, but then again, Deng's old home no longer belonged to a peasant. In Paifang, the officials were trying to transform the ancestral home into a local shrine, hoping to attract Chinese from miles away.

Deng was born in 1904 in a long wood-and-stucco house that has been restored to remarkable condition. The black-shingled roof twinkled in the sun, and the dull squares of concrete in the courtyard were swept and scrubbed clean, even the ones that had chipped at the corners. The charcoal-colored wood planks and beams, which criss-crossed the cement walls, were streaked with white and gray where cracks had been filled with putty, and there was an aroma of sweet pine as I walked up the doorstep to get a better glimpse of the plaques at the sides of the entrance.

"Welcome," said Chen Xiansong, the official caretaker. A tall man with a receding hairline and a blue Mao suit, Chen led us through the collection of fourteen rooms, most of which were tidy and empty. This amounted to a virtual mansion, and it underscored Deng's origins as a member of the landlord class. It was always curious how many of the Chinese Communist leaders—Mao Zedong, Zhou Enlai, and Deng Xiaoping—came from relatively well-off backgrounds and launched a revolution against their own social class.

Chen took us into a large bedroom that was unexceptional except for a wooden desk with a broken drawer that Deng had used and a large bed, carved from the wood of cypress trees. Deng was born in that bed. It was a gift from the parents of Deng's mother, a plump woman who, like many women of her generation, never had a given name. When she married into the Deng family, her name became Deng Dan Shi—"of the Dan family, married to a man named Deng."

Deng had seven sisters and brothers, although most were siblings by his stepmother. They all seemed to have had long lives, including Deng's eldest sister, Deng Xianling, who at the time was ninety-seven. A year later, I heard she had died. Their father, Deng Wenming, was a fairly wealthy landowner and also part owner of a silk factory and a small processing plant. He died in 1941, although there are different accounts of what happened to him. One version is that he simply died of an illness. The more interesting story is that he was killed by bandits who seized and beheaded him as he returned home from a long journey. But Chen denied this—possibly because it is untrue, or possibly because it seemed a macabre and undignified death for the father of an emperor. When Deng's mother died in 1927, seven years after Deng had left Paifang for the bright lights and good schools of the cities, the family purchased a grave site with an elegantly carved tombstone, but Deng did not even return for her funeral. By the time Deng's father died, the family's riches had dwindled, so his father's grave site was just a mound of dirt—an auspicious site, but no tombstone. Deng has never visited either grave site. We asked why. Chen fidgeted in his chair and finally came up with an excuse: "Deng Xiaoping was too busy."

"After he left in 1920, Deng didn't ever return, nor did he ever write a letter," said Chen. "He cut off the relationship. When he returned from France, he didn't even know if his father was still alive. He didn't know when his mother died."

It was a puzzle to me why Deng never returned, not even during the early 1950s, when he was based in Chongqing, about sixty miles away. Perhaps, as a Communist leader, he was embarrassed to have come from a relatively prosperous family. But Deng must have felt some kind of remorse, for he sent his daughters Deng Rong and Deng Lin on two separate occasions in the 1980s to tend to his parents' graves.

In some respects, Deng earned his imperial rank. Few leaders in recent history have so dramatically improved the lives of as many people as Deng did in his final years. Under Deng, Chinese learned what it means to own televisions, refrigerators, and washing machines. Deng took his two callused hands and yanked, pulling

China away from orthodox Maoist egalitarianism to a new world of stock markets and special economic zones. The police might still beat a retarded man to death to keep him out of the sight of foreigners, but this was not a typical experience. Such brutality, however revolting and inexcusable, was much less widespread under Deng than under Mao. A far more common experience in the Deng era was the thrill that families felt when buying a first cassette recorder, a first motorcycle, a first puppy.

An earthy, abrupt man with a peppery personality, Deng set in motion an economic boom that tripled average incomes, and he brought many Chinese villages the first opportunity to break through subsistence levels so that peasants could work to enjoy life, not merely struggle to survive. Instead of sitting on a regal throne issuing orders, he would slouch in an overstuffed chair, mixing his chatting with spitting and coughing as he cleared his throat.

Yet for all he achieved, Deng was in some ways a tragic figure. Although he dramatically accelerated the pace of change in China, and clearly improved the material lives of many Chinese, he seemed reluctant to bend to the new political demands that were the fruit of the nation's change. Many Chinese became increasingly annoyed that he would not fully withdraw from the country's political life. But in one sense it wasn't his fault; it was the system's. He was emperor, and an emperor cannot retire, even if he wants to. Deng Xiaoping didn't cling to power; instead, he gave up his seats on the Politburo and military commission, and even warned people in an internal speech not to listen to him if he went senile. He stopped meeting foreigners. He virtually disappeared from sight. But the only way to stop being emperor would be to commit suicide. So long as he lived, he was emperor. So long as he could mumble, he would be the ultimate arbiter of power struggles.

Nearly two hundred years ago, the same thing happened. In 1796, Emperor Qianlong stepped down at the age of eighty-six after a sixty-one-year reign. Qianlong retired because his grandfather, Emperor Kangxi, had also ruled for sixty-one years and he felt it would be unfilial to beat his grandfather's record. So Qianlong stepped down, and his son became emperor.

But, naturally, no one in the Forbidden City listened to the son. Everybody knew that Qianlong remained the real authority, and the son himself deferred to his father. Qianlong could retire from the formal post and step down from the throne, just as Deng Xiaoping could resign from the Politburo, but in an imperial system they were both stuck with their role as emperor.

Emperor Deng had a rival, a bitter enemy who may be the only other Chinese as stubborn as Deng himself. We did not get to meet this rival until the very end of our stay in China, for he had been in solitary confinement for nearly fifteen years.

Wei Jingsheng is the eldest son of a senior official, and even as a child he was the naughtiest kid in his compound. In the Cultural Revolution he was a Red Guard, a worshiper of Mao, but he gradually lost his faith. He was particularly shaken when his train stopped at a poor station in western China and he casually offered food through the window to a beggar. "Except for the long hair spread over her upper torso, that young woman—probably seventeen or eighteen years old—had nothing at all on her soot-and-mud-smeared body," he wrote later. "From a distance, the soot and mud had looked like clothing, and, standing among the other youngsters, she had not been conspicuous." Wei flinched and drew his hand back, and the beggars cried all the more loudly for food. "I saw that young woman, on tiptoe, her hands outstretched, fixing her piteous eyes on me as she pleaded in a dialect I didn't understand." How could this happen in a socialist country? The sight horrified young Wei, and it made him realize that Communist rule wasn't a panacea. It started him on the road to apostasy.

In 1978 and 1979, Wei Jingsheng emerged as the boldest and most farsighted of the young dissidents in the Democracy Wall movement. He was working as an electrician at the Beijing Zoo, but on the side he edited a magazine called *Explorations*. While other writers pulled their punches, praising the party at the same time that they asked for more openness, Wei crusaded for democracy itself—at least in some form. The Communist Party had called for "four modernizations," in agriculture, science, industry, and the army, and Wei wrote a famous essay calling for a "fifth modernization"—democracy. Without this, he said, the other modernizations would ring hollow.

Wei Jingsheng was also the first to warn that Deng Xiaoping could become a tyrant. He saw the crackdown coming in the spring of 1979, and he sounded the alarm. With his boldness, tenacity, and clarity of views, Wei tried to stand in Deng's way. Naturally, he was steamrolled.

Sentenced to fifteen years in prison for counterrevolutionary offenses, Wei was locked up in solitary confinement in Beijing No. 1 Prison. For the first three years, he was denied family visits and sunlight, and he was forbidden to talk to anyone at all, including the guards. He never knew what day or date it was.

"I couldn't even speak very well, since I hadn't had any practice for years," he recalled. "I spoke really slowly and awkwardly, like a foreigner." He looked at Nick and quickly added, "No offense—not like you, just like some foreigners when they speak Chinese."

We were having a long dinner together at a Cantonese restaurant a month after he had been freed from prison in September 1993. He had been released six months before the end of his fifteen-year term, apparently to improve China's image abroad and help it win the 2000 Olympics. After having written so many articles about Wei, we found it amazing to be sitting at a dinner table with him, hearing his account firsthand, laughing together at jokes. We had heard that Wei's teeth had fallen out during his imprisonment, and when the government released photos of Wei—with a full set of teeth—Nick had reported the fact but added that it was unclear whether the teeth were real. The Foreign Ministry was outraged at this. The officials complained that we were too suspicious, that we were always trying to be critical, that we never accepted any evidence. We told Wei about the episode and the Foreign Ministry's scolding, and he laughed. Then he reached into his mouth and pulled out his teeth. They were false. Most of his original teeth had fallen out in prison because of the poor diet and lack of sunlight.

After five years in Beijing No. 1 Prison, Wei Jingsheng was transferred to a labor camp on the Tibetan plateau of Qinghai Province and later to a prison in the eastern city of Tangshan. The food was terrible, and rats were everywhere. Wei repeatedly went on hunger strikes to demand better treatment, and usually that strategy worked. Gradually conditions improved, and Wei was allowed to speak with his guards. His next demand was for smarter guards.

I asked Wei what he thought of the economic boom in China. Was he surprised by how well China had done under Communist rule? Had he moderated his views on Deng Xiaoping?

"This wasn't his initiative," Wei said immediately, and I thought he was probably tired of the question. "He was pushed into the reforms by popular pressure; he was forced into them. As for the economy doing well, that's not the work of one man. That's the work of the entire nation. So it's not fair to credit Deng Xiaoping personally." After a sip of Coke, Wei kept on talking, making it clear that he felt vindicated by the changes that had taken place since his arrest.

"In 1979, most people weren't against the party as such. They criticized this aspect of the party or that. But now they're against the system itself. People come up to me and say, 'Old Wei, you were right back then. You saw that Old Deng was a dictator, and you were right.' Even party members, even Old Revolutionaries, are against the party now."

As I watched Wei hold forth, I thought that he would make a first-rate politician. We saw him again at his home, and he asked us to translate and edit his prison writings for publication abroad. We explained that we couldn't take on the project, but the world will hear more from him. Wei Jingsheng is a formidable adversary for an emperor. The government knows that, and it rearrested him on April 1, 1994. Wei has been imprisoned without charges since then, and the government will not discuss his case or even confirm that he is alive. He has been nominated for a Nobel Peace Prize. I'm rooting for him.

There was nothing particularly Communist about Deng's decision to lock Wei up in a rat-infested cell. Any emperor might have done the same; the difference is that any other emperor might not have let him out. Centuries ago, emperors used to inflict a punishment called *mie jiuzu* on people like Wei Jingsheng; it means to wipe out someone's entire clan, slaughtering even distant cousins. It says something about a country that it needs to come up with such an expression.

The term *totalitarianism* was first used in the 1920s, to describe Communist Russia and Fascist Italy, but some scholars believe the system first appeared thousands of years ago in China and other societies that depended on controlling and using water. To prevent flooding and to gain the benefits of irrigation, these civilizations came to be ruled by despots who exerted far more control over daily life than did kings in the West.

Back in the Northern Wei dynasty in the fifth century A.D., Chinese emperors developed an elaborate *baojia* system, in which neighbors watched other neighbors, regional militias watched one another to ensure that taxes were paid, and all were accountable to the center. Later dynasties inherited and modified the system, which is still recognizable in the 1990s in the form of neighborhood committees and party cells, each group run by a petty tyrant.

Local party officials cultivate their own fiefs outside the hazy legal system; they are the law. To the average Chinese peasant, Deng Xiaoping is a remote, barely comprehensible figure; real power lies with the village chief. In the 1980s and early 1990s, the economic loosening and rising prosperity had a side effect of promoting these little dictators and giving them bases of power. The decentralization led to a bloom of little Dengs all over the country. Take, for example, the village of Daqiuzhuang.

For years, the stony road to Daqiuzhuang was like a washboard. Trucks filled with glistening rods of steel made their way precariously down the road, pipes rumbling, clanging, dangling off the edge of the containers. The village chief kept the road this way. Some local drivers and workers speculated that he did so to maintain a bit of distance from the rest of China. It was a modern moat.

By the early 1990s, Daqiuzhuang was China's richest village. In 1993, it boasted an official average income of $23,000 for each of its 4,400 natives. This village, in other words, was richer per capita than the United States.

I kept hearing stories about Daqiuzhuang, and about its fabulous wealth and clever village chief, so in 1991 I decided to pay a visit. Only ninety miles from Beijing, near the city of Tianjin, Daqiuzhuang seemed to be an El Dorado—suspiciously so. The village head was Yu Zuomin, a wily, wiry sixty-three-year-old man with bushy eyebrows and a face full of wrinkles. In a guarded compound surrounded by a salmon-tinted wall, Yu lived in a three-story home with a lambskin sofa, a private bar, a bedroom for his bodyguard, and an elaborate video system by his bed, where he taped his lovemaking. When Yu traveled to Beijing, six bodyguards went everywhere with him. He wore Pierre Cardin suits, drove a Mercedes-Benz 600, and loved to watch videos. His fellow villagers also lived well, some dwelling in eleven-room houses with glass porticos, backyards, and purebred sharpay dogs worth thousands of dollars each. Wives didn't

work, and young girls coiffed their hair and wore short dresses and
pretzel-strap shoes. Gleaming cars with tinted windows whizzed
down dirt roads or parked by the local store, and men in designer
shirts and slacks scurried behind the panes of glass buildings.

I thought it extremely odd that a remote village could become so
wealthy so quickly. When I asked villagers about their secret, they
replied, "We work hard, we're efficient, our quality is good." Sure.
Such comments made me even more suspicious. The only hard work
in the village was done not by the peasants of Daqiuzhuang but by
the guest laborers, who were brought in from other provinces to work
fourteen-hour shifts in the village factories.

The Chinese government and news media became ever more
fulsome in their praise of Daqiuzhuang. It was the most famous village in the country, the model village of China, a symbol of the
prosperity that the party's policies could achieve. Yu Zuomin was a
national hero.

Then an accountant named Wei Fuhe, an outsider from a nearby
province, was accused of fiddling with the accounts. On December
13, 1992, four villagers held a private hearing to find out whether
Wei Fuhe had stolen money. The interrogators got carried away and
beat him to death, leaving a corpse barely recognizable after receiving 380 wounds.

The leaders of the city of Tianjin had been resentful of Yu
Zuomin and his canonization, so they promptly dispatched an investigative team to see if they could embarrass him. Unimpressed, Yu
detained the investigators for thirteen hours, releasing them only
after an appeal from the mayor of Tianjin. Then the Tianjin police,
who were in charge of security in Daqiuzhuang, tried to enter the village to capture the four suspects in the accountant's murder. But Yu
assembled a force of several hundred people, armed with guns, to
surround Daqiuzhuang. He blocked the police for three days.

When the police finally entered, they discovered that Yu had
assembled a private armory. But they didn't catch the murder suspects; Yu had spirited them away. He had also bribed officials in the
central government with thousands of yuan to acquire information
and block the investigation of his case. It didn't work. Tianjin was
intent on knocking Yu off his pedestal, and the central government
was embarrassed by foreign newspaper reports that Yu's private army
had kept the police out. The party realized it had to take tough

action, so Daqiuzhuang was transformed from a model village to a rogue village. The Politburo unanimously agreed to arrest Yu Zuomin.

Still, the mystery remained of how Daqiuzhuang had become so rich in the first place. Most Chinese insisted that Yu had a *kaoshan*—a high-level patron—but there were differing accounts of who this was. Some people said his *kaoshan* was a daughter of Deng. To learn more, I made another trip in the spring of 1993. Now the village looked like a ghost town, the streets deserted, the restaurants unoccupied, the stores empty, the music clubs quiet. But at the entrances to some of the large corporate headquarters, including that of a business run by one of Yu's brothers, Yu Zuozhang, I saw signs made out of two-foot-high metal Chinese characters: "Comrade Xiaoping, how are you!"

I learned that Yu Zuomin had tried to get Deng Xiaoping to visit Daqiuzhuang after the Chinese New Year in 1993. Yu must have thought that if Deng came to Daqiuzhuang, he would leave behind a trail of benefits, as he had on visits to other places, and the village would become invincible. One of Deng's daughters led an advance team to inspect the place. Then they encountered that road. They decided that if Deng were to visit the village, the road would have to be paved or the old man might suffer a heart attack along the way. So Yu started paving the road, but he had paved only about five miles before tensions over the murder exploded and spread throughout the country.

The official investigation revealed that Yu had periodically held a kangaroo court in a room equipped with video and audio equipment, electric batons, and whips. In one clandestine trial, Yu stripped three employees to the waist and interrogated them; then he hit one, and others began beating the defendants until they confessed to their crimes. Yu promptly rewarded the torturers with several thousand yuan in bonuses. Yu's own government trial was only slightly more meaningful, and he was sentenced to twenty years in prison.

Not that Chinese prosecutors need proof, but where did they get evidence against him? They discovered that Yu had videotaped the beating of the accountant.

To the public, it appeared that justice had caught up with Yu Zuomin, but since the government didn't execute him, one friend of mine remained skeptical. "You think he'll serve his twenty years?" she said, as her eyes narrowed. This friend lives in a compound for senior cadres and runs into former ministers and deputy ministers all the time in her elevator. She explained her doubt. A few years earlier, a high-level female official who lived four floors above her was convicted of bribery and embezzlement and sentenced to ten years in prison. It was mentioned on the television and radio news, because the government seemed to be trying to set an example against white-collar crime.

The disgraced official had been interrogated but had squealed on no one, so her friends got to work trying to obtain her release. No one knows how much money changed hands, but a year later the woman was out of prison and back in her apartment, receiving her friends and laughing over dinner.

At first I found it puzzling when I heard Chinese intellectuals talk about the need for more lawyers to tackle *renzhi*. I was used to American jokes about lawyers and complaints about litigiousness. My off-the-cuff response was to think that the last thing China should copy from the American system was the profusion of attorneys. Yet to my Chinese friends, the law was the weakest facet of Chinese society, and there was something reassuring about a country with lawyers chasing ambulances, something heartwarming about a society where criminals can get off on technicalities. During the Tiananmen Square movement, one young student at Beijing University put it this way: "We have rice, but we need laws."

China has laws, of course, and more all the time. At last count in 1993, it had several thousand law offices and 90,000 lawyers—as compared with 60,000 practicing in China before the Communists took power in 1949. And it aims to increase that number to 150,000 by the year 2000. But the government doesn't always understand the role of lawyers, as three attorneys in Taian County in Liaoning Province discovered in 1984 when they tried to defend a client. That was the problem—they weren't really supposed to defend him, or to allow him to plead innocent. So the city's prosecutors arrested them for shielding a criminal. They were detained in prison for nearly four years until the nation's top judicial leaders personally intervened to pardon them.

The government's concept of how the law operates was evident when it put on trial the students and intellectuals implicated in the Tiananmen Square movement. They were detained for many months before being formally arrested, and the so-called public trials were closed to foreign reporters, friends, and, in some cases, even family members. Most trials lasted little more than an hour or two, with virtually no debate, and their outcome had been decided in advance. At times, China's system reminded me of the Mouse's description of justice at the royal court in *Alice in Wonderland:*

> "*I'll be the judge, I'll be the jury,*"
> *said cunning old Fury:*
> "*I'll try the whole cause,*
> *and condemn you to death.*"

Chen Xiaoping, a short, scrappy Hunanese who is one of China's top constitutional lawyers, is one of our favorite counterrevolutionaries. He gives the authorities terrible migraines because of his refusal to buckle; he was even always willing to see us. One day he told me about his experience as one of four intellectuals tried for "plotting to overthrow the government" during the Tiananmen Square protests:

"On December 5, 1990, they woke me up in my jail cell very early," he recalled. "I knew something was up. They asked me if I wanted to shave. And they told me to dress up a bit, so I put on a blue cotton jacket they had given me, very clean, very new. Then they told me I was going to be put on trial that morning. They didn't give me breakfast, but put me immediately into a car with two policemen. They handcuffed me. It was the only time during my entire detention that I was handcuffed. They said they had to do this because every criminal must walk into the courtroom with handcuffs on, but they put the cuffs on as loosely as possible.

"We drove an hour to the courthouse on Justice Road in Beijing. The security was extremely tight around the courthouse. After I entered, they opened the handcuffs, gave me breakfast, and they started chatting with me. Then a man from the Special Cases Team came to say a few words to me. I think he just wanted to see my attitude toward all this. After he left, one of the judges came by to see me. He wanted to take another look at my personal statement. This was a 5,000-word speech that I had written over the past few months. This was where I had to admit to my mistakes, acknowledge my crimes. They had read it and edited it, then had me rewrite several sections at least three or four times. They were picky about every word.

"My trial was about to begin, but the courtroom was being renovated, so they held the trial in a big hallway. There were about 200 to 300 people there, and at a first glance, I saw my sister, my brother, and one of my professors. There were three judges. A prosecutor read out the accusations, and then my lawyer spoke for about ten minutes. I had met my lawyer only two or three times, each occasion for less than an hour. My lawyer of course couldn't say that I didn't commit a crime, but he tried to say that I didn't play a big role and that I had a good attitude. He hoped the court would give me a reduced sentence. Then they let me talk. At first I didn't want to speak at all, but they said I had to. So I began refuting each of the accusations before the judge cut me off. He wanted me to read out my Last Statement, all 5,000 words, which took about half an hour. That was it. We all left, and I ate lunch in the courtroom."

The judges were very happy with Chen's Last Statement, because in it he admitted to engaging in certain activities (although he didn't agree they were criminal), and they released him from jail two months later. They took him under police escort to the train station, and two university guards accompanied him on the train all the way back to Hunan, leaving him only after they arrived at the doorstep of his mother's house. The only problem was that Chen Xiaoping didn't want to go back to Hunan; he had been living for years in Beijing and wanted to return to his post at the University of Politics and Law there. The authorities, on the other hand, wanted him as far away from the capital as possible.

The university had expelled Chen Xiaoping from his post, and his arrest had cost him his Beijing residence permit. The authorities refused to give him a new residence permit or a new ID card, which he had lost. So he was left dangling in the system: For a couple of years, he had no *danwei*, no *hukou*, no ID card, no job. When he tried to marry a beautiful young woman, no one would approve it. He needed a permit from his work unit, but there was no place to apply. The other problem was that the woman's parents were Old Revolutionaries who were appalled that they had raised their daughter only to marry a counterrevolutionary. Against her family's wishes,

Chen and his girlfriend moved in together, and when she became pregnant the scandalized security forces found a way for them to marry. They had their first baby, a son, just a few days before we left Beijing.

The Communists started off by rebelling against the past. When they took power, they condemned feudalism, tore down Beijing's city walls, and seriously considered destroying the Forbidden City as well. In the Cultural Revolution, one of the favorite slogans was "Destroy the Four Olds": old ideas, old culture, old customs, and old habits.

Yet they never could really destroy the old ideas. Instead, bit by bit, the weight of history reshaped them and their administration. History formed the structure that governed the country: the imperial-style rule that had preceded them for forty or fifty centuries. In fact, the more I stayed in China, the more I came to see Communism not as a break with China's past so much as a continuation of it. Underneath all the talk about socialism, the "iron rice bowl," even stock markets and special economic zones, China still had the skeleton of a dynasty, of imperial rule.

The Communists were not the first new emperors to be seduced and overwhelmed by tradition. The Mongols defeated China in the thirteenth century and started the Yuan dynasty, only to be absorbed by those they had defeated. The same happened to the Manchus, who defeated the Chinese in 1644 and started the Qing dynasty. By the end of their dynasty, the Manchus had mostly forgotten the Manchu language and had lost such basic traditions as riding horses.

The problem is that when the Communists took power, one of the traditions they inherited was the concept and practice of unlimited power. Nominally, the Communists set up a legal system, and in China today the petty thieves are punished. But the real crooks get away with whatever they want, principally because they moonlight by running the country.

The Yugoslav dissident writer Milovan Djilas observed in 1957 that Communist leaders tend to usurp control over collective property. They replace the old elite with a privileged "new class," an easy task when there are no laws or watchdog organizations to prevent them from doing so. It was particularly galling that Mao and the other leaders of China's new class moved into the old imperial grounds of Zhongnanhai. The word means "Middle and South Lakes," and it was built as a playground for the emperors and their concubines. Surrounded by a fifteen-foot wall in the center of Beijing, with luscious trees and two shimmering lakes, Zhongnanhai is the modern Communist version of the Forbidden City, a place that many Chinese envision as a Shangri-la.

Popular anger at the supposed lavish lifestyles of the leaders was a passionate theme during the Tiananmen Square demonstrations. Secrecy fueled much of this public imagination, marring reputations sometimes more than they deserved. When Nick and I managed to visit Zhongnanhai, on one excuse or another, we were struck less by the opulence than by the ordinariness. Indeed, the buildings were spacious, but under the Communists, who had no flair for maintenance, the facilities had fallen into disrepair. This was especially so in the parts of the home that count, like the kitchen and the bathrooms: no coffee machines, no dishwashers, no garbage disposals, no comfortable showers. A friend who stayed for a time in the home of a Politburo member in Zhongnanhai later told us that our own home in Beijing was far more comfortable. Even Deng Xiaoping's home, until it was remodeled in 1992, had hot water for only half an hour each morning and three evenings a week. The Old Revolutionaries rode in Mercedes-Benzes but their toilets leaked.

In the early 1990s, however, the economy improved, and capitalism and its wild mores once again sailed into China. This time it came in big waves, sweeping in Western liquor and luxuries, cigarettes and caviar. The extravagance spread among the new class, from local warlords to Communist Party leaders. Members of the imperial retinue decided they might as well live like emperors. Former President Yang Shangkun, for example, is a stocky eighty-seven-year-old who praises the virtues of self-abnegation. But these days when he takes a bath, he steps into a $7,000 whirlpool tub made by American Standard Inc. General Secretary Jiang Zemin, a rotund fellow who likes to talk about self-sufficiency, installed the same model in 1992 in his own bathroom. The Communist leaders seem to like them, for they ordered eight more and even inquired whether they could obtain whirlpool bathtubs in which two people could bathe together.

This last request rather startled the general manager of American Standard, and he told me that he couldn't imagine why Zhongnanhai would need whirlpools for two. "We don't do that kind of stuff," he told the Zhongnanhai representative in early 1992. But he did fill a request to ship one hundred toilet-and-sink sets as part of an over-all renovation program. They were going to be installed in Zhong-nanhai and Beidaihe, the seaside resort where leaders go for a cool respite.

Yang Shangkun also adores *hamigua,* a popular Chinese melon that looks like cantaloupe and comes from the Xinjiang region in the northwest. One day in 1992, one of his assistants called up a buddy who worked for a businesswoman we know. The assistant asked his buddy to take the day off and took him to the airport, where they boarded a military plane on a special flight to Xinjiang. There they loaded some *hamigua* onto the plane and then returned to Beijing the same afternoon. We never knew whether Yang himself ordered the flight, or whether his assistants simply took the initiative to prove their devotion. In any case, it was the kind of extravagance that would have brought a smile to the lips of the old dowager empress, whose lavish tastes had helped bring down the Qing dynasty.

Only very rarely did we get a peek at the lifestyles of the leaders, partly because even their home addresses were state secrets. Still, I was once able to get a glimpse of the house of Hu Yaobang, the Com-munist Party leader until his ouster in 1987. Unfortunately, it was on the occasion of his death on April 15, 1989. We had heard that in the two years since his dismissal, he had written a number of essays criti-cal of Communist Party rule, and I wanted to see if I could obtain them from his family. Friends told me where Hu lived, so I carried a huge wreath from *The New York Times* to give to his wife and chil-dren. His son, Hu Deping, thanked me for the five-foot-high wreath and invited me into his house. He led me through the big green front gate and then through a small courtyard and several hallways and doors before we ended up in a small sitting room. But somehow I felt as though I were in a sterile conference room. There was a television and a few paintings on the walls, and the green sofa I sat on and the white-lace doily I leaned against all seemed to have been supplied by the Beijing No. 1 Furniture Factory. And there was Hu Deping, sit-ting way across the room, in as formal a manner as possible. In any case, my ploy failed. The family members said that they would arrange any publication of Hu's writings themselves, in China.

I tried to visit Zhao Ziyang's house as well, after he was ousted as Communist Party general secretary during the Tiananmen movement. He was under house arrest then, but we heard that he had been moved out of Zhongnanhai to Fuqiang Alley in central Beijing. We happened to know his date of birth, which was supposed to be a state secret, so on October 17, 1989, his seventieth birthday, I brought a small birthday cake and a bottle of wine and strode nervously through the crisp autumn air down the lane toward his courtyard home. I banged on the big door and a guard opened the peephole and said no one was home.

"May I see Wang Yannan, please?" I said with a smile, asking for Zhao's daughter, who was not much older than I. Then I waited. Ten minutes later a slight woman dressed in a white sweater and dark pants emerged through the red door. It was she. "What can I do for you?" she asked, motioning me toward another entrance of the compound. Maybe she thought I was a businesswoman, or passing on a message from a friend.

"Hi, I know it's your father's birthday today, and so I've come to give a token of our best wishes," I said softly. "I'm an overseas Chinese. I'm, er, I'm a reporter with *The New York Times*." Wang didn't flinch. She was poised and calm, but she stopped and didn't invite me further. We stood outside in the cold and chatted about the weather and her father's state of health ("not great, but okay"). I suggested that I would like to give the gift to her father personally, but she said that wasn't possible. It wasn't a good time for him to meet with foreigners. What about her? Could we meet for lunch? Again, it wasn't a good time for her to meet with foreigners.

We couldn't normally see the homes of current leaders, but the estates of former Communist leaders sometimes gave us visual proof of the prodigal, whimsical nature of their lives. In the summer of 1992, Nick and I took a trip to Beidaihe and discovered the Beverly Hills of China. The seaside resort is a rolling region of deep green grass and trees, with splashes of orchids, chrysanthemums, daisies, black-eyed Susans, and roses on the lawns of the vast estates. Fresh winds off the sea sweep salt air across the shore, and it is a rare place of peace, beauty, and quiet. Every important party and government organization has its own resort and white-sand beaches; we were staying in the Foreign Ministry's.

It was impossible to visit the resorts of the leaders. But rather foolishly, the authorities opened up the home of Lin Biao, the defense minister who had reportedly tried to stage a coup against Mao in 1971. Lin was killed in an apparent escape attempt after the coup failed, and since he is in disgrace it apparently is fine to poke fun at his expensive tastes. Set in a forest on a hillside above the sea, Lin Biao's home has two dozen rooms and an indoor swimming pool. Lin liked to swim in salt water, but the house is a good mile from the shore, and he was lazy. So he installed pipes to carry the seawater into his house and change the water in the pool every day. Hundreds of ordinary Chinese tour Lin Biao's house each summer day, admiring the luxury, envying the endless panorama of rooms, gazing at the pool. When we went, there happened to be a few dozen Chinese workers from inland provinces who were gleeful at the chance to see such riches but also privately chafing at the extravagance. A knowledgeable Chinese pointed out Deng Xiaoping's own estate just a hundred yards away. Armed guards keep people away, so you can only see the roof peeking through the trees. It's hard not to wonder if he isn't living in the same way.

"With the Communists, the peasants rebelled against the dynasty, and then they got into power," said Danping, the university professor who had lived for a spell in Zhongnanhai. "But the Communists became more corrupt than ever.

"In capitalism, you proclaim from the start that people are not equal and that some people are born with a silver spoon in their mouth and will rise higher than others. But here, we always proclaim that everyone is equal. Of course, our society isn't equal. So people see that and it causes resentment."

While most of the leaders seem personally honest, in that they aren't pilfering the treasury and opening up Swiss bank accounts, their children have fewer scruples. This infuriates many ordinary Chinese, and they refer scathingly to the *taizi*, or princes, who use their connections to accumulate huge sums of money. In the late 1980s, the sons of Zhao Ziyang were famous for their wheeling and dealing. Deng Xiaoping's children also had their forays into business. The eldest son, Deng Pufang, heads the national association for the handicapped and in the 1980s ran a huge trading company to make some money for the cause. To his credit, he certainly helped raise the status of the handicapped in China, but the company became so notorious that the government closed it down in 1989.

Deng's youngest son, Deng Zhifang, began his career cautiously. Zhifang earned a Ph.D. in physics from the University of Rochester, and his own son was born in America and thus is eligible for American citizenship. Zhifang took a job with the China International Trust and Investment Corporation, one of the largest and most successful state enterprises, and at first he set a fine example. He worked hard, lived frugally, and commuted on a bicycle. But beginning in about 1990, the temptations grew too alluring for many of the sons and daughters of senior leaders, and Deng Zhifang became more ambitious. He secured a job in the construction ministry as a way into real estate, then bought up large segments of the Pudong area of Shanghai. In fact, when he discovered that a Shanghai entrepreneur owned a piece of land between two large tracts that he had bought the rights to, he pressured the man into selling the land. In 1993, Deng Zhifang was cutting multimillion-dollar deals with the Hong Kong billionaire Li Ka-shing and joined a group to pay $75.3 million for a 74 percent stake in a Thai toy factory. It wasn't surprising that the price the mainland team was going to pay for the company represented a discount of 30 percent from the price of the stock the day the deal was announced. The *taizi* discount.

Deng Zhifang explained to friends that everything he did was legal, and that may well be true. But everybody knew that he was Deng Xiaoping's son, and everybody competed to give him special favors or sweetheart deals so as to build *guanxi* with him. When a friend quietly confronted him about his new, more explicit style of using connections to do business, he reportedly responded with candor: "I can't help it. I may only have a few years left to do this."

The son of a Politburo member once told Nick and me about his lucrative business plans, earning a $400,000 profit without putting in any of his own money. His contribution, he explained bluntly, was *guanxi*. He offered something that the other business partners could not: connections to the leadership and hence access to bank loans and the near-certain prospect of approval from local authorities for the development proposals.

But nobody used his connections better than Larry Yung, the son of Vice President Rong Yiren. In the 1980s, Vice President Rong headed the China International Trust and Investment Corporation. He installed his son as head of the Hong Kong branch, and Larry thrived in the fast lane—except for his proclivity for getting speeding tickets. Larry made plenty of money for his company, but he did fine for himself as well. In the spring of 1993, Larry paid about $10 million to buy Birch Grove, a 700-acre estate in England. This was not just any parcel. It had been the property of the late British Prime Minister Harold Macmillan.

By the early 1990s, Deng Xiaoping had mostly faded from the public scene. He appeared on television only once or twice a year, he never met foreign dignitaries, and he was rarely mentioned in the newspapers. It was almost possible to forget that he remained the emperor.

Then in early 1992, he went on a trip to southern China, and I was reminded once again that this is a country of *renzhi*. Deng said he traveled purely in a private capacity, as an ordinary citizen. But his trip changed China. The remarks he made on his tour were fashioned into special *hongtou wenjian,* or red banner documents, with red headlines to signify their importance. His words were hailed in nationwide study sessions, and some of his sayings ("Be bolder, Step more quickly!") were cited every time officials wanted to take a bigger dive into capitalism.

Indeed, his trip to the south was officially referred to as his *xun,* a description that is normally used in this context only for a journey by an emperor. No one else makes a *xun.* The television, the newspapers, the special study sessions all began calling Deng's speeches the *nanxun jianghua,* the "speeches from the emperor's southern journey."

In fact, even his speeches were modified to sound imperial. As he toured through the cities of Zhuhai, Shenzhen, Shunde, Zhongshan, and Shanghai, he made casual remarks like "Now that I am in Shenzhen, I cannot sit here and wait. I want to go out immediately," as he was quoted in the *Yangcheng Evening News* two months after his visit. Three months later, Deng's homespun remarks had been transformed into a 7,000-word speech with subheadings and neat categories.

"I saw three versions, and they were all so different," said Jihong, an elegant middle-aged woman we know. "The first one was very family-style. By the third version, there was all this economic stuff that wasn't in the first version. All of sudden Deng was exhorting people to push on the economy. It was his daughters, mostly Deng Nan, who edited his speeches and put in their views on the economy. It reminded me of Mao in his last days."

In Mao's later days, he was surrounded by young aides—mostly attractive women—who translated his grunts into commands. Zhang Yufeng, a former railway attendant, became Mao's mistress even though she was exactly fifty years younger than the chairman. She had a husband in Beijing but lived in the Zhongnanhai Swimming Pool quarters that Mao had taken over. At first Zhang lived in a small room like the other workers, but then she took over the empty bedroom suite that nominally belonged to Mao's wife, Jiang Qing, who was exiled to a guest compound four miles away. Zhang got away with a good deal, once even raging at Mao and calling him a "little puppy." She then stormed out and returned to her home in Beijing, and Mao had to send his top aides to plead with her before she relented and returned to Zhongnanhai.

Zhang has two daughters, and the younger one—born in 1974— resembles the chairman and may be Mao's. Many in Zhongnanhai believed that the baby was Mao's, even though it would have been quite a feat for an eighty-year-old man to father a child. The pregnancy and childbirth did, however, sideline Zhang. During this time, Mao became close to Nancy Tang, his thirty-year-old English interpreter and the model for the *Doonesbury* character Honey. A group of senior Chinese officials was once startled when Mao began stroking Tang's shoulder in the middle of a meeting. She then sat down on the floor and leaned back against his legs, as the other leaders tried desperately not to notice. Mao used to call her Miss Tang in English and encouraged her to call him Mr. Mao. That was a pun, for they pronounced *Mr.* as "Miss-Tou," and *tou* in Chinese means "to steal." So Mr. Mao became the "Mao who steals the misses." They both chuckled at that.

Nancy Tang and another top aide, Wang Hairong, used their proximity to Mao to gain political power, virtually controlling access to the chairman and even attending Politburo meetings on his behalf. At one Politburo session, they ordered Zhou Enlai to make a self-criticism; Zhou obeyed, for he, like everyone else, didn't dare challenge these two young women. It was never clear whether they were acting on a lark or whether they really did represent Mao. In any case, Mao in the mid-1970s was dying and no longer always lucid or intelligible. In China, the emperor rules even after he can no longer speak.

Deng's point on his southern imperial tour—or at least the point that his daughters arranged for him to make—was that China should hasten the process of economic change, not worrying if policies were capitalist or socialist. He stressed that officials should stop debating whether a proposed policy was "surnamed capitalist" or "surnamed socialist." Instead, they should simply consider whether it would be good for China's prosperity. Deng emphasized that China should learn from capitalism and that the country's aim was to build a market economy. Socialism does not mean a planned economy, he said, nor does capitalism mean a market economy. The result of Deng's speech was a burst of reforms throughout the country, as well as a growing confidence among investors that the changes were here to stay. Economic growth that year soared to 12.8 percent.

Deng apparently decided that the Communist Party would rise or fall on its ability to improve the economic well-being of the Chinese people. And the way to achieve prosperity, he determined, was through the market. He feared that if China continued to be loyal to central planning, the party would collapse as it had in the Soviet Union. In other words, in China only capitalism could save communism.

To Deng, however, political freedom was equivalent to political chaos. In his mind, it recalled the Cultural Revolution, when his eldest son was persecuted and either fell or was pushed out of a window at Beijing University and was left paralyzed for life. Of course, Deng knew that economic change was bound to bring in some of the democratic concepts of the capitalists. He himself wanted to absorb selected elements of *fazhi* to temper the *renzhi*. But he would not tolerate fractions debate about the system. The *fazhi* he sought was not the Bill of Rights but the Uniform Commercial Code.

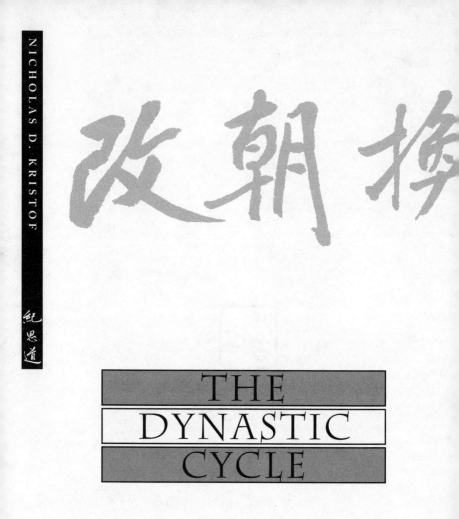

改朝換

紀思道

THE
DYNASTIC
CYCLE

*Every revolution evaporates, leaving behind only the slime of a
new bureaucracy.*

—Franz Kafka

5

Tibetan boy in Rangan village, captivated by a plastic bag that Nick had brought. He had never en plastic before. [Photo by Nicholas D. Kristof.]

One lazy summer morning I was sipping chrysanthemum tea and reading the Chinese newspapers with Haisheng, a prim forty-year-old employee of a government ministry. We were sitting at a table, the day's newspapers strewn about, when I asked her whether she thought the Communist dynasty was collapsing. She shrugged off the question, but the next time we met, she triumphantly handed me an article in the *Beijing Evening News*.

"Remember your question from last week?" she asked. "Take a look at this."

"Huh?" I said, perplexed. The article was a brief dispatch about a tide of crabs, 10,000 or more, that had abruptly landed on a beach on Hainan Island. Scientists were mystified about why the crabs should suddenly beach themselves, but there was no political angle.

"I don't get it," I said. "Why are you giving me this?"

"Think about it," she said, with a gleam in her eye. "Out of the blue, 10,000 crabs suddenly abandon the ocean and come pouring out onto the land. That's not normal in nature. Something strange is happening."

"Oh? Like what?"

"Well, in China, we think that when there is a miracle or tumult in the natural world, there may be one in the political world as well."

Personally, I'm not sure that a tide of crabs landing on a beach should be taken as an omen that the dynasty is in trouble. But the fact that some Chinese see it that way, that a college-educated woman like Haisheng should read about crustaceans and think about Communists, is indeed ominous for the regime. Haisheng's comment resonated in my mind because at the time I was searching for a new paradigm for understanding China, some new way of making sense of what I kept seeing around me. In particular, I was struck by the regime's loss of moral authority, the rise of superstition and religious cults, and the extent to which the Communist Party seemed to be losing control of the country. Sheryl and I had already come to believe that the best way to understand the Communist leaders was to see them as "red emperors"; now we found that we could push the metaphor further. Instead of seeing China as simply another Marxist-Leninist regime on its last legs—an Asian version of Romania or the Soviet Union—it seemed relevant to look at the regime in the context of China's imperial history, through the window of Chinese political philosophy.

More than 3,000 years ago, long before Socrates or any other major political thinker had emerged in Europe, the Duke of Zhou outlined the concept of the dynastic cycle. The duke, who lived in the twelfth century B.C., is a real figure, one of the earliest people in world history—outside the ancient Middle East—who is remembered today by name. Apparently a shrewd man, he faced a knotty problem in consolidating a new dynasty. His family had just overthrown the corrupt last emperor of the Shang dynasty. The problem was that the duke needed to justify this coup d'état.

The Duke of Zhou came up with an intriguing explanation. He said that any dynasty, any emperor, starts out with divine approval. But emperors have obligations, too, and they must treat their subjects fairly. When the emperors fall short, as the later Shang rulers did, the gods themselves revoke the Mandate of Heaven and give it to someone else. Likewise, if a dynasty collapses, that means that the gods disapproved of it.

"The Mandate of Heaven is not easily preserved," the Duke of Zhou declared. "Heaven is hard to depend on. Those who have lost the mandate did so because they could not practice and carry on the reverence and brilliant virtue of their ancestors."

Many of our Chinese friends think that the Communist dynasty is going the way of the Shang. They point out that it's difficult to find anyone in the leadership today who resembles a traditional "sage king" in a rising dynasty. But Prime Minister Li Peng strikes them as an obvious candidate for the part of the evil chief eunuch in a collapsing dynasty. There is something about Li, a combination of arrogance and hard-line political principles, which grates on many Chinese. After Tiananmen, he tried American-style political walkabouts, but once when he picked up a baby during a nationally televised broadcast, it began to shriek inconsolably. Most other Chinese feel the same way about Li Peng. He got where he is only because of support from his foster parents, Zhou Enlai and Deng Yingchao, who cared for Li after his own father died when he was just a few years old. Even Li's mother, when she was on her deathbed in 1985 in the Beijing Hospital, bitterly complained to all the nurses within earshot that her son was an ungrateful, unfilial wretch. Intellectuals mock Li Peng for his limited intellect, and it is true that he sometimes mispronounces Chinese characters—as he did that night I heard him on Tiananmen Square. The widespread contempt for Li Peng has spawned a number of jokes, including one about the dissident who is sentenced to twenty years in prison for shouting "Li Peng is an idiot" on a street corner. "Why did I get such a long sentence?" the dissident asks. "Other people say seditious things and get only five years." The judge replies, "Your sentence for sedition is only five years. Then there's fifteen years for revealing state secrets."

If the Communist dynasty has failed to rule wisely and humanely, then ancient tradition suggests that the gods should be sending us signs that the Mandate of Heaven is in jeopardy. A natural disaster, for example. That's why I thought it important that people like Haisheng exchanged rumors about crab landings and other bizarre events. The most important of these rumors always had to do with earthquakes, possibly because six weeks before Mao's death in 1976 China suffered a horrific earthquake in which at least 242,000 people died. So we took more than a geological interest when, beginning in 1990, our friends started to warn us of impending earthquakes. Every few months rumors would rush around Beijing that the end was nigh.

"You know about the earthquake, don't you?" the daughter of a Chinese leader asked us one afternoon as we picnicked in the botanical gardens. She and her husband were telling us anti-Communist jokes, which was more or less what we had come to expect from the leadership's offspring, and we were lying on the grass, stuffed with sandwiches, laughing at the punch lines.

"It's supposed to be two days from now, right?" Sheryl asked. "Friends have told us about it."

"Right, at noon," said the woman, who had a graduate degree from one of China's best universities. "Of course I don't know that I believe it, but you never know. The government's trying desperately to hush it up. I heard that the television news is going to deny the rumors."

"But won't that just make people even more worried?" I asked.

"Yeah, that's exactly the problem," the woman explained. "If the television news denies something, that usually means it's true. So the government's in a real bind. Actually, I hear that the State Council seismologists think that there will be a quake. You know, you two live in a tall building. You might want to be outside at noon."

In the end, of course, there was no quake.

While seismic rumbling and a rise in superstition were sometimes indicators of decline in past dynasties, the latest rumors would have startled the Duke of Zhou. A few of the superstitions underscore the peculiar public mood, which in a few places borders on psychosis. Perhaps the strangest panic occurred in 1993 in Chongqing, a huge riverside metropolis in central China.

A tale spread that an American-made robotic zombie had gone out of control and escaped from the United States to Chongqing. "The zombie specialized in eating children wearing red clothes, and it was said to have devoured several kids already," reported the *Chongqing Legal News,* an official newspaper. In the resulting frenzy, many children refused to go to school. Parents protected their "little emperors" by fashioning crosses out of chopsticks and putting cloves of garlic in their book bags. The result was a sudden garlic shortage in Chongqing. The mayor's office was forced to address the issue and order a new round of "ideological work on teachers and students to calm them down and make them at ease about going to school."

This is the kind of panic that is expected when a dynasty is coming apart. For the last four millennia, the dynastic cycle has been the dominant pattern of Chinese history. Almost every dynasty is founded by a vigorous leader with strong support: a fellow like Mao. The new emperor consolidates his hold on the country and establishes order, and the new administration hums along reasonably efficiently. But then the emperor's descendants become effete and corrupt, surrounded by a growing bureaucracy of officials and eunuchs. The later emperors, always cosseted in the palaces, become increasingly unpopular, remote, and unaware of what is going on.

In a Western country, the leaders at this point would be voted out of office. But in China, the rascals remain in the Forbidden City. They raise taxes and neglect public works—such as flood control projects—so that they can pay for new extravagances at court. The peasants seethe under the burden of taxation, and some turn to banditry. Neglect of public works contributes to floods and crop failures, and discontent begins to rumble throughout the land. Eventually the dynasty loses its Mandate of Heaven. Then the dynasty topples and the process is started anew.

The concept of the Mandate of Heaven was a remarkable development in global political philosophy. Four times as ancient as the Magna Carta, it provided a fundamental justification for resistance against repressive rulers. The philosopher Mencius, who lived in the third and fourth centuries B.C., further refined the notion of the Mandate of Heaven and of an explicit "right of rebellion." All this imposes a check on the absolute rule of the emperors: They have an obligation to be decent.

Now, why do people in a declining dynasty believe in child-eating zombies? The rise of superstition seems to have something to do with the collapse of traditional systems of belief. The society and economy are changing rapidly, but Chinese no longer know what to believe in, no longer have a source of values, no longer have a comprehensible code of morality. People now do not believe in Mao, or in Communism, but nothing has emerged to take their place.

A similar situation occurred during the late Qing dynasty a hundred years ago, when the official ideology—Confucianism—was moribund and people were searching for something to believe in. Some turned to Christianity and others to odd cults such as one founded by a man who proclaimed himself the younger brother of Jesus. He preached a rather muddled version of Christianity, urging people to save themselves by following him. They did, and what came next was a civil war that lasted fourteen years and for a time threatened to overthrow the Qing dynasty. The Taiping Rebellion, as it is known, was finally crushed in 1864. But millions of people died, and it was one of the bloodiest civil wars in world history.

These days as well, the dynasty is in trouble. The evidence that the Communists have lost the Mandate of Heaven is circumstantial but comes from innumerable glimpses of daily life. If this were a jury trial, the prosecution would be unable to summon any powerful eyewitnesses but instead would call scores of minor witnesses, each of them unimportant but collectively providing a compelling portrait of venality and dissipation.

The evidence that the dynasty is collapsing begins with the fact that, as in the late Qing period, the official faith is dying. The state church may be Communism, but the people are atheists or agnostics.

There are about as many believing Communists in China as there are Zoroastrians in the West. In place of Marxism, Christianity is rapidly gaining ground, and so are odd quasi-Christian cults in which charismatic peasants proclaim themselves Christ or declare themselves the new emperor.

A mysterious stranger showed up in a riverbank village in Henan Province in March 1990 and told local peasants that he could take them to Jesus. As in many villages in the area, a considerable proportion of the peasants were Christians, mostly converted in the last dozen years and now searching for an avenue for their faith. So the peasants listened as the stranger preached, and they followed him to the spot on the river where he said Jesus would appear. They waited all night, and finally twenty impatient villagers jumped into the river to see if Jesus was there. The water was cold and the current strong, and they never came out. In the morning, the other villagers found them downriver, drowned.

Even more popular than Christianity is *qi gong,* a breathing exercise that at its simplest is just a way of relaxing, a bit like hatha yoga. However, among the tens of millions of Chinese who practice *qi gong* are many who believe in it with a supernatural intensity, and some *qi gong* masters have attracted cultlike followings with their claims to be able to heal the sick, fly through the air, and burn objects by touching them. I had been puzzled by the popularity of these *qi gong* sorcerers for some time before I talked about them with Geremie Barmé, an Australian scholar, who put his finger on what was really going on. "It's a classic end-of-dynasty phenomenon," he said. "You always get this kind of weird stuff when the dynasty is collapsing."

Fortune-telling has also enjoyed a huge renaissance in the last few years, despite government campaigns against superstition. Even though the practice is banned, it has become fashionable in some areas to consult a fortune-teller before making major decisions. In the northeastern province of Heilongjiang, the wife of a peasant named Zhang Jingui asked a palm reader for advice about how to patch up their disintegrating marriage. The fortune-teller told Zhang's wife that she should cut off her husband's penis; supposedly it would then grow back, and the couple would again be happy together.

So the woman returned home and plied her husband with liquor. When he was drunk, she pulled out a pair of scissors and cut off his penis. Zhang nearly died from loss of blood, and his penis never did grow back.

New systems of belief are emerging to challenge the Communist Party all over China, but the confrontation is particularly menacing in the mountains and deserts of the Xinjiang "autonomous region" in the far west of China. More than four times the size of California, Xinjiang is a Muslim area whose 16 million inhabitants look less like Chinese than like Turks—which is ethnically what many of them are. They speak Chinese badly, if at all, and communicate mostly in dialects of Turkish. Throughout Xinjiang, the minarets of the mosques preside over every town, and the most respected people are not the party secretaries but the imams, the religious leaders, often distinguishable by their white robes and thick beards. Until the 1980s, the leaders in Beijing managed to keep a lid on unrest in Xinjiang, but Islam has been undergoing a renaissance in the region, and now it is becoming a challenge to Communist Party rule.

Xinjiang separatists got hold of some guns in 1990 and tried to launch a "holy war" against the government—just the kind of uprising typical in a decaying dynasty. The army crushed the insurrection, but at least twenty-two people were killed and hundreds or thousands arrested. As soon as I learned of that incident, I applied to go to Xinjiang. Impossible, the authorities replied—they were too busy to host me. It was not clear what was keeping them busy, since no other foreign journalists were allowed to go either, but whenever I applied to go there the authorities refused me permission. Even when friends at the World Bank and the United Nations invited me to join delegations touring the area, the Foreign Ministry ordered me excluded from the groups. As my time in Beijing came to an end, I became increasingly desperate to get to Xinjiang. In part, I wanted to see an area that seemed likely to be one of the first to spin off if China fragmented. And in part I wanted to go because I had been to the other twenty-nine provinces in China and wanted to visit the last one.

So when the authorities refused one last time to allow me to visit Xinjiang, I took matters into my own hands: I would go as a tourist. The Foreign Ministry wouldn't like it, but in fact the rules restricting foreign correspondents say only that we must get approval before making reporting trips. There is nothing prohibiting a reporter from traveling as a tourist and then writing about it afterward. So I quietly purchased an air ticket as a tourist, carefully avoiding mentioning my plans on the phone or anywhere that was bugged.

When it was time to go, I slipped down the stairs, all eleven flights, so that State Security would not see me on the elevator camera and get ready to follow me. I checked on the road to the airport that I wasn't tailed and checked again in the plane—occasionally, probably as a special treat, spies from Beijing were authorized to follow us on trips around the country. This time, nobody on the plane seemed to pay me any attention, and I was sure that I had no tail in the Xinjiang capital, Urumqi. My taxi left the Urumqi airport by a back way, over rutted paths and fields, so that it would avoid paying the parking fee, and there was no other vehicle in sight. I felt considerable relief—and exhilaration—as my taxi sped for four hours into the mountains surrounding Urumqi. After spending the night in a little hotel room miles and miles from nowhere, I hired the local equivalent of a Hertz: a Kazakh rent-a-horse to take me into the hills to talk to the nomadic herders. My guide, Khakhar, was a twenty-two-year-old born horseman who maneuvered his mount easily along the near-vertical muddy paths. My horse was less adept than his, and so was my horsemanship, and there were several times when my mare slipped in the steep mud.

After an hour's riding and slipping, Khakhar and I reached the felt yurt, or tepee, of his friend Fatima and her six children. It was about six feet high and fifteen feet across, with several layers of colorful carpets. A pot of tea bubbled over a fire in the center of the yurt, with the smoke wafting upward and out an opening at the top. Fatima was a stout fifty-five-year-old matriarch resting comfortably on the carpets, occasionally commanding her daughters to do this or that. The horses rustled outside, protesting at being left in a light drizzle, and children and grandchildren rushed in and out, muddier each time. Fatima offered some rectangular biscuits that seemed to be made of concrete, and I politely gnawed on one while we chatted about life in Xinjiang.

"What are the cadres like around here?" I asked.

Heads began shaking around the yurt. "They're corrupt," Khakhar said contemptuously.

"Nobody likes them," Fatima added. "They're all rotten."

"What do folks here think of the Han people?" I asked, referring to those normally known in English simply as the Chinese. The Han are the largest ethnic group in China, accounting for more than 90 percent of the nation's population.

"We don't like the Han Chinese," Khakhar said, frowning.

"Why not?"

"They're different from us. They don't herd. They don't ride horses. They're not Muslims. We just don't like them."

When I asked what they thought about the former Soviet republic of Kazakhstan's becoming independent, Fatima and Khakhar beamed and looked immensely proud. It was wonderful, they said.

Could Xinjiang become independent in the same way? "It could be," Khakhar said. "And that would be great." There was a long, delicate pause, as they all savored counterrevolutionary thoughts.

Throughout Xinjiang it was much the same. Public opinion is difficult to gauge in any tightly controlled society, but my sense was that most Muslims would love to have an independent state. The mood was particularly militant in the southern oasis town of Kashgar. I first realized that something was up when my taxi pulled into the gate of my hotel in Kashgar and two police stepped forward to search the car. It turned out that Muslim separatists had recently blown up the nearby Oasis Hotel, killing three people and shattering windows a hundred yards away. Muslim separatists had also set off three other bombs in nearby towns, including one in front of a police station.

A day later, a twenty-seven-year-old Kashgar trader, a short, thin man with a mustache, gave me a little lecture about freedom. We were in the bazaar, next to a stand selling sugary ice water. The trader and a half dozen of his friends were all sharing one bowl of the sugar water, which they kept thrusting on me. I took my turn, even though my stomach churned with every sip.

"The Uzbeks have Uzbekistan, the Kirgiz have Kyrgyzstan, the Tajiks have Tajikistan," the trader was saying fervently. "But here, we're still in China. Everything is still China, from Xinjiang to Tibet to Beijing.

"We're like Kuwait. We've been invaded, but no one will help us. There's nothing we can do." Then he pointed to the palm of his left hand and said, "This is Xinjiang." As I watched in puzzlement, he

pointed to the fingers of the same hand and said, "These are China."
He caught my eye for a long, quiet gaze, then he brought the fingers
in to crush the palm and make it disappear.

The complicating factor in Xinjiang is oil. The desolate Tarim
Basin in Xinjiang holds promising petroleum formations, and the
official Chinese press has suggested—based more on hope than on
evidence—that it contains more crude oil than Saudi Arabia. This is
particularly important because China is running out of petroleum
and by some estimates became a net oil importer in 1993. Xinjiang
offers its best hope for keeping the domestic spigots flowing. Of
course, if the Tarim Basin does prove as rich as the government says,
that will make China all the more determined to hold on to Xinjiang.
It will also make Xinjiang separatists all the more insistent on seces-
sion, for they will consider that Beijing is stealing their natural
wealth.

Still, the Chinese government may be able to maintain its grip on
Xinjiang, for all the discontent, because no single ethnic group dominates the region. The Uighurs are the most militant and the most
numerous, accounting for 45 percent of Xinjiang's population, but they
are still a minority. There are also large populations of Han Chinese,
Kazakhs, Hui, and other ethnic groups, and it is not clear how many
would support an uprising against Beijing. Moreover, the Chinese
Army for now seems unquestionably able to suppress any rebellion.

Yet an insurrection, if it came to that, could be a particularly
bloody one. Xinjiang's Muslims are getting support and training
from exile organizations based in Turkey, and Xinjiang's long border
is porous. It is relatively easy to smuggle in AK-47 assault rifles,
grenades, and bomb-making materials from Afghanistan and Pakistan, where weapons are abundant.

Whenever a dynasty is disintegrating, the emperors begin to lose
their grip on the country. These days, with people turning to new
faiths to replace the carcass of Communism, the party's authority
and control are fraying—along with China's system of public order.
Karl Marx may have called religion the opium of the people, but
many Chinese are also turning to the real thing. China's narcotics
problem would have been almost unimaginable a decade ago; it
seemed to come out of nowhere in the late 1980s, and by 1993 there

were already 250,000 registered drug addicts. The true number is, of course, far higher, probably well in excess of one million. These are not just marijuana users or pill poppers; almost all are heroin addicts.

One of Communism's greatest achievements in 1949 was wiping out the plague of opium that had crippled the nation for a century. In just a couple of years after the revolution, the authorities eliminated a problem that former governments had been unable to control. China was virtually drug free until the late 1980s, when international drug lords started looking for new ways to ship opium and heroin out of Thailand and the "Golden Triangle." They began to move the drugs across China to Hong Kong and Shanghai—where police were less vigilant—and on to Western countries from there. But, inevitably, there was some leakage. Local people not only trans-ported the heroin but they also tried it. Particularly in Yunnan Province, which is next to the Golden Triangle and shares borders with Burma and Laos, heroin use became epidemic. From there, the heroin spread to several other major cities, particularly Guangzhou, Xian, Shenzhen, and Lanzhou.

"There'll be more and more drugs," a forty-year-old heroin addict told me one humid spring afternoon in a garden in Yunnan. He had been a television salesman until his craving destroyed his business and turned him into a thief. He was attending a rehabilitation pro-gram in the hope of kicking the habit, but he wasn't optimistic that he would be able to stay off drugs. The craving was too strong, and the pressure from dealers too great. "The pushers make lots of money, unbelievable amounts of money," he said. "The profits are so high that even if the pushers are imprisoned for twenty years, they figure it's still worth it. Even if a guy's arrested for pushing drugs, his wife continues selling them."

A twenty-eight-year-old driver, also an addict trying to break the habit, added, "Young people think it's cool to take heroin. Everybody does it. Students, soldiers, even police. Then after a while they want to stop, but there's no way of stopping."

The bottom line for the Communist Party today has nothing to do with ideology or economics; it has everything do with power. The party's platform in the 1990s is that it will rule and that everything else is negotiable.

The hollowing of Chinese Communism has occurred even in Mao's hometown of Shaoshan, the Jerusalem of Maoism, the village that used to attract tens of millions of Red Guard pilgrims each year. It's a dusty little town surrounded by rich, brown earth that is divided into doll-size plots farmed by descendants of Mao's former neighbors. A couple of million people still visit Shaoshan each year, mostly in organized tours in which they can simultaneously prove their revolutionary credentials and have fun. They take photos with their new Japanese cameras, and the young people flirt in their colorful T-shirts with English-language slogans, like "Boys and Balls," which they don't understand but which scandalize occasional visiting Americans.

Nobody takes Shaoshan very seriously, but the high priests of Maoism feel that they still need to make a show of it. So when foreign correspondents turn up, the local officials trot out Wen Huikang, a middle-aged mandarin devoid of personality or ideas. Wen, who is vice president of the local Mao Zedong Thought Society, gives a much-rehearsed spiel about the continuing relevance of Mao's works and the importance of studying them diligently. I unfortunately didn't press him, but a couple of other reporters—Seth Faison of the *South China Morning Post* and Andy Higgins of *The Independent*—interviewed him later and got the same spiel about the importance of Mao's works. Finally, Andy lobbed a softball question: Of all Mao's innumerable speeches and essays, which was Wen's favorite? Wen paused and fumbled around a bit, and a look of panic crossed his face. His mouth opened and then closed. The silence grew longer.

It turned out that he couldn't name a single work by Mao.

At the universities and at cadre schools, China's best and brightest nominally study Marxism-Leninism; what they come away with is a heightened appreciation of capitalism. A middle-aged central government official, whose little kitchen turned out Beijing's best *jiaozi,* or dumplings, spent six months in a Communist Party school to make him a better leader. This official was a good friend but also a true believer, someone who always tried to convince us that the government had had no choice but to massacre students at Tiananmen. When he finished his party school course, we held a celebratory dinner for him and his family. "So," Sheryl asked as we sat around his kitchen table, "what did you learn?" Our friend reflected for a moment between *jiaozi,* and then summed it up: "I learned that we need to go capitalist."

When Sheryl and I arrived in China, we often turned to a senior official named Shenhou to demystify the country for us, to help us understand questions like popular attitudes toward the Communist Party. Shenhou wasn't really allowed to meet with us, for he worked inside the Central Committee headquarters in Zhongnanhai, but he did anyway.

The last time I saw him before he was purged was in May 1989, on the eve of martial law. He stood quietly, forlornly, by a leafless tree in front of the old Russian-designed Minzu Hotel, a bleak brown box of brick on the north side of the Avenue of Eternal Peace. Warm spring breezes danced in the air, and the avenue was clogged with exhilarated protesters who thought they had scored a triumph over the government. The students marched this way and that, waving banners, and some climbed the trees, echoing the proclamations that Tiananmen Square was theirs.

Shenhou was aloof from all this. He already knew that the students had lost. "It's all over," he said, speaking Chinese slowly, as if with great effort. "There's no hope."

Shenhou had devoted his life to the Communist Party. His public and private comments always suggested that he was unquestionably behind the party, and I had assumed he was a Communist to the core of his being. Until that day.

"We've lost the struggle," he said. "We're finished now. I'll be arrested, and so will everybody else. The students will be crushed. There'll be a white terror throughout China."

There was a long pause, and for a moment he sounded as if he were near tears. If so, his face did not show it. It was impassive, reflective, tired.

"There'll be a white terror throughout China," Shenhou repeated. "And it'll be terrible, but then people will finally understand the truth about the party. It's like the Gang of Four, which got a free hand and then ruled so murderously that people eventually rebelled and destroyed it. This time the terror will be the Communist Party's last act. The party is overthrowing itself. And I'll tell you something. The destruction of the Communist Party will be good for China."

I was shocked. We had been in China six months, and this was the first time I had realized that even senior party officials were against the party. Even in Zhongnanhai, the leadership compound, officials had lost the faith. Later off-the-record conversations with friends and officials confirmed that impression. A family member of a Politburo official confided to us that "none of them really believes in Communism anymore." The widow of a well-known Chinese leader told us, "By the end of his life, he saw clearly that it wasn't working. But what could he do? Of course he couldn't admit it to anyone but me." As I traveled the country, roaming from the alpine plains of Tibet to the fishing villages of Fujian Province, I came across one message: Almost nobody believed in Communism. It was a charade.

Although most of the evidence of alienation among Chinese is anecdotal, a survey research group at Beijing Normal University did conduct two important opinion polls during the Beijing spring of 1989—in the midst of the student movement and one of the few times when people might have dared to tell a pollster the truth. Asked about their attitude toward the student demonstrators, 95.4 percent of the citizens surveyed said they were sympathetic. Only 1.1 percent said they were opposed. The remainder were indifferent or did not respond.

The party also has an incredible knack for turning people off. After the 1989 crackdown, the authorities banned kissing and hugging on the campus of Beijing University. The result was simply that all the would-be kissers and huggers, who vastly outnumber the would-be Communists, feel more alienated than ever.

Sometimes we felt like Diogenes, who searched in ancient Greece for an honest man, only we were searching in contemporary China for a true believer in Communism. An acquaintance once suggested we contact Jihong, a woman he said was a true Maoist. Jihong had been active in the Cultural Revolution and was thought to be in touch with the castoffs from the Gang of Four. We invited her to dinner and expected a surly old fire-breathing hard-liner in a Mao jacket; instead she showed up with a touch of lipstick and rouge on a lightly powdered face, along with a thin black wool sweater and a long necklace. We became good friends and great admirers of Jihong, and it was clear almost from the start that she had lost the faith.

"My generation was very inspired by the revolution," she explained one evening. "When my friends and I get together, we miss the good old days of the 1950s. Life then wasn't so comfortable, but there was a tremendous sense of honesty and pitching in for the common good. Sometimes . . . I even think that time was more exciting to live in. People weren't so greedy. I guess we were all searching for something larger than ourselves.

"But that's gone, gone forever. Now everyone wants change, more democracy, more openness. People dream of a future that isn't necessarily socialist. Everybody's upset about corruption. The whole society seems to be growing more dishonest, obsessed by money.

"I'm worried about whether all this corruption will lead to a rottenness that will be difficult to correct without big change. And so many young people are fleeing abroad. In a way that's the most discouraging thing. You can't blame them for wanting to go, but still . . ." She paused and sipped her jasmine tea. "To see them all settling down over there and not coming back is somewhat depressing. My child, my niece, and the children of almost all of my friends. Almost every time a young person comes by my house to say goodbye, I have the feeling they're not coming back."

One of the shrewdest posters in the 1989 democracy movement quoted Lord Acton: "Absolute power corrupts absolutely." That traditionally was one of the reasons for the dynastic cycle. Chinese emperors ruled absolutely, each as the Son of Heaven, so no one dared criticize them or help them correct their errors. Dynasties fell not so much because they were venal as because they made catastrophic mistakes. China has never had any independent institution, such as a strong parliament or a free press, or even an organized church or autonomous university network, which could dilute this absolute power or at least check the hubris of the country's leaders. In Poland, the Catholic Church was an independent source of moral authority, even in the darkest days of Communist rule. But for China, the Communist Party has been the only game in town.

Like their predecessors, today's red emperors live in a Forbidden City, where they are isolated from reality. Deng Xiaoping and other octogenarian top leaders never talked to ordinary people, never walked the streets, and rarely left their homes at all. In November 1993, Deng took a one-hour fifteen-minute drive through Beijing, the city in which he was living. He drove along the main thoroughfare and then on the newly constructed airport road, and a subsequent report in a government newspaper suggested that it was mostly new to him. The newspaper suggested that Deng managed to recognize the Jingguang Center, Beijing's tallest building, but not much else. "Beijing has changed a lot," the paper quoted Deng as saying. "I don't recognize it."

China's leaders are so out of touch that they don't always know that they are out of touch. Like the emperors before them, they are victims of their ban on free expression and appear to operate on delusions and misinformation. That was one reason why they repeatedly miscalculated in handling the 1989 democracy movement; the Communists were stunned to learn that they were so unpopular.

"It's very difficult for leaders to know what's really going on," the son of a Politburo member admitted to us. "But Dad tries very hard, and he's learned a few tricks. For example, on his inspection trips he knows he's not going to find out anything himself. But he asks his secretaries to go and chat with the assistants of the local leaders and report to him later. He gets his driver to talk to the other drivers. It's not ideal, but he does learn something."

The degree to which officials are prisoners of their own repression, misinformed of public opinion, and unaware of what even their own colleagues feel became clear one spring day at an airport in central China. I was waiting for a plane back to Beijing, and I was having endless cups of tea with a senior provincial official. The official, in his late fifties, was a sincere, thoughtful man who appeared genuinely to believe in the regime. He was accompanied by two younger men, one on each side, who worked with him and agreed with everything he said.

"Why do you foreign journalists always report that many people are unhappy in China?" the official asked me, as I swirled my chrysanthemum tea and wondered how on earth I had ended up facing the only three people left in China who believed in Communism. "Sure, there may be one or two people in Beijing who are against the government. Every country has people like that. But I'll tell you, I've never met anyone who doesn't like the party. I never have. I think you foreign reporters really exaggerate the discontent."

I gave a spirited defense of foreign journalists. Many people did seem irritated with the government, I said, citing anecdotal evidence and a few public opinion surveys. The argument went back and forth for an hour, me on one side and the senior official—periodically backed by his two assistants—on the other. Perhaps the official was lying, but in this case there were no superiors to impress and the words seemed to come from his heart.

Then the official excused himself to go to the bathroom. As soon as he was gone, his assistants became radiant. It seemed that their boss, who had worked with them every day for many years, had no idea what they really thought.

"You tell him!" one assistant said. "You're exactly right, everything you say! Nobody's happy in this country."

"It must be nice to be a foreign journalist," said the other with a heavy sigh. "You can tell the truth."

Part of me would like the process of dynastic disintegration to continue, so that this brutal regime might rot away completely and be replaced. That is what many of my Chinese friends want as well. But even if the Communist dynasty is on the road to collapse, we may want to hold off on the champagne. What comes next could be worse. As officials from Deng Xiaoping down have warned, Westerners should not be so gleeful about the possibility of the Communist Party disintegrating. The officials suggest that such an event could trigger the largest human migration the world has ever known, with millions of people fleeing a war-torn China. Ma Yuzhen, the Chinese ambassador to Britain, made the point in a speech in 1992: "Should there be a disintegration of China or a continued chaos with the 1.16 billion people divided and fighting and starving, the disastrous consequences would spill over the border and endanger the stability of our neighbors, and Hong Kong may witness a flow of millions of people across the border."

That is one reason why many Chinese intellectuals, even those who are bitterly against the Communist Party, are fundamentally apprehensive about the future. It is far from clear what would take the party's place. Just a few years ago, many Chinese feared the return of hard-liners, but that has faded as a risk. Instead, what people today worry about is chaos.

"What we want above all is stability," said the official who made the best *jiaozi* in Beijing. "You Americans can just never understand how important stability is to us. Democracy would be nice, but it's a luxury. What we care about most is just stability, so that we can get on with our lives."

Historically, the collapse of a dynasty has often been followed by years of turbulence and even civil war. Even now, civil war remains a possibility. After all, for decades and sometimes centuries at a time, China has been more like Europe, sometimes like Europe at war, than like a single unified country. In the years following the collapse of the Qing dynasty in 1911–12, China was a hodgepodge of fiefs run by competing warlords.

Few questions may be so important to Asia over the next few decades as what follows the Communist dynasty. On the one hand, there is the risk that the new national "cement" to replace Communism will be aggressive nationalism, threatening other countries in the region. On the other hand, there is the risk of chaos, or *luan*, a four-letter word in Chinese.

Fundamentally the problem is that the old cement that held China together was a dual epoxy of ideology and fear. But ideology and fear are both fading in the 1990s, and corruption is eating away at the remaining superstructure of the Chinese state.

"There's nothing to hold us together," Zhang Weiguo, our journalist friend, now freed from prison, told me over lunch in early 1993. "It's only a question of time before everything falls apart."

Not everyone offers such a bleak view of the end of the dynasty, but it is clear that empires have had a way of falling apart in the twentieth century. The Austro-Hungarians, the British, and lately the Russians have all discovered that. Today the Chinese empire— stretching from Buddhist Tibet to Korean enclaves in Manchuria, from Muslim Xinjiang to Cantonese-speaking Guangdong—is arguably the last great multiethnic transcontinental empire left in the world. With the dynasty in jeopardy, there is a good chance that even if most of China sticks together, even if chaos is averted, a few pieces will break loose.

That's what Tsereng hopes. He's a rickshaw driver in Lhasa, the Tibetan capital, and he drove me from my hotel to the holy Jokhang Temple one evening in 1990. As an experiment, the Chinese Foreign Ministry had allowed me and a Japanese reporter to visit Tibet for a week. The experiment apparently was a failure, because the authorities did not let any other Beijing-based reporters make such a visit for three more years.

Born in a Tibetan area in Sichuan Province, Tsereng is in his late twenties, a compact man who speaks rapid-fire Mandarin. As we raced through town, swerving by pedestrians and bicyclists, Tsereng gave me an over-the-shoulder introduction to life in Tibet.

"This is a volcano, and it'll explode," he announced. "But nobody knows when." He pointed to the neat shops and restaurants and beauty parlors on both sides of the road. "You see these shops? Most of these shops are owned by Han Chinese. They come in here and make lots of money, and most Tibetans don't like them. We don't think in the same ways as the Chinese. And we don't like their repression and terrorism. Many people here have been arrested and tortured."

Tsereng dropped me off at the temple, and I tried to interview some people. This proved difficult. There were a couple of hundred people in the public square, and all were ethnic Tibetans. It was clear that they were intrigued by me, because I found myself the center of a clump of strangers wherever I walked around the square. Yet when I turned to my right to try to talk to them, they all hurried away. I turned to my left, and the people there walked off as well. I confronted an old man and tried to start a conversation.

"I don't speak Chinese," he said, and rushed off. I blocked the path of a young couple and asked if this was the Jokhang Temple.

"Yes, it is," they shouted over their shoulders as they raced to safety. Several more people claimed to speak no Chinese or else answered "I don't know" to all my questions. It was like trying to interview a department store full of mannequins. The fear of the authorities seemed to have a basis: One young man nodded silently to the top of a nearby building, and I spotted Chinese troops with machine guns in a rooftop bunker.

In desperation, I entered a little restaurant in a side street and began making small talk with the customers. It was dark, with crude wooden tables, and I sat in a corner facing the crumbling wall and a little window. Opposite me was a thirty-two-year-old doctor, a neat, well-groomed man with short hair. He leaned forward on the table, over the remains of dinner, and spoke beautiful Chinese with a mournful intensity. In the darkness, surrounded by his friends, he bared his heart.

"You've got to help us," he began. "We need foreign help." He looked around and continued in a low voice, "Nobody dares to say anything. Oh! The repression! If I say anything, I'll be like this in the morning." He held out his hands together, as if they were hand-cuffed, and pointed a finger at the side of his head, as if it were a gun.

"The repression is terrible," he continued. "We're arrested and beaten, so we can't talk about politics. But everybody wants independence. Everybody wants the Dalai Lama back." He bowed his head at the mention of the Tibetan spiritual leader and paused for a moment. "We hate China and what it has done. We can't speak now, but after independence you should come back. We'll give you a good welcome."

Suddenly there was a commotion outside, and someone on the street began shining a flashlight through the window, as if looking to see what was going on inside the restaurant. The Tibetans all ducked, leaving me staring back, like a deer caught in the headlights. The flashlight focused on me for several seconds and then moved around the restaurant. I could see that an army jeep had materialized outside the restaurant.

"What can we do?" the doctor moaned in terror, as he crouched below the window. "They're everywhere."

We all fled the restaurant, and the Tibetans quickly disappeared in the darkness. The troops did not try to arrest anybody.

Over the next few days, I was determined to get out to the "Real Tibet," the herding areas where 90 percent of the population lives. The authorities allowed me to travel in the countryside only if I was escorted by an official, a Han Chinese, but it proved easier than I'd expected to escape his clutches. My "minder" had not lived in Tibet long and so suffered from altitude sickness, which became acute when we went into the mountains surrounding Lhasa. As soon as the official interviews were concluded at 4:00 P.M. each day, he disappeared into his hotel room to vomit and sleep. However, the Chinese keep Tibet in the same time zone as Beijing, so after my minder disappeared, I still had about six hours of daylight on my own to roam around and visit little villages like Rangan. Surrounded by barley fields, Rangan is perched on the central Tibetan plain, with a steep Himalayan mountain rising in the background. As I walked through the barley to the first tumbledown house, I met a lean fifty-seven-year-old peasant coming back from the fields. The man, who said his name was Dorje, wore a red cape and carried a spade that he leaned on as we chatted about the harvest and his family. Then I tried to steer the conversation toward politics.

"I don't worry about big things," Dorje said with a shrug. "I just worry about my little life, and I don't really know whether the Chinese are good or bad." Then Dorje began to fret over one of those little things. Spotting me pulling out my camera, he politely asked not to be photographed. He explained that he might die soon and that, in the Buddhist tradition, it would be inappropriate for images of him to linger after his body is gone.

Rural Tibetan villages like Rangan are humble places, where the bodies of the dead are left outside to be torn apart by vultures, and where babies are sometimes given names like Dog Droppings to avoid attracting the attention of evil spirits. Per capita incomes in Tibet average only about one-third of the level in the rest of China, and the illiteracy rate is 70 percent. Infant mortality in two backward counties of Tibet is officially reported to be among the highest in the world: For every 1,000 births, 300 babies die in their first year of life.

Punjiong, a small woman whose fifty-five years are etched deeply in the lines on her face, understands the human dimensions of those statistics. She showed me around her hovel in Rangan and told me that of her eleven children two have died and only one has attended any school. Her home is made of mud, two tiny rooms plus a storage area for barley. There is no running water, no decoration on the brown walls, not even a kerosene lamp or any other source of light. When it gets dark, she goes to bed. She has no change of clothes: Punjiong wears her entire wardrobe. There's a small cooking area, a primitive stove that burns dried grass or animal dung, but there is no fire to provide warmth during the bitter winter.

The only thing her home seems to have is rats, but because of her Buddhist reverence for life Punjiong doesn't try to kill them. Instead, each day she leaves a handful of barley on the mud floor, sharing what little she has with the rats.

Punjiong has never been to Lhasa, has no radio or television, never sees newspapers, and has very little idea of what is happening outside the village. She said she had never heard of the pro-independence protests in Lhasa. I asked if her village had electricity, and there was a moment of bewilderment. "Electricity?" she repeated. "What's that?"

Gong Liefu, the acting director of the Tibet Foreign Affairs Office, complained to me and my Japanese colleague about our independent forays in the evenings. We should go out of our hotels only with an escort, he said. I reached for my notebook and asked if this meant we were banned from going out on our own. Not banned, Gong explained quickly, but for our own safety we could go out only with a guide. I explained that I wanted to be able to tell my readers whether I was allowed to go out on my own. Finally, after about twenty minutes of obfuscation, Gong acknowledged that while we would be best off with a guide, we were not legally prohibited from going out without one.

At the time, I regarded Gong as a slippery liar, for he kept insisting how happy Tibetans were under Chinese rule. Later I realized that he was simply another cog in the system, as afraid of his superiors as his subordinates were of him. In the end, the Chinese authorities were unhappy with my articles and those of my Japanese colleague, and Gong was reprimanded and demoted. Gong might be a slippery liar, but he was a victim of the repression as well as an agent of it.

Even with the best efforts of people like Gong, Tibet may well spin off into its own orbit in the coming decades. Rebellions in both Tibet and Xinjiang are distinct possibilities in the 1990s, and under the present government the result would be a harsh crackdown and perhaps massacres of civilians. Under a more restrained government, one reluctant to open fire on crowds, the result would be some kind of a crisis and perhaps eventually independence. Relations with the local people, particularly in Tibet, have reached such a low that only force seems able to sustain the link with the rest of China.

All this suggests that an international furor may lie ahead. But while ethnic minorities will be a challenge, this need not be an insurmountable one. Tibet and Xinjiang account for 30 percent of China's territory, but the terrain is mostly mountain and desert on the fringe of the country. The inhabitants of the two areas account for only 1.5 percent of China's total population. Han Chinese account for 91 percent of China's population; other ethnic groups such as the Zhuang in the south make up the difference. In contrast, non-Russians accounted for a bit more than half of the Soviet Union's population. Non-Russian areas of the Soviet Union included the breadbasket of the Ukraine, and their loss was far more traumatic to Russia than the loss of non-Han areas would be in China.

What kind of person will bring down the Communist dynasty? Traditionally, it would make sense to look among powerful generals or regional leaders, or else to search for a prospective peasant rebel. There is also a strong possibility that some existing senior official—a Chinese version of Boris Yeltsin—will abandon the party and lead an alternative force. Americans occasionally ask me who in the Chinese leadership might be a Gorbachev or a Yeltsin. The answer is: almost all of them. Very few of the leaders today have any real faith in the system. Show me a Communist leader, and I'll show you an opportunist.

Yet today a rival power center may be emerging in China: the industrial labor force. Indeed, it may be a charismatic labor leader who presents the greatest challenge to this dynasty. This would be someone, like Lech Walesa in Poland, who can mobilize workers to strike and shut down the economy. Intellectuals have been at the vanguard of the democracy movement throughout this century, but one reason they have not succeeded is that there was no broad coalition of workers marching behind them. University students are still a tiny fringe of society, accounting for just one-fifth of one percent of the population, whereas workers total 150 million and dominate the cities (the rest of China's population of 1.2 billion is composed principally of peasants, children, and old people). The workers have enormous leverage because of the possibility of a general strike, and no one was more aware of this than Deng Xiaoping himself. Deng in his private speeches warned about the "Polish disease," and it was the growing participation of workers in the 1989 Tiananmen protests that convinced him to send in the tanks.

It may be idle speculation, of course, to look at what might bring down the dynasty. There are innumerable termites boring away, and it is hard to measure the impact of each. But as a case study of a single termite, Han Dongfang is fascinating. He is an ordinary railway worker—now an ordinary dismissed railway worker—who is trying to organize an independent labor movement in China.

Han had been released from prison in 1991 only on condition that he not see foreigners, so I was afraid that my arranging a meeting might get him in trouble. Still, I desperately wanted to see him, and I contacted him through a mutual friend. Finally, in March 1992, I got word that Han had agreed to give me an interview, his first full, on-the-record discussion with a reporter for a Western publication. I figured that he was a consenting adult, aware of the risks of talking to the press, but even so, I was deeply worried for him.

I hid on the floorboard of a Chinese friend's car as we left my compound so the guards at the gate wouldn't see me, and after reaching our destination I ambled through back alleys to make sure I wasn't being tailed. But when I got to Han Dongfang's building, I couldn't find the right apartment. As I wandered around in frustration, I turned a corner and almost stumbled into the arms of a security officer. His eyes widened with surprise.

"Please sign the register book," he suggested, beaming at me. "What work unit are you from?"

I was busy making excuses when Han walked by and spotted me. I was ready to feign ignorance and slouch away, but Han calmly greeted both me and the policeman, then led me to his apartment.

"I'm so sorry," I told him. "I hope I haven't gotten you into trouble."

"No trouble," he said serenely. "Everything I do, I do openly. I'm not hiding what I do from the government."

Over the next few hours, as we spoke in his apartment—two bare rooms, the whitewashed walls decorated only with a wildlife calendar from many years earlier—he boldly left the door ajar, his denunciations of the regime wafting into the corridor.

Like most Chinese, Han Dongfang grew up as a loyal believer in the Communist Party. After graduating from high school in 1980, Han was delighted to learn that he had been accepted to join the People's Liberation Army. "From when I was little, I'd believed that to serve in the People's Liberation Army was a glorious calling," Han recalled, speaking in his deep, rich Mandarin Chinese. "I was seventeen then, and I worshiped the army."

After just three months, Han was promoted to squad commander and nominated for Communist Party membership. With his tall frame, easy manners, and casual good looks, he seemed to be on the road to a fine career as a military officer or Communist cadre. But something bothered him: While the troops ate miserable rations, rice and *wotou* cornmeal buns, the officers dined on meat and sipped wine. When a political commissar called a large meeting with divisional and regimental commanders present, Han stood up and protested the difference in rations. "I'm upset and disappointed," he declared. "The Communist Party tradition is that when troops are eating so miserably, the officers should share in the unpleasantness." The next day he learned that an angry officer had ripped up his Communist Party application.

"My idealism was shattered," Han remembered, his thick eyebrows shooting upward for a moment, as if in puzzlement at the perfidy. "That was a starting point. It was when I began to feel the injustice around me."

Han left the army after three years and was assigned a job riding on refrigerator railcars to make sure that they were working properly. When the Tiananmen Square demonstrations began in April 1989, Han emerged as head of the newly formed Beijing Workers Autonomous Federation, an independent labor union that operated from a tent on the square. Because it sought to mobilize workers rather than students, and aimed to become like Solidarity in Poland, the independent union was seen by the regime as a serious threat. When the tanks arrived at Tiananmen Square in the predawn darkness of June 4, 1989, one of their first missions was to knock down the union headquarters.

After the crackdown, Han hid for a few weeks in the countryside. Then he decided to confront his accusers, and he returned to Beijing and showed up at the big gate next to Righteousness Street, the headquarters of the Public Security Bureau.

"I'm Han Dongfang," he explained politely to the policeman at the gate. "You're looking for me."

"Huh?" the guard asked, not understanding. "Who are you looking for?" But another guard recognized him from the wanted posters and called out, "Are you Han Dongfang?"

The police were initially thrilled that the nation's most wanted labor leader had turned himself in, and they poured him tea. But Han soon annoyed them by declaring that he was not a criminal and that he had come only to set the record straight.

"We just executed some people the other day," an interrogator replied icily. "You know, a bullet can enter your skull as well."

Han was assigned a crowded cell at the Paoju Detention Center, a prison squeezed behind fourteen-foot red- and gray-brick walls amid the narrow lanes of an old-fashioned neighborhood in northeast Beijing. Twenty-odd prisoners shared a small room, with no beds, nothing to read, and only two identical meals a day: a half bowl of vegetable soup and two *wotou* buns. As in most Chinese prisons, inmates were constantly hungry. Interrogators grilled Han nearly every day, sometimes far into the night, and they and the jailers were furious at his obstreperousness. Han refused to acknowledge wrong-doing, refused to write self-criticisms, refused to grovel. The guards never beat him—although they threatened to—but they found other ways to punish him.

When Han complained about a stomach ailment, which left him so weak that he could not stand, the prison refused his demands for a hospital checkup. Instead, they summoned a prison acupuncturist, who forced a long needle lengthwise through several inches of flesh on his hand. There was little pretense that this was meant to ease his ailment; the acupuncturist raked the needle back and forth through the wound to increase the pain.

Han protested his treatment by going on a hunger strike. This won him a trip to the hospital, but the doctors there couldn't diagnose the stomach ailment he complained of. That tended to confirm the guards' suspicion that Han was faking the illness. To teach him a lesson, they installed him that winter in the outermost cell and left the two doors down the corridor open so that the winds rushed in. As he lay on the floor, sick and miserable, Han felt as if he were freezing to death. Other prisoners, who respected him for his role at Tiananmen and for his courage in talking back to the guards, gave him their blankets. The guards then ordered the extra blankets taken away.

One day the warden ordered the other prisoners to pick up the sickly Han and lean him with his back against the wall, arms outstretched, as if he were being crucified. The prisoners obeyed, warily and gently. They feared hurting Han, who seemed near death and couldn't even stand on his own.

"Now let go," the warden said, with a flicker of a smile.

"But he's too weak!" one prisoner objected. "He'll fall down!"

"What did you say?" the warden thundered menacingly. "Are you disobeying orders?"

The prisoner looked away and whispered into Han's ear, "I'm sorry, big brother, but there's nothing I can do." So he and the others released their grip, and watched anxiously as the semiconscious Han wobbled and then teetered forward like a tree that had been sawed off at its base. Han was too weak to take a step, too weak to bring his hands up in front of his face; so he simply fell forward and smashed face-first into the wooden floor.

"Han Dongfang," the warden sneered, towering over him, "you had this coming! This is how guys like you end up."

The warden and the guards soon devised a more ingenious punishment.

"We've been too nice to you, too polite to you," a guard told him one day in late 1989. "We've given you face, and even though you're ill we haven't put you into the contagious diseases unit. But that's what you're going to get now! You're afraid of illness, so that's what we're going to give you."

"You're criminals!" Han retorted. "You know that my illness isn't contagious."

The guards moved Han into a cell with more than twenty other prisoners, more than two-thirds of whom suffered from tuberculosis. The remainder mostly had hepatitis or gonorrhea. Han spent four months in the contagious diseases unit before being moved in March 1990 to another prison, where conditions improved. His stomach ailment gradually disappeared, and he felt much healthier. But then another ailment began to manifest itself. Han weakened quickly and began coughing. Soon he couldn't stand, couldn't roll over, couldn't even speak. It didn't help that he was kept in leg irons.

The prison authorities paid little attention to Han's sickness, but two state prosecutors who came to interrogate him one day were horrified at his condition. The next day the authorities put him on an IV drip, and two days later he was taken to a military hospital, where doctors misdiagnosed his case as Legionnaires' disease. For two months, Han lay with a 104-degree temperature, not responding to treatment. Word reached the outside world that Han Dongfang was mortally ill, causing indignation in the West, and the Chinese leadership apparently feared that he would die while in custody.

So, at the end of April 1991, prison officials released him on a temporary medical discharge. Outside doctors quickly diagnosed his ailment as tuberculosis, which he had caught while confined in the contagious diseases unit. New drugs eventually cured Han, but half his right lung is useless, and he tires easily and has pains in his chest. Still, by early 1992 he could walk about and talk. That was when I met him for the first time.

As his strength returned, Han Dongfang began to resume his work to unite China's laborers. He even applied to hold a legal one-man demonstration in behalf of worker rights, handing out leaflets on labor issues. Of course, the Public Security Bureau rejected Han's request, but the application itself served as a cannon shot across the bow, a warning that Han has not been cowed and intends to continue as a labor organizer. He says he plans to work openly, within the law, to oppose the Communist Party and win improved health care for workers.

Han traveled to the United States in 1992 to receive medical treatment, and he tried to return to China in the summer of 1993, slipping across the border at a remote checkpoint where guards had never heard of him. A couple of days later, however, secret police charged into his hotel room in Guangzhou and bundled him back into Hong Kong. When Han tried once more to return to China, the border guards turned him back again. The Chinese government announced that it had revoked his passport, apparently in an effort to strip him of his Chinese nationality. So for now Han Dongfang is stuck abroad. He'll be back.

Whatever happens to Han, it is clear that a growing number of Chinese are jostling the Communist Party and dislodging it. Still, all this shouldn't be taken too far. History shows that declining dynasties can take centuries to collapse, so a terminal illness—if that is indeed the correct diagnosis—does not necessarily mean that the Communist dynasty is going to expire this year or even this decade. Moreover, foreigners sometimes point to China's new problems and get a bit hysterical. Corruption, religious zeal, and public skepticism may be the hallmarks not of a disintegrating country but simply of a normal nation. Normal countries, after all, have drug problems, crooked cops, and alienated citizens. It was only in the abnormal era of Mao that China was too sterile for any real life.

Moreover, there is one crucial aspect of China today that does not fit the pattern of dynastic decline: the flourishing economy. People are getting richer rather than poorer, public works projects are getting more funding instead of less, and rather than facing floods and starvation, Chinese are learning to shop till they drop.

This paradox is, of course, central to China in the 1990s. But when I pointed this out to Chinese friends, they snorted with derision. The economic boom does not create support for the Communist Party, they said. Many Chinese credit themselves—or capitalism—for their gains, while blaming the party for corruption and inflation. And once people see how quasi capitalism can improve their lives, they wonder why they wasted so much time with a centrally planned economy.

Our octogenarian friend Luhui, who had played bridge with Deng, even insisted that Chinese are no better off in the 1990s than they were in the 1970s. "Look at the price of shrimp today!" he complained. "Look at the price of everything! People can't afford to live."

In reality, of course, prices are higher but so are incomes. And at least goods are available in the stores. It wasn't much use to have cheap shrimp in the 1970s if you couldn't buy any, but Luhui refused to see that. By any statistical measure, his position that Chinese are no better off than they were in the Maoist era is ludicrous. But since perceptions often matter more than reality, Luhui's is a telling view. And it isn't unique. Most of our friends acknowledged that living conditions had improved, but it was surprising how a minority—perhaps 10 percent—insisted in the face of all evidence that economic conditions had deteriorated since the Maoist period. Luhui is not a dumb man; on the contrary, he is brilliant and fairly cosmopolitan, and that made his lack of appreciation for the economic changes even more remarkable.

Luhui also had a keen interest in history. So one day when his maid was out of earshot, I asked him if the Communist Party resembled a declining dynasty. "Of course!" he said immediately. That's exactly what's happening. It's just like the late Qing.

"I'll tell you, in 1949 I hated the Nationalists. I went to welcome the Communists when they entered Beijing, and I cheered for them. When a Communist soldier was shot, I went to get help for him. At a meeting in my office to discuss what to do, I was the first to speak out. I said we should support the Communist Party.

"Now I would welcome the Nationalists back. In fact, I would go out and lead them into Beijing."

SHERYL WUDUNN

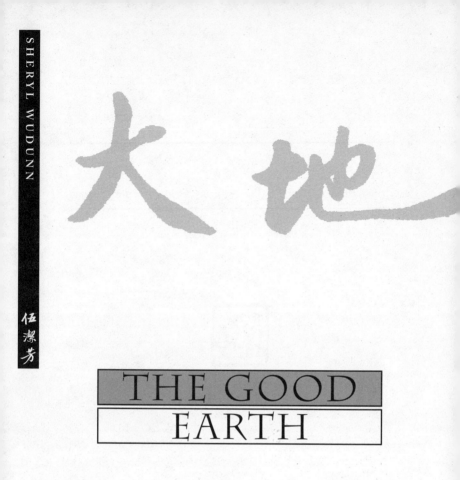

大地

伍潔芳

THE GOOD
EARTH

When I grow up, I am determined to be a peasant!

—Cultural Revolution children's song

6

Three siblings playing outside their home, which had to be rebuilt after Guizhou Province officials tore it down as punishment for violating the one-child policy. [Photo by Sheryl WuDunn.]

In the undulating hills of Sichuan Province, peasants like Zhao Qingnan toil in the rice paddies and in the nearby coal mines. Per capita income is less than a hundred dollars a year, so every bit of grain counts.

That's why the party secretary of Zhao's village likes to "borrow" rice from the villagers. He never pays it back, of course, any more than he paid back the thousands of yuan he pocketed from family planning funds raised as taxes from the peasants. Nobody dares complain. Zhao Qingnan did, and look what happened to him.

Zhao's family was particularly poor, and he was desperate for grain. He was also only twenty-one years old, and—with five brothers in the village—perhaps he felt invincible. So he asked the party secretary to repay the grain and ten yuan that he had borrowed. The party secretary turned him away. Zhao kept trying. He went five times and was turned down five times. Each time as he walked down the street on the way to the party secretary's house, the curious, hopeful eyes of the villagers followed him to the door, waiting to see what would happen.

"The party secretary got angry," Zhao Qingyou, Zhao Qingnan's thirty-nine-year-old brother, recalled to me one hazy evening. "He felt he'd lost face, so he punched my brother." That was only the beginning. The party secretary then hired the Flying Tiger Gang—a local group of hooligans—to beat up the younger Zhao. The Flying Tigers seized him and pounded him with sticks and clubs for thirty-nine hours, leaving him as good as dead. He survived, but neither his brain nor his body recovered. Zhao Qingnan now is senseless, crippled, and unable to talk. He helps out with cooking and minor household chores but is able to do nothing else. His wife, not wanting to live with a handicapped man, is trying to divorce him. And since he had tried to fight back while he was being beaten, the party secretary fined him 100 yuan, or $17.50, in "ruffian fees."

Zhao Qingyou is seeking justice on behalf of his injured brother. He wanted to sue, so he borrowed 1,000 yuan to cover his costs. Unfortunately he didn't have a safe place to put the money, and the party secretary broke into his house one day and stole it. The township leaders, one notch above the party secretary, quietly helped recover some of it, and Zhao Qingyou made his way to Beijing. That's where I met him, as he stood patiently outside a government office set up to receive public complaints—but only very rarely to act on them. He limped on his right leg and held a small wooden pipe in his left hand. His thick black hair hadn't been combed in weeks. As he stood before me in his ripped blue Mao jacket, his frayed sandals, and his wrinkled pants, a picture of dirt and misery, Zhao Qingyou could have been any one of China's 900 million peasants.

Except that he was fighting back.

Party secretaries weren't supposed to be beating up peasants in the Chinese countryside. When I went on my first trips to the villages, I was overwhelmed by the bustle and construction: the new stores by the road, the pigpens going up, the piles of bricks to replace old mud homes. Everybody was getting richer. Life looked sweet. Peasants seemed content.

Gradually I realized that there was far more to the picture. The villages are home not only to the sweetness of newfound prosperity but also to the bitterness of age-old injustice. And some of the anger in the countryside is now welling over.

For 5,000 years, China's history has been punctuated by peasant revolts—including the one five decades ago that put the Communists in power. Since then, the Communist Party leaders have worried principally about disgruntled students and workers, for protests and demonstrations were concentrated in the urban centers. Now Chinese officials and foreign specialists seriously debate whether a new peasant rebellion is possible, and the government itself acknowledges that the discontent in the villages could sound the death knell for the Communist Party.

A peasant rebellion in the 1990s? It seems scarcely imaginable. China's 900 million peasants account for one person in six on this planet. Even if the rebellion did not spill across the borders, any large-scale domestic upheaval in China's countryside would involve far more people than were touched by all the fighting in World War I.

Yet some peasant rebellions have already broken out in recent years. Most are small-scale riots in which the peasants protest one injustice or another, but a few have had broader resonance. In 1992, a thirty-eight-year-old peasant named Li Chengfu had an extraordinary fantasy: He wanted to overthrow the Communist Party and establish a new dynasty with himself as emperor. Both charismatic and superstitious, Li Chengfu lured several party members into his clique and aimed to surround the cities in Henan Province with his army of peasants. If victorious, they would all join him in building a new dynasty called the Heavenly Kingdom of Everlasting Satisfaction. The government arrested the members only after infiltrating his ring with a spy who posed as an expert in traditional divination.

The conventional view is that the peasants are pretty happy with their lot. There is something to this, in that peasants tend to be more acquiescent than urban workers; the peasants are the shock absorbers of the system. Moreover, even when the peasants protest against various injustices, they don't necessarily want to overthrow the Communist Party. The signs of rural unrest perhaps can be seen as no more than the violent growing pains of a rapidly changing society.

Yet whenever officials tried to tell me how happy the peasants were, I thought of Pan Qunying. Thirty-seven years old, Pan was a meek, frightened, uneducated woman who lived with her husband and two children in a tiny village called Zhao in the southern province of Hunan. Because her first child was retarded, she was allowed to have a second child, and after that she was sterilized. But on May 13, 1992, the authorities arbitrarily ordered her to pay birth control fees of 100 yuan, plus a special construction tax that local officials were assessing to build an apartment building. There was no justification for these taxes except that the local officials needed money. Nevertheless, the authorities assessed Pan Qunying and her family 319 yuan, or nearly half the average annual income for a peasant.

She borrowed fifty yuan, and one official said he would put up the money for her for a few days while she found a way to borrow the remainder. For two days, she couldn't eat or sleep. Where would she get the money for the assessment, let alone money to feed her children? Pan Qunying had no idea. She felt ill and weak, and she told the officials that she couldn't pay right away. When they heard this, the township officials sent over a collection brigade and confiscated her family's bicycle, television set, and everything else they could find. When she clung to the bicycle, her family's only means of transportation, the deputy party secretary of the township cursed her. He stomped on the back wheel, crushing the spokes.

The next day, when another young woman was walking by the village's pond, she heard a scream and a loud splash. The passerby rushed over and found that Pan Qunying, unable to face her huge tax bill, had plunged into the pond and was struggling in the water, her arms waving frantically. The woman called the village officials. They came, but no one tried to rescue Pan. So she drowned.

There is no group of 900 million people about whom so little is known as the Chinese peasantry. Even many of China's city residents often have only a rudimentary idea of what is going on in the countryside. Diplomats, scholars, journalists—we all live in the cities and pay too little attention to the peasants. In the 1930s and 1940s, that tendency led to a monumental intelligence failure: the inability to predict the Communist takeover. Now we may be making the same mistake.

Part of the problem is our own, and part is caused by the Chinese government. The authorities refuse to allow most foreign specialists to travel unescorted in the countryside, and in particular to stay in a village for any length of time. A few scholars, particularly Chinese-Americans, have managed to wangle their way into villages to stay for a few months and conduct research, but this doesn't happen nearly enough. Nick and I tried to obey the rules for journalists in China, particularly at first, and the result was that most of our trips to the villages were stage-managed by local governments. They chose the village, prepared the people for our interviews, and hovered in the background as we talked to the peasants. The exercise was virtually meaningless. I always finished such trips with a sense that the officials had colored the grass, painted the houses, and brought in sacks of rice to make the peasants look sated and happy.

In 1993 I arranged a trip to Guizhou, an impoverished southern province famed for its pebbly soil and rocky hills and valleys. My "handlers" were a young woman named Wan Shengwen, who had just graduated from college, and a middle-aged editor named Ling Yuming. They promised me that we would visit a "very poor" village.

As we drove through a relatively wealthy area, dotted with two-story shingled-roof houses and checkered vegetable fields, I wondered how poor these peasants would be. At the regional government office, we picked up a couple of officials; then, at the township headquarters, we picked up a couple more. At the village, the party secretary and village chief greeted us and ushered all seven of us into the home of a "typical" villager.

I should have known better.

The peasant was Li Zhuo, a quiet twenty-nine-year-old man who raised six pigs and grew red peppers, peanuts, corn, and green vegetables on one and a half acres. He belonged to one of China's largest minority groups, the Miao, and his average income per family member was $150. So this "poor villager" earned far more than the average income of $88 per year among peasants in Guizhou Province. He even exceeded the national average earnings among the peasantry, which were about 700 yuan, or $123, in 1993. As I walked onto the porch of his house, I noticed a motorcycle—a purchase that would require several years of an average family's income.

Well, I thought, even the rich have to pay taxes. One of the purposes of my trip was to find out how much peasants were paying in taxes, so I asked Li how much he paid each year. He hesitated, then turned to the party secretary and mumbled something in the local dialect. The party secretary barked back.

"I turned in seventy-five *jin* of rice," said Li. That was eighty-three pounds, worth about $1.31, less than one percent of his income. Li laughed at the amount of taxes, leaving the impression that they were so trivial that he was willing to pay more. With the seven officials in tow, I interviewed a couple of other peasants, but their stories were the same. They insisted that they were paying very little in taxes. I wondered if they were lying, but it was impossible to know.

In Guizhou, it was hard to get even a dinner to myself, for my handlers did a good job of accompanying me practically everywhere I went. I puzzled over how I could escape them.

"I'm afraid I've got a stomachache," I told my hosts the next morning.

"Too bad," Ling, the editor, said. "We have a whole day planned for you. First we'll interview private bus companies. Then, if you don't have any more requests, Little Wan will take you sightseeing."

"I really need some rest. I think I'll just spend the afternoon in my room."

"There's a special painting exhibit this month, and foreigners are coming from all over to see it. You shouldn't miss the chance. Little

Wan can take you this afternoon, and she can also take you shopping. Would you like to buy some wax-dyed material?"

"Why don't you let me rest awhile, and I'll give you a call if I need you?" I said. Half an hour later, he gave in.

"Okay, but remember we have dinner promptly at six," Mr. Ling said. That came as a surprise.

"Oh, there's really no need, and anyway, I don't think I'll feel like eating much," I pleaded.

"We'll pick you up at your hotel at six." I lost that argument.

When he had gone, I slipped out of the hotel, hired a car, and headed south to an area that President Jiang Zemin had once visited. We drove more than two hours into the wild clay mountains, down roads where passenger cars probably hadn't ventured for weeks. Patches of rock peeked through the fields in the hills and valleys, and peasants bent over their terraced rice paddies. Miao women, dressed in red and white and blue hemp cloth, balanced large bamboo baskets on their heads as they walked at the side of the road. It was a market day, and they had put on their best clothes, the wedding outfits that they would keep and wear for the rest of their lives.

I stopped in a village by a main road. It turned out to be a different China from the one I had visited with officials.

A sturdy, talkative thirty-five-year-old woman, who wouldn't reveal her name, was fuming at the variety of taxes she and her family of five had to pay: grain tax, land fees, a head tax, local management tax, educational fees, and contributions to the families of soldiers. Altogether, she paid twelve dollars, or 17.5 percent of her family's gross annual income, plus more than one-third of the grain her family had brought in the preceding year. Moreover, during a provincewide drought that lasted two months, local authorities raised the fee for pumping water for crops from forty-four cents an hour to fifty-three cents—or three days' income. In the cities, even in Beijing, residents pay much less: only a fraction of a cent for a ton of running water.

"Fees!" cried out Guo Duancheng, a man who lived nearby. "If you offer to go pay the fees yourself, you'll be charged less. But if you wait for them to come to you, you'll get stuck with a huge bill."

The peasants I talked to were furious, but they gave no hint that they were going to do anything about it, that they had any intention of organizing a resistance. Instead, there was fear, plus a lifelong tradition of obeying officials. "It's not a matter of guts," said Peng Dagui, a sixty-year-old peasant who told me he paid 16 percent of his grain in tax the preceding year. "There's just nothing you can do."

I returned to the car, and we headed into the mountains. We passed by a township, and then all of a sudden I noticed that the road had become a bright cement gray, smooth and wide. The driver, who was familiar with the area, explained that the road had been paved in preparation for President Jiang's visit. Jiang made it to the township, but never to any villages. The money for the road, the driver said, probably came from peasant taxes.

We turned off the paved road and kept driving, then decided to stop at a quiet village, a sprawling hamlet in the stone-covered countryside. I looked up toward a small hut on an incline, where a man in tattered clothes stood barefoot next to his tiny children. He was Luo Qingguo, a skinny thirty-six-year-old peasant, the father of four children, including a retarded, crippled, mute son. Two of his sons wore no clothes below the waist. "I can't afford to give them pants to wear," Luo explained with an embarrassed laugh.

He took me into his shack, a fairly large room, dark and dusty, cluttered with wooden scraps and stacks of wheat. In one corner was a bed where three of his children slept, and in another was a clump of frayed straw and a rag, the nest where his retarded son slept alone. Luo and his wife retired upstairs to a loft, and he led me up the ladder to show it off: another messy pile of straw and dust. Downstairs, taking up one entire side of the room, was a sunken, smelly pen. I peered inside and was startled to find three chickens and a big, flabby pig. Man and animal, they lived all together here like one family.

Luo said that the previous year his family of six averaged earnings of only fifteen dollars each—compared with the provincial per capita income of eighty-eight dollars—and this put him in the bottom third of the village strata. Part of the problem is that he has to feed his family of six from land allocated for only two, himself and his wife. "There wasn't enough food to eat last year," Luo explained. The two smaller kids looked malnourished; they had distended bellies. At least the children fared better than the family cow, which had died from sickness earlier in the year.

When I mentioned local taxes, Luo bristled. About six months earlier, a group of local officials rode their spanking-clean motorcycles into Luo's village. They were tax collectors, and they seized 110 pounds of his rice and corn, a month's food for his family, forcing Luo to go out and buy more rice at a high market price. The officials also took a few more dollars in various other taxes, arbitrarily calculated: There was land rent, irrigation tax, housing insurance, electricity fees, the subsidy payment to local officials, and the contribution to help support the elderly.

Luo had a single lightbulb in his shack, and he dashed over to turn it on and show it off. "Do you use it often?" I asked him. He lowered his head in response, clearly embarrassed to say that he hardly ever used it. Then I glanced toward one of the beds and noticed a water hole, a deep black cavity in the ground. It was open, mud particles and clods of dirt peeking out from the mottled surface. The pigs and the people drank from the same water hole. As I edged out of the shack, I debated whether I should give him the lunch I had brought with me. I was a reporter, not a social worker, but Luo needed the food much more than I did. I ran back to the car and returned with some packages of instant noodles and candy for his children. Then I slipped out.

"I never imagined there would be such poverty so close to the city," said my taxi driver, both angry and shaken by what he had seen with me. "This area is administered by the provincial capital, and they still let these people live so poorly!"

As I left the village, a crowd of villagers followed me around. None of them asked for handouts; they were too proud or too intimidated, and anyway they didn't have the slightest expectation. This made me think that all the other outsiders who had come to their village had demanded something: money, grain, sterilization. I had come, not asking for anything, and they were glad. I reached out the window and emptied a bag of candy into the hands of a dozen children.

Back in Guiyang, the provincial capital, I had a grueling dinner with Ling, Wan, and another foreign affairs official. They talked about how wonderful life was in Guizhou, about how they had shown me a poor village (with a motorcycle), but my eyes glazed over as I sat across the table. They told me that there were poorer areas, and that Nick had visited one of the poorest areas in Guizhou a year earlier. I remembered Nick telling me that he had been to a poor area but that the person he was taken to see was a local tycoon with a two-story villa.

The officials glossed over the province's problems, and I wasn't even certain how much they knew about them. I was sure, however, that Wan had never seen poverty. She grew up in the city of Guiyang, and the trip to the village with the motorcycle was the first time she had ever been to the countryside.

That night, I hardly slept. I thought of Luo Qingguo and his little children, the ones with no clothes. I thought of the tax collectors, coming to harass the peasants and seize their property. It was the first time I had ever seen such desperate poverty in China, and I wondered how many millions of other Chinese live like Luo Qingguo.

After that visit, Nick and I concluded that officially arranged visits are sometimes not only misleading but actually counterproductive. Even on our first visits, we knew we were being manipulated, but still we figured that we were getting something, a heavily veiled glimpse of reality. But with time it became clear to us that the authorities do not just manipulate the truth. They lie. They invent. So you don't just get a distorted view of reality. You get absolute falsehood. And unless you go on your own, unescorted, you have no idea what reality is like.

We now know that the best reporting during the Maoist era came not from journalists who were allowed into China but from those who were obliged to sit outside the country in Hong Kong, interviewing refugees as they escaped. In 1961, for example, a writer named Felix Greene wrote *Awakened China*—a book whose title sends shivers up our spines, for it was so obviously premature. Greene included a chapter on foreign press coverage, with extensive examples of harsh reporting by the many journalists who never entered China and much more positive accounts by those few who traveled around the country.

Greene's point was that most Hong Kong and foreign accounts were unfair. In fact, three decades later, what is most striking about his remarks is how wrong they were: Those who never entered China reported far more accurately than those who visited the country. Most of the critical reporting, which Greene ridiculed, stands up fairly well to the test of time. But travelers to China wrote gushy pieces about how happy the Chinese were with the communes, and these portraits now come across as naive and ridiculous. It is obvious that the travelers made the mistake of trusting what they saw and heard; in China, when you are talking to officials and being taken on government-arranged visits, that is a mistake.

So Nick and I increasingly began to test the limits of the rules. We did this carefully, remembering what had happened to one of our *New York Times* predecessors in Beijing, John Burns. In 1986 he wandered into a closed rural area without permission, and he was promptly arrested for espionage and later expelled from the country. So, like most other foreign journalists, we tried to bend the rules without quite openly breaking them. For example, all our reporting was supposed to be arranged through the government, but the rules say nothing of pleasure excursions for tourism, so Nick played tourist. The Foreign Ministry complained, but Nick explained that he had decided to write articles only when he was in the middle of his tourist trip.

When friends asked us for suggestions about visiting China, we offered similar advice: Avoid the authorities. Officials never say anything new anyway, and "field trips" are so manipulated that you don't know whether you're getting anything real. It's much more useful simply to go out and talk to people without any minders present. Unlike journalists, tourists may visit the countryside without permission (so long as they keep to open areas, which cover much of the country), and they can always find an interpreter. Of course, it's not always possible to show up at a factory door and ask for a tour. But sometimes it does work, and in that case the factory manager's lies at least won't be rehearsed.

In some of my own private conversations with peasants, I discovered the insidious dynamics of power and *guanxi* that can rule a village. Take the case of Xu Yanhua, a short, bony, middle-aged peasant from the Tianjin area in northern China. Xu and his older brother had improved their status in peasant life the honest way, by joining the army. For a peasant, the military is a way out of a rural rut, a way to see the country and perhaps spend time in the nation's capital. The villagers thought they'd never return. Unfortunately, it was while they were in the army that the brothers' luck ran out. Xu's eyesight failed him—one eye grew bloodshot and partially blind—and he was discharged, and his brother was never promoted, so they decided to return home, penniless and loveless. Xu eventually wandered to the county seat in search of a job, while his brother tilled the land in their home village.

By the mid-1980s, the Xu brothers still hadn't found wives, and their prospects for marriage and heirs were looking grim. Meanwhile, another villager named Wang, a fifty-year-old bully with an eye for money, wanted the Xu brothers' land to set up a store selling sugar, fruits, cigarettes, and wine. One morning, Xu's older brother vanished. Days later, a peasant found the body and summoned Xu to come home. Somebody had poisoned his brother with pesticides and then tried to make it look like a disappearance: The body had been mutilated and hidden in a hemp bag in the fields.

By the time Xu returned to the village, Wang had taken over his home, his furniture, and everything his brother had owned. Xu, who had to beg village friends for food and shelter, fretted every night for two years; finally he pounded on the doors of the township police station. But it was too late, the police told him. Twenty times Xu petitioned to the higher authorities, sending letters to the Public Security Ministry, the Ministry of Civil Affairs, even the State Council. Finally, a plump official in a Mao suit visited the village to investigate. Months later, another official paid a visit with a mysterious message: "Your money has arrived." What money, Xu wondered. "You petitioned to the authorities, and they're distributing some money to you," the official said curtly. "Don't file any more complaints," he warned. "We'll give you some money, help you find some work, and arrange for the village to build you a house." Xu was to receive 5,000 yuan.

It was hush money, but even that never came. "To this day, I've received only 200 yuan," Xu said. I furrowed my brow in puzzlement over how peasant Wang could get away with so much, and the explanation finally came out: Wang's relatives included the village party secretary.

The Communists didn't expect their revolution to turn out this way.

Mao learned early on that no revolution in China would spread and be victorious unless it attracted the peasantry, the largest stratum of Chinese society. He knew that the peasants' lives were awful: They lived in mud shacks, slept on straw mats or coal-warmed beds, ate *wotou*, spent their days in the fields, and then turned over a large portion of their harvest to the landowners. They could barely feed their children, and sometimes they even had to sell the kids for a few bags of rice. The suffering was widespread, and Mao seized on this as the basis for the revolution. Indeed, the secret to the Communists' success was their support among the peasants.

After the Communists came to power, they dramatically improved the lives of the peasants. Land reform, the first major achievement of the revolution, was a mind-boggling step in China. It meant that for the first time every family had a bit of land that it could farm for itself. In the late 1950s, Mao took back the land, turning it over to the communes, but twenty years later, Deng Xiaoping returned the farmland to the peasants. Nominally the land still belongs to the state, but in fact it is "contracted" out to the peasants in exchange for a portion of the crop. Every few years, a village may adjust the size of each family's plot, to account for births and deaths, but the land is the peasants' to use. They cannot sell it, yet it is theirs to make them rich or poor.

This division of the communes, which began in the late 1970s, caused an agrarian revolution in China. Agricultural output soared, particularly from 1980 to 1985, and peasants for the first time began to buy consumer goods like bicycles, televisions, and watches. In 1980, only one rural family in three owned a bicycle; by 1985, four in five did. Poverty and malnutrition nose-dived, and since 1978 China has managed to reduce the number of poor people—almost all of them peasants—by 170 million, a number greater than the entire population of Japan. China, which had been notorious for its famines, began to export grain.

By the late 1980s, however, this revolution in agricultural output was petering out. The problem was that the gains in productivity had resulted simply from a gift of land to the peasants, and that could happen only once. But Deng Xiaoping, in a stroke of genius, engineered a second agricultural revolution. Traditionally in developing countries, peasants stream to the cities and get jobs in factories, creating the huge slums that mar the outskirts of Calcutta, Lagos, Mexico City, and other third world metropolises. In China, by contrast, Deng Xiaoping discouraged the peasants from migrating to industry; instead, he brought industry to the countryside.

To help employ surplus rural laborers, Deng encouraged townships and villages to start their own enterprises. They were happy to do this—indeed, many were already doing so before the national government gave its blessing to the idea—and these businesses became a phenomenal success. Typically, these *xiangzhen qiye,* or township and village enterprises, were owned by the local government and employed fewer than a hundred people, making everything from metal pails to teddy bears to silk rugs. The number of these countryside enterprises soared from 1.5 million in 1978 to 19 million in 1991, by which time they were contributing about 30 percent of China's gross national product, far exceeding the share of agricultural output. These *xiangzhen qiye,* in other words, marked an intermediate step in the industrial revolution, a way to ease peasants into assembly lines and industry without the traumas and dislocations of urbanization. These enterprises were often market oriented, because local governments would not bail out the failures, so they quickly taught people the discipline of profits and losses. To be sure, the *xiangzhen qiye* were sometimes hugely inefficient and polluting, but by and large they were a terrific idea, employing about 112 million idle farmers across the country. They were one of China's best economic innovations and provide a useful model for Eastern Europe and the third world.

Even with the *xiangzhen qiye,* though, China may well have 100 million more rural laborers than it needs. Mechanization means that the problem is getting worse, and that the government needs to figure out how to accommodate these people. Some of these surplus laborers simply have nothing to do during the slack season, as I was reminded one day by Fu Sunin, a short, thin, eighteen-year-old peasant who had graduated from middle school in Guoshan Village in Sichuan. Fu couldn't really explain what he did during his days, although he admitted that he took long naps, slept late into the mornings, and leaned on his hoe a lot in the fields. The country has millions of peasants like Fu Sunin, so it's not surprising that beginning in the mid-1980s the peasants' socioeconomic escalator slowed down. In fact, from 1985 to 1993, the real average growth in farmers' earnings was 2.2 percent per year. The *xiangzhen qiye* helped enormously, but they predominated in coastal areas rather than in the poor interior.

Worse yet, the central government began running out of money and cut payments to peasants for their grain. Instead, the local grain bureaus issued *baitiaozi*—white slips, or IOUs—to the peasants, redeeming them with cash only months later. The cash shortages in the countryside also meant that some peasants working for the government were not getting paid. In 1993, for instance, some teachers in Hunan Province weren't paid their salaries for six months. When our octogenarian friend Luhui returned home to his *laojia*, or ancestral home, he discovered that the employees at the county-run guest house had not been paid their salaries for months. "They got free food and lodging, but they were paid IOUs instead of cash," he said.

Meanwhile, local authorities became steadily more avaricious, raiding homes to seize taxes and grain. A friend of ours, the son of a senior general, told us about seizures he had heard about in Gansu Province. The local officials had confiscated the grain that the peasants depended on to carry them through the winter. "That's the kind of thing that led my papa to join the Red Army in the 1930s," he said, shaking his head in wonderment.

Peasants shared their ire by quietly chanting a countryside *minyao*, a ditty satirizing the officials' drive to make money:

> You raise money, I raise money, he raises money,
> The peasant raises his blood pressure;
> You collect money, I collect money, he collects money,
> The peasant collects worries.
> Take a deep breath.

In the early 1980s, the income gap between the cities and the villages diminished, so that in about 1985 the average city dweller earned only 1.7 times as much as the average peasant. But then the disparity gradually increased. These days, taking into account subsidies to urban residents and taxes on farmers, an urban resident's income rises to four times as much as that of a peasant.

The ratios are growing more skewed with each passing year. In 1993, when gross national product grew by about 13 percent, rural incomes grew by just 2 percent, making the improvement in the quality of life barely perceptible to a peasant. In contrast, industrial growth galloped at a rate of 20 percent.

Partly because farming was unprofitable, peasants have simply stopped cultivating the land in some areas. High taxes and the state's low purchase price for grain make agriculture a money-losing venture. In Anhui Province's Chu County, for instance, one-third of the peasants threw down their hoes and left their land idle, according to a confidential government report. Many of the rest just cultivated a portion of their land. Moreover, peasants are abandoning the land all across the country to search for work in the cities—even with the success of the *xiangzhen qiye*.

By 1993, peasants had something else to worry about: *lutiaozi*, or green slips. These are IOUs that the post offices issue to peasants who receive money orders—the main way people send money from city to city. Many peasants migrate to the cities to work and send money payments back to their families through the postal system, but their families sometimes have to wait months before they can cash their green slips. While the authorities made sure that urban banks had cash, the rural areas once again got the short end of the stick.

Sometimes peasants complained. But it is the thorny logic of *renzhi* that operates in the countryside. Take the case of Cai Yutang, an elderly peasant in Pingyu County in Henan Province. Local officials wanted to collect money from the peasants to pay for an electricity station, but Cai refused to pay. He saw no point in paying for electricity that he regarded as uselsss, and he had no savings anyway. "Ah! I'm old," he explained to his daughter. "These eyes of mine can't even see. What good is hooking up a television?" Then at three o'clock one afternoon in November 1992, a band of nineteen officials stomped into Cai Yutang's house. They squeezed the contribution out of him, then took all 218 pounds of wheat and 22 pounds of sesame seeds that he had stored in his house. When an official tried to grab a last bag, half-filled with sesame seeds, Cai protested.

The official threatened him: "We'll tie you up." So Cai Yutang let them take the seeds, and the officials left. A few days later, some young students were walking by Cai's house on the way to school when they discovered his body. He had hanged himself from the pear tree by his door.

After Cai died, the local officials, feeling somewhat remorseful, returned the wheat and sesame seeds. But then they demanded that his family pay $263, or two years' income for a typical peasant, for his burial.

The Communists seemed to have forgotten their original source of support. Many peasants found themselves again exploited, this time by the Communist Party. Whereas the Communists had once been seen as saviors for a nation of peasants, they were now becoming instruments of growing oppression. Moreover, the one infallible rule of Chinese politics seems to be this: In any conflict between city people and peasants, the peasants get screwed.

The party extracts funds from the peasants and subsidizes city dwellers, largely because of fear that disgruntled urban workers might take to the streets to protest. This is a common third world phenomenon. In Europe and North America, governments subsidize farmers and pay them not to produce, or else pay them above-market prices for corn, milk, and wheat. In developing countries like China, governments are worried about urban unrest, so they pay farmers below-market prices for their cotton, cocoa, and rice, ensuring that city dwellers can eat their fill cheaply.

The government subsidized the fine universities and "key schools" in the cities, while in the countryside there was not even really a system of free public education. The fees, even for elementary schools, kept many children from attending classes beyond the third grade. To be sure, the government periodically launched literacy campaigns in the countryside, but by and large educational opportunities are far fewer in the villages than in the cities. Of the one-fifth of the nation's population that is illiterate, nearly all are peasants.

The proposition that the central government always favors city dwellers over peasants was tested in 1990, when the Huai and Yangtze rivers flooded in central China. In some areas it was the biggest flood of the century, and the waters threatened industrial and semi-industrial areas around major cities like Suzhou and Shanghai. To protect the cities, the authorities blasted dikes farther upriver, in impoverished Anhui Province. The waters flooded poor villages, so that the overall economic damage was far less than it would have been had the cities been ravaged. It was a perfectly rational decision. But the result was that those who had almost nothing lost what little they had, while those downriver in the cities were untouched. Some 3,000 people died in those floods, almost all of them peasants, and millions were left homeless. Many were still living in temporary housing more than a year later, when Nick visited the area to look at the consequences of the tussle between city and village.

I began to realize that for the Chinese leadership the peasantry doesn't matter. The government worries not about people getting angry at the voting booth, but about their taking to the streets. Throughout the 1980s and early 1990s, the main constituencies that worried the leaders were the university students, the intellectuals, and the workers—all of whom lived in the cities. The peasants never took part in the Tiananmen Square protests, except in their roles as soldiers who fired on the students.

In other countries that have experienced far-reaching changes in recent years—the Soviet Union, Eastern Europe, the Philippines— the peasants have also been somewhat irrelevant. Russian peasants didn't trigger the collapse of the Soviet Communist Party, nor did Filipino peasants matter much in the "People's Revolution" of 1986. In each case, the urban middle class was the greatest force for change, followed by urban workers, who are powerful because of their ability to go on strike. Perhaps the Chinese government is right; perhaps the peasants don't matter.

Still, I think it is a dangerous gamble for any government to neglect and alienate 80 percent of its population. The peasants increasingly are conscious of their status as second-class citizens, and they are groping for ways to take charge of their lives.

One day when the State Security censors perhaps were napping, we received a letter from a group of peasants in a village in northern China. I can't say precisely where it is, for reasons that will become clear in a moment. The peasants complained bitterly that their village chief had used their land to set up a brick factory for his personal profit.

The peasants had no telephone, of course, and I didn't dare communicate by letter for fear of alerting State Security. So we sent a summer intern, an American named Ben Read, to the village to check things out and set up a time when we could go. Ben followed a potholed dirt road to the village and found K. G. Sun, one of the letter writers. Sun was a short but muscular man in a tank top and black cotton pants. He wasn't very familiar with dates, but he said he was born in the Year of the Dog—1958. As for his two kids, he said, "One's a 'Dog,' the other's a 'Pig' "—meaning that they were ten and twelve years old. "But I don't know which one's which," he added.

"Big cadres eat big, little cadres eat a little, and if you're not a cadre, you don't eat," Sun complained, using a stock phrase in which *to eat* means "to make money off other people." His complaint was that the village chief had reallocated all the village's land in the fall of

1992, giving everybody a bit less than before. He then allocated twelve acres—enough for about seven families—for a brick factory. The factory is supposed to pay the village for the use of its land and clay, but instead the payments are made to the village chief. Moreover, the factory is privately owned, with profits going to a group of investors, including the village chief and several high officials.

Sun and the other peasants protested to the township, but the village chief foiled them by giving 2,560 yuan worth of apples—purchased with public village funds—to county officials. The peasants continued to pursue the case, signing petitions and raising funds among themselves to finance trips to the county seat and provincial capital. About half the 400 families in the village openly supported this insurrection against the village chief. They even had a letter of complaint formally printed. It read:

> *To All Comrades in Positions of Responsibility:*
> *We are not acting in the least out of private interests, but rather we are reacting with indignation to the reckless takeover of farmland in our village by a small number of people who built a brick plant to fatten themselves. . . . In the face of these perverse acts, can we, as ordinary peasants, stand by and do nothing? Can we allow ourselves to be trampled upon? We cannot! We absolutely cannot!*

I was amused and intrigued by the conflict, but I had no idea which side was right. It might well have been that the brick factory would be good for the village as well as for the village chief. What I found surprising was that the peasants had dared to complain—even to *The New York Times.*

Before I could arrange a visit, we got an urgent call one morning from one of the peasants, Sanheng. He was in Beijing, having just taken the overnight train, and he needed to see us urgently. We met him in the coffee shop of the Friendship Store, and he looked tired. The village chief had learned of Ben's visit and had called in the county authorities. The police interrogated all the peasants whom Ben had talked to and accused them of "leaking state secrets." Sanheng had sneaked into Beijing to warn us not to go to the village; if we did, he said, the peasants would be severely punished. Above all, he said, we should not identify the location of the village in any articles we wrote. Sanheng also asked us to write a letter to the county police explaining that Ben's visit had been a casual excursion rather than a formal interview. We agreed, feeling guilty that we had inadvertently caused the peasants such problems.

A few days later, the phone rang at 7:00 A.M. and it was Sanheng again—sounding more worried than ever. "I'm in Beijing again," he explained in his thick rural accent. "I've just arrived. Can we meet again, same place?"

Sanheng came dressed in a blue cotton flannel shirt and faded pants. He had borrowed a couple of hundred yuan from friends to finance his escape, but it wasn't enough, although it certainly represented a large portion of his annual income. The authorities say that peasants in his village earn an average of 560 yuan each year. "But it's actually just a quota they set for our village," he explained to me. "I've never counted my income before, so I have no idea if they're right."

The authorities were pressing their investigation, Sanheng told us, and had subpoenaed him and all the others for interrogation. The police were threatening to contact his girlfriend, in another village, and advise her family that he was a counterrevolutionary so that her family would break off the relationship. They were also talking about denying him the licenses he needed to run his sideline business. In the old days, the police told him, he simply would have been shot, and he and the others expected the subpoena to end with their detention and imprisonment. So he had decided to flee the village for a few weeks. Then he would sneak back at night and see if it was safe to return.

I listened to his tale, feeling sickened by his torment. We had never imagined—nor had he—that our response to his letter could cause such a furor. We talked for a couple of hours that morning, and it was clear that he was an extraordinarily bright and motivated young peasant. It was also striking that although he had many reasons to be outraged at the government, he was much kinder to the leadership than many of our friends in Beijing.

"Overall, life has gotten much better," he said. "My family eats meat maybe four or five times a week now. Ten years ago, we never had meat. Kids get an education now, and we can travel around—we can even go to Beijing and see some of the world. That used to be impossible. What's more, kids can go to the city and earn eighteen yuan a day or so in construction or odd jobs. Sometimes twenty yuan! Not bad! I've done it myself.

"So peasants are content and feel pretty good about the government. Of course, corruption is terrible and getting worse. It's much worse in the villages than in the cities. If you're a peasant, you need to pay people off to do anything."

Sanheng said that life in the village was reasonably harmonious, even if someone did celebrate Chinese New Year by heaving a brick through the village chief's window. And of course everyone hates the peasant in charge of enforcing family planning rules. Eight people reported him anonymously after he tried to shield his own son and daughter-in-law when they were expecting a second child. There was much glee when the township authorities forced the woman to have an abortion.

I asked Sanheng what would happen if there were a free election. "We'd vote for the government, of course," he explained, puzzled. "Otherwise we'd get in trouble."

"No, no," I replied. "What if it were a really free election? What if there were a choice, a Communist and a non-Communist, and you could vote in secret for either one. You wouldn't get in trouble."

"Of course we'd vote for the government," he said, still confused. "We would have to. How could we not vote for the government?"

Finally, after more explanation, he caught on, at least a little bit. "Really free? A choice?" He thought for a while and tried to understand what that would be like. "Most of us would still vote for the government. Especially older folks, those born before Liberation. They really like the Communist Party. Younger people, well, mostly we'd still go along with the government, I guess, though there're things we don't like—such as corruption. But I think only a few peasants would actually vote against the government."

"Don't the peasants ever think about getting together to oppose the leaders?" I asked.

"No, not at all," he said.

"Why?" I asked.

"When a peasant buys a defective pair of shoes, he doesn't even dare report it," he replied. "He just thinks of himself as unlucky. When I was at the Beijing Train Station last time, I bought a box lunch that was supposed to cost three yuan. After I ate it, the guy wanted twenty yuan. I gave it to him. I was afraid he'd beat me up. We're afraid. All of us! We're all afraid of officials and other people."

I was bemused and intrigued. Here was a peasant who had been mistreated by the government, someone who had a reason to be against the government. But if given the chance, he probably would still vote to support it. How many peasants were like him? No wonder the Communists had decided that the peasants weren't all that important, that it simply didn't matter if their lives stagnated.

After a couple of hours, it was time for him to go. I thought of the long journey Sanheng had ahead of him. I knew that he had spent a good share of his savings making two trips to Beijing, and that he was now going into debt to escape the consequences of our inquiry. Part of me wanted to offer him some money, at least to pay for the train rides to Beijing. Part of me cautioned against paying someone who had given me information—journalists shouldn't pay their sources. Yet here was an alert, intelligent peasant, someone whose bright future was now likely to be marred by events Nick and I had set in motion. And after all, I wasn't a journalist at the moment, since I was then on book leave from *The Times* . . . I tucked fifty yuan into his pocket and handed him a bag full of fruit and sandwiches.

We never heard from Sanheng again. I would love to know what happened, but it would be much too dangerous to try to contact him.

For all their qualms, the people of Sanheng's village did write us that letter, and, in many other areas of China as well, the peasants are beginning to signal that they're not sheep. In January 1993, for example, some 10,000 peasants in a poor part of Sichuan Province attacked local government offices. The peasants, some of whom armed themselves with iron rods, scythes, and rocks, were incensed because officials had demanded levies of thirty to fifty yuan per person to build a highway. Through a Chinese reporter who had conducted interviews there for a *neibu*, or internal publication, I heard that the villagers burned a police car and trashed the elegant homes of township leaders. The dispute, which took place in Renshou County, was temporarily resolved after the deputy governor made a special trip to the area and ordered that the peasants be repaid their money with 7.2 percent interest.

But for all the soothing words, not much changed in Renshou County, and local officials continued to demand taxes and fees from the peasants. So in late May and early June, the peasants took to the streets again. Nearly 10,000 villagers attacked officials, blocked traffic, smashed buildings, set fires, and took a police officer hostage. The crowd hurled rocks at the police and burned five vehicles, and the police used tear gas to dispel the protesters.

We heard many other reports of small-scale peasant rebellions, but they usually took place in remote areas and were difficult to verify. In addition to these incidents, there have been a series of clashes among clans, clusters of Chinese who share the same surname and ancestry.

Throughout history, clans have always been a source of pride, jealousy, wealth, and war. On my mother's side, for example, my clan is the Mak family (Mai in Mandarin), and we've been feuding with the Lei clan (Li in Mandarin) for centuries. My forebears would expect me to punch any Lei or Li that I meet.

My mother's ancestral village in Taishan came into being because of such warfare two hundred years ago. Until then, members of the Mak clan had lived together with the Lei clan. Then for some reason lost to history there was a battle between the two clans, and many Maks, including my ancestors, fled to form their own hamlet, called Pan Shi. Nevertheless, Pan Shi was near enough that the feuding continued. At the beginning of the twentieth century violent clashes led many residents, including Mak Sik-chew, my grandpa, to join a growing wave of peasants fleeing to Macao, Canada, and the United States.

Now, in Pan Shi, my mother's ancestral home, villagers believe that clan warfare erupts every several decades. Romances across clan lines often blossom during peacetime, but sometimes unravel—like something from Shakespearean drama—when warfare breaks out again. Lei Yuk-kam, a woman from the Lei clan, explained to me what happened when she fell in love with a Mak. After they got married, a clan battle broke out in the late 1960s, and for a time Lei had to seek refuge back in her parents' village to avoid being attacked by the Mak clan in Pan Shi.

"No one knows why it's this way," Lei told me when I visited Pan Shi. "Everyone knows that it has been this way for a couple of centuries. It doesn't make sense. But our life is better now. It's stable. People are educated. Maybe we won't fight again."

In fact, the clan fighting seems to be on the rise. With a persistent dearth of work and entertainment in the countryside, and particularly with the decline in the control and prestige of the government, the clans again have become a prime source of identity for local peasants.

Near the central Chinese city of Xiaogan, a place famous for its peanut candy, peasants now mark the traditional winter Lantern Festival by fighting. Peasants from Xiaogan and a neighboring county battle one another with torches and other weapons. In each of the last few years, one peasant has died and about ten have been injured in the fighting. In Guangdong, vicious clan wars have broken out several times over ownership of land. In 1993, residents of two neighboring villages near Guangzhou took it upon themselves to resolve a dispute over a plot of forestland. The peasants battled for four hours with hunting rifles, swords, and wooden sticks. Two peasants were killed and thirteen injured.

Then, shortly before we left China, 5,000 peasants from rival clans in the south-central province of Hunan started a small war. The peasants were from the Liu clan in Matian Village and the Li clan in Jinggang Village, and they were pursuing a blood feud that had started in 1927. In that year, a small-time warlord from the Li family used the pretext of "wiping out Communists" to slaughter twenty-seven members of the Liu clan. Tensions have flared ever since, and in 1993 the peasants began arming themselves with homemade guns, bombs, and spears that they hurled from battle stations in the school, the hospital, the village headquarters, and their own homes. Two hundred policemen had to use tear gas to dispel the crowd, and, when the smoke cleared, they discovered that the Liu clan had managed to steal twenty-three barrels of gunpowder and 2,300 sticks of dynamite from a coal mine.

The peasants fought for four days, leaving five people killed and twelve seriously wounded. The fight ended when 200 armed policemen "braved a hail of gunfire" to charge onto the battlefield, according to an official account. "Smoke filled the air, gunfire rumbled, and battle cries mingled with wails of agony," a Guangzhou newspaper reported.

As peasants in China grew bolder, Chinese officials became alarmed. At the end of 1992, a long analysis hinting at the leadership's worries appeared in *Selected Reference Articles,* a classified publication for officials in the central government:

> *Many of the numerous taxes have a deadline, and the small income of a peasant often makes it hard for him to pay up. . . .*

So the local officials establish "fee collection work teams," "branch brigades," or "attack teams" that go to the peasants' homes to collect grain and money.

These "work teams" pay no attention to how much a peasant actually earns or how much he can afford to pay. They neglect the law and legal regulations. Whatever the peasants have, they take. Sometimes the "work teams" even carry handcuffs or police batons to threaten the peasants. If the peasants don't obey, they use violence or take the peasants into custody.

One of the members of the investigative team described the severity of the situation this way: "This work affects the relationship between the party and the masses, and it weighs on the critical question of the life or death of this country."

The peasants are a wild card, and they have been so throughout China's history. One conflagration occurred in 209 B.C., when two common peasants, Wu Guang and Chen Sheng, were ordered to report for work at a site far from their homes. That was during the Qin dynasty, which for years had abused the system of conscripting workers—unpaid—to build roads, bridges, and the Great Wall. Peasants obliged, and no wonder, for the penalty for late arrival to an assignment was death. Unfortunately, it was storming when Wu Guang and Chen Sheng received their work orders, and many roads were destroyed by floods. This prevented Wu and Chen from getting to work. It also meant they had only two choices: execution or rebellion. They convinced other peasants to rebel with them, and the effort turned out to be the first large-scale peasant uprising in Chinese history. Two years later, the Qin dynasty collapsed.

In April 1993, Wan Li, then head of the National People's Congress, warned other Chinese leaders about the plight of the peasants. "In many rural areas, peasants were forced to revolt . . . they surrounded the township government office, beat up party-member cadres, and refused to pay levies and taxes. This was because we failed to bring a change to the countryside in the last forty years."

The peasants, he observed with a shudder, were calling for Wu Guang and Chen Sheng.

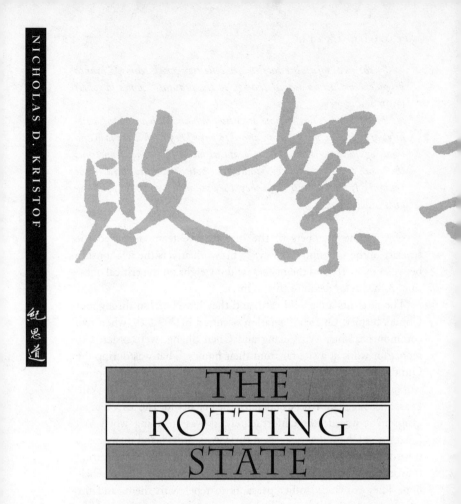

NICHOLAS D. KRISTOF

紀思道

THE
ROTTING
STATE

We've seen the most hideous corruption spread everywhere. Magistrates sell justice to the highest bidder, and Mandarins at every level—instead of protecting the people—use every imaginable means to oppress them and pillage them.

—Abbé Huc, *L'Empire Chinois*, 1854

7

Liu Xiang in New York City, 1991. [Photo by Adam Stoltman.]

Down a winding alley not far from the Forbidden City is a walled courtyard from which one can hear the babble of excited young voices. The brick wall encircles one of China's best elementary schools, the kind of institution that helps students prepare for the tests to get into a good junior high school, so that they can get into a good high school, so that they can pass the university entrance examination and earn a B.A. in sixteen years' time.

A senior government official, a former ambassador, was trying to get his five-year-old grandson into the school's first grade. First the official arranged for his friend Jihong—the woman we had found in our search for a believing Maoist—to pretend that she was the boy's aunt. Jihong told the school that the child was living in her home, well within the school district. In theory, the school was obliged to take the child, but these days good school districts often ignore their obligations. The principal demanded a "fee" equivalent to $400. The former ambassador, who happened to be relatively honest, went in to explain that he didn't have that much money.

"Well, you've got an important job," the principal said. "Get us a school bus. Or a van."

The ambassador, being only relatively honest, agreed. He figured he could use his *guanxi* to get a van assigned to the school. Sure enough, the ambassador managed to divert part of a foreign aid program so that funds were spent to buy a van for the school. The problem was that the van still hadn't been delivered by the first day of the new school year. "Where is the van you promised?" the principal asked the ambassador.

"It'll be here any day now," the ambassador explained. "Just give me a week."

"Okay. But your grandson isn't entering the school with the other kids. We'll wait for the van to get here first."

The school could afford to be greedy, for it was overwhelmed with other bribes. One day when the ambassador went to negotiate with the principal, he encountered a delegation from a cashmere factory. The factory paid $4,000—and gave a cashmere sweater to each teacher—in exchange for permission to enroll ten children of the factory's employees.

Few things surprised me so much about China as the ubiquitousness of the corruption. I had expected a repressive state, maybe a stupid state, but not a rotten one. Yet China today sometimes seems not so much an autocracy as a kleptocracy.

For ordinary people, getting a passport, changing a job, moving from one apartment to another—each may require bribes worth several months' salary. A survey of 3,300 people in 1992 found that those questioned spent an average of 118 yuan, or several weeks' income, on "gifts" each year for people from whom they sought assistance. Nationally, that amounts to about $20 billion a year. So if you ask ordinary peasants and workers what upsets them the most about the government, usually the answer is not the restraints on the press or the torture of dissidents, but graft. The Tiananmen protests in 1989 were triggered as much by outrage over corrupt officials as by a yearning for democracy. It was too unwieldy to describe Tiananmen as a "pro-democracy, anti-corruption, anti-inflation movement," but that's what it was.

If and when the Chinese Communist Party collapses, corruption will surely be a major reason. Moreover, graft has flowered with economic liberalization, and they have become so intertwined that at some point the corruption may choke the economic vine itself. While it is possible that the Chinese mainland will sustain its economic miracle and turn into another Taiwan, it is also possible that corruption and regionalism will turn it into another Nigeria.

The notion of China as a disintegrating dynasty was just beginning to jell in my mind when Sheryl and I started hearing more and more complaints from Chinese friends about corruption. Their tales reminded us of the kleptocrats who had dominated past dynasties in their eleventh hour. Luhui, our octogenarian friend, said that it was corruption that had driven him to support the Communists in 1949. But now he finds that the graft has come back. "Corruption is much worse now than it ever was under the Nationalists," he complained during our last visit to his home before we left Beijing.

In any case, despite a series of anticorruption campaigns, it is clear that graft is growing steadily worse, and that it is far more severe than when it helped provoke the Tiananmen protests. A private factory manager from Fujian Province had dinner with us one evening and spoke with typical exasperation. "Government officials are bandits!" he wailed. "Chinese cadres used to have only two hands each. Now they have thirty or forty hands each, all of them busy grabbing for money."

Foreigners are partly isolated from the corruption. But when we needed to install a fax line in the *New York Times* bureau in 1991, a three-man team from the Beijing Telephone Office dropped by, looked grimly at the setup, frowned a good deal, and advised us that it would cost $800 to move the telephone cord thirty feet to the site of the fax machine. I couldn't reason with the men. Rules were rules, they said, and the fee structure was something they could not control. A Chinese friend rescued me. I followed his advice and gave each of the men a case of Marlboro cigarettes—a form of currency in China—in appreciation for their inspection. The workmen expressed their thanks, and a moment later they got to work. The $800 fee had been waived.

During our time in China, Sheryl and I noticed two fundamental changes in the corruption around us. The first was a huge increase in the sums involved. When we arrived in Beijing, crooked cops might take payoffs of a couple of dollars at a time, or a principal might take $500 to admit a pupil. By the time we left, corrupt officials were stealing hundreds of thousands of dollars at a time. In the summer of 1993, the Agriculture Bank of China even disclosed a fraud case involving letters of credit totaling $10 billion. That's a sum equivalent to the annual gross national products of El Salvador, Nicaragua, and Honduras combined. It probably was the biggest single theft ever attempted anywhere in the world. The scheme failed, but it underscores how corrupt Chinese officials and bankers are becoming more ambitious.

The second change we observed concerned the nature of the corruption. In the early 1990s, the graft turned from individual bribery to Mafia-style organized crime. In some towns, like the riverbank community of Shenqiu in central China, the crooks took over the government.

Shenqiu is a county town in Henan Province, in the cradle of Chinese civilization, not far from where the Duke of Zhou propounded the notion of a dynastic cycle more than 3,000 years ago. But peasants don't think about that; they think about their chickens and hogs and how to keep them healthy.

Keeping them healthy was supposed to be the mission of the Zhoukou No. 1 Veterinary Medicine Factory, a collectively owned business in Shenqiu. Wang Zhiqiang, the factory manager since 1986, was the kind of hardheaded entrepreneur now sprouting all over China. He turned the factory into a bustling enterprise that employed 350 workers and diversified into human medicine as well. There was only one problem: Everything the factory produced was a fake. The "antibiotics" were made of cornstarch and talcum powder. The "intravenous solution" was MSG dissolved in tap water. The factory produced twenty kinds of fake medicines and never turned out a single genuine pill.

The peasants quickly caught on. There was a string of complaints and protests, and the County Health Department found that the medicines were fakes and instructed that the factory be closed and Wang be fined. But the top county leaders countermanded the order. The official explanation: "This is a brand-new enterprise, and, after all, it's not so easy to start up a factory."

The real reason, of course, was that Wang knew how to do business in China. He gave a luxury imported car to the county chief and another to the county Communist Party secretary. When the party secretary's brother-in-law ran into financial trouble, Wang gave him $20,000. Wang gave the local police money for a new police station and provided bonuses for the staff of the county agriculture department. He paid the bribes to get urban *hukou*, or residence permits, for family members of all the people he needed in his pocket: the deputy county chief, the deputy county party secretary, the head of the county tax office, the head of the county electrical company, and the head of the county commerce department.

"I was like a spigot of tap water," Wang explained later. "Everybody came to suck my blood."

That explanation is a bit self-serving, because Wang got plenty for his money. The party secretary personally approved a special permit for Wang to carry a pistol, and the police department gave him a police ID card and allowed him to use a police license plate on his car. The police even allowed him to put a flashing light on top of his vehicle, and they supplied members of the militia and People's Armed Police to guard his factory. Wang established his own private court and jail inside the factory and maintained strict security. A curious peasant who wandered in to have a look was "arrested" and severely beaten.

In December 1988, a veterinary station in nearby Taikang County discovered that the medicine it had purchased from Wang's factory was all fake. The station's accountant, Liang Dezhi, refused to pay. So Wang sent the police and militia, armed with pistols, to Liang's home in the middle of the night. They kicked open the door, dragged Liang out of bed, handcuffed him, and took him back to the factory. Wang and his aides badly beat Liang and imprisoned him in the factory.

Taikang County wasn't so pleased about this and sent an official to ask for Liang's release. Wang then arrested that official as well, finally releasing him with a message to his superiors that Liang would be freed only if a ransom of $2,000 was paid. Taikang County bargained Wang down to $500, and Wang let his prisoner go. As the bruised Liang left, he warned that he would sue.

"Go ahead," Wang told him fiercely. "I'm the king of the law around here. I run the law shop. Whether you go to the county or to the provincial government, I've got my people everywhere."

Meanwhile, Wang's factory was churning out such huge profits that two of his employees, Sun Yinping and Sun Zhirong, decided to go into business for themselves. They set up their own fake veterinary medicine factory and soon were reaping huge profits. Wang sent the police to bust their operation and destroy their equipment. He confiscated their profits and severely beat them in his torture chamber. At the same time, Wang took credit for closing down the factory and wrote an article for a major national newspaper under the headline "Henan Province's Greatest Success in Cracking Down on Fake Medicines." At the same time, Wang was repackaging under his own labels the fake medicine confiscated from the other factory.

The county officials were so impressed by Wang's entrepreneurial talent that they gave him award after award, twelve in all. He was named a model worker and given the May Day Labor Prize, while his factory was awarded the Red Flag Work Unit prize. The factory was also given a prize as an outstanding quality and name brand enterprise. Partly in recognition of these achievements, Wang was given the title deputy head of the county agriculture department.

The national Agriculture Ministry in Beijing had heard complaints about Wang, so it decided to investigate. In 1991, it summoned the director of veterinary medicine for Henan Province, along with a few other officials. They all arrived in Beijing in cars provided by Wang, with Wang paying their expenses. Just to be sure that they said the right things, he accompanied them as well. When they got back to Henan, the county officials proposed that the provincial leaders formally declare Wang's innocence and "restore his honor." Still, the authorities in Beijing pursued their investigation and traveled to Shenqiu; when they arrived, the county officials announced that unfortunately Wang and other factory leaders were away. It is true that they were not at the factory; they were staying at the county guest house. In the meantime, nobody dared tell the investigators the truth.

The national authorities persisted and, not inhibited by Western concepts of due process of law, arrested Wang at the end of 1992. Then, gradually, people dared to speak out against him, and the authorities were able to gather their evidence. Even so, it wasn't until March 1993 that Henan Province suspended the officials of Shenqiu County. Six months later, the central government decided to make an example of Wang by sentencing him to life imprisonment. The county party secretary received an eight-year term for accepting bribes, and eleven others were given prison terms ranging up to seventeen years.

Corruption is one of the oldest problems in China. Indeed, among the earliest songs in Chinese history is a complaint from 3,000 years ago against high taxes and grasping officials:

> *Big rat, big rat,*
> *Don't eat my millet!*
> *Three years I've worked for you,*
> *But you won't care for me. . . .*

Anger at the crooked "big rats" in government helped bring down the Nationalist regime of Chiang Kai-shek in the 1940s. A similar fury at the graft in the Forbidden City helped bring down the Qing dynasty early in this century.

Among the most notorious of the figures in the Qing court was a tall, wrinkle-faced eunuch named Li Lianying. He had been a cobbler's apprentice when he saw how much money a court eunuch could make. So as a teenager he castrated himself with the cobbler's knife (carefully preserving his organs, as all the eunuchs did, so that after he died he could be buried as a "complete man").

Around the turn of the century, Li Lianying was administering 6.5 million British pounds each year running the empress dowager's household, spending the money on such things as the pearls that were ground up for her to eat every ten days or so, the better for her complexion, as well as the hundreds of dishes that were set out for her at every meal. In fact, Li and the others quickly learned that the empress dowager always ate the same handful of dishes, so they brought out the same bowls of other foods day after day, even when weevils were crawling through the dishes. What they saved went into their pockets. Through such savings, and through the bribes he accepted, Li had become one of the richest men in China by the time he died in 1911. It was said that his estate was worth 2 million pounds sterling.

Sheryl and I weren't the only ones who noted that corruption is a sign of disintegrating dynasties. The authorities quietly drew the same historical parallels, and in 1991 I noticed an editorial about graft in a provincial newspaper, the *Hubei Daily News*, which noted, "In the past, many dynasties collapsed because they were corrupt. . . . If we do not effectively carry out the struggle against corruption, it will spread like a pestilence, and the Communist Party will destroy itself." Shortly afterward, the *Gansu Daily News*, another official newspaper in the provinces, warned that corruption "is a malignant tumor on the body of the party. If we let it spread unchecked, our cause will be ruined. An anticorruption struggle is a matter of primary importance and concerns our ruling party's life or death."

It may be difficult for Westerners to comprehend the degree of public indignation at the graft, but there are two reasons why it arouses real fury among ordinary Chinese. The first is that salaries are so low in China that corruption has an exaggerated impact on living standards. A policeman in New York who accepts payoffs might double his salary; a dishonest cop in Beijing can easily earn twenty times his wages. Second, the beneficiaries of corruption in China are overwhelmingly public servants, or their children and relatives.

Furthermore, during the first few decades of Communist rule, people got used to the idea of honesty in government. Then, beginning in the 1980s, bribery and avarice multiplied at an enormous rate until today it sometimes seems that everyone is trying to deceive everyone else.

Take Leili, a bright-eyed single woman of twenty-four from the northeastern city of Changchun. I met her at the Changchun airport, where she tried to *bang dakuan*, or pick me up. A university graduate with permed hair and passable English that she liked to practice with me, Leili was a rather mixed-up young woman facing her share of tragedy. She knew that her mother was probably dying of stomach cancer, an ordeal similar to that in the West—long afternoons and evenings spent in hospital corridors, frowning doctors, hopes gradually eroding—with one exception. On top of their grief, Leili and her father had to present "gifts" to the doctors to make sure that her mother got the best treatment. They gave cash, awkwardly, but the doctors took it without embarrassment. Other families gave television sets, radios, jewelry, whatever they could afford. Leili was outraged that government doctors should take bribes in exchange for caring for their patients, but that was how it was. And Leili herself was scarcely more honest. She arranged an illicit leave of absence for herself so that she could go south to Guangdong Province to look for a high-paying job.

"It was very easy," she explained. "I got a doctor to write a letter saying that I was ill and needed a medical leave for three years— that's the maximum medical leave at my company. Of course, I had to give the doctor something, but it was worth it because while I'm on medical leave I still get 70 percent of my wages even though I'm not even in town. If I didn't have the doctor's letter, I would have to quit my work unit, and then I wouldn't get a penny. Anyway, my company was state owned, and so my bosses don't really care about my salary. They know I'm not really ill, but this is what everybody does now.

"So I went down south, and a friend helped me get a job at a joint venture factory in the city of Dongguan. Really rich place, Dongguan is! Right near Hong Kong. You heard of it?"

"Of course," I said. "I've been there."

"The factory makes sweaters, and I was the personal secretary to the manager. I got 900 yuan a month—that's more than six times what I was getting in my old job. I should have known it was too good to be true.

"My boss gave me a room to live in, right next to his. But my room didn't have a door that locked, and he used to come in all the time. Any time at all, no matter what I was doing. And then he began to hint that maybe I should sleep with him. A lot of girls do that, you know, especially in the south. The secretaries are always the prettiest girls in the factory, and they all sleep with their bosses. But I wasn't ready for that, and so I told him I was quitting."

Leili went back to her job in the state-owned company, drawing her monthly wages of 150 yuan, or $30. But after two months of that, she began to miss the paychecks from the job in Dongguan.

"I've pretty much decided I'm going to go back to my job in the south," she said. "It's a lot of money."

"What about your boss?" I asked.

"We'll see." She shrugged. "Anyway, it wouldn't be the worst thing in the world. And it's a lot of money. Nine hundred yuan a month."

One problem with graft is that it snowballs. At some point, the corruption reaches a critical mass and people begin to say: Everybody else is doing it, so why not me? It then accelerates and becomes almost impossible to uproot.

While small payoffs are common in many societies, corruption in China often takes strange forms and seems particularly institutionalized. Special "receipt markets" have emerged, for example, where low- and mid-ranking Chinese officials pick up receipts useful in padding their expense accounts. The receipt market at Xizhimen in Beijing is on a busy sidewalk outside the railroad ticket office. Two dozen men and women stand around, thrusting cigarette lighters at passersby. They keep receipt booklets sticking out of their pockets, and if someone strolling by looks as if he's from out of town, the vendors go into overdrive. "You want receipts?" one asks. "Blank receipts! Make plenty of money? Real cheap!"

When the buyer pauses, the vendor reaches into a bag and pulls out a stack of blank receipts for hotels, restaurants, and shops. Receipts in China are typically preprinted forms, on which the restaurant or hotel stamps its name with a chop or seal. At the time of the purchase, the clerk fills in the amount by hand. With blank receipts, a Chinese traveling on official business stays at four-dollar-a-night hotels while turning in receipts for twenty-dollar-a-night hotels. He claims reimbursement for banquets that he never hosted, for courtesy gifts that he never purchased, and for medical treatment that he never received. The blank receipts cost from forty cents to four dollars each, depending on how high a sum can plausibly be filled in.

Some of the receipts can be used even by those who are not traveling. As an experiment, I once purchased a blank receipt from the Taoranting Hospital in Beijing. Because it was stamped "emergency," any Chinese could fill in a sum and claim reimbursement on the ground that there was no time to go to his regular hospital.

"It may be that somebody inside the hospital is selling the blank receipts," said Li Zuogui, the deputy director of the hospital. "Or the receipts may have been stolen or lost. But in any case, it doesn't happen very often."

Many of the receipts bear chops from nonexistent hotels, restaurants, and department stores. It used to be that chops were sacrosanct because each company had only one and nobody would dare to forge a chop. But in recent years a growing number of craftsmen have begun carving chops for anyone who will pay for them.

"If the cops come over, then we just run away," said a receipt vendor, a young man in a gray sports jacket. "And even if they grab you, things can be worked out. If you're also selling cigarette lighters, maybe the policeman will grab five of them and say to you: 'I've confiscated four of your lighters, right?' Then you say, 'Four, that's right,' even though you know he's got five. So instead of hauling you in, he returns four lighters, pockets one, and lets you off."

A related growth industry, one that annoys Chinese whenever they travel, is the counterfeiting and scalping of train tickets. This is supposed to be illegal, but the scalpers—known as *huangniu*, or yellow cows—openly solicit business at major train stations around the country. One bright fall afternoon in 1992, I drove to the Beijing train station to find out how the business worked. The station, as always, was crowded with peasants from villages all over China. Some sprawled on the ground beside their bags, trying to nap before boarding their trains; others prepared meals in little pans; others played cards or simply stared wide-eyed at foreigners like me. I looked around for anyone who might be trying to sell tickets, and several *huangniu* quickly found me.

"Ticket?" inquired a short man of about twenty-five, in atrocious English. "You buy ticket-ticket?"

"You're selling tickets?" I asked, switching to Chinese. He looked relieved.

"I've got any kind of ticket you could want," he said. His lip bristled with a few hairs of an attempted mustache, and he spoke in a Manchurian accent that seemed intended to convey the image of a gangster. "I can get you as many tickets as you want. No problem."

"What about a second-class sleeper to Guangzhou?" I asked. "Day after tomorrow? Three tickets?" I had checked, and I knew that the official price was twenty-seven dollars—but that all tickets were sold out for the next month.

"No problem," he said, quoting me a price equivalent to ninety dollars.

"What about the police?" I asked, looking around, wondering if my State Security followers were photographing me.

"The cops won't interfere," the *huangniu* said. "We know the cops; they know us. In fact, they buy their tickets through me, too."

Some of the scalpers get their tickets in the conventional way, by lining up, but many order them in bulk through friends in purchasing offices of large companies or government ministries. Others bribe ticket sellers to get a bundle of tickets each month at the official price. Still other *huangniu* simply forge train tickets. As China has loosened up in recent years, it has become possible for crooks as well as entrepreneurs to buy printing equipment and travel around the country making sales. One of the pioneers in the industry was Lin Liangxi, but his manufacturing venture collapsed in 1992 after he tried to get a refund for three train tickets. The clerk at the train station suspected that they were forged, and police seized Lin and confirmed that the tickets were fakes. In Lin's hotel room, the authorities found 254 more fake tickets hidden in two packages of instant noodles. But that was just the beginning; the police later found that Lin had set up a ticket-making factory in his hometown of Wenzhou. The factory was stocked with a printing press, a paper-cutting machine, and 1,200 pounds of the cardboard used to make tickets.

The earnings of people like Lin have become an increasingly important part of the economy. Some crooks manage to earn hundreds of thousands of dollars, which they spread around in dozens of bank accounts. Or they send the money abroad. Bankers in Hong Kong tell us of a boom in mysterious Chinese clients who sometimes open accounts with a million U.S. dollars or more. It has become a joke in China that the best sleuths of corruption are burglars. To understand why, take the typical case of Pan Qinghai, the deputy director of the Public Security Bureau in Qianguo in northeastern China. He had a fine career until 1991, when robbers stole 200,000 yuan in cash, or about $40,000, from his home. Pan did not report the crime, but the robbers were caught, and they confessed where they had obtained the loot. That was hard for Pan to explain, since his monthly income was only about 200 yuan. An investigation found that Pan and his mistress, Liu Hui, who also worked for the police, had been taking bribes for five years. The mistress was sentenced to life imprisonment. As for Pan, he was led to the execution field, his hands tied behind his back, his eyes blindfolded. He was forced to kneel on the ground. A policeman standing behind him fired a single bullet into the base of his skull.

The Communist Party woke up to the political risks of corruption after the Tiananmen protests. A few anticorruption campaigns were announced, and the government shot a few people like Pan who had been convicted of corruption. Still, the crackdown has had no impact. The odds of being caught are not much worse than those of being struck by lightning. The potential profits are so huge, and so many people seem to be indulging, that very few officials are deterred. Of all our Chinese acquaintances, the one who probably understood most clearly the risks of corruption was a young Beijing judge who handled bribery cases. Every week he sentenced people to prison, or worse, for corruption.

We knew the judge simply because he was a member of the same health club we belonged to, in a five-star Western-managed hotel. I lifted weights with him and chatted in the locker room about recent events. The judge's salary was about $500 a year—yet he somehow managed to spend many times that much. The health club membership alone cost $500 a year, and he also owned his own motorcycle, which allowed him to zip around the city. He ate out in nice restaurants and owned an endless variety of fine Western clothes. I used to watch the judge peel off his expensive black leather motorcycle outfit and wonder if he ever worried that he would one day end up on the other side of the bench.

A particularly bad omen for China's development is that corruption tends to be worst in the most open, reformist areas, places that to outsiders represent the nation's best hope for the future. In Guangdong and Fujian provinces, for example, traditional Mafia organizations, known as triads, have reestablished themselves and formed close links with the triads in Hong Kong, Taiwan, and New York. Several triad leaders live in refuge in southern China and from their headquarters there oversee the bank robberies, prostitution rings, and gambling dens in Hong Kong. One Chinese "godfather," Paul K. F. Wong, lives in Fujian Province and from there directs the Green Dragon gang in New York City's Chinatown. Wong is wanted in connection with murder in New York, but naturally Fujian authorities can't seem to find him to extradite him.

The triads are criminal gangs, with blood oaths of secrecy and special handshakes. Punishment for betraying a triad is to hack off the traitor's arms and legs and leave him to bleed to death. The big difference between the triads and the American Mafia is that in New York the Mafia and the FBI are adversaries. In China, the triads and the police don't believe in confrontation; they often work together.

In 1993, the minister of public security held a press conference for the first time. I asked him about the links between the Chinese police and the triads, because I was curious to see how vehemently he would deny them. Instead, to everyone's surprise, he acknowledged that the authorities maintain ties to the triads, and he described them as patriotic organizations. He went on to say that the triads had helped provide protection for a Chinese leader traveling abroad; we later heard that he was talking about Deng Xiaoping's trip to the United States in 1979.

The best way to understand the cooperation between the triads and the Communist Party apparatus is to rent a Mercedes-Benz in Hong Kong and park it on the street overnight. In the morning it may be in China. Hong Kong thieves will have stolen it, driven it to a deserted dock, and loaded it onto an armored speedboat for the ride to Guangdong Province. The triads use a kind of boat called the *tai fei*, specially designed with a steel hull, bullet-proof cabin, and up to five 300-horsepower engines. The *tai fei* is based on a design for a Canadian racing boat but modified with a sharpened bow for ramming other vessels and bullet-proof plates to protect the crew. Banned in Hong Kong, the *tai fei* is typically kept in small coves along the southern Chinese coast and used each night to smuggle cigarettes, videos, and stolen cars. The scale is enormous. According to official estimates, more than one million video recorders are smuggled into China each year, accounting for 90 percent of all those sold. As for cars, the demand is for luxury models like the Mercedes-Benz; in 1992, one Mercedes-Benz was stolen in Hong Kong every five hours, and nearly all are suspected of having ended up in China. The latest car to win the compliment of being stolen in large numbers is the Mazda 929. It made an appearance at a car show in Guangzhou, and people were so impressed that they started placing orders—not with dealers but with the triads, for Mazdas stolen in Hong Kong and smuggled into China.

Naturally, Hong Kong car owners are concerned about theft, and dealers have come up with all kinds of alarms to keep cars from getting stolen. However, the only technique that has worked is the one pioneered by the Toyota distributor in Hong Kong to prevent its Lexus model from being stolen. Toyota's strategy is to make it useless for triads in China to steal its cars. Toyota does not market the Lexus in China, and it sells spare parts in Hong Kong only to people who can prove that they are legal owners of a Lexus. Toyota even took out advertisements in Guangdong newspapers, urging mainland Chinese not to buy its cars. The ads reminded people that the Lexus will break down after 20,000 miles unless it has unleaded fuel, which is unavailable in China.

The Hong Kong marine police used to think that they were battling just the triads, but then a few funny things started happening. Several times the police intercepted boats engaging in smuggling, only to discover Chinese troops onboard. In 1991, the police were trying to board a smugglers' boat in Hong Kong waters when two uniformed Chinese police emerged from the cabin. The Chinese police pointed machine guns at the Hong Kong police and summoned two other Chinese police boats, which rescued the smugglers and escorted them to safety in Chinese waters.

For some time, we wondered who in China would dare to buy and use a stolen Hong Kong Mercedes-Benz. Such cars stand out, not only because they have no registration but also because they have the steering wheel on the right-hand side, in the British style, while cars sold in China have the steering wheel on the left. Who would dare to drive around in a car that was so obviously stolen and smuggled into the country? The police, of course! And Communist Party officials. And the army. And those with *guanxi* with the police. "It's hard to get a new car registered for the road if it has right-hand steering," a Guangzhou taxi driver told Sheryl. But he admitted that the problem could be solved by anyone with good *guanxi*. The driver knew what he was talking about: His own taxi was a right-hand-drive vehicle from Hong Kong. The *South China Morning Post* in Hong Kong collected independent evidence of where the stolen cars end up. A photographer for the newspaper shot pictures of a new black Lexus, with right-hand steering, in front of a five-star hotel in Guangzhou. The car was accompanied by another vehicle full of assistants and bodyguards, and its license plate showed that it belonged to a senior army general.

These days, Hong Kong isn't big enough to supply southern China with cars. So the triads are buying stolen cars in the United States and shipping them to China. Anyone can go to Guangdong Province and visit the lots where American cars are lined up, with their original license plates still attached. Some American reporters traced the cars' owners and called them up; the owners said that the cars had been stolen a couple of months earlier, and they were very surprised to hear that they had been found—in China.

The harder question is what all this corruption means. A skeptic can say that widespread graft clogs the wheels of commerce in most of the developing world, and certainly a number of other countries— South Korea, Taiwan, Indonesia, Mexico, and Thailand—have done very well for themselves despite mind-boggling levels of bribery.

I'm not sure that China's graft is necessarily worse than that of other countries, but I do think it may be more threatening. China has none of the democratic mechanisms that normally help make a government legitimate in the eyes of its people. Italians and even Mexicans may regard their leaders as crooks, but they at least elected them, after a fashion. In China, by contrast, the leaders came into power without any legitimating mechanism, and their moral authority rests solely on their performance.

In China, in other words, the current social framework of Communism is already so weak, and the ideological underpinning of the state so flimsy, that the regime may not be able to take much more. The corruption risks creating a bog that impairs economic efficiency, and it also risks irritating people to the point that they take to the streets just as they did in Tiananmen. In 1989, with Deng Xiaoping and the other elders still alive, the party could withstand the challenge. Next time it may not be able to.

The rot has a tremendous corrosive effect on the Chinese political and social structure—and on the Chinese people. It is particularly evident among young people, those who grew up in the moral vacuum of the Cultural Revolution and its aftermath. Some of them subscribe to only one value: the importance of getting rich. It has been disheartening to watch our reformist friends in the years after the Tiananmen crackdown. Journalists, who had championed the right of freedom of the press, now frequently are absorbed by only one thought: getting payoffs in exchange for writing nice stories about companies. Intellectuals, who used to quote Patrick Henry— "Give me liberty or give me death"—now adhere to a Wall Street credo: "Greed is good."

Private business owners may complain about officials who demand bribes, but their own moral standards are often primitive. Owners of food stands have taken to lacing their food with opium poppies in the hope that their dishes will become, literally, addictive. I don't know whether it works, but restaurateurs seem to swear by it. Restaurants and food stalls in six provinces have been caught adding poppies to their food, and in 1993 the Public Security Ministry had to issue a formal circular pledging a crackdown on the practice.

Even peasants have been infected by the greed. A village called Haotou, in Guangdong Province, discovered a particularly lucrative way of entering the modern market economy. The peasants kidnapped women and girls from other areas and locked them up in their homes, forcing them to work as sex slaves. Many of Haotou's peasants ran brothels out of their homes as a sideline business. Officials took notice only after a Guangzhou newspaper dared to write about the village.

Corruption has not only corroded community values but also eaten away at the efficiency of China's autocracy. From outside its borders, China may seem a smoothly functioning dictatorship, but in fact the rot has clogged up the apparatus so that it often barely works. Li Peng may order somebody arrested, but that person may be able to make a ten-dollar payoff and slip free.

People like Liu Xiang, a physics student cum fugitive, showed me how the corruption is breaking down the system. Liu introduced Sheryl and me to the underbelly of China, where the apparatus of repression is not an ominous, well-oiled machine but a leaking, jerry-rigged contraption that is constantly breaking down. He also showed me how the most decent of people, even a public-spirited activist, can get stained by the mess.

Sheryl met Liu Xiang during a protest early in the Tiananmen student movement. He was easygoing, tall and gangly, with close-cropped hair framing a long face and a crooked smile. Liu Xiang had a Boy Scout eagerness to help us; he became our contact at Qinghua University, helping set up interviews there and calling frequently with information. He spoke some English, so instead of using our Chinese names he would call up and inquire in throaty English, "Hello? Is that Nikko? Sherry? I am Liu."

Then twenty-three, with an occasional pimple that made him look younger, Liu Xiang symbolized the problems the regime had in cultivating support. His father, an army officer, had been killed in a battle during the Cultural Revolution and subsequently declared a Communist martyr. Liu himself was raised on the party's nursery rhymes—"The party is just like my mommy"—and he was a member of the Communist Youth League. But he was angered by corruption, by the lies in the newspapers, by the arrogance of the leadership. The Tiananmen crackdown transformed him from a mere critic to an outright rebel. Roused from his dormitory bed in the early morning hours of June 4, 1989, by news that troops were firing on protesters, he rushed to Tiananmen Square. At one point the man next to him was shot in the shoulder, and Liu dragged him to the hospital. He also helped a group of workers disable an abandoned armored personnel carrier. They couldn't figure out how to set it on fire, but he applied his physicist's know-how and had it burning in no time.

It didn't make a difference. The troops consolidated their hold over the capital and detained thousands of workers and students. The security forces began daily interrogations of Liu at the Qinghua campus. The authorities didn't know that he had helped set up a broadcast system at Tiananmen Square; instead they grilled him on his contacts with student leaders and with Sheryl and me. They knew that he had registered us as his guests when we visited the Qinghua campus.

"Write down everything about the *New York Times* reporters," the head interrogator ordered him. "Write down how you met them. Write down each time you met them—the date and the time and the place—and what they asked you. Write what you told them, what secrets you gave out. You must tell everything!"

"Of course you couldn't tell them the truth," Liu told me later in a series of interviews while still in hiding. "Then you'd go to prison. So I lied. I figured if I lied, I'd be able to get a diploma and resume a normal life. So I told them I wasn't involved in Tiananmen. I told them I just met Sherry on the street—she was asking for directions—and because she was an overseas Chinese, it was my duty to help. I thought I should be friendly to an overseas Chinese, so I met Sherry and Nikko a few times. I invited them to visit the university. But we never talked about politics. I wasn't interested in politics. That's what I told them."

Even with all this pressure on him, Liu continued to meet Sheryl surreptitiously—on an alley near Tiananmen Square—to brief her on the situation on campus. We were then writing about the hardliners' calls for a major nationwide crackdown on participants in the democracy movement, and what astonished us was how almost everywhere the crackdown was deflected by passive resistance. Students, professors, and Communist Party officials all took part in a massive cover-up. At Qinghua, several officials secretly met regularly with Liu and other students who were under investigation. "They would tell us, 'The authorities know this much—so tell them that, and no more,'" Liu said. Another official helped Liu obtain a photocopy of his university diploma (which had been withheld from him), so that he could pretend to have graduated.

Then, abruptly, some of his university buddies were arrested, and Liu began to worry that time was running out. So at the end of the summer of 1989, he obtained false documents from a friendly official and fled Beijing for the southern city of Shenzhen, a special economic zone adjacent to Hong Kong. Shenzhen is a boomtown like something from the Wild West; it's also the place where Tang Rimei saw her brother beaten to death. Ordinary Chinese are not allowed to enter Shenzhen without a special certificate, but Liu was able to go through *guanxi* and obtain the necessary certificate. His new papers, which were under his own name, proclaimed him a worker who had never participated in the democracy movement and who was going to Shenzhen as a buyer for a factory.

"I had some friends already in Shenzhen, and they were a big help," Liu reminisced. "On my third day there, I found a job in a small office, assigning sailors jobs on ships. The boss asked me if I had participated in the student movement, and I said no. I showed him a copy of the diploma, and said, 'How could I have gotten this if I'd joined in the movement?' "

Liu cultivated *guanxi* the way some people collect postage stamps, and through his network of friends he managed to find someone who had connections to the Public Security Bureau. By paying a ten-dollar bribe, he extended his stay in Shenzhen, and he also made connections with the criminal underworld. As a backup, in case the authorities caught up with him, Liu used his job to obtain an ID card in the name of a sailor whose papers Liu was handling for the agency. "It was a bit of a problem, because the ID said I was thirty-four years old, but people didn't look at it all that closely."

Unfortunately, Liu Xiang did his job so well that his boss decided to hire him permanently. While on a trip to Beijing at the beginning of 1990, the boss dropped by Qinghua University to check Liu's *dangan*, his personnel file. The boss was horrified to learn that his star employee was being sought by the university authorities for fleeing in the middle of investigations. Upon returning to Shenzhen, the boss promptly fired Liu, who now joined forces with the underworld and helped some criminal friends run a money-changing business and smuggle computer printers into China from Hong Kong. "We made a lot of money in a short period," he said, flashing a grin.

Meanwhile, Qinghua officials had tipped off the Public Security Bureau in Beijing that Liu was working in Shenzhen. Soon two Beijing policemen arrived there, questioning people about Liu's whereabouts. Liu felt the net tightening around him and decided that the only solution was to escape to Hong Kong. He arranged to make his escape on Zhong-Ying Street, a shopping district straddling the border. Residents of China need special permission to visit the street, but Liu and two friends paid a bribe equivalent to $106—several months' salary for a factory worker—so that the Chinese People's Armed Police on duty there would look the other way. Once on Zhong-Ying Street, Liu and his buddies sneaked onto the Hong Kong side, then paid a boat owner twenty dollars to take them across a channel of water to the main part of the British territory.

Liu and his friends turned themselves in to the Hong Kong government and requested asylum. He called me up, and I sent him a faxed testimonial about his role in the student democracy movement. He also had photographs and other documents proving his participation. But on his seventh day in Hong Kong, a long bus pulled up at the detention center, and Liu's heart froze. It was not the van used to take people back to the center of Hong Kong but the bus used to repatriate ordinary illegal immigrants back to China.

"There must be some mistake," he protested, but the police forced him and his friends onto the bus and across the border. The Hong Kong authorities were sacrificing him at the altar of Sino-British relations. On the bus, Liu frantically ripped up the faxes from me, then shoved the tiny pieces through the grate in the window.

In his interrogation with the Chinese police, Liu lied about his identity: He claimed to be a worker from Xian and gave a false address. He asked a detainee who was about to be released to telephone a friend in Shenzhen and explain the situation. The Shenzhen friend promptly went to great lengths to bribe the guards to release Liu. "The guards took the 'gifts' but said that to release me they needed proof that I didn't have a criminal record," Liu said. "My friend tried to get that, but it was very difficult to get one forged. In Guangdong it's usually easy to get things done with money, but in this case we had some difficulties."

Meanwhile, Liu Xiang was stuck in prison, where each cell housed up to forty prisoners, with up to ten sleeping in a single, oversize bed. In addition to the beds, the cell contained a basin of water and a hole in the floor for a toilet. Toilet paper? Liu laughed. "Of course not." Meals consisted of cold rice with warmed-over vegetables. "The biggest problem was that there wasn't enough food," he remembered. "If somebody spit out a rotten or disgusting vegetable on the floor, then someone else would pick it up and put it in his mouth—even though the guards would beat us if they saw us doing that."

As soon as he entered the detention center, Liu learned that order is established in each cell by the "boss"—a prisoner who bullies his way to the top of the heap and orders the other prisoners around. In a bit of good fortune, the boss in his cell was a fellow northerner and Mandarin speaker.

"Big Brother, please take my watch," Liu told the boss as soon as he was in the cell. The boss warmed up to such flattery (no doubt he would have taken the watch in any case), and soon Liu became one of the boss's strongmen. When anybody was newly assigned to the cell, Liu and the others would rough him up and search for any money that he had hidden from the guards. The money could be used to buy cigarettes, food, and clothing. When the boss was moved to another prison, Liu took over. The boy from Qinghua University forced other prisoners to wash his underwear and give up their money and sometimes even their food. When they disobeyed, he ordered his strongmen to beat them up.

"Originally, I didn't want to do it, but then I realized that in prison everything depends on this," he said, clenching a fist. "If you don't beat them up, then others will beat you up. And then you'll end up washing their underwear. In there, the only thing that matters is violence. There's no morality, just power."

Liu's obsession was escape, and he thought an opportunity might come while he was working on the prison farm. "I decided the best time to escape was during a rain, because then it's harder for them to drive their motorcycles around looking for you, and they won't try as hard to find you," he said. So on June 12, 1990, after a thunderstorm, Liu made his move. He was working in a large vegetable field with seven other prisoners. On that day, only three guards were on duty, and the prisoners were scattered about the field. Liu began to work near the guard who was paying the least attention.

"When the guard wasn't looking, I slipped behind a hedge," he said. "I was ready to say that I needed to relieve myself." Liu crawled to the edge of the field and then through another hedge that functioned as a kind of fence. Since Liu had not been charged with any offense, he was wearing ordinary clothes and was able to hurry along the road and hitch a ride on a truck. A sympathizer had smuggled him some money, enabling him to make his way to Guangzhou, where he hid with friends. Not long afterward, Liu made his way by train back to Beijing and called me up. "Nikko, I am Liu," he said.

I met him for dinner at a back table in the coffee shop of the Traders Hotel in Beijing. Over his soup Liu spilled—rather boastfully—the fact that he was an escaped felon. I nearly fell over. To me, Liu Xiang as a fugitive seemed a changed person. He was no longer an idealistic university student but a prison-hardened young man who had a taste for the fast life in Guangdong. He boasted of his underworld connections and of invitations to join the criminal gangs.

Now I'm a bit embarrassed to say that his request for help in fleeing to Hong Kong set off alarm bells in my mind. I liked Liu and admired him, and I felt I owed him one, considering all he had suffered for helping us out. But at the same time, I couldn't stop my mind from playing with strange ideas: What if this was all an elaborate plot by State Security to frame me for protecting a fugitive? And even if it wasn't a plot, what if State Security found out? I figured that even if he had escaped to Hong Kong once, the odds were against Liu's getting away twice. And if he was arrested, the police would beat the truth out of him.

Sheryl returned from a trip, and together we debated what to do. Sheryl argued for helping him; I was afraid of getting caught, afraid of being kicked out of China. I also felt that it was generally wrong for journalists to get involved, to help fugitives escape, to break the law, and that we owed *The Times* the obligation not to get in trouble. "But, Sheryl, what if it's a setup?" I asked. "What happens if he's caught? You know he probably will be!"

"I can't imagine he would be setting us up," Sheryl countered. "And anyway, we can't just abandon him, after all the help he gave us. Then he'll be caught for sure, and he'll spend a lifetime in jail. The guards will pulverize him! How can that be the right thing to do?"

As it happened, the Chinese Foreign Ministry had taken away Sheryl's press credentials on a technicality, so at that point she was not accredited as a reporter. We figured that this gave her a little extra flexibility in what she did. So just before Liu fled Beijing, Sheryl met him in the Friendship Store and hustled him up and down staircases until she was sure no one was following them. Then she passed him an envelope. Inside was a letter from her to show the Hong Kong police, if he was caught at the border, attesting to his status as a dissident and hinting that if they returned Liu Xiang it might be in the paper the next day. Tucked inside the letter was $300 in cash.

Liu arrived in Shenzhen that fall and renewed his underworld connections to see if they could help him flee to Hong Kong. Working through his *guanxi*, Liu was able to join a tour group of Shenzhen citizens scheduled to visit Zhong-Ying Street. He timed it for Christmas Day 1990, because he figured that Hong Kong's borders might be understaffed on a holiday. As the other tour members gawked, Liu slipped through the back doors and alleys on the Hong

Kong side of the street, then took a boat across the water. On Christmas evening, our phone rang. I picked it up.

"Wei?" said a familiar voice. "Is that Nikko, Sherry? I am Liu. I'm in Hong Kong."

I flew down to Hong Kong the next day, partly to do what I could to make sure that Liu was not repatriated once more. But, to my horror, the Hong Kong authorities refused to give him any protection. The British colonial rulers, headed by Lord Wilson, the governor, knew every aspect of his case, including the fact that he was an escapee from prison and would face severe punishment if he was returned, but they still turned him down. Even when the United States agreed to give Liu refugee status, the Hong Kong government refused to allow him to go. An American diplomat had to escort Liu through the Hong Kong airport and onto a plane. But in the end he made it. Now Liu Xiang is studying computer science in California.

Liu Xiang's odyssey opened my eyes to the way China is changing. The alienation from the government that caused him to protest, the brutality that provoked him to rebel, the corruption that allowed him to escape, the support from friends and criminal gangs that sustained him—all these arguably are signs of a collapsing dynasty. His case, after all, is far from unique. Several hundred Chinese dissidents have escaped on a modern Underground Railroad to Hong Kong and Europe, even though wanted posters of some of them were in police stations throughout the country. One of the students on the national most-wanted list, Zhang Boli, spent two years underground before escaping to Hong Kong. Then a filmmaker named Iris Kung managed to take a film crew around the country, under the noses of the police, and make an underground documentary about Zhang's escape.

Such episodes probably would have been impossible in the Maoist period, for China then was still a tightly run totalitarian country. But these days, as Liu Xiang's journey suggests, China is not very effective at being a police state. It tries to be, but to many Chinese the Communist Party is more pitiful than terrifying. It is too corrupt, too putrescent, to be very successful at being totalitarian. Beijing tries to rewrite history, to indoctrinate its subjects, to ban heresy, but while it dominates the stage, most people in the vast audience sitting in the dark either pay no attention or giggle at the performance. China can still be a horrifyingly brutal and capricious place. But try as it might, it no longer succeeds at being Orwellian.

Corruption, I came to feel, is too frail a word for what is happening. More and more, I felt not only that the regime was in political trouble but that the entire state was decaying, layer by layer. This suggests a far more profound challenge. A repressive government directly threatens only those few urban intellectuals who dare to demand human rights. A rotting state affects everyone.

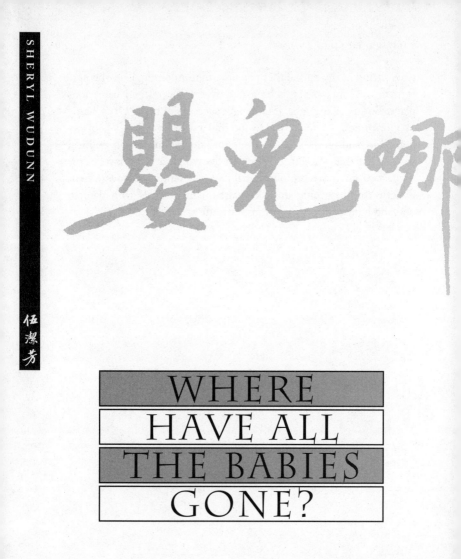

SHERYL WUDUNN

伍潔芳

WHERE HAVE ALL THE BABIES GONE?

For a woman to starve to death is a small matter, but for her to lose her chastity is a great calamity.

— A neo-Confucian saying in the Song dynasty

Men cannot make rules for women that they do not keep themselves.

— Lu Xun, "My Views on Chastity," July 1918

8

裏去了？

Wives for sale in rural China. [Photo from the cover of the 1989 book *Gulao De Zui'e* (*An Age-Old Horror*).]

Ohne day in late summer a thirty-year-old woman, slightly frail and innocent-looking, was sitting on a hillside near the grain fields of Liaohepo Village in Henan Province. Zuo Dechang, a young hoodlum who had been in and out of the local police station for various crimes, spotted her and cozied up to her. She wasn't much for conversation, for she was mentally retarded, but Zuo didn't mind. He brought her back to his village and tried to find a man who might buy her as a wife.

"I have no money," an unmarried peasant told Zuo, as the two negotiated a deal. "But I have a small calf. What would you think if I gave you this calf in exchange for this woman you've brought to our village?"

Well, Zuo thought, I could sell the calf for a bit of money. "It's a deal," he told the farmer, and the woman changed hands.

Her new husband gave her hardly anything to eat and little clothing to protect herself against the cold. A few months later, on a wintry day in 1990, she died.

A woman for a calf.

Something, I decided, was wrong with the picture of Communist equality that I had initially absorbed. When I first arrived in China, I was impressed that almost every woman I met had an occupation or a career. I did not notice any discrimination against women, and I met intelligent and capable women in academia, business, and journalism, as well as gutsy female vegetable merchants, engineering consultants, and toy makers. When we got to the Chinese border on Macao during my first trip into China in 1987, a crowd of ambitious, pushy cabdrivers crowded around Nick and me in pursuit of our fare. The most reasonable price was quoted to us by the most levelheaded of them all, a twenty-seven-year-old woman who owned her own taxi, and we chose her.

I thought, This is equality! I felt better about China itself, for as a Chinese woman, I was troubled greatly by the traditional distaste and discrimination that women faced. It was fine to be proud of the Great Wall but not of a 4,000-year legacy of abandoning female babies, of binding girls' feet, of keeping girls illiterate. Until the turn of the century, many Chinese girls were not even given names: They were called

Eldest Daughter, Second Daughter, and so on, until they married and took on a combination of their fathers' and husbands' surnames. Deng Xiaoping's own mother had no given name, and Luhui, our octogenarian friend, said that the same was true of his mother. We asked what his father had called her, and he thought for a long moment. Then his face lit up with the memory. "Eh!" He beamed. "He would just call out, 'Eh!' "

These days, girls do get names, even in remote areas. But some of these names are none too flattering. If the firstborn child in a peasant family is a girl, she is occasionally called Laidi, Zhaodi, or Yindi, all variations on the meaning "Bring a Little Brother."

I felt the weight of tradition in part because my own grandmother had had her feet bound as a young girl. This was an excruciating process, typically begun when a child was five to ten years old. Long strips of cloth were tightened around a girl's feet and maintained until the late teens. The binding forced the bones to break and the skin to rot. Toes sometimes dropped off, pus and blood covered the wounds, and the smell was sometimes overpowering. When Grandma moved to Canada with my grandfather in the 1920s, she unbound her feet, but it was too late: They had turned into flat, stubby blocks.

Mao tried to end all that. Foot binding itself had pretty much died out by 1949, but the Communists pressed relentlessly to admit women into the ranks of human beings. One of the Communist Party's greatest achievements—and one for which it is not given adequate credit—is its elevation of the status of Chinese women. The Communists emphasized from the start that power would be shared by women and men equally: As Mao said, women would hold up half the sky. The party outlawed prostitution, child marriages, the use of concubines, and the sale of brides. Women's associations were formed throughout the country and often intervened to help girls and women. Neighborhood committees began knocking on doors and scolding men who beat up their wives.

The party encouraged women to join its ranks, to become officials, to run factories, to do things they had never done before. The number of women in the industrial labor force soared, from 600,000 in 1949 to more than 50 million today, so that now some 82 percent of working-age women in the cities hold jobs. These gains gave women some economic independence and self-confidence. Side by side with their husbands, they built huts and tilled the fields. Above all, the party oversaw a revolution in educational practices, mobilizing peasant girls to go to school. For the first time in Chinese history, large numbers of peasant women graduated from the status of donkeys; they became almost human beings and not just walking wombs.

To be sure, even under Mao there was still a great deal of discrimination. But factories and offices were motivated to improve conditions by enthusiasm for change as well as fear of central leaders. And society was much more prudish then, so it was hardly possible to emphasize sexual differences. Cosmetics were effectively banned, and everyone wore the same blue or gray Mao jackets. Wolf whistles would have been unrevolutionary.

So when I arrived in China, I was generally impressed by the status of women. And with the new opportunities generated by a market economy, I expected life for women to get even better.

Then one day, I met Yang Yanru, a middle-aged peasant near Tianjin whose husband had become rich doing business. He asked her to stop working, and she was happy just to stay at home tidying up the house. That nagged at me. I could understand that now that she was rich she had better things to do with her time than to slave away in a factory for measly pay. But the same thing was happening all over China, and it seemed funny to me that economic progress in China would mean more housewives and fewer career women. What ever happened to Mao's belief in equality?

As I talked to more women and got better acquainted with their status, it became clear that the problems ran far deeper. The obstacle was not just the strength of traditional beliefs but the invisible hand of the market itself. The market economy raised living standards for women along with men, but it also led to the return of the male-dominated Chinese society—coupled with the sexist features of Western society. Advertisers quickly discovered that the best way to market their products was by airing commercials showing lovely young women, preferably wearing as little as possible. To promote sales of weapons abroad, the army began publishing a calendar with a pinup each month of a buxom young woman clutching a gun. In the 1994 calendar, for example, Miss February wears a bikini top and a red skirt slit to the waist, accompanied by an AK-47 assault rifle.

Miss November wears a strapless formal, high heels, red gloves—and carries a submachine gun in her right hand.

Nick once visited a school in Tianjin and was shown a twenty-minute introductory video that the principal had prepared. It began with a five-minute scene of the newly arrived high school girls scrubbing themselves from head to toe in the shower. The principal seemed to think that this was a tribute to his open-mindedness. Likewise, pornography and prostitution spread rapidly throughout China beginning in the 1980s, and bosses began to hire pretty young women as ornaments or playthings.

"These days if you're a woman, you're as good as a commodity," said Lihong, a young Chinese businesswoman whose work in a joint venture brings her in contact with men and women of many ranks and backgrounds. "You're worth either six pounds of gold or two tons of aluminum."

When Miaoxia, a twenty-eight-year-old married woman with long hair, olive skin, and sleepy, almond-shaped eyes, interviewed for a summer job one year, she was flattered that an employer decided to hire her immediately. Miaoxia went to her first day of work at the Beijing office of a machinery company to find her boss beaming with an envelope in his hand. He gave her a bit less than $1,000 to go out and buy clothes, makeup, and other accessories "to make you look prettier."

"I was so excited," she told me one afternoon a year later. "After I went out and bought a bunch of clothes, I was determined to go in and impress the boss with my skills. I thought I had better do a terrific job, or else he might be disappointed that he had spent so much money on me the first day."

The office was small, with only five other employees, and often they were out. On her second day, Miaoxia found herself alone typing a letter in English. All of a sudden, her boss walked up behind her and kissed her on her cheek and the back of her neck. She pushed him away with her shoulder, but he did it again. "I told him, 'I don't like this sort of thing.' You know what he said? He said, 'I'm a rich businessman, and I can buy almost any woman I want. Many women would love to use me to climb to the top. Others would just love to *bang dakuan*' [the colloquial term for finding a sugar daddy]. Not me, I told him. I'm not that kind of girl."

Later the other office workers told her that he made passes at female employees all the time, that in fact he'd been through many secretaries. "I stayed a week, and didn't get paid. But then again, I didn't return any of his money either."

Women face greater economic opportunity than they did under Mao but also more discrimination; they can find work more easily, but many of the jobs are on assembly lines in the noisiest, dirtiest industries; they may drive buses and taxis, but they usually take only one-third of the spots in universities; they enjoy excellent maternity benefits, but they are the first workers fired during times of economic austerity; while they are sometimes allocated land in the countryside, valued possessions are handed down from generation to generation through the male line.

Worst of all, the rising market economy now embraces women themselves as tradable commodities. A huge market emerged in the 1980s in the trafficking of women and children. Typically, a con man goes to a rural area and announces that he is recruiting young women to work in a restaurant or factory. He leads several of them away, often by public bus, on a long journey to some distant village. Many of the girls have never been outside their township before, and they have no idea what to expect. If they ask questions, they are reassured that they will get to the factory soon. Finally they end up in a village that has a shortage of young women, and some men in their twenties are eyeing them and offering prices of a few thousand yuan each. Or a calf.

Often the women are raped by the brokers who handle them along the way. This makes them feel as though they are damaged merchandise, unable to attract a first-rate husband even if they escape to their home villages. In addition, the women are sometimes tied up, and they certainly have no money with which to make the long journey home. Moreover, many peasants regard the practice as perfectly normal, and they sympathize with the man who spends good money—often many years' savings—to buy a wife. If the woman escapes, their pal's money is wasted. So the husband's neighbors keep an eye out to make sure the wife, almost always a complete stranger in the village, doesn't try to sneak away. When the authorities try to rescue a woman, the local peasants often erect barricades to keep the police out. In some places, peasants have fought pitched battles for several days to prevent the police from rescuing a kidnapped woman.

My Chinese friends told me all this. Even so, I couldn't really understand why more of these wives didn't try to escape. I understood that a naive girl of sixteen, kept under guard 1,000 miles from her home, might find it difficult to sneak away. But it is impossible to keep a wife under lock and key indefinitely, and I kept asking why the women didn't eventually run away—even if they had to wait months or years. Sure, some of the women have babies by that time and decide to stay put. Others don't have the guts or know-how. But if only one-third of the wives ran away within a year or two, the business of woman trafficking would collapse. Men would stop paying for livestock that kept escaping.

An investigative reporter named Jia Lusheng helped me understand why women often don't dare escape. Jia had coauthored a book about the trade in women. He had traveled throughout China, sometimes posing as a potential client, and he went to many of the poorest areas in Sichuan, Anhui, Henan, and the western corner of Shandong. It was in these pockets of poverty, where the grain grows sparse between vast patches of sand and scrub, where the children wear hand-me-downs if they wear anything at all, that he saw how women were bought and sold. He also saw what happened to them when they tried to escape.

"I saw her in the hospital in Shandong," Jia told me one afternoon, as he described a woman who had been sold as a wife to an uneducated Shaanxi peasant. "The first time she tried to flee, the peasant tied her to the bedpost. The second time she tried, he beat her. The third time, he gouged out her eyes. When I saw her in the hospital, she had white gauze covering the top of her head. The only thing you could see left of her eyes were two deep holes."

This was a slave trade. It appalled and fascinated me, and it occasionally alarmed me. A graduate student in Shanghai was kidnapped and sold to be the wife of a peasant in central China, and I occasionally wondered what would happen if a slave trader tried to grab me off the street of Beijing and peddle me to the peasants of Sichuan. I searched for more information, asking about wife trafficking whenever I visited the countryside and pressing my Chinese friends for anything they knew.

Once a friend gave me a confidential government document that provides some indications of the scale of the problem. The document, prepared for leaders of the National People's Congress, said that the authorities had investigated 18,692 cases of the sale of women in 1990. It said that in 1989 and 1990, a total of 65,236 people were arrested for trafficking in women and children. At about the same time, the *People's Daily* reported that in a twelve-month period in 1989–90, some 10,000 abducted women and children had been rescued by the authorities. Presumably many more, the great majority, were never rescued.

With so many abducted women out there, I wanted to find one to interview. I cast my net, mentioning my aim to all my friends, but they were urban intellectuals and didn't know any peasants who had been sold into slavery. They didn't know people like Zhu Li.

Zhu Li is a young, dark-skinned woman, with a tired-looking face, rough and unrefined, and big brown eyes that, alas, are very timid. She is twenty-two years old, but the wind and the sun have taken away her youth. She looks old and haggard. She is short and silent, the kind of woman I wouldn't even notice if I walked by her on the street. But she is neatly dressed, and she seems very innocent.

Zhu is from a poor area in Henan Province, and her family of five earns only about $125 a year in gross income. From that her parents have to pay school fees for her brother and sister—Zhu herself dropped out of school after the second grade to help out at home—as well as a $9 fee to pave a nearby road. That leaves just enough to survive. Her village is also installing electricity now, and her family has been assessed $25 to help pay the costs—but they don't know where they'll get that money. The family also has to send people on work teams, just as peasants have had to do for thousands of years under the emperors.

"Our village organizes mine-digging groups," Zhu said. "When you go, you go for a full month. If you don't go, you have to pay fifty yuan. No one has that kind of money in our village. The officials send their thugs to the homes of whoever refuses to go, and they take grain as collateral for the money."

Then Zhu casually dropped the fact that she had been sold—that she was one of the examples of merchandise that I was looking for.

"Actually, I'm from Sichuan, from Daxian," she explained. "I still have a younger sister in Daxian. Eleven years ago, my mother was abducted by traders and sold to Henan. They sold her to my current father for coupons to buy eighty *jin* worth of grain. [A *jin* is a bit more than a pound.] I was taken along with my mother. The traders then tried to get more money from my stepfather. They said that if he didn't give them money, they'd take us away from him. He was stuck. He gave them 350 yuan, which in those days was about a year's income.

"Luckily, my stepfather is a kind man. He was very good to me and my mother, so we stayed with him. Now I have an eleven-year-old brother in Henan."

When I talked to officials, they acknowledged that women were bought and sold, but they said it occurred on only a small scale and only in isolated regions. "It happens in the remote mountainous areas, where the economy is backward, in places where women don't want to go to marry," said Wu Baoyu, an official in the All China Women's Federation in the southern boomtown of Xiamen. But then I began hearing that the Beijing labor market was a center for the female slave trade. The labor market is a narrow paved road, dusty and cluttered with garbage, where peasants gather every morning to look for work. Beijing residents go there to look for nannies, for construction laborers, for people to do odd jobs—and for women to kidnap. It is a strange place, a truly free market, for there are no regulations. In fact, it is outside the law. The police scoot everyone away several times throughout the day, and there are plainclothes policemen crawling throughout the place. In many ways it is as dangerous as it is filled with opportunity.

In the summer of 1993, the police caught a slave-trading gang that had abducted 1,800 women from the Beijing labor market and sold them to a remote area in Shanxi Province. It had taken a while to crack the case, for in one village a year earlier, a rural official had led the police to a suspect only to have the villagers knife the official.

A few months after those arrests, I was wandering through the market, trying to find a woman who'd been sold, when I found myself standing behind an old man in his sixties. He wore a gray windbreaker and a hat that partially hid his wrinkled forehead and beady eyes. He was walking up to some of the prettier out-of-town girls on the street.

"I'm looking for someone to frame pictures," he said as he approached one attractive, plump-faced young woman.

"Why are you looking for someone from out of town?" the woman asked, with extreme skepticism. "Framing pictures requires skill. Why don't you get someone from Beijing?"

"Well, er, I also want someone to help out in the house. I have three sons and a daughter, and I need a maid. We're a family of intellectuals. I need someone to help me out and to help frame pictures."

"Are you a painter?" asked a young man, butting in on the conversation. The old man didn't pay any attention to him.

"Do you paint? Are you a painter?" the young man asked again. "If you're an intellectual, what is your specialty?"

Finally, the old man turned to his challenger and said, "Why, I'm an intellectual. I do everything and anything."

The old man, whose uncouth way of speaking suggested he was a manual laborer, certainly did not look like an intellectual. So was he trying to deceive this woman, using the lure of a lucrative job to take her away and sell her as a wife? Sensing the suspicion around him, he beat a retreat. But it was easy to see how a naive peasant girl could be tricked. He offered what he said would be very good wages, a huge temptation to girls who have borrowed money from their families to get to Beijing and are trying to find any kind of work. I talked to some young women who were sleeping in front of the train station and starving themselves because they had no money but couldn't bear to return to their villages and disappoint their families.

"Old men are the ones we have to look out for the most," said a woman in her twenties who was sitting on the ground in the labor market. "They even treat you to nice meals, and you'd never suspect them. But they're the worst scoundrels. I've seen it. We're all warned. They come here and want you to be a maid, and you get there, and you're finished."

Where were the police when this old man was wandering through the labor market? The police don't need an excuse to detain someone, as Honggan, a Chinese intellectual, discovered one day. Honggan was helping me look for kidnapped women, and a plainclothes policeman finally detained her for interrogation. "Why are you here?" he asked. "Are you working for foreigners? This place is banned to foreign reporters." Honggan insisted that she wasn't working for any foreigners, and she was released. But it seemed to me that the police might be more useful if they looked for slave traders instead of for people helping foreign correspondents.

I was still eager to find a woman who'd been tricked by the slave traders. Zhu Li had been sold, but only as a girl accompanying her mother. I was searching for someone who had been marketed as a wife. Then, just a couple of weeks before I left Beijing, on a bright fall day in 1993, I met Zhu Qianyun.

Adorned by a new red sweater, Zhu Qianyun has long, jet-black hair and a face almost equally long, with smooth white skin surrounding a pair of dull and cautious eyes. It was only after I bribed her with some peanuts—she hadn't eaten for three days—that her story tumbled out, in a thick rural accent. "I was tricked for two and a half days," the twenty-four-year-old Zhu said. "They cheated me for two and a half days. I was cheated by traders."

Zhu was a proud woman who had come to Beijing from a small city in Henan Province. (Despite her name, she was not related to Zhu Li.) As soon as she arrived, there was a cold spell, so she ran out and spent most of her money on warm clothes. "Then three men and a woman in her thirties, a pretty woman, they came to me on the corner here and said they'd find me a job at a restaurant," she recalled. "We kept switching buses. We took the public bus and kept switching. We were somewhere near Dahongmen in the south of Beijing. They kept saying they would find the restaurant, but they never did. That made me suspicious. They kept saying for two days that they would find the restaurant.

"Finally we were having lunch at a noodle joint, and they started talking among themselves. I heard them say that they could sell me for 10,000 yuan. They wanted to go to Baoding to sell me.

"There was a small boy, too. He was really ugly. He was about this tall," she said as she held her hand out at chest height. "I think he was seven years old. I think they were going to sell him, too.

"When I heard them say these things, I ran away. Me, look at me. My life? I don't care about my life anymore. So I fought like hell, without caring if they'd kill me. I didn't care if I died. I just kicked and screamed with whatever was in me. I kicked one of the men down there, real hard, with my heels. You know, in his crotch. I kicked the woman in the same place. They reeled over in pain. They were afraid that I'd injured them for life, so the other men didn't dare touch me. They let me run, and I ran and got a bus back to the Beijing train station.

"I don't dare go to the police because I don't have any ID on me. I didn't take it with me when I left home. And I don't want to go back home because I got into a big fight with my sister. Besides, there's no money back where I live."

It would be too simplistic to say unequivocally that Chinese women lost ground in the 1980s and 1990s. The market economy gave them new opportunities and in some cases independence as well. But, on balance, it seems to me that while women gained on any absolute scale, they lost ground relative to men. As the party stopped fighting for equality, traditional attitudes reasserted themselves.

One measure of that was simply the presence of women in the top leadership of the country. In 1978, on the eve of the reforms, two women served on the Politburo. Since the late 1980s, however, no woman has held so lofty a post, and today no woman is even close. In 1978, 11.1 percent of the Central Committee members and their alternates were women; the proportion is 7.5 percent today. In 1993, the government selected women for just three out of the forty-one ministerial jobs, and there are indications that the proportion of female party members has also dropped.

The official line is that there are not enough women with the training to be promoted to senior positions. This is partly true. Seventy percent of China's illiterates are women, and one-third of women between the ages of fifteen and forty-five cannot read a newspaper. But in hamlets throughout China, the problem is being perpetuated. Visit any rural school and the principal will tell you that 100 percent or 98.6 percent or 96.9 percent or some other impressive proportion of elementary school–age children are attending school. Then drop by the nearby villages, and you see it's a lie. Everywhere there are young girls who have dropped out in the third grade, or the fifth grade. School fees often amount to twenty dollars a year in rural areas, a huge sum that parents often think isn't worth it—particularly for a mere *yatou*, or girl, who will soon be married into someone else's clan. So rural parents frequently keep their daughters at home to help with the chores while sending their sons to school.

Nick once traveled to a rural area in the Dabie Mountains of central China to find out about the dropout problem. In America there are "college towns" to serve as the intellectual focus for a region, and in the same way in rural China there are "elementary school villages" serving as the scholarly locus of a larger area. Nick visited the Yejuao Elementary School, whose 130 students come from about thirty little villages in the surrounding hills. Most stay six nights a week at the school, hiking home only on Saturday afternoons and returning the next night. In Yejuao, as in many such remote schools, there are 50 percent more boys than girls.

One of the star pupils at the school was Dai Manju, a shy, pint-size thirteen-year-old who wanted to be a craft teacher when she grew up. Dai's parents were peasants in a hillside village two hours away by muddy trail, and they owned almost nothing. When Nick dropped by their home, about their only possession was a coffin for the girl's great-aunt. She was in fine health, they explained cheerfully, but it was best to be prepared. Dai was an ace student who loved school, even though she had to share a bed with several other girls, wear the same clothes all week, and put up with atrocious facilities. The school had no hot water, and the toilets were a set of three outdoor pits surrounded by a low wall. There was no lighting, so students and teachers did not lightly answer the call of nature at night. Nevertheless, Dai fervently wanted to stay in school, to pursue her dream of becoming the first in her family ever to graduate from elementary school. Dreams weren't enough, though. When Nick met her, Dai had already dropped out of elementary school four times.

The problem was that her parents said they couldn't afford the school fees of about thirteen dollars a year, including room and board. When Nick saw Dai Manju, she was in school only because some teachers had hiked to her house and offered to pay part of the fees out of their own wages.

There was an epilogue: Nick's story about Dai Manju and other elementary school dropouts landed on the front page of *The Times*, with a woeful picture of the girl. We were then flooded with inquiries from readers who wanted to pay for Dai's education. Most checks were for thirteen dollars, but some were for larger sums. One reader went to the trouble of going to Morgan Guaranty Trust and getting a bank draft for Chinese yuan, equivalent to one hundred dollars. Morgan Guaranty, unused to dealing with yuan, mistakenly dropped the decimal point in the exchange rate, which meant that the bank sent the equivalent of $10,000 instead of $100. After the money had safely arrived at the school and was being used in a fund to keep dropouts in class, Nick called up Morgan Guaranty and pointed out the error. The bank decided not to ask for the money back from the school. "Under the circumstances," said John M. Morris, a bank spokesman, "we're happy to make a donation of the difference."

It is a nice little tale—except that there are kids like Dai Manju all over China. The situation is improving, but rural China is still a terrible place for a girl to grow up.

Even the mortality statistics bear this out. In all parts of the world, male children die more often than girls. At birth there are more boys than girls, but after that it is the girls who are the survivors. In the first year of life, boys are 30 percent more likely to die. In Japan, for example, there are 133 dead infant boys for every 100 girls. In the United States the ratio is 131 to 100. But in China, only 112 boys die for every 100 girls.

What is skewing the statistics in China? Why are boys doing relatively better in China than in other countries? Presumably, because people treat sons better than daughters. They give them more food. They pay more attention to them. They are quicker to summon medical help for sons. It is not that they intentionally expose their daughters to mortal danger but that they take marginally greater risks with girls than with boys.

"If a boy gets sick, the parents may send him to the hospital at once," acknowledged Li Honggui, an official in China's State Family Planning Commission. "But if a girl gets sick, the parents may say to themselves, 'Well, we'll see how she is tomorrow.'"

Life is particularly harsh for women who are peasants. Liming, a twenty-eight-year-old peasant, taught me that. Life had left myriad lines on Liming's face, so that she looked more like thirty-five. She was bitter and almost ugly, a woman with a dark, long face that bore a perpetually sallow expression. Her lips were dry and her small eyes expressionless as she sat on the sidewalk one autumn day relating her story. Liming lived in Zhumadian in the north-central province of Henan, in a small village where the nation's regulations don't seem to matter.

China's marriage law stipulates that men can marry at age twenty-two, while women can take a husband when they are twenty. But in Zhumadian, most villagers get engaged when they are seventeen years old, sometimes even when they are fifteen, and they start living together right away. When they turn twenty, they can pay one hundred yuan as a bribe to buy a marriage certificate from the local officials. Liming herself wasn't exactly the village beauty and was still single at eighteen—and thus humiliated—while her younger brother was already engaged.

"My father was furious and often scolded me for bringing such disgrace to the family," she said. "He found a matchmaker, but I rejected the men that the matchmaker sent until finally, after I could take no more of my father's yelling, I agreed to marry a boy, a nineteen-year-old. That year, I was twenty-three."

"How was I supposed to know that this young guy had gotten his former girlfriend pregnant eight months earlier?" Liming said, as tears streaked down her dirty face.

"We were basically married, but I soon learned that my man, who was a nice-looking man on the outside, I soon discovered that the only thing he was good at doing was riding a bicycle everywhere like a feudal prince on tour. He was good for nothing. He didn't do any work, and we had no money. I had to borrow grain from my family, and so my father and my brother looked down on me. My man and I argued all the time. My father had given me a hundred yuan when I got married, but my man took that from me and spent it all. When that was gone, he started hitting and kicking me.

"Six months later, when I was five months pregnant, my man found a new woman. Me, with my big stomach, I ran back home. In my village, if you return home, you disgrace the family. My father lost face. He wouldn't let me return home. I could only run to my cousin's house, and that's where I gave birth. The baby was a girl. I wanted my man to give me money to raise my daughter, so I complained to the police station. The police told me that since I never got an official marriage certificate, my daughter wasn't protected under the law.

"At home, my mother was mistreated by both my father and my younger brother. But after this happened, I left my daughter with my mother and took a plunge by coming to Beijing.

"I had just given birth, but I needed money to raise my daughter. So I did everything, even heavy manual labor. I was weak and then got sick. I worked in a restaurant, but because my hands and legs were slow, I was fired.

"I was only twenty-four when I came to Beijing, and I was really naive. One evening, a sixty-year-old man told me he wanted to hire a maid, and so I went with him to the high-tech district, where his wife's mother and father lived. The old man took a shower, and when he finished, he told me to take a shower. When I came out, he raped me. I told him I would go to the police station. He laughed. 'I work in Tianjin. I've no home in Beijing. This is my wife's parents' home. It'll do you no good to go to the police station. Hmph! All I have to tell them is that you came here in the middle of the night to sell your body.' I was scared out of my wits. The old man threw me fifty yuan. I took it and quietly ran out of the house.

"Luckily, I found a nice family that took me in as a maid. But they moved to Hainan, and I was put out on the streets again. Someone then introduced me to a place outside Beijing called Yangzha. I became a waitress in a restaurant there, but the boss often laid his hands on me. He scolded me often, too. After ten days, I couldn't take it anymore, so I left to learn how to become a hairdresser at a place in the neighborhood. The boss there was Fujianese. He had hired a northeastern girl and a Sichuanese girl to help him. Those two girls, they would cut hair during the day and then sell their bodies at night. Once, when I was cutting the hair of a young man, he put his hand on my leg. I scolded him. That northeastern girl turned and criticized me. Then she turned to the customer and said, 'That woman is an old virgin. You won't get any sex from her.' A few days later, the boss came up to me and said, 'You aren't suitable for the work here. Why don't you leave?'

"Then I met someone from my hometown. He worked in a slaughterhouse. His boss asked me to work for him. The boss said to me, 'Even though you're married, there's no need to be old-fashioned around here. You shouldn't be offended by things around here. If you do what you're told, I'll give you some extra money.' I knew right away that this guy had something in mind, so I refused. That guy was a scoundrel. He hit me, so I ran away.

"Then I was a maid for a family named Jin. They are descendants of court officials in the Qing dynasty, and even now, they follow a strict code of manners. They always scolded me for not having refined behavior, and they were offended when I called the head of the household Big Brother. I worked there for half a month, and then I caught a cold. The family kicked me out. They originally agreed to pay me 100 to 150 yuan each month. But I didn't get a penny.

"I don't want to stay in Beijing any longer," Liming finally confessed. "But my father doesn't want me to go home. I don't know what I'm supposed to do. All I know is that I must find out whether I can get money from my husband to raise my daughter."

Only gradually did we become aware of the most outrageous way in which females have suffered since the reforms began in China. Women, after all, suffer discrimination in countries all over the world, and kidnapping and rape occur in the West as well as in China. But since the 1980s there has been a dramatic rise in the worst kind of discrimination: that which denies females even the right to exist.

Female infanticide has a long history in China—and for most of that time, it was not even frowned upon. Certainly, there was a vague sense that one ought not to kill infants, but infanticide was just one minor sin among many. For example, a popular moral text that was distributed widely during the sixteenth and seventeenth centuries orders people not to kill babies. But the injunction against infanticide is simply one of a long list of things that people should not do, such as leaping over food served on the floor; stepping over a person lying on a floor mat; weeping, spitting, or urinating when facing north (the direction of the emperor); spitting at a shooting star; or pointing at a rainbow. If you committed these sins, the Arbiter of Human Destiny would shave three or three hundred days off your life. The text does not indicate that infanticide is any worse than, for example, urinating when facing north.

Infanticide was not considered terrible in part because babies were not considered fully human until they were one year old or had grown a full set of teeth. An old Chinese fable even describes a young couple who were rewarded by the gods for trying to kill their baby. The parents worried that their infant would take food that could better be used by the man's sick mother, so they buried the baby alive. This act of filial piety so touched the gods that they arranged for the couple to find a pile of gold as they dug their baby's grave. Clearly Chinese tradition placed more emphasis on filial piety than on parental responsibility.

Still, the Communist Party virtually eradicated female infanticide after 1949. Subsequent censuses showed no shortfall of infant girls— until the 1980s. Then the statistics showed hundreds of thousands of baby girls going missing each year, rising to more than a million a year in the early 1990s.

What changed? The population policy. In the 1950s, Mao purged a famous advocate of family planning and declared that more babies would make China more powerful. But in the late 1970s, China's leadership introduced the most coercive family planning program the world has ever known. One-child policy is a misnomer, because in some circumstances parents can have two or even more children. Herding families in remote parts of Xinjiang Province are in some cases even allowed to have four children. But for all the exceptions, the new policy was a draconian attempt to curb family size, and peasants typically found themselves limited to one or two children.

Particularly if the first child was a girl, they didn't want to "waste" the last opportunity on another girl. Peasants want sons, not daughters, for many reasons. Lineage passes down through only the male line, so a man with daughters but no sons has no descendants. Moreover, daughters marry into other families while sons have the obligation to look after their parents in old age. Boys also are regarded as more adept at field work. Finally, there is peer pressure. A woman will be scolded by her mother-in-law until she produces a son, and she may even be divorced by her husband if she does not. Many rural couples feel that they have not accomplished life's mission until they have produced a baby complete with a penis.

Before the new family planning policy, a couple could afford to raise daughters and simply try again for a son. Now that is no longer feasible. A woman who breaks the rules by having an extra child faces huge fines, the prospect of her home being knocked down, and the likelihood of being forced to undergo sterilization. Some parents figure this would be worthwhile if the pregnancy resulted in a son, but not if it led to another daughter.

The scale of the problem is evident only as a shadow in the statistics. Normally, people of all races have 105 or 106 male births for every 100 female births. Since males die at higher rates than females, the sex ratio should even out by marriage age; then in old age there are typically far more women than men. The problem is that in China the sex ratio at birth is much higher than 105 to 100. We started seeking explanations from officials and scholars in the late 1980s, when new statistics showed a ratio of between 110 and 112 newborn boys for every 100 girls. The State Family Planning Commission temporized, suggesting that it was arrogant of Westerners to assume that China would necessarily have the same sex ratio as other countries. In fact, however, the People's Republic of China had a normal sex ratio in its 1953 census and its 1964 census, the only ones conducted before the one-child policy was adopted. In 1953, there were 104.9 newborn boys for every 100 girls. In 1964 there were 103.8 boys for 100 girls. It was only in the 1982 census, after the family planning crackdown, that the ratios began to creep up.

Moreover, even now, for firstborn infants, China has a fairly normal sex ratio, of about 106 to 100. It is only the later-born infants that are disproportionately male. Among fifth-born children, the ratio is more than 125 to 100. Presumably this is because couples will accept a daughter if she is their first child, because they expect that they can find a way legally or illegally to have another child.

Meanwhile, the problem is getting worse. In 1992, the authorities were stunned by the results of a new government-sponsored survey which showed that the sex ratio for newborn infants had reached 118.5 boys for every 100 girls. If the norm is taken to be 105.5, then more than 12 percent of all Chinese baby girls go missing each year. That adds up to more than 1.7 million missing girls annually.

This does not mean, of course, that 1.7 million girls are killed each year. The majority are probably born safely but simply never reported to the authorities. One study found that several hundred thousand girls are informally "adopted" by friends or relatives each year, and others are quietly raised by their own parents without anybody paying attention. Only a small minority are likely to be killed, drowned in the bucket of water that some midwives keep at the bedside in case the baby is a girl. But whether a small minority means 10,000 cases of infanticide a year or 100,000 or 300,000 or even more, nobody knows.

Technology also conspired against females in the 1980s. As early as 1979, China began manufacturing ultrasound scanners, which use sound waves to generate a picture of the inside of a human body. By the end of the 1980s, China each year was importing more than 2,000 ultrasound scanners and making 10,000 of its own. One Chinese demographer has estimated that 100,000 ultrasound scanners were in place around the country by 1990. The scanners are supposed to be used to help doctors see problems in livers and other internal organs, as well as to check whether fetuses are developing properly. In addition, the family planning authorities use them to confirm that women are still wearing their IUDs. The catch is that ultrasound scanners can also be used to gain a rough idea of whether a fetus is male or female. As a result, expectant parents found that they could get an unscrupulous doctor to tell them whether they were likely to have a boy or a girl. If they were told to expect a daughter, they requested an abortion.

This practice had become hugely popular by the early 1990s. It may well be that in China today the modern machine that is having the most far-reaching impact on society is not the personal computer, the fax, or even the car but rather the ultrasound scanner. Of the 1.7 million missing girls each year, perhaps the largest number were simply detected before birth by ultrasound and aborted.

In 1993 Nick traveled to a series of rural villages in Fujian Province and chatted with the peasants about ultrasound. Even the most uneducated hillbillies had heard of it. And they loved it. As a violent rainstorm pounded the paddies of one village, a half-dozen peasants sat around a stone hut and spoke with glee about the new age of ultrasound.

"Everyone has boys now," Y. H. Chen said in a tone of awe, as the others nodded agreement. "Last year we had only one girl born in the village—everybody else had boys. You go to the doctor and pay him 200 or 300 yuan. He tells you if your wife is pregnant with a boy or a girl. Then if it's a girl, you get an abortion."

Chen's brother, Y. C. Chen, interrupted: "One family here in the village has five girls. They were desperate for a son, so they kept on having another child in the hope that it would be a son. But now you don't need to do that. Now technology is changing things."

The emergence of a market economy is partly to blame, for more and more doctors are setting up private practices, and even state-run hospitals are becoming more attuned to the need to raise funds. In either case, they buy ultrasound equipment because such machines are among the most profitable medical equipment available. In a busy clinic, an ultrasound machine can be used on more than a hundred patients a day, and the machine operator faces little risk of being caught taking bribes in exchange for revealing the sex of the fetus.

The Chens' brother-in-law, for example, is a private pharmacist who last year bought his own ultrasound machine. A Chinese-made machine costs only a bit more than $1,000, and he can charge pregnant women up to $50 each for a brief consultation on the sex of the fetus.

One problem is that ultrasound scans are not very reliable for sex determination, not nearly as reliable as more complex tests like amniocentesis. Moreover, a doctor cannot make an educated guess about the sex of the fetus until the second trimester, when an abortion is a much more difficult procedure than at the beginning of pregnancy. There are many stories of women going to clinics late in the second trimester to ask for abortions, even though they have government permission to give birth. Usually the fetuses turn out to be female, but when one is a boy—about 20 percent of the time, presumably because the ultrasound operator made a mistake—the mother becomes hysterical with shock and grief.

A Chinese newspaper, *China Information News,* reported that ultrasound was used in 2,316 cases in one county to determine the sex of a fetus, resulting in the abortion of 1,006 female fetuses. Another official newspaper, *Public Security News,* said that in a district of Ouhai County in Zhejiang Province, a survey of seventy-four aborted fetuses found that sixty-eight were female.

"Ultrasound is just like nuclear technology," *Public Security News* lamented in late 1993. "It is a wonderful thing for society, yet it also brings great tragedy." In a sign of alarm at the sex ratio, the official press is beginning to warn that today's infant boys will be unable to find wives in twenty years' time. Yet aside from vague warnings about "bachelor villages" multiplying in the countryside, no one is exploring the social consequences that may arise in a nation with a huge surplus of males. To be sure, China is not the only country facing this problem. Throughout Asia, with its historic preference for boys, ultrasound scanners and other medical technologies are being used to check the sex of fetuses so that females can be aborted. Apparently largely because of ultrasound scans, the sex ratio of newborn children in South Korea is about 113 boys to 100 girls. But in China the problem is unusually severe because of the family planning policy. As the Communist Party loses control and authority, it is difficult to see how it will control the illicit use of ultrasound for sex selection. Although the practice has been banned since 1987, it has steadily gotten worse. In five of China's thirty provinces, the sex ratio has risen to 120 boys for every 100 girls.

What will China be like in fifteen or twenty years if there are far more eligible men than women? What will its society be like if one-fifth of all its men never find partners?

The starkest indication that women face problems in China is statistical: At least 30 million females are missing in China.

Partly because women ordinarily live longer, they should outnumber men. In most industrialized countries, where males and females get equal access to food and medicine, there are about 5 percent more females than males in the overall population.

In China, however, the 1990 census showed only 93.8 women for every 100 men. Moreover, the imbalance is getting worse, for in the 1982 census the ratio was 94.1 females for 100 males. The statistics are extremely complex and subject to different interpretations, but even a conservative analysis suggests that 5 percent of Chinese females are missing. Thirty million of them—that means little girls, teenagers, young women, and old grandmas.

Where are these missing females? Some were killed at birth in the 1930s and 1940s and so are not present as elderly women today. Some died as girls because they were not given adequate food, clothing, and health care. Some died in the 1958–1961 famine because their parents saved the rice for their brothers. Some are the female fetuses of just the last few years who were discovered by ultrasound and then aborted.

Other countries, such as Afghanistan and India, also have huge numbers of missing women. But not all poor countries are discriminatory: Sub-Saharan Africa has more women than men. The problem, it seems, is particularly acute in Asia and the Arab world.

What if Grandpa hadn't left China, I thought, and I'd been born in China. I was born in 1959, early in the great famine in which 30 million died. Would I have had to compete with my younger brother, Darrell, for food? And if there hadn't been enough food to go around—what then? Would I have been one of those 30 million females missing from China's population today?

That thought certainly wasn't on my mind when I first arrived in China. I was then quite sympathetic to China's family planning efforts, for the country clearly has a huge population problem. It seemed to me that one major reason to be more optimistic about China than about India is that China appears to have defused the population bomb.

Yet at what a cost! The family planning authorities routinely force young women to undergo abortions and sterilization. The township authorities send teams into the villages once or twice a year to collect

all the women who are due to be fitted with an IUD or to be sterilized. Some run away, in hopes that they can remain fertile and have
another baby, and the authorities then send goons to the women's
relatives in other villages, even in other provinces, to find and steril-
ize them. Usually they do not have to drag a woman to the operating
table; when half a dozen young men surround her home and order
her to come out, she may not see much sense in fighting back.

Take Wu Xinlian, a thirty-year-old peasant who was born a
member of my clan, the Wu family of Shun Shui village in Guangdong Province. I met her when I returned to my ancestral village to
interview people about family planning, among other topics. Wu
grew up in my village and later married into another clan. She had
two daughters—she was bouncing her younger one in her arms as
she talked to me—but her dream was to have a son. The problem, of
course, was that since she already had two children, the officials
insisted that she be sterilized.

The women in my clan are a plucky lot, however. When the family planning authorities swept into the village where Wu lived with
her husband, preparing to take her and other women to the clinic to
be sterilized, she fled to her parents' home in Shun Shui. She stayed
there, planning to meet her husband secretly and become pregnant.
But the authorities discovered her whereabouts and sent two dozen
officials to take her to a hospital for her tubal ligation. She didn't dare
refuse. How could she?

"I have no idea how they found out I was here," Wu told me, cud-
dling her younger daughter. "I really wanted a boy."

Another member of my clan, a man named Wu Tiaoyuan, was
luckier. He and his thirty-three-year-old wife hid for several months
while she was pregnant with their third child. She finally gave birth
in February 1992 to the son they had always wanted. "We kept moving around from village to village," he told me. "It was very hard, and
I was scared."

My mind raced as I listened to these distant relatives of mine. I
wondered what Wu Tiaoyuan and his wife would have done if, after
their months of hiding, their third child had turned out to be a girl as
well. It would have been impossible to remain in hiding for two or
three more years and have a fourth try (rural mothers often breast-
feed their babies for a year or two, delaying the chance of becoming
pregnant again). So would they have accepted fate and returned to

their village with their infant daughter to accept the fines and steril-ization? Or would they, in their torment, have told the midwife to plunge their baby daughter into a bucket of water?

My other thought as I stood in Shun Shui, near the house where my grandfather had lived, was more personal. As I listened to Wu Xinlian talk wistfully and painfully about her yearning for a boy, I began to wonder about how my grandparents had felt when I was born. Grandpa had left his first wife back in the village because she didn't bear him a son, but it would all have been to no avail if Dad had failed to have a son as well. The family line would have ended with Dad, and there would be nobody to sweep the family graves and bribe the gods to look after Grandpa. I thought, with sudden pain— and anger—that they must have been enormously disappointed when their only son's first child was a girl. Perhaps in some way I had brought shame to the family.

My parents never ever gave the slightest hint that they had first wanted a boy, and I have never asked them about this. If it had mat-tered at one time, I know it doesn't matter now—in part because my brother, Darrell, has dutifully pursued the Chinese-American dream by earning both an M.D. and a Ph.D. and practicing medicine. I know that Mom and Dad are open-minded, but even if they had no personal preference, I wondered if they had felt pressure for their firstborn to be a son. Was I a disappointment? Were their two other wonderful daughters also a letdown? The thought gnawed at me. I know the burden of these pressures, for when I was pregnant my Chinese friends kept taking guesses at whether my baby was a boy or a girl. It was clear that many thought a girl would be fine but a boy would be better.

In the United States, I never could decide whether I wanted boys or girls as children. But in China, when I had Gregory, I was a bit relieved that he was a boy. It just made life easier, and China is not even my home. I remember calling up Lihua, a Chinese journalist friend of mine, to tell her about my newborn baby. At first, there was silence on the other end of the line, and she asked, "Is it a boy or a girl?" I told her, and only then did she extend congratulations. I can imagine the anxieties the millions of Chinese mothers must feel when they are about to give birth, particularly those who will not be allowed to have another baby. Many around them will see it as life's most important exam, a pass-fail test in which half the people fail.

Infanticide and ultrasound sex selection appall me, but I can understand how—when faced with such an important exam—people feel the urge to cheat.

Whatever one thinks of the one-child policy, this is not just the Communist Party looking after its own interests. People often debate whether the party has any principles anymore, but I think that the family planning policy is proof that it does—warped principles, perhaps, but principles nonetheless. The restrictive family planning policy earns the party no favor; in fact, it is one of the most hated features of party rule. Most peasants don't care much about democracy, but they often have a visceral hatred for anyone who prevents them from having more sons. So the party is exercising genuine leadership and it is paying a political price in popularity to do what it thinks is right.

But is it right? Whenever we went to villages, we asked about family planning, and we found that the policy caused enormous pain. It often punished the poorest and most miserable peasants by destroying their homes and taking what little they had.

One particular vignette stays with me, from my unauthorized taxi ride around Guizhou Province (the same ride that introduced me to Luo Qingguo, the man who couldn't afford pants for his children). It happened in a tiny hillside hamlet when I peered inside the dilapidated makeshift hut of a couple who had had a son the previous year. The father's parents lived next door, in a larger hut put together from thick branches, brush, straw, and stones gathered along the hillside. The floors were dirt. It was not a countryside view of lush green fields and fresh air. Instead, everywhere I looked there was brown dirt and mud, gray stones and dry wood. The only fragrance I could pick out was of human and animal waste.

The family had had the misfortune to be caught up in a nationwide crackdown by the family planning authorities. The baby was a second child, and the parents had not waited the full four years before a second child is allowed in that area. The baby was born five months before it would have been permitted.

Four days after his birth, a brigade of ten men and women came from the township to spoil the celebration. They demolished the family's original home, strewing stones and straw all over the place.

Then they demanded the equivalent of forty-five dollars, or one year of the couple's meager income, and when the family could not pay, they smashed the parents' chest of drawers—their only furniture aside from a bed.

"They took away our family cow," said Peng Dagui, the sixty-year-old head of the household and grandfather of the baby boy. "I wouldn't let the cow out of my sight. I followed it all the way to the township and pleaded with the officials there. But they didn't care."

Three months later, two dozen officials appeared in the village to take the baby's mother, Wang Zhengmei, to the clinic to be sterilized. Wang, a twenty-seven-year-old with long hair and frightened eyes, did not dare refuse, and, in any case, she was told that she would get $3.50 if she had the operation. She had a tubal ligation, but the officials never gave her the money.

At least rebuilding a home was easier in the Guizhou countryside than it would have been in a city. The baby's father, Peng Fagang, rebuilt the hut in a month from stones and dry grass collected in the fields. The only consolation for the Pengs was that they were not alone: The officials had done the same thing to another family in the village.

This crackdown, which began in early 1991, was the product of a new strategy to get localities to tighten enforcement of the rules. The nation's leaders announced that they were implementing a "responsibility system" for family planning targets. They called in the provincial governors and party secretaries and warned them that if their provinces had too many births, they would be held personally accountable. In other words, they would be fired. The provincial governors became alarmed, called in the county leaders, and passed on the warning. And so it went down to the village level. The result was that the rules were tightened only modestly, but enforcement and punishments were made much harsher.

There was not much impact on people in the cities, but for the 900 million peasants the consequences were enormous. In 1992, the total fertility rate—the expected number of live births for a woman in her childbearing career—dropped to 1.86, the first time it had ever dropped below two births per couple. China had reached targets it had not expected to meet until the year 2010. It would be difficult to imagine any policy anywhere in the world having such a huge effect on the daily lives of so many people.

Where were we at the time? Asleep. I'm embarrassed to say that, for two years, we didn't notice this extraordinary event. Neither did diplomats, scholars, or Chinese intellectuals. It was one of the major policy decisions of that period, but because it happened in the Chinese countryside, nobody had a clue. That is a pretty good indictment of the state of China watching today.

The matriarch of the family planning system is a tubby, beaming grandmother named Peng Peiyun. One of eight children herself, Peng has four children of her own, all born before the one-child policy was dreamed up. Now she oversees the sterilization of millions of women each year. Peng claims that the authorities use persuasion to encourage families to have fewer children. Force, she says, is prohibited—although she can't cite a single example of a family planning worker who has been punished for using force.

She should talk to the people I met in Guizhou.

"Please, can you tell me, ultimately, what is the nation's family planning policy?" a forty-five-year-old grade-school teacher asked when I was in another small village in Guizhou. In 1983, he and his wife had a second child, three years after they had had their first. He had thought that this was permissible. But the policy had apparently changed, so officials fined him $2,456, about seventeen times his annual salary at that time. Since he did not have the money, they deducted it from his salary, docking about 80 percent of his wages for a decade. These fines by installment plan turned out to be common, probably because otherwise no one could pay them.

"They often take things, your furniture, your cow, your pig, your chickens, your preserved meat," said a thirty-five-year-old woman in another village in Guizhou. "If you get sterilized, they take your stuff, and if you don't get sterilized, they beat you. Some people have been beaten badly, family members and women. They take electric batons, and they hit whomever they see."

She and other villagers were gathered in the house of Huang Guohai, a thirty-seven-year-old peasant who has two children, six years apart. Careless with formalities, as peasants in remote areas often are, Huang never got a marriage license when he married eleven years ago. Because he had no license, a brigade of ten people, wielding sticks and screwdrivers, came to his house in 1992 at one o'clock in the morning to punish him for breaking family planning rules—he wasn't quite sure which ones. They took away his wash-basin and black-and-white television. What upset Huang the most, however, was that they confiscated the coffin and funeral clothes he had prepared for his aged mother, to be used when she dies. But there was nothing he could do: "If you don't let them take your things, you'll just get beaten."

Under the responsibility system for family planning, local cadres went out of control all over China. In 1993 we obtained a classified document, *Cankao Xuanpian*, with an account of obstetric atrocities in Hunan Province. Under China's complex quota system for births, the county officials wanted certain babies born in 1992 rather than 1993. "Some district and township officials feared that they would be fined for not meeting the family planning targets, or would not receive their bonuses," the report declares.

So at the end of December the family planning officials formed an "early birth shock brigade" to round up nine women so labor could be induced before the end of the calendar year. On December 30, the team showed up at the home of Li Qiuliang, a twenty-three-year-old who was seven months pregnant. Li had a permit to have her child, and she had broken no rule. Li's mother-in-law pleaded with the officials: "My daughter-in-law's health isn't good, and she may not be able to get pregnant again," the report quotes the woman as saying. "So let her have one baby, someone to look after her and my son when they grow old. It doesn't matter if it's a boy or a girl. After it's born, she'll go get sterilized."

The officials rejected the plea. And at the first-aid station, when the doctor said Li was too frail to undergo induced labor, they swept his protests aside and ordered him to proceed. Li bled severely, fell unconscious, and almost died. As for the baby, it lived for just nine hours.

Family members took Li to the township clinic, which saved her life. Now she has returned home, but the report says she is crippled, without specifying the nature of her injuries. A local official who confirmed the accuracy of the report also told Nick that the only governmental response had been to summon the officials responsible for the early birth shock brigade to a meeting, where they were told not to induce labor in the future. The State Family Planning Commission declined to comment. After Nick's story on Li Qiuliang appeared on page one of *The Times,* the Chinese government was furious. Neither Peng Peiyun nor any other top official had been interested in the case when it appeared in *Cankao Xuanpian,* but now that it was in *The Times* they swung into action. Shortly afterward, they published a rebuttal stating that the classified report had been wrong: Li Qiuliang's baby had been due in mid-January, not in March, and she gave birth on December 31 at the end of the normal gestation period. The rebuttal finessed the question of whether labor had been induced and suggested that the baby would have died anyway.

It is of course entirely possible that the classified document was false. It is conceivable that the county official reached on the telephone also chose to lie. Government reports normally whitewash problems, but it's impossible to prove that in this case the officials preparing the report didn't exaggerate the case instead.

Of course, I tend to believe the original document, because I've found Chinese officials to be pathological liars. But until the government allows people to travel freely, so that journalists can interview Li Qiuliang herself, we can't be sure.

When Nick and I wrote stories about forced abortion and sterilization, we received reproachful letters from organizations like Zero Population Growth that support family planning programs. On the other side of the spectrum, the die-hard congressional critics of abortion were delighted with our stories because they gave them tools with which to attack China. Such reactions distressed us, because people often seemed to have formed their own conclusions long before they looked at the evidence. Even experts debated the policy in a vacuum, without ever going out and talking—without an escort—to some ordinary peasants. Visitors would be far better off talking to peasants and skipping the State Family Planning Commission, rather than the other way around.

Views of China's family planning program are so polarized that almost no one ever tries to wrestle with the hard question: How much coercion is legitimate in controlling a nation's swelling population? The family planning lobbies refuse to acknowledge the enormous suffering that China's policy causes in the countryside. And the antiabortion crowd refuses to recognize that China really does have an urgent need to control its population: 22 percent of the world's people are living on 7 percent of the world's arable land.

As for me, however much I sympathized with China's need to control its population, it was impossible not to feel that the one-child policy was out of control. I now regard China's family planning policy as a major mistake, for two reasons.

First, I find it morally offensive. It puts too much power into the hands of corrupt local officials, who sometimes pocket the family planning fines themselves. The policy also leaves hundreds of millions of peasants miserable. Forced sterilizations and forced abortions strike me as particularly repugnant. It is one thing to support legalized abortion as a choice—among other forms of contraception—but quite another to support a system in which township cadres swoop down on villages and abduct pregnant women.

Second, China may have a brighter future if it has a smaller population, but not if there is a 20 percent shortfall of girls and young women. I see no way in which China can maintain a very restrictive policy without aggravating the imbalance in the sex ratio, particularly as ultrasound machines and eventually amniocentesis become more common. I suspect that China would be a healthier place with a larger, more balanced population than it would be with a smaller population masking a large surplus of males.

I agree that China desperately needs some sort of family planning policy, but I hope that it can move to a less brutal kind of coercion, like the kind that gets Americans to pay taxes or to obey parking rules. Coercion, in the sense of reasonable rewards and punishments, may well be legitimate. But the government needs to retreat from forced sterilization and forced abortion, from knocking down homes, from confiscating the cows of impoverished peasants. Instead, it should rely on fines and subsidies, coupled with intensive counseling, education, and rural development programs, particularly aimed at raising the status of women. We shouldn't fool ourselves: This won't work as well as contraceptive terrorism. China will end up with more people and will perhaps be a poorer country. But at least on my next trip to the hillside villages of Guizhou, I won't see penniless peasant women who've had a baby a bit too soon and consequently lost their homes, their livestock, and their ovaries.

NICHOLAS D. KRISTOF

紀思道

箝口術

CASTRATING
THE
THINKERS

Families, when a child is born
Want it to be intelligent.
I, through intelligence,
Having wrecked my whole life,
Only hope the baby will prove
Ignorant and stupid.
Then he will crown a tranquil life
By becoming a cabinet minister.

— Su Dongpo, eleventh-century poet

9

Ren Wanding, one of China's first human rights activists. [Photo by Nicholas D. Kristof.]

Qin Benli was a crusty old bear of a man, a newspaper editor in his seventies who had proven himself one of the bravest journalists in China. As editor of the *World Economic Herald*, he almost single-handedly redefined the limits of what could be published. Then around the time of the Tiananmen crackdown in 1989, his newspaper was closed, his reporters were tossed into prison, and he was put under house arrest.

At that time I was looking for someone in China to interview on the record for a long profile. Privately, most people were scathing about the Communist Party, but they refused to be quoted by name. To make the story come alive, I searched for someone who could speak openly about his disillusionment, his personal anguish, his own tangle of feelings. One person after another refused me. Finally I thought about Qin Benli.

Qin was then suffering from cancer, with just a few months to live. He had nothing to lose, and I thought he might want to get some things off his chest. He was nominally under house arrest, but at that time he was in a Shanghai hospital under loose guard. I figured that I might be able to get into the hospital and slip by the guards in some way. So I sent messages through trusted friends, asking Qin if he would see me again. Soon the message came back: "Thank you for your interest, and I hope you and Sheryl are well. But please excuse me for not meeting you. The party has asked me not to see any foreigners, and I must oblige."

That got me thinking. What was behind this culture of silence in China? Why did no one protest against the regime? Where did Chinese keep their principles?

In the Soviet Union, a succession of brave dissidents stood up for what they believed in. In China, by contrast, almost no one protested openly. Most leading intellectuals publicly supported what they privately denounced. They appeared on television, earnestly scribbling notes as various party officials delivered speeches about the virtues of socialism. Abroad, people blame Deng Xiaoping and Li Peng for the repression in China; that is true enough, but a share of the blame also must be laid at the feet of the ordinary citizens who accept it.

I began asking my friends why they were moral wimps. Gradually I realized that the question led to ethical dilemmas that go to the heart of the relationship between the citizen and the state in China. In the West, we have the luxury of being able to say publicly what we think. We scarcely understand the concept of being forced into repulsive compromises. But in China, everyone makes these compromises and the question is simply where to draw the line. Nearly all Chinese show up at political study sessions and lie through their teeth. Virtually all Chinese are collaborators. Some of the rest are dead.

Moreover, the liars and the cheats may be taking the honorable path. I thought of Gregory, whom we would have sent to a Chinese school if he had been a little older. What if I were a Chinese father, wishing the best for my son? What would I tell him to do in political study classes? If the exam called for assessing Chairman Mao's contributions to the building of Chinese socialism, would I really counsel him to mention the deaths of 30 million people in the famine of 1958–1961? Of course not. I would tell him to parrot back what the teachers wanted. I would tell him to lie.

If I didn't train him to lie, then he would never get into a first-rate high school or into any university at all. He would end up as a factory worker with no chance for ever getting ahead. So of course I would urge him to lie, even teach him how to do so if necessary. And if Gregory resisted and said he wanted to write his exams with a clean conscience, I would yell at him that he had to think of his future. I would order him to lie.

Ren Wanding is one of the bravest, most principled people I know. I admire him enormously. But he is a terrible father.

Ren is a small, lean accountant whose Coke-bottle glasses make him look like a great horned owl. He is unimpressive when you first meet him—he wears old, rumpled clothes and has a ragged haircut—yet he is essentially the founder of China's human rights movement. Other dissidents focused on democracy; his interest was human rights. Ren helped lead the 1978–79 Democracy Wall movement and was sentenced administratively, without benefit of a trial, to three years in prison for his political activities. Even in prison, Ren refused to acknowledge any mistake, and he used the nib of a discarded pen to write a four-volume book on human rights—on toilet paper. The warden was so outraged that he kept Ren in prison for another year after the sentence expired.

After he was released, Ren found work as an accountant for a factory and kept quiet for a few years. Then at the end of 1988, after much soul-searching, he decided to take on the regime once more. We met at the coffee shop of the Jinglun Hotel, and afterward he came by our house—where he turned up the stereo to drown out the bugs. My story about him was my first front-page article from China, and he was the first dissident whose safety I agonized over. After the story appeared, I was terrified that he would be arrested again. But he wasn't, and he grew bolder. He participated energetically in the Tiananmen democracy movement, giving speeches on the university campuses and at Tiananmen Square.

When the troops moved in with tanks and machine guns, we all knew that Ren was headed for prison again. His wife, Zhang Fengying, pleaded with him to flee. "Everyone else is running away," she said. "Why don't you?"

"I'm not leaving," Ren replied. "I believe that what I am doing is right, and I'm going to take responsibility for my actions. Besides, where would I go? And if everyone runs away, who will be left to explain what really happened?"

Zhang had no answer for that. Ren stayed in their little home above the factory where he worked. One evening after the crackdown, there was a wire report that he'd been arrested, so I called up to check. He came to the phone, and I explained with some embarrassment that I was calling to find out if he'd been imprisoned.

"Do you think they'll arrest me?" he asked me soberly. "I haven't done anything wrong."

"I just don't know, Old Ren," I said softly. "Sometimes it doesn't matter whether you've done anything wrong." How could I tell him that I was sure that the police would arrest him and sentence him to prison for many years?

Sure enough, a few hours after our conversation, they came for Ren Wanding. A court sentenced him to seven years in prison for counterrevolutionary offenses, and he is serving the term in the rundown Beijing No. 2 Prison. His eyesight is failing because his cell has little light, and the warden and guards have had other prisoners, common felons, bully him and humiliate him.

My point, though, is not to talk about what Ren is going through. At least he knew what he was getting into. At least he chose this path. His family didn't.

After Ren was arrested, his wife and daughter were evicted from their home. When they stayed with friends, the police threatened the friends and forced them to turn Zhang and her daughter out on the street. Neither the mother nor the daughter had a Beijing *hukou,* so the police tried to force them to return to Zhang's parents' home in the city of Tianjin. Zhang wanted to be in Beijing, near her husband, and finally she found a miserable apartment in the suburbs. But their daughter, without a Beijing *hukou,* wasn't allowed to go to school. The girl, who was born in 1977, had been just a tiny child when Ren was first arrested. She was twelve when he was arrested again, and the shock and the persecution proved too much to bear.

"She was scared sick," Zhang explained to Sheryl. "She was mentally wounded. Her heart was upset, and she would scream at night. She was afraid. It's best for a child to have her father with her. She didn't understand why her papa was not there, why the police were treating us the way they did."

Zhang took her daughter to a hospital in Nanjing, where they both stayed for about six months. When they finally got back to Beijing, they found their tiny apartment boarded up with a metal sheet—with all their possessions inside. During the next six months, Zhang moved six times, often squeezing in with sympathetic friends. Finally, the authorities helped her find living quarters: about two hours by bus outside central Beijing.

That's where Sheryl met with her one rainy afternoon in the fall of 1993. Zhang's room was fairly spacious, but the walls and the roof were taped up with pieces of square white paper, like a hundred patches on a torn quilt. In one corner, the rain seeped in, all the way to the floor. Zhang had brought all her possessions: her husband's books, her clothes, her daughter's school notepads. Her daughter was attending a rural school, with peasant boys and girls. Between her hospitalization and the refusal of the authorities to allow her to attend Beijing schools, she had missed two years of schooling, so she is older than most of her classmates.

"I'm so muddled," Zhang said. "I have no regrets about my husband. If he were an embezzler or a murderer, then it'd be different.

Then I'd dump him. But Ren Wanding is trying to push China forward.

"Still, I thirst for a home, my own place. Sometimes I feel I want to die. Really! But I can't. I have a responsibility. If Ren Wanding doesn't come out and my child's still young, what would happen to her? I've got to figure everything out for us now—where to live, what we eat, what we wear.

"I'm a traditional Chinese wife. I want to marry only once, and I think my husband's not bad. But sometimes I get tired of life, and now I have to be both mom and dad. When I cut my hand or run into some problem, I think, oh, if you were only here, life would be so much better!"

What a lousy husband! What an irresponsible father! Was it right for Ren Wanding to campaign for human rights, knowing that he was risking not only his own freedom but also the well-being of his daughter? Or would he have been a better man, a more honorable man, if he had put his family first? The last thing I want to do is criticize Ren Wanding, who is one of the people I respect most in the world. But I do not think it is necessarily wrong for someone to keep quiet in similar circumstances, to turn a blind eye to human rights abuses, out of concern for his daughter. In China, to speak out is to invite punishment not only on oneself but also on one's loved ones. That makes for an agonizing moral calculus.

This is not a new problem. For thousands of years Chinese scholars have struggled between their ambitions and their consciences. Confucians were supposed to tell emperors frankly what they thought of them, and the result was a large number of dead and battered Confucians.

One of the greatest Confucian scholars of the Ming dynasty was Fang Xiaoru, a brilliant scholar who was born in 1357. By all accounts, he was a nice fellow as well as a genius. When Fang was eighteen, his father was imprisoned and Fang applied to be punished in place of his father. The request was rejected, and the father died in prison a year later.

Fang became a close adviser to the second emperor of the Ming dynasty, but perhaps his advice wasn't very good—another member of the imperial family launched a rebellion and civil war and overthrew the emperor. The new emperor, who chose as his imperial name Yongle, or Eternal Happiness, badly needed Fang's endorsement to legitimize the usurpation. He asked, apparently nicely, for Fang to remain at court and approve the new regime. Fang responded by denouncing him as a criminal, and the new emperor applied all the imaginative tortures available at the time. By one account, the Emperor of Eternal Happiness threatened to execute Fang and all his relatives to the ninth degree. Fang supposedly replied that it would not matter: The emperor could execute Fang's relatives to the tenth degree, but he would not change his stand.

Eternal Happiness obliged. He had Fang cut to pieces in the public square. He then exterminated all Fang's relatives, however distant the relationship. More than 900 people were killed, including all members of Fang's extended family and his neighbors, students, friends, and anybody else who had ever had contact with him. Fang's wife and four children were a bit quicker; they committed suicide.

It's an impressive story, and it's clear that Fang was a principled Confucian. But I wonder what his wife thought about all this; perhaps she would have preferred that Fang be more of a family man.

Han Dongfang, the labor leader who was infected with tuberculosis while in prison, is at least a family man. He's as bold and brave as any Chinese, yet I once saw him flinch. It was at the end of six hours of interviews, and I had stood up and was preparing to go. His wife, Chen Jingyun, a pretty woman with long, smooth hair, came to say good-bye. I pulled out my notebook to ask her a few questions.

"She's not involved in any of this," Han said hurriedly, trying to shoo her away. "This is something that I'm working on alone." I asked her how to write her name, and Han grew more flustered still. His wife seemed to find it amusing that he should be so protective of her, but I found it reassuring: He abruptly seemed a bit less of a hero and a bit more of a human.

Chen told me something else: She was two months pregnant, even though she did not have permission to have a baby. After some soul-searching, I mentioned that fact in my article. I thought it was relevant to their story that the authorities might punish them by forcing Chen to have an abortion, and that it was a risk they were prepared to take. But I also worried that my article would be the avenue for informing the government of the pregnancy; I didn't want a forced abortion on my conscience.

In the end, it worked out all right. The authorities did not force Chen to have an abortion, and my article may have protected her—which is what I had hoped at the time. The couple was allowed to leave for the United States before the birth, and the government pretended not to know that she was pregnant without permission.

More and more, I came to see that one major reason for the culture of silence is that people don't want to get their family members in trouble. Conversely, one of the government's most effective sanctions is the fear that it will punish not only dissidents but their children, siblings, and parents as well.

After Wei Jingsheng was released from prison after fourteen and a half years, Sheryl and I asked him over dinner whether his family had suffered. He eagerly recounted how his sister and brother had been refused permission to travel abroad, how his brother-in-law had been denied promotions, how his niece had been discriminated against in school. And then I asked him whether he felt it was right that he had made his family members pay this price.

"Every time my brother and sister visited me in prison, I apologized to them," he said slowly. "And they told me to shut up. They told me not to waste visiting hours by apologizing.

"And there's no other way. If you're going to take this road, you've got to take it to the end. Lots of people are ready to sacrifice themselves for democracy. But not to sacrifice their wives, their children."

"So, Wei Jingsheng," I asked, "what if you had been married, with children, at the time of the Democracy Wall movement? Would you have been more careful? Would you have held back?"

There was a long silence as he considered the question.

"Maybe," he said finally. "Maybe I would have."

I had the chance to watch firsthand as one young man, Xu Yiruo, grappled with the question of whether to speak out. Xu, a Catholic from Shandong Province, is a serious, anguished young man with bushy hair and glasses. He spoke to me in a grassy glade by Beijing's second ring road, with shrubbery surrounding us so that no one would spot him. He had reason to be careful; he had already served three stints in prison by the time of our conversation in 1993. In each case, the reason was his support for democracy.

Xu was trying to escape from China, and he contacted me partly to ask if I could help. But I explained that I couldn't, and he understood. We talked about his experiences, which I found fascinating. Here was a student whom no one had ever heard of, who had played only a very minor role in the Tiananmen movement, and his life had been sheer hell ever since the crackdown. Moreover, during his latest stint in prison, he had been mining clay for export to Japan and manufacturing Christmas tree lights for export to Britain. That was explosive information, for the Chinese government was denying that prison-made goods were exported—and there was something wrenching about the idea of Western families gathering around a Christmas tree and enjoying the sparkle of colored lights made by political prisoners working eighteen hours a day, seven days a week, in Shandong Province. It was fairly easy to confirm the exports, partly because the Shandong authorities offered over the phone to sell me prison-mined clay so that I could ship it to America.

I asked Xu if I could write about his story, but I told him that I would need to use his name. I laid out as fairly as I could the consequences for him, and I acknowledged that it would make it more difficult for him to escape from China. But he reflected and agreed. What he worried about wasn't his own safety but that of his family.

"I know this is dangerous, and I thought about it over and over before giving an interview," he told me. "But there are so many things that foreigners don't know about China. If I don't speak out, then none of this will be known. I figure this is the time to get the word out about what is going on, to encourage the world to put pressure on China to stop violating human rights. So I think it's worth the risk to speak out."

Then, in a rush, his facade crumbled. Tears welled in his eyes, and his voice caught. "Do you think they'll do anything to my parents?" he asked. "What about my sisters? I've got two older sisters. Will they be punished?"

We talked for another hour or so, as the sun set, and he made me promise to send a copy of my article to his parents. That way, he said, perhaps they would understand his motives. "I'm afraid that if I'm arrested, there'll be no one to explain to them why I'm speaking out. But I've got to do this."

I received a few phone calls from Xu Yiruo after that, and I learned that he had sneaked as far as Shenzhen—just across the border from Hong Kong. Then the calls stopped. I feared that he had been arrested, and perhaps punished more severely than ever for cooperating with me. But in early 1994, while I was in New York, I received a call from Xu Yiruo and met him several times. He, too, was in Manhattan, having escaped by speedboat to Hong Kong and then won political asylum to come to the United States. He said that the police had visited his family after my article appeared, but that the authorities did not harass his parents.

For all the fury that people felt after Tiananmen, I know of only one official who resigned in protest: Zhang Wei, a rising star in the city of Tianjin. Zhang was kept under house arrest for more than a year, and he courageously agreed to see me. But even he did not want to be quoted by name. Likewise, even the bravest of the dissidents— Fang Lizhi, the physicist; Zhang Weiguo, the journalist—calculated carefully what they could get away with. I know not a single person in all China who speaks absolutely candidly.

I later heard that Qin Benli, the dying newspaper editor, had decided not to see me because he was afraid of what the party would do to his family. Like many older party members, he had also absorbed the culture of acquiescence, in which open protest is almost unimaginable. He had worked all his life for the Communist Party, and to criticize it publicly would be to abandon his life's work, to betray every principle he had ever learned about party discipline.

"You have to understand what they've gone through," a midcareer party member said of people like Qin Benli. "A lot of them have given most of their lives to the Communist Party. You can't just throw that away like an old shirt. And when they first got in trouble, in the Anti-Rightist Campaign, a lot of them spent the next twenty years in disgrace or in prison or work camps. Probably half of them died during that experience. So the survivors have learned to go along, to live through the political campaigns, and not to disagree lightly."

Except for occasional (and often short-lived) mavericks like the Ming dynasty scholar Fang Xiaoru, intellectuals in China have always tended to be lackeys of dictators—ever since the time of Sima Qian in the first and second centuries B.C. One of the greatest figures of ancient China, Sima Qian wrote a monumental history that is still an important record. He is to East Asia what Herodotus is to Europe, and he was one of the leading courtiers in the retinue of the Han dynasty emperor Wu Di. But Sima Qian made the political mistake of speaking up on behalf of a defeated general who he thought was being criticized unfairly. Sima Qian had a point: The defeat wasn't the general's fault but the emperor's, for the emperor had failed to send reinforcements as the general requested. Nevertheless, the emperor was outraged that someone would stick up for the general.

As Sima Qian later wrote to a friend: "I could not make myself fully understood. Our enlightened Ruler did not wholly perceive my meaning. . . . So I was put into prison, and I was never able to make clear my fervent loyalty. Because it was believed that I had tried to deceive the Emperor, I was finally forced to submit to the judgment of the law officials."

The government at that time had a system of allowing condemned people to pay a fine in lieu of punishment. Indeed, when it ran short of cash it convicted some wealthy figure of an invented crime so as to raise funds. Sima Qian was sentenced to be castrated, but he had so many rich friends that he should have been able to raise the money he needed. Unfortunately, his friends abandoned him once he was in disfavor.

"Of my friends and associates, not one would save me," Sima wrote.

Among those near the Emperor no one said so much as a word for me. My body is not wood or stone, yet alone I had to face the officials of the law. . . . I was thrown into the "silkworm chamber" [where castrations were performed]. . . . I have brought upon myself the scorn and mockery even of my native village and I have soiled and shamed my father's name. With what face can I again ascend and stand before the grave mound of my father and mother? Though a hundred generations pass, my defilement will only become greater. This is the thought that wrenches my bowels nine times a day. Sitting at home, I am befuddled as though I had lost something. I go out, and then realize I do not know where I am going. Each time I think of this shame, the sweat pours down my back and soaks my robe.

Sima Qian finished his great historical work as a eunuch, "a mutilated being who dwells in degradation," as he told his friend. Ever since then, Chinese intellectuals have all been a bit like that.

"Most Chinese intellectuals still feel castrated, in that we don't dare stand up for what is right," Huali, our friend the university lecturer, said glumly. "We don't have outspoken dissidents, the way the Soviet Union produced Sakharov. We don't have that tradition, and anyway, those in power are so strong that you can't hope to get away with challenging them."

The culture of silence derives in part from the traditional Chinese emphasis on keeping one's head down. A popular saying reminds people that "the roof beam that sticks out is the first to rot." Even if Confucian scholars were supposed to give candid advice to the emperors, they were not encouraged to go public with their criticisms. Scholars were always part of the state apparatus, and independent academic analysis was virtually unknown in China.

The Chinese Communist Party added to the traditional conformist pressure by insisting that citizens not only comply with all laws but also positively declare their support. To do this is to *biao tai*, or express one's personal position. This began before the Communists even took power, and it has been an integral part of the control mechanism ever since.

After Tiananmen, every office in the country called a series of meetings in which employees had to stand up and *biao tai*, thanking the army for suppressing the "counterrevolutionary rebellion." In some cases, even those who had lost family members were supposed to do this. And, for the most part, they did. Virtually all the people I knew went to these meetings and lied about their most fundamental beliefs.

For some people, it was a joke. For others, it was a game, no more lying than an author is lying when writing a novel—everybody knows that it is fiction, so there is no deception. For still others, lying was a painful necessity, and they had to be coaxed each step of the way by the person leading the discussion. Finally, there were those, particularly older people, who seemed to have become disoriented by their decades in the Communist Party. They couldn't tell truth from falsehood.

After the June 4 Tiananmen crackdown, for example, one of our more courageous friends went to the home of a senior official. The official was horrified at what the army was doing and bitterly denounced the party leadership. "Those fascists!" she kept saying. "Those fascists!" My friend agreed and openly criticized the Communist leaders.

A couple of weeks later, after the hard-liners had reestablished party discipline, the *danwei* party committee called a meeting to expel my friend from the Communist Party. Some other young people were refusing to go along with the expulsion and were threatening to vote against it. The government minister in charge threatened to dissolve the entire department if my friend was not expelled. Everyone would be sent off to another job. So my friend convinced the party members to go along with the charade and expel him, and a party meeting was called to denounce him. He was expecting it, but even so, it hurt to have people rise one by one and criticize him. Among those who did so was the senior party official who earlier had condemned the leaders as fascists.

"It wasn't a trick," my friend said later, after his release from prison. "She believed what she was saying. The party changed her mind. That's what the Communist Party does: It changes you, it takes away your personality, it turns you inside out."

"Let me tell you about my mom and dad," Louli, a doctor friend of ours, suggested to Sheryl and me over lunch. We had asked her how the party warps its members, and she put down her chopsticks and became terribly serious.

"Dad was an intellectual, a brilliant scholar who placed number one out of 2,000 people taking the exams in his province. He had a terrific future in the Nationalist Party, but he was infected by the 'New Thinking.' He was revolted by the corruption. And so he fled to Yanan to join the Communists.

"Then he supported Wang Shiwei's call for more democracy in 1942. Dad saw what happened to Wang Shiwei, and he was afraid for himself. He knew that Wang Shiwei wasn't a Trotskyite, wasn't a spy, but Dad didn't dare say anything.

"Then in the 1950s, Dad was investigated as a possible rightist, and he missed being labeled a rightist by a hair. Mom was the same. She had been the only daughter of a landlord, but she was appalled by society then, and she stole her parents' money to run away to

Yanan and join the Communist Party. But then after the revolution she kept getting in trouble because her pedigree was bad. She was of landlord stock.

"When the Cultural Revolution began, Dad was a university president. So he got in trouble right away. He was struggled against every day. I remember when I was twelve years old, and I was called to the stage of a big struggle session to denounce him. He watched me, and I stood there, and they ordered me to inform on him, to tell about the bad things that he had done. I hesitated, and I could see him looking at me. And then I told the crowd that when I got a good grade in school, Dad was very happy and gave me a reward, a little present. That was unrevolutionary of him. So I denounced my father.

"But he didn't hate me. He knew I had no choice.

"Then he was sent off to prison for eleven years, and Mom and I were sent away to work in a chemical factory. We visited him once, and he was in rags, in cotton clothing that was falling off him. He was gaunt, famished. We couldn't bear to look at him.

"So after Dad got out, he knew that there were problems in the Communist Party. But then he had a new burst of hope when Deng Xiaoping rose to power. Dad thought everything would be different. Sometimes he urged me to join the party, because it would help my career, give me opportunities to go abroad. But I never would join the party.

"Finally, after June 4 [the Tiananmen massacre], Dad gave up on the party. He lost all hope in it. He told us that he regretted ever going to Yanan. He was sorry that he had devoted his life to the party. He stopped urging us to join. And it wasn't just the killing of the students. It was also the corruption. Dad joined the party in the 1930s because of his disgust with the corruption then. And he says that now it's worse than it was then. The Communist Party is more corrupt than the Nationalist Party ever was. He says these things openly to his old buddies from Yanan. They all think like that. They've all given up.

"But people like Dad, they've been left handicapped by a lifetime of being struggled against. Dad's fine on the outside, but the party has destroyed him on the inside. He has no courage. When I was going to college, Dad didn't want me to study Chinese or journalism or any topic like that. He thought I would end up in trouble, end up the target of some political campaign. He got me to study medicine, because he said it would be safer. I'd be shielded from politics. So I became a doctor. But I'm not like his generation. I told you, the party destroyed them from the inside out. They're shells. People of my generation are bolder. We can't be intimidated so easily. We won't put up with so much."

As a foreigner, I was not gagged nearly as much as my Chinese friends. But even I sometimes found myself forced to lie. As we were preparing to leave Beijing in 1993, Sheryl and I decided to buy several Chinese silk carpets to take with us. We called up Xixu, a peasant from Henan who in the previous few years had become a carpet dealer in Beijing. He showed up one night in a taxi with a dozen carpets, and we met him at the gate of our compound so that the People's Armed Police would allow him inside. After forty minutes of admiring his rugs and bargaining fiercely, we picked one striking red carpet. He lugged the rest with him and said he would find a taxi at the gate to the compound.

An hour later, he telephoned us, practically in tears. "They took my carpets," he said. "All of them!"

"Who took your carpets?"

"The guards at the gate of your compound. They confiscated them. Every one of them. They said I wasn't allowed to do business inside the compound, and so they took all my carpets."

I was outraged, for there was no such rule against doing business. The loss of eleven carpets would be a terrible blow to Xixu, wiping out all his profits for six months or more. The State Security agents at the gate had probably decided that they could use silk carpets in their own homes. I told Xixu to come back immediately, so that I could try to use my status as a foreigner to get his rugs back. Usually Sheryl's face was more suited to dealing with Chinese and getting information, but this was one occasion when I figured it would help to have a Western nose. The officials were unlikely to dismiss me rudely in the way that they would Sheryl or any other ethnic Chinese. So Xixu said he could be at the gate in twenty minutes, and I told him to meet me there.

We marched together to the nearby third-floor State Security office of the compound. It was 10:00 P.M., and the door was locked.

Peering through the window in the door, I could see that the hallway was dark—but that the carpets were stacked up against a wall. I pounded on the door. Silence. I pounded again, and someone inside shouted in Chinese to be quiet. I pounded on the door again, to show that I was not intimidated and would not back down. Finally, a middle-aged man emerged in the corridor, wearing only boxer shorts and a T-shirt. Seeing a foreigner, he disappeared and threw on a pair of trousers, then came to the doorway to meet me. Unfortunately, he spotted Xixu beside me.

"You!" he roared. "What are you doing here? Have you brought this foreigner? I told you to go home! Now, go! Go! I'll deal with you later."

Xixu slinked backward and seemed ready to oblige.

"He didn't get me," I protested. "I got him. You took his carpets. I invited him into the compound, and then you took his carpets. I want them back now."

"This has got nothing to do with you," the man told me politely, and then he shook his fist at Xixu, who was cringing near the stairs. "Go away, now!" the man ordered Xixu.

"We're not going until we get the carpets," I declared, but Xixu was tugging at my arm. "Let's go," he was saying. "We can come tomorrow."

It became a triangular conversation. I was yelling at the State Security boss, who was yelling at Xixu, who was pleading with me to drop the matter. Finally I declared that I would return the next morning and that we expected to get the carpets then.

On the way to the office the next morning, Xixu coached me on being nice and apologetic and conciliatory—the opposite of the emotions I felt. He said that if I criticized the confiscation of the carpets, he would never get them back.

The State Security boss was in his office, and Xixu began by apologizing for everything but his birth. "I'm so sorry to have disturbed you and caused this fuss," Xixu said. "I know you're very busy, and I don't want to trouble you. I'd like to apologize for breaking your rules and causing you this nuisance."

The State Security boss's eyes gleamed with satisfaction, but then he tried to wring from me a statement that it had been absolutely proper to seize the carpets in the first place. "We have to look after the compound's security, and protect the foreigners from businessmen who might take advantage of them," he said. "You must admit that's proper."

I grunted ambiguously.

"Some of these people sell things that are poorly made, or else they charge too much," he continued. "That's why there's a law that foreigners can buy only from state-owned companies like the Friendship Store."

"Oh," I said brightly, pulling out my notebook. "I didn't know about that law. I should write an article about that law, because most people have never heard about it. What is the citation?"

"Well, it's not really a law. But you're best off buying from state-owned companies. Safer! And you must admit that all countries sometimes confiscate goods when it is necessary to protect consumers."

"Yes, I believe that in North Korea the authorities act in the same way," I said pleasantly. The State Security boss was puzzled, and Xixu looked reproachfully at me.

"All countries have such rules to protect consumers, right?" the State Security boss repeated.

"Yes," I said wearily. I could feel Xixu's eyes burning into my face.

"So what we did was really quite reasonable, right?"

"It's certainly reasonable to try to protect people," I said weakly.

The State Security boss tried to wring from me not only a statement that he had done no wrong but actually a thank-you for protecting me by stealing Xixu's carpets. I felt like slugging him. Instead, mindful that Xixu would slug me if I did so, I meekly nodded my head a lot. In the end, after a week of hassles and some expense to Xixu, we got his carpets back. But I lost my honor.

What distressed me was that I had been forced to lie, to abandon my principles, to hide all my true feelings—to suffer the fate of the Chinese. If I had used the words that were on my mind, State Security would have punished Xixu beyond just stealing his carpets.

So even I as a foreigner had to make compromises from time to time. I never wrote a self-criticism, as a few of my journalistic colleagues were forced to do, but I did go out of my way to try to be nice to Foreign Ministry officials. I regularly thanked them for their kind cooperation, even when they were being most obstreperous. I once went a bit further, and I still feel a bit uneasy about it. It was May 1992, and the Foreign Ministry and State Security apparatus seemed to be preparing to expel me from China. I was being summoned to the Foreign Ministry on a weekly basis for "stern warnings," and the government was refusing to give Gregory a visa or residence permit. The tax authorities were auditing my taxes, and we understood from Chinese friends that there was a move afoot to expel us.

I enlisted the help of three visiting American delegations, and each of them obligingly brought up the topic in their discussions with Chinese officials. Expelling an American journalist would harm Chinese-American relations, they emphasized. And, especially, don't kick out *The New York Times*! Shortly afterward, there was a reception with more than 1,000 Chinese officials and several hundred Americans. A minister-level acquaintance sought me out to discuss the problem.

"The matter is very complicated right now, and it's extremely delicate," he said. "It could go either way. But it would help the people who are arguing in your favor if they had something to hold up, something that they could point to, to say that your attitude had improved. Now, speaking as a friend, what I would suggest is that you write a letter to the Foreign Ministry. Don't apologize. Don't write a self-criticism. Just say that you have noted the Foreign Ministry's concerns and that you believe that journalists should engage in fair and accurate reporting. At least your supporters could point to that, and it would help them in the internal arguments that are now going on."

I thought about it all day, and talked to Sheryl about what to do. I didn't like the idea of writing such a letter, because it could be interpreted as an admission that I had done something wrong. I didn't want to play politics with the Foreign Ministry. And yet, there was nothing particularly objectionable about the wording of the letter. Moreover, I thought I owed it to *The Times* to try to maintain a bureau in Beijing—plus I wanted to stay as well. So, with my lip curled in disgust, I wrote the letter and had my driver deliver it by hand the next morning. It worked. A few days later, the harassment stopped. I heard through Chinese friends that my problem had been solved.

For a journalist, of course, the most pressing moral conundrums involved Chinese friends. What right did we have to contact Chinese acquaintances, to befriend them, to ask them about politics, to ask them for documents, when that could get them into huge trouble? A Chinese official who gave us a classified document could easily be sentenced to a long prison term. Bai Weiji, a Chinese friend of my *Washington Post* colleague, Lena Sun, is now serving a ten-year sentence for giving her confidential documents. Bai's wife was imprisoned for six years, and, with no one to care for their baby daughter, they almost had to put the child up for adoption.

The only clear rule that Sheryl and I established was that we didn't ask friends to give us classified documents. If friends offered, then we accepted; it happened surprisingly often, given the risks involved. Beyond that, we wandered through a minefield, probing with our toes—or, more accurately, those of our Chinese buddies. When visiting sensitive friends, we always tried to establish that we were not being tailed, and we never used our own telephone to set up meetings. But we knew that we would eventually make a mistake. In fifty meetings, State Security would manage to tail us once. We could reduce the risks to our Chinese friends but not eliminate them.

One of the last military people I met in Beijing was a midcareer official, an extremely nervous fellow with highly classified information that he wanted to sell. In particular, he claimed to have firsthand information and photos relating to Chinese shipments of M-11 missiles to Pakistan. The M-11 is a medium-range missile that can carry a nuclear warhead, and it is at the center of a nasty dispute between Beijing and Washington. The United States accuses China of having sold the missiles to Pakistan, a charge that China denies.

At first I thought the man was a State Security or Military Intelligence agent trying to trap me. It seemed too much of a coincidence that he should offer precisely the kind of classified information that was in the most demand. I explained to him that I could never pay for information. He asked me to introduce him to an American diplomat, and I said I couldn't do that either. While American intelligence would love to have a spy in the M-11 program, it would compromise my independence as a journalist if I acted as a procurer for the CIA. We haggled and haggled. I wanted him to give me the information, no strings attached, and he wanted to get some access to a diplomat who might pay. He asked what would happen if he telephoned the American Embassy, and I told him that the line was surely bugged. He asked for a home phone number of a diplomat, and I said I couldn't give him that either.

Gradually, my suspicions faded to some extent. I quizzed him about his story, and it held together. He showed me his identification cards and answered a variety of questions—I can't quite explain what kind, for fear of helping the authorities track him down—that left me thinking that he probably was legitimate. Moreover, he insisted that the M-11 sales to Pakistan not only had taken place but were continuing. It seemed unlikely that State Security would send an agent out to confirm the world's suspicions of China's proliferation. I met him two more times, and he explained that he simply wanted to make a buck.

"If my neighbor's kid gets a toy, then my kid wants it too," he explained during a tense meeting one night under a streetlamp. "Life's a competition now. Everybody's trying to make money. Everyone! Hey, I'm just trying to cash in on what I have."

The first time I saw him, to build rapport, I asked him about his family. He talked lovingly about his wife and child, who knew nothing about his bid to be a spy. The next two times, I also asked about his wife and child, and I thought about them a lot. If he did give me classified information about M-11 shipments to Pakistan, then it would be a major story. But there was some chance that the counter-intelligence authorities would track him down and figure out that he was the source. And then he would be shot.

I didn't want to deal with that. In our last meeting, I found myself suggesting that he just call it quits and give up trying to be a spy. I stopped pressing him for information about the M-11s. I didn't want to create an orphan.

In the West, we have the tradition of Antigone, of the righteous person who is obstinate and unreasonable and ultimately pursues justice until enveloped by disaster. We may not want to go to prison, like Thoreau, for refusing to pay taxes for causes we do not believe in. But we admire that kind of unreasonableness, that kind of principled obstinacy.

The Chinese, by contrast, appear to be more sympathetic to unprincipled reasonableness. The Chinese historical figure whom young people most admire, according to one poll, is Zhou Enlai. It is an interesting choice, because Zhou was a master of compromise. He abandoned his friends right and left, even leading struggle sessions against them, to maintain his own position. He might well have said in his own defense that as a result, by remaining in power, he was able to intercede in modest ways to improve the conditions for his friends. In some cases he saved their lives, and he certainly helped keep China together. But even his ability or willingness to intercede was limited: He allowed his own foster daughter, Sun Weishi, whom he loved dearly, to be kidnapped and imprisoned by his rival, Madame Mao. Only after Sun had been tortured to death did Zhou Enlai risk taking a stand, by rushing in a rescue team. It was too late; the torturers had already cremated the body.

· A Tibetan friend in Beijing reminds me in many ways of Zhou Enlai, in the best sense. Phunkhang Goranangpa is a cheerful, earnest mountain of a man, with a voice that rumbles alternately in Chinese, Tibetan, and English. First his father, and then he, faced the vexing question of how best to serve Tibet. And each chose to work within the system, to be a collaborator, as it were. His father, Phutsog Wangyel, came to China to study and became a Communist in the 1930s. "The Nationalists were repressing ethnic minorities, so it was natural for my father to choose the Communist Party," Phunkhang reflected in his office in Beijing. Phunkhang's father then supported the Communists' "liberation" of Tibet: "My father didn't want to see bloodshed in Tibet. He thought that whatever would happen, the Chinese Army would go into Tibet. So he thought it would be better if there were less bloodshed."

Once Tibet was firmly under Chinese control, Phunkhang's father became the prototype collaborator: the highest-ranking Tibetan in the country. He was the only Tibetan to serve on the regional political-military committee that controlled southwestern China, and he accompanied the Dalai Lama to Beijing to meet Mao. Yet he used his influence and mastery of Chinese to urge the central government to adopt a more sympathetic policy toward Tibet. As a result, he came under suspicion and was removed from Tibet and relocated to Beijing in 1958. Two years later, after an abortive Tibetan rebellion in which the Dalai Lama fled, he was arrested and disappeared into the Chinese gulag. Phunkhang was then ten years old.

Phunkhang's mother was pressed to divorce her husband—to *huaqing jiexian,* to draw a clear line between them, as the Chinese say. Perhaps if she had, it would have been better for her and for her family. Many other men and women divorced their spouses in times of political difficulty. Even Deng Xiaoping's wife divorced him in 1933 when he was in disgrace, dumping him for another man who at the time seemed to have better career prospects. But Phunkhang's mother adored her husband and stood by him. So after the Cultural Revolution began in 1966, both Phunkhang and his mother were arrested. His mother died in 1969, supposedly after committing suicide by slashing her wrists on a radiator. More likely she was beaten or starved to death.

As for Phunkhang himself, he was kept in isolation for two years. In that time he never saw the sun and never had a conversation with another human being. He suffered from severe lung disease and almost died of it. Finally, after six years in prison, he was released in 1975. Three years later, his father was released as well, after eighteen years in prison.

Phunkhang went to the United States in 1981 to attend university, and he tried to do what his father had done: to play the role of an intermediary between the Dalai Lama and the Chinese leadership. He had the implicit support of General Secretary Hu Yaobang in these efforts, but the talks collapsed after Hu was dismissed in 1987. Phunkhang next started the International Fund for the Development of Tibet, which raises money to give scholarships for Tibetans so that they can study in the United States. The fund also promotes Tibetan culture and holds conferences and sports exchanges.

Everyone was suspicious of Phunkhang. The Communist Party tried to figure out what he was up to, and so did the Dalai Lama's people. In fact, Phunkhang has no hidden agenda. He simply wants to help his homeland. He returned to China in late 1989 and since then has been based in Beijing. He has never married, and his entire life is consumed with his work for Tibet. Although he tries to remain nonpolitical, that is impossible. He is working in Beijing, the capital of what many Tibetans see as the occupation government. He must work through this government, through the authorities. He cannot advocate independence. He is a captive of his position. The political climate on the Tibet question has become so polarized that Phunkhang, simply trying to improve the living standard of his people, is caught in a minefield. "I've been working on this for ten years, and so little has been accomplished," he acknowledged.

I told Phunkhang that I thought he was trying to make compromises in an area where opinions were polarized, and he understood immediately what I was saying. But he didn't entirely agree. "These things are good for Tibet," he said. "Tibetans need a better life, they need a better education. So it's not just a question of compromise. No matter how much ugliness has happened, there has been a change, and the direction is good. I'm disappointed, but I do see a future. That's why I gave up the good life in the States to come back.

"You know, Nick, I really envy you. You've got a beautiful wife, and now a child as well. I don't have any of that. My family is my work for Tibet. But it's hard sometimes."

Phunkhang agonized over his moral responsibilities, I knew, and I respect his decision to collaborate. Few people have ever compromised their moral principles out of such noble motives.

As Sheryl and I grappled with the moral dilemmas that the Chinese face, we became obsessed with finding the mystery man of the 1989 crackdown: the man who betrayed the leaders of the democracy movement.

He was at the center of the great puzzle of the 1989 crackdown: How had State Security busted the Underground Railroad that was whisking the most important dissidents out of China? In October 1989, State Security agents suddenly made a series of arrests in several cities, crushing an entire escape network of Hong Kong and Chinese activists. Among those seized were Wang Juntao and Chen Ziming, the two "black hands" who were later blamed for organizing the entire protest movement. Wang and Chen were both longtime democracy campaigners in their thirties, and they formed the core of a group of intellectuals that represented China's best hope for orderly change. Each was sentenced to thirteen years in prison (although they were released in the spring of 1994 in a concession to the West), and various Chinese and Hong Kong people who had helped them were given lesser terms.

The arrests were a shocking blow to China's underground democracy movement and to the Hong Kong organizations that were helping fugitives escape. Sheryl wrote about one of the Hong Kong men, Luo Haixing, a businessman who had taken on the extraordinarily dangerous task of entering China to contact Chen and Wang and help them escape. Luo was arrested on what was supposed to be his last trip and sentenced to five years in prison. At that time no one knew how State Security had found out about the Underground Railroad, and everybody had a horrible feeling that State Security had infiltrated the democracy movement.

When Sheryl was looking into the case of Luo Haixing, she found disturbing evidence about one of the stars of the dissident movement, Fei Yuan. Thirty-five years old at the time of the crackdown, Fei is a tall and handsome economist and was a close friend of both Wang and Chen. Indeed, they had appointed him director of their research institute, and he proved an outstanding choice. Brilliant, hardworking, well-connected, and blessed with a talent for organization, Fei was one of the leaders of the intellectual movement pressuring the Communist Party for change.

Yet Fei, almost alone among the leaders of the institute, was not added to the national wanted list after the crackdown. Instead, he was interrogated but not arrested. Then he set out to find where his buddies Wang Juntao and Chen Ziming were hiding, saying that he wanted to help them escape to Hong Kong. He was Luo Haixing's contact in China, and he apparently was the last person to visit the Underground Railroad safe house where Chen was hiding before police swooped in to arrest everybody. A few days later, Fei arranged to meet Wang at the railway station in the city of Changsha. Wang showed up on schedule—and was promptly arrested.

The others were all arrested and sentenced, but Fei Yuan was never charged with anything, even though he had appeared to play a key role in helping them escape. Moreover, court documents referred to him as Fei XXXX, as though the police were trying to protect the identity of an informant. I was pretty sure that Fei had turned traitor, probably because of threats from State Security. I wanted to find him. I wanted to see what he looked like. I wanted to see if he became defensive, or angry, or embarrassed, when I brought up the issue of his betrayal.

There was so much courage in the democracy movement that I wanted to see what a chicken looked like. Friends of mine like Han Dongfang were enduring torture and risking death for their beliefs, so I wanted to see the ignoble and craven as well. I wanted to understand what would make a fellow like Fei Yuan crumple, to learn what kind of awful threat had been mustered against him. Had State

Security threatened to kill him, to kill his children, to rape his wife, to flay him alive?

We searched Beijing for Fei Yuan. We had many friends in common, but these friends had all abandoned him after the crackdown. They suspected what we suspected, and they would have nothing to do with him. We heard that he had offered to meet with his old friends and explain what had happened but that they had collectively decided not to listen. "It won't do us any good to hear him out," explained one. "We've got to wait until Wang Juntao and Chen Ziming are released from prison and can explain things fully. Until then we won't know if Fei Yuan is telling the truth or lying." We tried to send messages to Fei, asking him to call us, but since no one was speaking to him, the messages never got through. Even Fei's wife— who had also been involved in the democracy movement—had divorced him.

Finally, just ten days before we were going to leave Beijing, someone gave Sheryl a telephone number for Fei Yuan. She called, but even the person answering the phone seemed contemptuous of him. "He's out," she said, hanging up the phone as Sheryl asked to leave a message. Later Sheryl tried again and got through to him, and he agreed—a bit reluctantly—to meet us in the lounge of the Great Wall Hotel a few days later.

He looked good, smartly dressed in a black pinstriped suit, a white shirt, and a red and blue tie. He was nervous, chain-smoking frantically, but very polished, making easy small talk in formal Mandarin. His smoothness annoyed me. As we talked, one thought was pounding away in my mind: So this is what a traitor looks like.

Normally, when we were having a meal or a drink with a Chinese friend, the conversation paused or took a different turn when a waitress approached. Some hotel staff work for State Security on the side, and the Great Wall Hotel is particularly suspect: Sheryl and I sometimes were followed by tails on long chases up and down the escalators and through the lobby of the hotel. But I noticed that Fei Yuan wasn't intimidated by the waitresses. When one was pouring his drink, he told us what good friends he was with Wang Juntao and Chen Ziming. Of course you're not afraid, I thought, with a gust of bitterness. You're safe. You and the eavesdroppers are all on the same side.

I was impatient and wanted to confront Fei immediately. But whenever we broached the topic of the crackdown, he digressed. We hinted at the suspicions people had of him, and he acknowledged them and didn't deny that he had betrayed his buddies. But then he kept turning the conversation around. I was tired of this and disgusted by him, and at one point I excused myself to go buy a newspaper and stretch my legs. When I returned, I listened distractedly as I scanned the front-page headlines. Fortunately, Sheryl played Fei brilliantly. She listened sympathetically to his accounts of the Cultural Revolution, of his family, of all kinds of other irrelevant topics, and finally he seemed to run out of things to say. He paused, took a deep breath, and told what I think is a true account.

"I wasn't arrested after my first interrogation because I hadn't done anything," he said, emitting a cloud of smoke. "They asked me to write about all my activities during the democracy movement, and I wrote it all down. And they asked me where Chen Ziming and Wang Juntao were, and I said I didn't know. I didn't, then."

The police did not bother Fei anymore, probably because his background was squeaky clean. But as the summer wore on, Fei and several friends decided that they had a responsibility to help their old buddies out. They began spreading the word, and they found out from a family member of Chen Ziming the address of the safe house where he was staying in the southern Chinese city of Zhanjiang. Then Fei linked up with Luo Haixing and the Hong Kong terminus of the Underground Railroad to arrange safe passage out of China. After the last meeting with Luo, on October 8, 1989, Fei traveled to Chen's safe house to meet his old buddy and assure him that everything was almost ready. Next, Fei rushed to Wuhan, where Wang Juntao was hiding, and met the contacts who he knew were helping Wang. Those people checked and double-checked Fei's background, even asking Wang—who apparently was delighted that his old friend had shown up to help. Finally, on October 16, Fei arranged to meet again the next day with Wang's friends and set final plans for Wang's escape.

That night, at about midnight, Fei told us, the police burst into his hotel room. They took him to a police station, and teams of interrogators worked on him all night and all the next day. They informed him that Chen Ziming had already been arrested—which was entirely true. Shortly after Fei's visit to Chen, teams of police moved in and arrested everyone in that safe house. Apparently they had followed Fei when he visited the safe house, revealing its location.

"Wang Juntao can't escape," the chief interrogator told Fei. "We don't know his precise location, but we know roughly where he is. We know how to get to him. But we want to wrap this up quickly, so we'll give you an opportunity. If you cooperate with us, we'll give you a break."

The situation seemed hopeless to Fei, yet he resisted. He asked to be released in exchange for trying to persuade Wang to turn himself in, but the police refused. They warned that Wang himself would be in danger if he remained on the loose. They pointed out that Wang was a fugitive, and that police might shoot him if they saw him but couldn't catch him. It was in Wang's own interest to be caught, the police said.

Here Fei broke off and looked ruefully at us.

"Of course, there's lots of things I can try to say in my defense. But I don't want to defend myself. Basically, I was frightened silly."

That wasn't a very good reason. I wanted to reach across the table and grab Fei by the collar and shake him. Others had put up with torture, with vicious threats, and now Fei was saying that he had simply been frightened.

"Did they beat you?" I asked.

"No," he said, shaking his head sorrowfully.

"Did they threaten your family?"

Again, a shake of his head. "I asked them how they would treat Wang Juntao, and they said that he would be punished according to law. I answered that he hadn't broken the law. They said that if that was clear, if the court found that to be the case, then he would be released.

"You know, I was afraid, but that wasn't it alone. I thought that the police had a point. I figured that he would be tried according to law. I thought that maybe he wouldn't even get a prison sentence."

The interrogations continued for twenty-one hours. When the regular interrogators took a break, a handful of young toughs guarded Fei, and they whispered among themselves that perhaps he would be killed. Fei became terrified. No one knew that he had been arrested. The authorities could do anything to him. On the other hand, they promised that he would be released without prosecution if he cooperated. He asked for a pledge that other people involved in the escape, aside from Chen Ziming and Wang Juntao, would not be prosecuted. The police said they would consider this but made no promises.

Finally, late in the evening, Fei Yuan caved in. He told everything he knew, although he says that he portrayed some of those involved in the escape as doing less than they really had. He also agreed to take four Hong Kong democracy activists to see the man protecting Wang Juntao, even though one of the four was a State Security agent. It turned out that State Security had infiltrated the ranks of the Hong Kong democracy movement, and that may be how Fei himself had been captured. He thinks that someone in the Hong Kong movement informed State Security of Luo Haixing's trips into China, and that State Security followed him from those meetings and then tailed him to Chen Ziming's safe house. Fei admits he wasn't careful enough when he went to the safe house, and that that is probably how Chen was caught.

When he led the four Hong Kong activists to Wang Juntao's "stationmaster" on the Underground Railroad, Fei hoped that somehow he would have a moment alone to warn Wang. But State Security made sure that didn't happen, and Fei set up a rendezvous with Wang. He told the stationmaster that Wang should take the train down to the Hunan Province capital of Changsha. He, Fei Yuan, would be waiting the next evening in the Changsha railway station to meet Wang and conduct him to the next stage of the Underground Railroad. The stationmaster agreed to pass on the message.

State Security took Fei Yuan—heavily guarded—to Changsha on an early train. He spent all the next day waiting at the railway station, guards a few feet away from him. Plainclothes police were everywhere in the cavernous railway station.

"Suddenly at about 8:00 P.M. they took me away," Fei Yuan remembers. "I heard the guard behind me say that Wang Juntao had been grabbed. Until then, I'd been hoping that he wouldn't show up. Now that hope was gone."

So that was it. That was how the two leaders of the democracy movement had been captured. That was how a brave man—brave enough to have tried to rescue his friends—had been induced to betray them. There was a long silence at our table. Fei Yuan's nervousness seemed to have eased slightly, but he still smoked one cigarette after another.

My anger toward Fei was ebbing, but I still wanted to rub his nose in it, to make him realize that he had betrayed his buddies. I pressed on: "Do you regret what you did?"

"Of course I regret it," he said quietly.

"What did you feel when you found out that they had been sentenced to thirteen years in prison?"

"If I had known the aftermath, I would never have cooperated at all."

"Do you think that what you did was morally wrong?"

"From a moral point of view, I didn't do what was right. I was a close friend of Wang Juntao and Chen Ziming. I really regret what happened. I feel a burden because I failed. I should have done better. My friends don't understand what I did. I've lost my core of companions. I've lost my network. That's the worst thing, the most painful thing. I can't stay on this road, and I can't go back and start another."

There was another long silence at our table. Sheryl and I had been expecting to hear that State Security had beaten Fei to a pulp, that police had threatened to carve up his wife or lock up his parents. The case was such a hugely important one in the annals of China's democracy movement that it seemed that there should be more. Here was the biggest turncoat in years, yet it was all so banal. They hadn't laid a glove on him.

Nonetheless, I found that my anger had disappeared and had been replaced by compassion and sympathy for Fei Yuan. I wondered if I would have crumbled. Perhaps. We began chatting a bit about mutual friends—people who had deserted Fei—and about his divorce from his wife, who had been a member of the same informal club of intellectuals. He said that the divorce was complex, but that the episode with his buddies had played some role. It grew on me that Fei Yuan was paying as high a price from the political repression as anyone I knew. He had saved his own skin, but at the cost of his honor, friendships, and self-respect. If he had refused to cooperate, he would have been imprisoned for a few years and emerged a hero. Instead, he may be scorned for the rest of his life as the Man Who Crumbled. In other circumstances, he might have played a leading role in some post-Communist government. Now his political career is finished. The regime, I realized, had forced him to make a decision when he was frightened and exhausted, and his misjudgment would haunt him for the rest of his life.

At the end of our conversation, we exchanged addresses and telephone numbers. "Here's my home number," he said, writing it down. "I'm usually home in the evenings. I don't go out much now."

One of the most heartening changes under way in China in the 1990s is that fewer and fewer people have to make these kinds of excruciating moral compromises. In the Maoist era, such choices were daily occurrences, for lies were woven into the fabric of life. In the Anti-Rightist Campaign of 1957, every office was given a quota of rightists it was supposed to denounce. For those in charge, it was an agonizing choice: Which of their colleagues would they destroy? So officials in every office around the country looked through files and discussed their employees, then fingered a few as rightists. Those people were sent off to labor camps, and often to death by starvation. In effect, officials in each unit had been forced to choose a few colleagues to murder.

During our time in China, it was easier. You simply had to lie, and you had to teach your children to lie. During political campaigns, you had to gang up on those who were in political trouble. But people became adept at wiggling out of their responsibility to tattle on their friends and neighbors. It was even a sign of change that Fei Yuan risked punishment to tell us of what he had done—and that he regretted his conduct in 1989. Political study sessions became a bit of a joke, so that in many units it was no longer necessary to stand up and lie. In some more relaxed units, it became possible to tell political jokes—even to criticize the party—during the meetings.

"Nobody takes our political study sessions seriously these days," a university professor friend told us in 1993. "Lots of people come up with excuses about why they can't attend, or they bring newspapers and openly read while the session is going on. Or else we just sit around and gossip about this and that. It's worse when they really try to get something done. A couple of weeks ago, they were announcing the new anticorruption campaign, so we were supposed to discuss it. In the old days, we would have gone around and said how wonderful the party was to try to solve these problems, and how it should be carried out seriously, and so on. But this time, one fellow stood up and said, 'The party is always announcing anticorruption campaigns, but corruption always gets worse. If they really want to stop it, why don't they arrest the kids of the leaders?'"

The most searing image I ever saw on television was of a young Chinese woman being praised by the government for turning in her own brother to the police. The young man, Zhou Fengsuo, was a leader of the Tiananmen democracy movement. After the June 4 army assault on the protesters, he fled to his hometown of Xian and sought to hide out there in the apartment of a brother. But, according to the Chinese television account, his sister turned him in on June 13. The television report showed her sitting in her living room, and it showed him being led away to prison.

The tale fascinated me. What kind of monster would turn in her own brother for supporting democracy? Ever since the dawn of Chinese history, the family has been the core of Chinese society. Confucius himself had come across a local governor who boasted that the morality of his subjects was so sophisticated that a son had testified against his father for stealing a sheep. Confucius was appalled. In his part of China, he responded dryly, a son would shield his father and a father would shield his son. How could a society survive if its cement, the family relationship, crumbled?

Many of my Chinese friends in Beijing were also deeply distressed by the story of the sister's betrayal. It reminded them of the worst days of the Cultural Revolution, when Red Guards joined in struggle sessions against their parents. My friends pondered how, in a country where family ties traditionally have been so important, a woman could turn in her own brother.

I traveled to Xian to try to find the answer to that question. The authorities refused to allow me to interview the woman, Zhou Wenrong. But I talked to countless other people in the city, and what emerged was very different from the government version of events. For starters, it seems that all of the neighbors knew that the family was hiding Zhou Fengsuo, but none of them reported him to the police. Moreover, it seems that the sister didn't intend to turn in her brother at all. A friend of the family later explained that the sister and her husband, an air force officer, simply decided to go and persuade Zhou Fengsuo to turn himself in, for his own good. To get to the apartment where he was hiding, they asked to borrow a jeep from the air force institute where the husband worked. That caught the attention of the security agents, who knew of the relation to Zhou Fengsuo, and they apparently shadowed the jeep to the apartment and caught Zhou Fengsuo.

What's more, it seems that family ties still do count for something. Everyone in Xian knew of the incident, and most were scathing about the sister. Even if she had not intended to get her brother in trouble, she had been foolish and careless, they said. There was such ill will toward her that she did not even dare leave her apartment.

"Everybody hates her," said a woman in her early thirties. "She's afraid to go out on the street because of all the threatening letters she has received. People say she is going crazy. If she does go mad, her parents will have lost both children."

I found it encouraging that the sister had become the pariah of Xian. It suggested that China had come a long way, and that people were now making moral choices in a more humane way. I hope that in another decade or so, this chapter will seem like an oddity, a curiosity from another era, and that the only works on China that will address this topic will be history books.

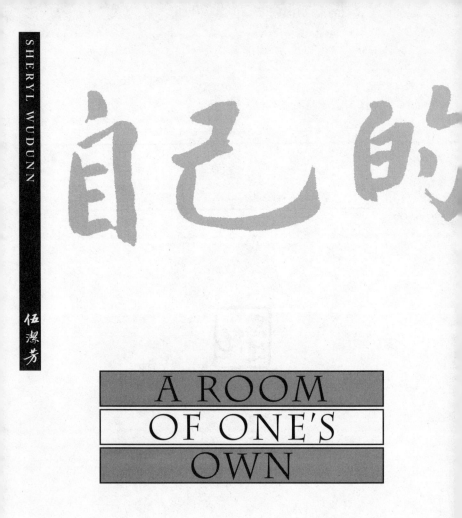

SHERYL WUDUNN

自己的

伍潔芳

A ROOM
OF ONE'S
OWN

Stopping up the mouths of the people is more dangerous than stopping up a river. When a river is blocked and then breaks through, many people are bound to be injured. It is the same with the people.

—Duke of Shao, complaining to the tyrannical
King Li in the ninth century B.C.

10

天地

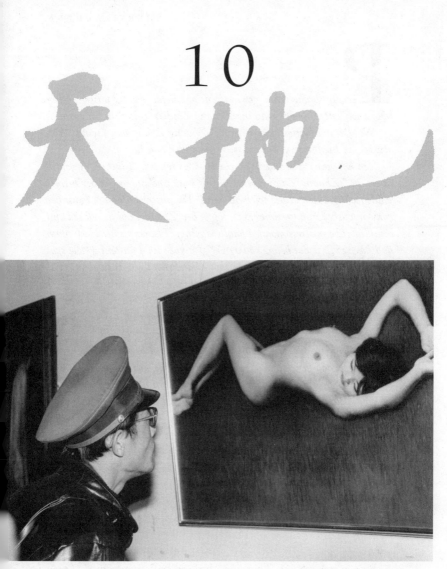

reaking old taboos: A man admires a painting at a show of nude art in a Beijing museum. [Photo by umiyo Asahi.]

Peering through the crack in the door, Liuyue saw the mistress lying in bed with nothing on, grasping Zhuang Zhidie's "thing" in her hand.

"No, I'm not going to do it again," Zhuang Zhidie was saying. "You always say I seduce you, but today it's your turn to seduce me."

"I'm not going to seduce you," the mistress replied. "I just want you to caress me." Zhuang Zhidie then bent his head, sucking one of her breasts while feeling down below with his hand. The mistress began to twist her body and asked him to climb up on top of her. Zhuang Zhidie refused and chuckled. The mistress moaned loudly, saying, "Please, please! How much do I have to flow out before you agree?" Liuyue saw a glistening wet spot between the mistress's legs, and she immediately felt light-headed. . . . The door fell open, and the couple looked up from the bed and saw her.

"How the hell did you get in?" Zhuang Zhidie screamed at her. . . . Zhuang Zhidie chased Liuyue to her room, finding her lying on her bed, panting. Zhuang Zhidie asked, "Are you going to tell?"

"No," Liuyue replied. Zhuang Zhidie embraced her immediately and began peeling off her clothes. Liuyue resisted awhile, but submitted after he pulled off her shirt. When Zhuang Zhidie took off her pants, he saw she was completely wet already. He said, "I thought Liuyue didn't understand these things, but she's a ripe persimmon already." The two locked together on the edge of the bed. . . .

"Liuyue, how come there's no blood?" Zhuang Zhidie said. "You're not a virgin. Who is he?" "No, I never have, never have." Liuyue could no longer control herself, twisting her body like a snake. The mistress had been watching from the very beginning at the door. When the two finally separated, she went up and embraced Liuyue, saying, "Liuyue, now we're really sisters."

Pardon me, readers. That was a little spicy fiction from *A City in Ruins*, a novel that hit the book stands in 1993. The author, Jia Ping'ao, a gruff chain-smoker in his early forties, knew that sex sells even in China, and his book shattered every Communist taboo. The main character, Zhuang Zhidie, likes to suck milk from a cow; the son of a painter snorts cocaine; a young woman dies from masturbating with corncobs. Few people thought it was much of a book, but it was a publishing sensation, blanketing the street stalls in Beijing and other cities. It would have jumped to the top of the best-seller list if China had such a list.

A City in Ruins appeared not long before we left China, and it left me gasping in surprise at the revolution in the Chinese social and cultural world—a metamorphosis that is touching people every day in every way. Literature, music, and the popular press have largely wriggled free from the commissars' grip, so that these days almost anything is permitted if it does not directly challenge the party. The information revolution is also sweeping through the land, with satellite dishes sprouting from rooftops in the major cities and faxes and electronic mail messages blipping across the optical fiber circuits. In the early 1990s, a computer virus spread around China, underscoring the leadership's difficulties in the information age. The virus generated a question on the computer screen: Do you think Li Peng is a good prime minister? If the computer operator answered no, the message disappeared and nothing happened. But if the person said yes, Li Peng was a good prime minister, then the virus wiped out the computer's entire hard disk.

The government, it seems, has lost control of the cultural world, the information channels, the social forces, the individual's mind. What is emerging is the embryo of a civil society.

Cut back to the Maoist era.

Classic poetry and novels are banned, traditional landscape painting and Peking opera are in disgrace, and the best-seller is Mao's little red book of quotations. Popular songs include tunes like "Socialism Is Good" and "Night Soil Collectors Coming down the Mountain." Revolutionary exhortations boom over the loudspeakers to wake people up in the morning and follow them throughout the day. The Communist Party determines everything: the clothes you wear, the city you live in, the job you hold, the amount of rice you eat, the clinic you go to, the person you are allowed to marry, even the kinds of activities for which you "volunteer."

Such totalitarianism grew out of a Chinese imperial tradition that recognized no place for individual rights. Obligations—to one's father, husband, or emperor—were absolute. For centuries, the patriarch was the tyrant of the family, allowed even to kill his children. And the emperor was the tyrant of the nation, allowed even to kill his subjects. The result was that everyone tried to blend in according to the social norms; otherwise, the authorities would *qiangda chutou niao*, "shoot the bird that flies in front of the flock."

Then Mao went even further in subordinating the individual to the community, effectively putting all Chinese through a homogenizer. People were supposed to become virtually identical: They dressed alike in Mao suits, cut their hair in the same way, rode the same black bicycles, shared a faith in Communism, and—like parrots—spewed forth the same lines over and over. The party even advised people how often to have sex: "very often" for newlyweds, meaning once every three to seven days, and once every week or two for everyone else. The party controlled absolutely everything, from the kindergarten curriculum to the crops grown on each commune. Visitors could be pardoned for likening the Chinese to a hill of blue ants.

There was no specific scope for politics, because everything was politics. One of our Chinese nannies used to teach Gregory the nursery rhymes that she remembered from her childhood in the 1950s, when Chinese troops were fighting Americans in Korea. I did a double take the first time I heard her teaching Gregory these words:

> *One, two, three, four, five,*
> *Climb the mountain, hunt the tiger,*
> *Tigers won't eat a human,*
> *They just eat Truman.*

Mao wanted no outside force, no independent institution, to survive. Fearful that freethinking writers were threatening his absolute power, he launched the 1942 "rectification." Communist writers were tortured, imprisoned, and abused, as Mao laid down the cultural guidelines that China then endeavored to impose. Mao declared that his purpose was to "ensure that literature and art fit well into the whole of the revolutionary machine as a component part." Half a century later, the commissars were still adhering to that dictum. The purpose of culture was not to enlighten or entertain, they insisted, but to spread political propaganda.

In China today, however, the commissars' work has become more and more difficult. Artists and writers fight back, and the introduction of a market economy means that studios and publishers aim to please audiences as well as party hacks. Thus China is now seared by a cultural and social war that in many respects is as fierce—and as illuminating—as the one about economic policies. A market economy expands people's wallets, but freedom in the arts and society opens their souls.

What do I mean when I say that the embryo of a civil society is emerging in China?

James Madison employed the expression *civil society* in the *Federalist* papers, but in a more modern sense the term arose recently in Eastern Europe to describe the birth of pluralism. The sharpest contrast is to a totalitarian society—whether Communist, imperial, or theocratic—in which the state encompasses every aspect of life. Mussolini once defined such a society as: "Everything within the state, nothing outside the state, nothing against the state."

A civil society, by contrast, is one in which the role of government is narrowly circumscribed. Labor unions and industrial groups disagree with each other and also squabble among themselves. Newspapers and magazines are independent of any authority, free to denounce the government or each other. Individuals can worship God, Satan, or no one at all. Fundamentally, in a civil society the role of citizens is not to be subjects but to be participants.

The United States was thus a civil society long before civil rights and women's suffrage made it a democratic one. Toward the end of our stay in China, I picked up our copy of Alexis de Tocqueville's classic *Democracy in America* and blew off the dust. In Tocqueville's analysis of early-nineteenth-century America, I saw more clearly the notion of civil society that I hope is emerging in China. Tocqueville emphasized the respect for law in the United States, the general acceptance of the principle that the majority has the right to rule, and the tremendous number of groups and associations that give Americans experience in self-rule. Aside from such associations, he said, "I see no other dike to hold back tyranny of whatever sort, and a great nation might with impunity be oppressed by some tiny faction or by a single man."

China still lacks many of the elements of a civil society: the broad educational base, the respect for law, the sensitivity to opposing opinions, and, perhaps more than anything else, an understanding that the turbulent clash of private and group interests is a sign not of fearful chaos but of a healthy free market in opinions.

Yet slowly, painfully, the tiny seeds of a civil society are sprouting in a few large Chinese cities. The number of private associations is increasing, having reached 180,000 by 1993. One in Beijing brings together many Chinese who have studied abroad and returned home; others unite people with an interest in stamp collecting or foreign languages. These associations are government sponsored, but increasingly they are creating their own autonomy, sometimes functioning as lobbies or business clubs where contacts are made. The legal structure is steadily becoming more meaningful, with a growing number of laws—particularly in commerce—that the government itself increasingly obeys. Since the early 1990s, for instance, when a new administrative law went into effect, Chinese individuals have begun to sue government bureaus, and a few have even won their cases.

Shortwave radios, satellite dishes, and fax machines are finding their way into more offices and even some homes, helping to encourage a freer flow of information. Some intellectuals are beginning to divorce themselves from the government, setting up their own research institutes, their own consulting firms, their own commercial projects that sometimes link them to universities and companies overseas.

Education, which in other countries has helped create the basis for a more tolerant and pluralistic society, is spreading in the urban areas. Perhaps more important, the older, uneducated leaders are dying and being replaced by college-educated technocrats. The nucleus of a middle class is also beginning to emerge, and so are semiautonomous power bases, such as large enterprises. Moreover, as the state becomes less centralized, governors and other local leaders are arguing more forcefully for their interests, and several recent party plenums have been marked by bitter wrangling because provincial governors object to turning more taxes over to the central government. There are even hints that labor, which could emerge as the most powerful independent actor of all, is becoming more assertive, with a growing number of wildcat strikes. Perhaps most important of all, in the artistic and cultural world, an incipient "Free China" is emerging.

Perhaps the single most subversive person I know in China is not Wei Jingsheng, the charismatic dissident who spent fourteen and a half years in prison, or Wang Dan, the student leader of the Tiananmen democracy movement. Rather, in the broadest sense the most subversive person I know may well be Wang Shuo.

Huh? Never heard of him? Wang Shuo, a thirty-five-year-old with a mischievous grin, is a Chinese version of Jack Kerouac. Almost single-handedly he brought the Beat Generation to China. Wang isn't a dissident, but if anything he's more dangerous. He doesn't criticize the party; he laughs at it. The party, in his eyes, is Uncool.

I met Wang Shuo soon after he had released a four-volume collection of his works. As he sat busily signing copies of his books at the New China Book Store in Beijing, young readers rushed in and out, clutching stacks of his novels, often buying several sets at a time. Back at his three-room apartment in northeast Beijing, Wang dressed casually, a bit sloppily, in a white T-shirt and running shorts. The apartment's furnishings were simple—a plain wooden table, a soft couch, and nothing on the walls. I was also puzzled: There were hardly any books. On the table was a translation of a Joseph Heller novel, and in a study there was a small bookcase with a few Chinese books inside, but I was accustomed to the homes of intellectuals, where rooms are filled with books. Wang seemed impatient with talk of intellectuals and politics, and he didn't give any indication of wanting to play a political role. Instead, his ambition is commercial success. "I want to become famous," he explained, "I want to be motherfucking famous till I'm dizzy."

Wang is subversive because he can transform the ordinary into the extraordinary. He turns hoodlums into heroes, he colors his dialogue with curses, and he writes about sex, alienation, and failure as perfectly normal things. Wang has become one of China's most popular, provocative, influential, and seductive writers, churning out words with a fury—novels, short stories, detective stories, film scripts, love stories, television dramas, even songs. Almost everything he writes brims with satire, and much of it focuses on the predicament of China's working-class urban society: the struggles of salesmen, prostitutes, homeless vagrants, and common workers.

Wang's young readership is entranced. When I interviewed Wang, he had another guest, a friend named Heizi, or Blackie, an affable man in his early thirties. Toward the end of the interview, Wang went to answer a telephone call. It had been nearly two hours of shared jokes and laughs, all of them inspired by Wang's magical, slippery words, his cartoonlike gestures, and his crooning voice. Heizi turned to me, and I thought he would swoon like a teenage girl with a crush on a movie star. He beamed. "Miss Wu, isn't Wang Shuo simply enchanting?"

Wang Shuo finished two years of high school in 1976 and never went to college. Instead, he joined the navy, training to become a sailor. Then he drifted from job to job, from woman to woman, with no particular ambitions in mind. For an empty, rambling while, he lived off the salary of his girlfriend, an airline stewardess, before he ran away with a dancer, Shen Xujia, who then became his wife. He finally ended up with a pen in his hand. A quiet cultural blossoming was taking place, and Wang tested its limits. Literary critics call his works *pizi wenxue*, "hooligan literature," because he frowns on intellectuals, and his most interesting and even charming characters are hooligans.

"All the impetus for openness and reform comes from hooligans," Wang said, gesturing wildly. "Hooligans do business, hooligans do commerce, hooligans build factories, and hooligans open shops. Their craziness is what makes the society tick. Because China's economy is not perfect, isn't completely built up, those who are really successful— that is, those who have gotten rich—all of them are hooligans."

Take Zhang Ming, the main character in Wang's novel *Hot and Cold, Measure for Measure*. Zhang is a hoodlum who seduces a naive college student. She falls for him, becomes a prostitute, and commits suicide when the gang is arrested. In the scene when they first meet, Zhang throws jabs at the girl's boyfriend, a successful student leader certain to become a Communist Party member. As he narrates:

> *"Which university are you at?" I'd noticed the university badge on her sweater.*
>
> *"I suppose this is your pickup line. Then you'll tell me where you study, how close our campuses are and how easy it would be to see a lot of each other . . ."*
>
> *"Do I look like a student?" was my reply. "I'm an ex-con from a labor camp. At the moment I'm trying my hand at blackmail."*

"I don't give a damn what you are." She smiled down at her toes as if they were terribly amusing. "I really couldn't care less."

We sat there in silence for what seemed an eternity, gazing contentedly at the setting sun and the rapidly approaching darkness. The clouds were still visible and quite magnificent.

"Look, that cloud looks like Marx, and that one over there looks a bit like a pirate, don't you think?"

"How old are you?"

She turned and studied me. "You haven't had much experience with women, have you?"

"No, I haven't." I delivered this line totally poker-faced.

"I knew it the moment I saw you. You're just a kid. I could tell from the way you hovered there in the distance, trying to pluck up the courage to come over and talk to me. You were afraid I was going to say something to embarrass you, weren't you?"

"Actually I've slept with more than a hundred girls."

She shrieked with laughter.

"You have a moronic laugh," I told her.

She stopped laughing and threw me a resentful look. "Look, I'm not dumping on you, so lay off me. O.K.? To tell you the truth, I've been going out with someone for over a year." She smiled smugly.

"Who is he? Some . . . classmate of yours?"

"He's a cadre in the Student Union!"

"You can't get much worse than that."

"Hmph. You should talk. Your mother is the only woman who's ever kissed you, that's for sure."

"If I were him, at least I'd be man enough to sleep with you," I said with a smirk. "Tell me, does he?" Although it was already dark, I could see she had turned bright red.

"He respects me!"

I sniggered.

The hard-liners just don't know how to deal with people like Wang Shuo. They fuss and harrumph, but harrumphing isn't enough. There's now a huge appetite for entertainment rather than propaganda; people want new books, new films, new music. Chinese are discovering that the arts can be something other than political education and brainwashing.

Capitalism has changed China in fundamental ways, so that there are new avenues for cultural works. In part this is because publishing houses and other cultural organizations have been made responsible for their own profits, so they are beginning to print books that people want to read. They publish works by people like Wang Shuo—nothing overtly counterrevolutionary, yet not what the commissars want. The hard-liners rush hither and thither, banning works, but the cultural arena is so wide that they cannot control everything.

So, Wang Shuos are proliferating in China. Films are becoming bolder, testing taboos on the Cultural Revolution and other topics. Theater is more rambunctious, exploring themes such as the way power corrupts. And in music, Cui Jian, a long-haired Chinese version of Bob Dylan, is the nation's rock star, a hero to urban youth in every province. He is generally barred from television, and his concerts are sometimes canceled, but his raspy outbursts of alienation have become the anthems of his generation. In a 1991 cassette that evaded the harried censors and sold wildly throughout China, he even suggested that the Golden Road—a byword for Communism—is a dead end:

> Look all around, at men and women, kids and old folks,
> Look—we've come to the end of the Golden Road.

The Communist Party may never willingly admit political pluralism, but it has already been forced to accept social, economic, and cultural pluralism. The "poisonous weeds," as the hard-liners call cultural works they want to ban, keep growing luxuriantly.

Even more significant, the government is losing control of the information game. As they become wealthier, more and more Chinese buy shortwave radios and have access to real news: BBC, Voice of America, and French Radio, all broadcasting in Chinese. In southern parts of Guangdong Province, most homes tune to Hong Kong television. In Fujian Province, multisystem TV sets are the norm, so that people can receive Taiwan broadcasts.

Personal satellite dishes are nominally illegal, but they began proliferating in the early 1990s. The Ministry of Electronics operates a factory in Gansu Province that turns out some 70,000 satellite dishes a year, and various private companies and army units also sell large numbers of the receivers. By mid-1993, hundreds of shops in Beijing and Shanghai were selling cheap satellite dishes, with a five-foot dish and electronic receiver costing just $500.

In October 1993, Prime Minister Li Peng approved a new national law restating the ban on most satellite dishes, and shops again became more careful about breaking the law. They still sold the dishes, but under the table—and for a greater markup. In any case, a growing number of cable systems make satellite dishes less necessary. Cable systems are being set up in almost every city, and even in many county towns, neighborhoods, military compounds, and villages. In southern China, cable systems sometimes offer Hong Kong broadcasts, including news programs.

The market economy also is beginning to transform the official news media, so that at times they actually provide news. This is a true breakthrough, for except during occasional periods of relaxation the official newspapers used to contain only pabulum and propaganda. Many of my Chinese friends used to laugh at me because I always studied the *People's Daily,* whereas they hardly ever read it.

A former editor of the *People's Daily* explained that there was only one truthful thing in the newspaper each day: the date. What about the weather? "No, even the weather report is skewed. If the weather is too hot or too cold, the rules say that people don't have to go to work. But of course, we can't have everyone stop working just because of the weather, so if it's really cold, we report a temperature a few degrees warmer than it really is. If it's really hot, we report a slightly more tolerable temperature."

In the fall of 1990, Nick wrote an article about the *People's Daily* and explained that while it is the most powerful newspaper in the country, few people read it. As a result, Nick was summoned to the Foreign Ministry for a scolding. "Some of your articles have slandered China and hurt the feelings of the Chinese people," Wan Jisong, our official liaison, said in the airy conference room on the ministry's ground floor. Nick was separately summoned for a lecture by two officials from the *People's Daily* foreign affairs department.

"Your article is untrue," complained Gao Fuyuan, the department's deputy director. "The *People's Daily* has a very big circulation. Three million people."

"Well, it may have a big circulation, but I've got to tell you that my Chinese friends say they just don't read it," Nick replied. "Offices and factories subscribe to it, so the circulation is huge. But that doesn't mean people read it."

The conversation went around and around for an hour, with Gao insisting that the public closely read each edition of the *People's Daily*. As they were finishing up, Nick decided to be conciliatory and end on a favorable note: "By the way, I thought the editorial you had in the paper two days ago was very interesting."

"Which editorial?" Gao looked flattered but puzzled.

"The one on the front page, top of the front page, about the cultural world."

"Culture?" Gao's brows furrowed. "When did you say it was?"

"Day before yesterday," Nick replied. "The one calling for more controls on culture."

The two men racked their brains unsuccessfully for some memory of it. "It was on the inside pages?"

"No, on the front page. Top of the front page. Lead article. It was the one saying that the government must watch out for 'poisonous weeds.' "

"Yes, well, we've been quite busy lately," Gao said awkwardly. "We haven't had much time to read the paper."

While the *People's Daily* is still filled with propaganda, other newspapers are changing. New papers are fighting for readers, partly because the government is cutting off subsidies, and so the pages are filled with juicy stories. The *Beijing Youth Daily* revealed China's aspirations to build an aircraft carrier; the *Peasants' Daily* wrote about a man suing the police; the *Beijing Evening News* described a little boy who was living in terrible poverty, abandoned by his parents and neglected by the authorities.

The electronic news media have undergone a similar revolution. Television stations in Guangzhou and Shanghai began airing public meetings, in which citizens could discuss some of their gripes. They also began covering the news without waiting for the Propaganda Department to tell them what to think. When a neighborhood flooded in Shanghai, East-China Television and East-China Radio rushed to the scene and went on the air with live reports. The reporters even had the gall to thrust microphones in the faces of officials and ask them what they were going to do about the flood.

Most striking of all, talk radio has come to China. Whenever we tuned in to radio stations during the evening hours, we encountered *rexian dianhua*—"hot line calls," as talk radio is called in Chinese. Callers are subjected to a fourteen-second delay, and they sometimes have to leave their names with the producer to make sure that they do not get too hotheaded. But they are allowed to complain about minor problems: rude shop assistants, poor garbage collection, difficulties redeeming government bonds, factories belching smoke. In just one evening on a talk radio station in Guangzhou, listeners called to discuss:

—Whether incompatibility is a valid reason for divorce.
—Whether high school girls can insist on keeping their bras on during medical checkups at school.
—How workers should deal with a boss in a private factory who forces employees to work sixteen hours a day and illegally intercepts their letters.
—How out-of-towners should make friends in Guangzhou. A computer programmer named Dong complained that she was "out of tune with the Cantonese people" and so depressed that she felt "like a glass of distilled water."

To be sure, Chinese journalists are still frustrated by all the restrictions that remain. When I met a reporter who had written an exposé on Yu Zuomin, the corrupt and now imprisoned chief of Daqiuzhuang, China's model village, she told me about the fights she had had with her editor while trying to get her story printed. "It finally did come out, and I was criticized," she said. "But you know, the article contained less than one-tenth of what I found out."

Many of our friends and sources were Chinese journalists, in part because they had a lot of information and could not use it. But this is a dangerous game, and journalists at *People's Daily* are banned from meeting with foreign correspondents. I sometimes crept through a back entrance, hurrying past the guard and prepared with a phony excuse if he asked what I was up to. One Chinese journalist, Wu Shishen, an editor at the New China News Agency, discovered how risky the information trade can be. One day in early October 1992, just over a week before hundreds of Communist Party delegates descended upon Beijing to attend the Fourteenth Party Congress, a

Hong Kong reporter asked for Wu's help. She wanted to know if she could get a glimpse of the keynote speech—no matter how boring—that Jiang Zemin, the party's chief, was going to give. Wu obliged. He had access to the speech, and in a few hours he could make a copy of it. His bosses wouldn't notice.

They certainly did, especially when the Hong Kong paper published the full text of the bland speech before Jiang gave it. The government caught Wu, and he is now serving a life sentence in prison.

Nonetheless, there is a metamorphosis under way in China, as it makes the transition to a civil society. The best way I have found to explain it is to recall the distinction that Jeane Kirkpatrick made between totalitarian and authoritarian societies. I used to be very skeptical of Kirkpatrick's analysis; it seemed to be an excuse for covering up the faults of those dictators that the United States liked. But after seeing the changes in China, I think the distinction is not only valid but also very important. The difference is that in totalitarian countries, citizens are mobilized to join political movements supporting the regime, while in authoritarian countries they are simply banned from opposing the government. Fundamentally, in an authoritarian state, citizens can opt out of the political system: So long as they do not criticize the government, it leaves them alone. There is also a difference of degree. In authoritarian countries, dissidents face arrest and torture; in totalitarian countries, so do their family members. This may be the difference between murder and mass murder, but it still is a significant distinction.

China is now becoming an authoritarian country, instead of a totalitarian one, and it is likely to remain authoritarian for years to come. It will continue to imprison and torture those who challenge the Communist Party, and I wouldn't be surprised if there are further massacres of Tibetans or other protesters. But it is no longer very totalitarian. The average Chinese can now tune in to Voice of America without fear, he can send his kids to private schools, he can mutter jokes about Li Peng, he can bellyache about graft, he can listen to Taiwanese pop singers. China still has political prisoners, but not a billion of them.

Totalitarianism is also no longer the way the Chinese leadership makes policy. The central government must cajole provinces and local governments, and even so they often disobey quietly. Resistance from bureaucrats and local officials means that central decrees are often not implemented outside Beijing's second ring road. Or the central decrees are manipulated for local purposes. There was the time, for example, that the State Family Planning Commission funded a clinic so that it could develop better contraceptive methods to slow down population growth. A year later, the authorities returned and found that the clinic had switched roles. It had determined that it could make more money by helping peasants conceive children. So it had become a fertility clinic.

When the State Council imposed a ban on the manufacture of aluminum cans because it felt the process uses excessive amounts of electricity, Nick telephoned a half dozen aluminum plants around the country. They all said blithely that they would continue making the cans.

"Of course we're going to keep on going," said a factory manager in Guangdong. "We heard about the State Council order, but we'll keep on producing until our local officials tell us to stop." And the local government, which owned the factory, would never tell it to stop production.

No wonder there's a Chinese expression: "The central bosses create policy; the local bosses create counterpolicy."

The social loosening is accelerating, and the Communist Party's domain has been squeezed into a much narrower space, so that it presides over the political realm but not much else. This is particularly evident in matters of faith, for it used to be that only one religion was permitted—Maoism. Now other faiths are allowed, within limits, and most are thriving. A growing number of young people are turning to Christianity and other mystical movements. Indeed, one of the great paradoxes of modern China is that Christianity may well be gaining converts at a more rapid rate today, under a sometimes repressive government, than it ever did early in this century, when missionaries were free to evangelize at will. The fundamental attraction of Christianity is that it offers young people a spiritual anchor at a time when they have little else to believe in. Kids also sometimes regard Christianity as "cool," a fashionable Western product analogous to McDonald's hamburgers, hula hoops, and Coca-Cola.

"Maybe I'm not a believer," Peter Zhu, a thirty-four-year-old travel agent, said at a Catholic church in Beijing. "But this is Western culture, and I want to learn more about it. This is a very famous religion."

China has established official church organizations for both Catholics and Protestants, and these "pet churches" are the only ones allowed. Official figures indicate that China has 5.5 million Protestants and 3.5 million Catholics. But these numbers don't include the parishioners of the underground house churches, who may number even more than those in the official church, and who are sometimes far more serious in their beliefs than many official churchgoers.

One evening I paid a visit to Daxin, a friend of mine, who lives in a densely populated area in southwest Beijing. That night, he and five other Christians were holding a Bible session, an illegal get-together where they discussed fundamental questions about religion that they never could talk about openly in church. Daxin had already turned his apartment into a small shrine. As soon as I entered, I noticed a wooden box with a slot for cash offerings. Above the couch in the small living room was a red tapestry of a cross, and nearby was a picture of Christ. The room was impeccably clean and sparsely furnished. One of Daxin's friends unraveled a T-shirt that said, "God Loves China." Then he quickly folded it up into a ball and stashed it away in a bag.

The six men read for a spell from the Bible, but the conversation soon turned to politics and to their frustrations about being Christians in China.

"My boss has tried to talk me out of it," explained one short man who worked in a factory. " 'Why do you believe in God?' he interrogated me once. 'Don't you believe in Communism?' I told him, 'I believe in God because God teaches us to help each other.' Then he raised his voice and asked me, 'Did God give you this factory? Did he build it up from the land or did Communism give it to you? Aagh! Our control over religion is too weak.' "

Another friend, a tall, studious-looking man who had been quiet, suddenly cleared his throat and spoke up: "There is a conflict between Christianity and Marxism. In the future this conflict will become more acute. Christianity doesn't have many believers now, but in the future, it'll be a stronger force. It'll challenge the government."

"So are you a political group as well?" I asked, wondering whether these men were closet dissidents.

"We don't engage in politics," the solemn man said calmly. "We believe in God. But we feel we must do something to cure the ills of this sick society. We are oppressed, and if we are going to do anything about it, inevitably we run into politics. Throughout history, religion and politics have been intermingled. Now, in China, however, the two must be separate. But when Christians see social problems, how can we not stand up? Freedom of religion, freedom of the press, freedom of speech, they're all the same."

Dozens of small cults, most of them loosely based on Christianity, have also sprung up around the country in recent years. There are said to be tens of thousands of "shouters"—so named because they shout in unison "Jesus is Lord!"—in half a dozen provinces.

Perhaps the oddest of the cults is the one that began in 1990 to worship Mao Zedong. This cult began in southern China, when taxi drivers started putting Mao pictures in their vehicles because they believed doing so would protect them from car crashes. Truck drivers caught on and carried the fashion all over. At its peak, in 1991 and 1992, cars and trucks throughout the country carried Mao's image dangling from their rearview mirrors. Naturally, reasons varied. Some did it out of respect for the Chairman, or out of annoyance at today's leaders. But the most common answer I heard, in conversations with drivers from many different provinces, was that it amounted to cheap car insurance. "I heard there was a convoy of fifteen cars, and every one of them got in a bad accident except the two that had Chairman Mao's picture," a twenty-nine-year-old driver told us in Beijing. "And in some places, like Shandong Province, I hear that for traffic safety reasons they don't even let you on the road unless you've got your Chairman Mao photo out." Another taxi driver put it more succinctly. Pointing to the Mao photo dangling beside him, he said, "He's become a god."

At least two temples honoring Mao have been set up, one in Fujian Province and another in Hunan, so that peasants can go and offer him a suckling pig and ask for a son, a good crop, or whatever else they want. This isn't quite as strange in China as it might seem in the West. The Chinese pantheon is cluttered with folk gods, rather like saints in the West, to whom one can pray for help. Most of the important ones, like the god of war, the goddess of fishermen, or the kitchen god, were once humans. Deification is more unusual for recent figures, however, and Mao may be the first atheist to become a deity.

Other systems of belief are also gaining converts. Tens of millions have turned to *qi gong*, the breathing exercise that helps people meditate and relax. Some *qi gong* masters entrance huge crowds and claim to be virtual messiahs who can heal the sick, make people taller, or even fly across the country. Deng Xiaoping and other Chinese leaders use a *qi gong* master named Zhang Baosheng, a mysterious man who is supposed to have all kinds of magical powers. A thirty-five-year-old high school dropout, Zhang supposedly became aware of his abilities when, at the age of two, he used his mental powers to transport some cookies out of the cabinet where they had been hidden from him. Some people insist that Zhang can weld metal with his fingers, remove pills from sealed bottles, and move objects just by thinking of them. Nick once saw a video in which Zhang appeared to burn clothing simply by touching it. I'm still rather skeptical, but the Chinese government isn't. The army supplies Zhang with bodyguards and prevents him from leaving Beijing without permission. When we applied to interview Zhang, the authorities said no. "We can't make him available," said a spokesman for the Public Security Ministry. "He's a national treasure."

Another *qi gong* master who has attracted a devoted following is Li Hanxiang, a fifty-two-year-old former electrician, tall and hefty, with a shock of hair careening over his forehead. We have a friend in common, so we arranged to interview him one day and accompany him to a healing session. Despite our skepticism, we wanted to see for ourselves what all the excitement was about.

Li held court one afternoon in an old people's home, a dusty and dilapidated room in which a handful of retirees sat on rickety wooden chairs. Li beamed at them and shook their hands, then picked a couple of patients to start with. He stared inside their ears, then purported to diagnose their ailments and those of their family members. He stood in a trancelike state, vibrating slightly, with sweat pouring from his body, as he tried to transmit his *qi* to cure several lame men and women. With a cough he came out of his trance and shouted at the patients to throw away their crutches. "You can walk now!" he shouted. "You can dance!" The patients eagerly hobbled a few steps. "You see!" Li thundered. "It works! You can dance again!"

Li came by our home to talk about his powers, and one of our Chinese office assistants asked to sit in on the interview. The assistant, a Beijing woman in her forties, entirely believed in *qi gong* and told wild stories about how a *qi gong* master had restored a friend's eyesight and discovered a cancerous tumor before it became serious. After an hour of the interview, Li asked us to get some wine so that he could turn it into fruit juice. We didn't want to waste a new bottle of wine, so Nick poured a glass from an opened bottle of Cointreau instead. Li placed the glass in front of him and began to concentrate, putting one hand on his brow and the other over the glass. He shook violently for several minutes, and then there was a sudden spasm. Li looked up, wiped off the sweat, and announced confidently that it was now fruit juice.

The office assistant took the first sip. "Oh, it's changed!" she said. "It's orange juice. No alcohol at all!"

We tried it, and, sure enough, it tasted like Cointreau. The lesson was that belief is more powerful than reality: If you wanted to believe the *qi gong* master, then he became real. On a larger scale, for us, it also suggested that many Chinese were looking for something to believe in, searching for a spiritual center for their lives.

The rise of cults is a typical late-dynasty phenomenon, as people seek to create a new belief system to replace the disintegrating official one. Yet cults can also be seen as harmless fads, as signs that society is becoming less restrained and that people are feeling freer to pursue personal choices. In this sense, cults are emblems of the emerging civil society.

So which is it? Are Christianity and *qi gong* signs of a collapsing dynasty? Or of a rising civil society? I wavered in my answer to that question. In my first few years in Beijing, I tended to see such activities as omens of a crumbling regime. But increasingly I came to see a more reassuring side to such phenomena, for many people weren't just fleeing to these fads out of desperation over the loss of faith in Communism. They were curious and experimental, and the government was for the first time letting them pursue their interests. Ultimately, therefore, I think the two phenomena are happening simultaneously: The old dynasty is crumbling and being replaced by a civil society. As Tocqueville said, the birth of freedom is never orderly: "Liberty is generally born in stormy weather, growing with difficulty among civil discords, and only when it is already old does one see the blessings it has brought."

The search in China for something to believe in was a wacky process, just as it often is in the West, but it brought a smile to my face.

Chinese were breaking rules and doing their own thing. They were carving out their own personal space, marking parts of their lives off-limits to the government.

The emphasis on community interests in China, indeed in most of East Asia, is in some ways a valuable legacy, but for a flower garden to dazzle, the individual plants must bloom—and that is what is finally happening to China in the 1990s. I began to cheer up as I saw more and more signs of individuals and not just groups. China seemed to be turning into a patchwork quilt of individuals, and no longer just a hill of blue ants.

Social pluralism, of course, manifests itself not only in the heads and hearts of Chinese but also in their loins, as the success of books like *A City in Ruins* demonstrates. Since sex is such an important undercurrent in any society, I decided to poke around the Chinese bedroom a bit. Okay, perhaps it was partly prurience on my part. But I convinced myself that to understand the flowering of individualism I should understand the sexual revolution in China. After all, nothing so reflects the need for privacy and personal space as sex.

One of the first peeks we gained into this realm came in July 1992, when Nick, Gregory, and I took a break for a long weekend at the beach resort of Beidaihe. First developed by Europeans early in the century as a place to seek refuge in the hot summer months, Beidaihe was taken over after 1949 by the Communist leaders themselves, and it was on this trip that we saw how Lin Biao, the former defense minister, built a grand saltwater swimming pool in his villa. Today Beidaihe is a sleepy little town, dominated by resorts and hotels, with public beaches that are so packed with vacationing Chinese that it is difficult to see the sand. Separate private beaches are available, fenced off and guarded by troops, for senior government officials.

I had quietly arranged to meet up with a dozen Chinese, all employees of a Beijing trading company. The office manager, a friend of ours, had made some money on black market foreign exchange deals and had decided that instead of giving the profits to the head office the staff would all take a paid vacation together. We stayed at the same hotel as they did, went to the beach with them, and followed their gossip. To our surprise, the main topic seemed to be whether Little Zhao, a well-dressed young man in his midtwenties, would sleep with Little Li, a secretary who had been flirting with him for some months. Both were virgins, both were willing, but both were also wondering about the propriety of an intraoffice affair. To us the most surprising thing was the openness with which the topic was discussed. Everybody in the office knew what was happening and debated whether or not Little Zhao and Little Li should "do it." One man in his thirties complained contemptuously that Little Zhao was just wasting everybody's time with his indecisiveness and should get on with it. Another employee, a young woman, disapproved heatedly: "I don't think they should do things like this!" she exclaimed. "It's not right." Everybody else laughed.

The group had arranged for an extra hotel room to be vacant, and Little Li was rubbing her hands and clearly looking forward to the event with great apprehension and expectation. But after dinner, Little Zhao settled down with the rest of the group to watch the Summer Olympics, which were then being broadcast on television from Barcelona. In the back of the group sat Little Li, her arms crossed in ire and exasperation, as the hours passed. Little Zhao, in contrast, chatted with the others about the hundred-meter dash.

"Don't you have something to do?" one of Little Zhao's friends finally reminded him at 11:00 P.M. Little Li perked up at that, but Little Zhao simply shook his head. "No, this is too interesting."

In the morning, the question on everybody's lips was *Xiao Zhao banle meiyou?*—"Did Little Zhao get it done?" But his roommate asserted that the matter had not been taken care of. The following evenings Little Li was sufficiently annoyed and disillusioned that she was no longer interested. The soap opera ended without a consummation.

Historically, Chinese have not been particularly prudish. For example, an erotic novel called *The Golden Lotus* was written three centuries ago. And visiting Westerners once regarded China as a center of iniquity. One visitor wrote in 1727: "The abominable sin of sodomy is tolerated here, and all over China, and so is buggery, which they use with both beasts and fowl, in so much that Europeans do not care to eat duck." But as in many parts of the world, sex in China was considered suitable entertainment for men but not for women. The traditional words for virginity, *zhenjie,* and for a virgin, *chunu,* both refer only to a female.

Communism ushered in a new puritanism, but that gradually eased after Deng came to power in 1978. Even so, China remains straitlaced by Western standards. A hint of sex education has been gradually introduced in Shanghai and other major cities—both in the schools and in special classes for engaged couples—but it seems that some Chinese are dizzyingly incompetent. An official newspaper in 1990 described a couple of peasants who had been married for five years but despite their best efforts could not conceive a child. The husband accused his wife of being infertile, and finally they saw a doctor in the central Chinese city of Zhengzhou. The doctor discovered why they had not conceived: For five years they had unwittingly been engaging only in anal sex.

Even today, China is extraordinarily businesslike about intercourse. Particularly in the countryside, sex is about producing babies, especially sons, or else about meeting biological appetites. And most Chinese sate themselves not with high cuisine but with fast food. One survey found that only 60 percent of Chinese "often or sometimes" make love while naked. There are other indications of how hasty and purposeful sex usually is. For example, 34 percent of peasants reported less than one minute of foreplay. Indeed, the Chinese term for foreplay, *qianxi,* is not widely understood except by academic specialists. The expression for orgasm, *xing gaochao,* is also not widely known, and so researchers have difficulty asking about it. In any case, only a third of urban women and one-quarter of rural women said that they "very often" felt a *kuaigan,* or happy feeling, during intercourse.

Clearly one dampener is the cramped housing. It is difficult to establish personal space when there is almost no physical space. One large survey found that 46 percent of those interviewed sleep in the same room as their children. Of this group, about half sleep in the same bed as their children.

Yet space is increasing, and so is libido. Among younger people, particularly university students, attitudes are changing rapidly. Asked about premarital sex, 78 percent of university students said they approved.

One of the oddest testimonials to the sexual revolution comes in the form of grumbling from CAAC, the Chinese airline. My experiences with the flight attendants had convinced me that CAAC's principal criterion for hiring them was their surliness, but apparently the airline has its own equally peculiar guidelines. It has repeatedly said that it will hire only young women who are virgins. Reporters called up CAAC to double-check: Surely the airline simply meant "single women," not necessarily "virgins." No, the airline said. It meant "virgins." Then in June 1991 CAAC complained that it was difficult to find flight attendants who met its requirements. The airline said that while there were plenty of applicants, "many are unhealthy, nearsighted, or no longer virgins."

Creating your own personal space does not, of course, mean that you have to hold an orgy in it. Puritans and philanderers now exist side by side; the point is that they are making their own decisions about private conduct, that there is such a thing as private conduct.

This in itself is a revolutionary concept in China. There is no appropriate word in Chinese for "privacy" or "private." Of course, if you look in a dictionary, you'll find a few Chinese translations of *privacy* or *private*—words like *yinsi*. But these suggest something that has been concealed or kept secret. All the expressions that correspond in some way to *privacy* are pejorative or at least vaguely negative. The idea of every individual's having his or her own bit of living space, "a room of one's own" in Virginia Woolf's phrase, doesn't really exist in China. Even words like *individualism* have an unpleasant ring in Chinese, connoting little more than selfishness.

When we needed to talk through an issue, to hold an idea up to the light and look at it from several angles, we always found it helpful to chat with Dai Qing. Dai, the fifty-one-year-old stepdaughter of a Chinese marshal, was one of the boldest and bravest writers in the country, and her essays about the dark side of Communist history have earned her the regime's bitter hatred. Nick met her for lunch at the Shangri-La Hotel to talk about the emergence of a civil society. The setting was a bit surreal, because State Security tailed Nick to the meeting and sent a woman in her thirties to eavesdrop on them from the next table. The coffee shop was almost deserted; then the State Security spy sat down two feet away from them.

"I guess the spies have expense accounts," Nick said, and Dai roared with laughter. The young woman at the next table looked mortified and buried her head in her menu. Dai Qing was not at all worried—she had once worked for the military intelligence agency herself, and one of her missions then had been to spy on a foreign journalist. By the late 1980s she had crossed the Rubicon and was so outspoken that she didn't care what the government knew about her. (In fact, the spy at the next table didn't take her mission that seriously either: Instead of scrupulously eavesdropping, she took advantage of her expense-paid meal to make four trips to the buffet table.)

"When the Communist Party took power, it destroyed the personal space of the people, and this destroyed civil society," Dai reflected as she munched on her salad. "But now that personal space is coming back. The worst thing in the old days was that there was no pluralism whatsoever. You depended absolutely on your niche in the vertical hierarchy. If you stepped out, you had nothing.

"Look at me," she said, recalling what had happened after her two-year imprisonment following the Tiananmen crackdown. "Now I have no job, no housing of my own, no salary, no status, no official trips abroad. But at least I can speak out. In the 1950s, I wouldn't even have been able to do that. Now at least I can survive. I have that much personal space.

"When the *Guangming Daily* fired me, well, in the past I would have had absolutely nothing. But now I can work for others, for a magazine in Taiwan, for example. I can have friends. I can get a passport, and I can go to Harvard for a Nieman fellowship. Some people in my position are starting companies and getting property of their own, so that they can cultivate some autonomy in that way. They'll eventually be able to start publishing companies, media outlets, and other organizations. That's the start of a civil society.

"Now the party lets people do what they want as long as they obey the law. If you don't interfere with them, they leave you alone. And this civil society can't be changed. I think it's irreversible."

While the trend toward cultural pluralism may appear unstoppable, many intellectuals are in fact disappointed with the result. Artists whom the Communist Party subsidized for four decades were suddenly told to fend for themselves. And the market's choices are cruel. Traditional Peking opera is in particular disarray, because few young people like to see it. It is all incomprehensible screeching, they say, and they would much rather see a Hong Kong martial arts film.

Many artists had anticipated that greater freedom would inspire powerful works of literature, bold new poetry, daring new plays. Instead, it inspires pornography. Ordinary folk, the *laobaixing*, are more interested in sex than in poetry, and the taboo that artists are most interested in breaking has to do with nudity rather than with politics.

At a street stand in Wenzhou, Nick picked up a magazine whose cover displayed 160 bite-size pictures of parts of a naked woman's body. The title page boasts warnings about the dangers women face in society—that is its excuse for publication—but the pages inside are filled with titillating episodes of sexual relations between men and women. The Shanghai Youth Drama Theater staged Harold Pinter's play *The Lover* and included a spicy sex scene. The audience watched through a frosted glass panel as a couple "made love" onstage. The play was a hit. A few months later, the official *China Culture News*, the newspaper published by the Culture Ministry, had a shocking cover-page photo: an insolent-looking Western woman wearing only a leather jacket, unzipped to reveal much of her breasts. The Chinese character for the word *nude* appeared in the corner, and inside, one photo showed two nude women, while another showed a woman wearing only a G-string.

"The government still maintains control," Feng Xiaogang, a thirty-five-year-old film director, explained to me during a break in production of one of his television series. "But it's a bit looser now. There are some films that just tick the edge of the Ping-Pong table— that are allowed, but just barely—and that's great."

Films have had a penetrating influence in China, and because of this, the government tirelessly scrutinizes and strictly regulates them. But now a few serious artists are hammering away at the fetters and beginning to liberate the moribund industry. One of the most accomplished figures behind this transformation is Zhang Yimou, a forty-three-year-old so self-effacing and ordinary-looking that he scarcely seems an artistic revolutionary who keeps doling out headaches to the authorities. Zhang has a square jaw and large, sunken, striking eyes that stare as though they could bore through a brick wall. Even his hair, which is cropped, crew-cut style, seems to revolve around his eyes. He wore blue jeans and a black work shirt, and he smiled almost shyly when we shook hands for the first time in a Beijing restaurant. A waitress recognized him and asked for his autograph. Zhang nodded, with a touch of modesty, and signed her scrap of paper.

He is cautious, if a bit calculating, in his approach to film, and part of this stems from his experience during the Cultural Revolution. He labored for three years in the countryside and then seven years in a textile factory, washing cars and machines, transporting loads of materials. In his spare time, he took pictures and developed them under a black cloth in his dormitory room. "It was a bitter experience, but I saw many different aspects of life; I saw the real China," he recalled.

In 1978, the Beijing Film Studio advertised that it was looking for students from eighteen to twenty-two years old. "I didn't have a particular love for movies, but I wanted to study something so that I could change my fate," Zhang said. "I applied and sent still photos that I had taken. They liked them, but said I was too old."

At age twenty-eight, Zhang was six years past the cutoff, but he made a special trip from the southern region of Guangxi to plead his case and deliver his portfolio to the culture minister. Spotting talent, the minister made an unusual intervention on Zhang's behalf. Zhang entered the academy, and Chinese film underwent a revolution.

Years later, when Zhang was scouting for a lead actress for his film *Red Sorghum,* he paid a visit to the Central Drama Academy in Beijing. He picked Gong Li, a strikingly beautiful second-year drama student, and her career took off along with his. Zhang and Gong have been together ever since, and Gong Li is now sometimes regarded as China's answer to Marilyn Monroe. It adds to Zhang's mystique that they are lovers and that his wife, Xiao Hua, the mother of their nine-year-old daughter, refuses to grant him a divorce.

Zhang first tested the limits of cultural freedom with *Judou,* a film about the owner of a dyeing factory who buys a pretty young wife to bear him a son. But the owner is impotent and takes out his frustrations by beating the girl, Gong Li. She seeks solace in an affair with her husband's hired hand and bears him a child who grows up believing he is the son of the factory owner and ends up killing his real father.

To avoid political problems, Zhang deliberately dated his film before the Communist Revolution, but it was not the cheerful kind of movie the party likes. Moreover, some people inferred that the despotic, impotent old factory owner was a symbol of a traditional, decaying China—or even of Deng Xiaoping himself.

So the Chinese government banned *Judou* when it was released in late 1990. But the movie received rave reviews abroad and became the first Chinese film to be nominated for an Oscar. Disconcerted officials at the Chinese Film Bureau tried desperately to get the Academy Award nomination revoked, but this only gained the film more attention, although in the end it did not win the Oscar.

Zhang's next film, *Raise the Red Lantern,* was also nominated for an Academy Award—and also banned. In 1993, hard-liners even banned Chen Kaige's landmark film *Farewell My Concubine* on its opening night in Beijing. The film had won the top prize at the Cannes Film Festival, a first for a Chinese movie, but the authorities worried that it spent too much time depicting the Cultural Revolution. Worse, one character commits suicide after the Cultural Revolution has ended—in the Deng Xiaoping era. Blasphemy!

Yet the hard-liners are fighting a rearguard action. Commercial pressures are growing increasingly important, and movie audiences are shrinking at a rate of 10 percent a year, forcing the closure of more than 6,000 theaters in the first half of 1993 alone. With viewers losing their tolerance for boring propaganda, studios and movie houses are desperate for entertaining films. And the government is increasingly embarrassed about banning movies that win prizes abroad. So eventually all these films were released in China. The temporary bans simply made them more appealing.

More important, Chinese filmmakers, writers, and other artists are finally producing interesting art, art that makes people laugh and cry and think (though not too hard). They are beginning to taste the kind of artistic freedom that people in the West have been enjoying for centuries.

One fundamental question is whether a market economy and civil society will nurture more refined art as well as more vivid pornography. For half a century, China's cultural world has been crippled, and writers bemoan the fact that no Chinese has ever won a Nobel Prize in literature. There were some great writers in the 1930s and 1940s—Lu Xun, Ba Jin, Shen Congwen, Lao She—but none after 1949. Lu Xun died, and the rest were stifled by the party. Lao She was driven to suicide in the Cultural Revolution. Ba Jin became head of the Writers' Association but essentially stopped writing.

Liu Xiaobo, a literary critic who was jailed for his role in the Tiananmen Square democracy demonstrations, doubts that his generation of Chinese can produce real art. "Chinese intellectuals are very shallow, and the society is becoming even more superficial," he told me one afternoon. "I have difficulty writing anything of value. People of my generation, we weren't properly educated. We grew up in a desert. I didn't read any Western literature until I was over twenty. It was too late. The result is that we don't think very deeply."

I'm more optimistic. I see an experimentalism and seriousness in Zhang Yimou, Wang Shuo, Chen Kaige, and Cui Jian that bodes well for the future of the arts in China—and for their success abroad. Wang Shuo is also more optimistic. At dinner one autumn evening, as he scooped a forkful of fried noodles into his mouth, he told me, "We might see a real Enlightenment by the end of this century. And you'll see, China will have a Nobel laureate in literature."

"And who'll that be?" I asked. "Do you have any inkling?"

Wang grinned and said impishly, "You're looking at him."

NICHOLAS D. KRISTOF

向 "钱"

纪思道

MARCHING
TOWARD
MONEY

What kind of society isn't structured on greed? The problem of social organization is how to set up an arrangement under which greed will do the least harm; capitalism is that kind of system.

—Milton Friedman

11

Improved health care and living conditions mean that it is now rare to see people like Du Dayi (*right*), a peasant disfigured by leprosy. [Photo by Nicholas D. Kristof.]

Sheryl and I were feeling pretty grim about China in the spring of 1992. The Foreign Ministry was summoning me for regular "struggle sessions" with my handler, Zhao Xingmin, who was threatening to kick me out of China. To put pressure on me, the ministry was refusing to give newborn Gregory a residence permit. And some of the most admirable Chinese I had ever met were still sitting in horrid prison cells.

Then I fled Beijing for Jiangxi Province, a poor, landlocked region in eastern China that had once been a revolutionary base for the Communists. It was there, in the little hamlet of Yujiang, that I experienced an epiphany of sorts.

The first I saw of Yujiang was the gnarled old peasants slogging barefoot behind water buffalo in the rice paddies. The countryside was a brilliant green, with periodic blotches of mud—the only time I had ever regarded brown as a warm color—all under a spectacular blue sky. My car entered the town, and the pedestrians all turned to look; no other vehicles were anywhere in sight. Yujiang consists of small, low buildings, except for one ten-story office tower that seems very out of place. My car weaved among the pedestrians and bicyclists and pulled through an iron gate. We came to a stop by the ten-story building.

This was the fief of Zhang Guoxi, a balding, thirty-nine-year-old tycoon who may be the richest man in China. If Boss Zhang, as he is universally known, chose not to use the two spittoons by the elevator, he could spit from the top floor of his headquarters in an arc that would reach the rice paddies next door. But from this remote spot he became an industrialist with assets worth $40 million or more. Perhaps much more.

"Sure, I live very well," he said, grinning, when I asked how many homes he owns. "Very well!" It had taken me two days, by plane and car, to get to Boss Zhang's headquarters, and after those hours of driving by rice paddies on gravel roads it seemed all the more peculiar to encounter a tycoon in the middle of nowhere. It was also refreshing, after being cooped up in the car with my Communist Party escort, to talk with someone who seemed eminently straightforward. Boss Zhang shook my hand, looked me in the eye, installed me in his private hotel—and charged me the going rate of twenty dollars a night.

Most of the buildings around Yujiang are dilapidated brick homes with propaganda slogans proclaiming "Socialism Is Good!" or "Control the Population Quantity; Raise the Population Quality!" Boss Zhang's corporate headquarters rises abruptly from these surroundings, a gleaming office tower with international direct dialing and fax service, in a sprawling compound that also includes a goldfish pond and two marble arches. His buildings have their own slogans, nonpolitical ones like "Guard Against Fires!"

An energetic man, constantly in motion, Boss Zhang chainsmokes up-market Zhonghua cigarettes but speaks Mandarin with a rural accent, so that he sounds like a hick. He wears a white shirt underneath a banker's suit, but his bright yellow socks are distinctly out of place.

Boss Zhang is rich in China in a way that can scarcely be fathomed, rich in a way that the Rockefellers are rich in America. He sips Napoleon brandy and Remy Martin cognac, and he has a chauffeured car waiting for him in each city where he has an office. Zhang keeps his family in Hong Kong, where he lives much of the time, and he is powerful enough that a few years ago he fathered a third child—a clear violation of the one-child policy—while obsequious local officials all looked the other way. The state even provides him with his own police station of a dozen officers solely to protect his company and serve as his bodyguards.

One of the most unusual tributes he received was to have an asteroid named after him. The asteroid—No. 3028 in the international register—was discovered at an observatory in Jiangxi, and the local government decided to name it after Zhang as an expression of admiration. Some asteroids have been named for Chinese cities and famous people, but this is the first one that the Communists have named for a capitalist.

Zhang Guoxi's name means "fruit of happiness," because at birth he was only a bit more than four pounds, the size of a fruit. His mother died when he was two, and after finishing elementary school he dropped out and began work as a carpenter. Then in 1973, in the dark days of the Cultural Revolution, he sold his family home for

$250 and used the money to start a company. Initially it made carved wooden chests, when Zhang wasn't fighting off criticisms by Communist ideologues who denounced his business as the "tail of capitalism."

"I'm fine now, and people see me going abroad and praised in the papers, and so on," Boss Zhang said soberly, as he relaxed on a leather couch in his office. "But back in 1973 to 1977, it was really rough, and I was often hungry. If I told you about those years, you'd be in tears. My life was terribly bitter then. The officials were really upset by the way I did business, and they said I was engaged in capitalism. The police came all the time to investigate. The party secretary denounced me."

After Deng Xiaoping came to power in 1978, Boss Zhang's company prospered and began to export the wooden chests and other carved furniture to Japan. Then it branched into the manufacture of gold-plated Buddhist altars, which in Japan sell for about $10,000 each. As business grew, Boss Zhang opened offices in three Chinese cities, as well as in Japan, Hong Kong, Canada, Thailand, and Germany. The Guoxi Group became a general international trading company, with interests ranging from stock trading in Hong Kong to Chinese restaurants in Germany. The company also built a nine-story hotel in the southern Chinese resort of Sanya.

Boss Zhang took me around one of his factories, where dozens of craftsmen were sawing and sanding wooden desks, and explained why he has done better than his competitors. "One difference is that the state-owned companies have the 'three irons'—iron wages, iron chairs, and iron rice bowl. In other words, wages never go down, managers can sit in their chairs all their careers no matter what kind of a job they do, and workers know that even if they never do a lick of work they won't lose their 'rice bowl,' their source of income. But in my factories, if workers are no good, they're out! And if they have talent, then they're promoted. Look at that manager there—he came up from the bottom.

"Here, you get paid according to how much you put in. My workers are paid according to a formula. They get paid by the piece, with deductions for any supplies they ruin by bad workmanship, and then it's adjusted based on the quality of the work. This way, they try to work as fast as they can, while still doing first-rate craftsmanship."

The person that Boss Zhang most admires is Lee Iacocca, whose autobiography he read in 1985 after it was translated into Chinese. Mostly Boss Zhang reads trash novels about martial arts fighting—the Chinese equivalent of Westerns—but Iacocca's book had a powerful impact on him, and he talks about it often. Indeed, his most treasured possession is a copy of the English-language edition with the autographed inscription "To Zhang Guoxi: From what I have heard about you, you'll soon write your own book, and I'll be quoting you! Best regards, Lee Iacocca."

While he doesn't bother holding political study sessions for his workers, Boss Zhang is clearly no subversive. He doesn't seem to care much about politics, and he's an optimist about China. "I'm very confident of China's future," he said. "Only a few areas have really opened up so far, and they've done very well. Look how many more provinces we have left to open up. Think what the impact of that will be."

I came back from a couple of days with Boss Zhang feeling much more hopeful about China. In Beijing, surrounded by Communist Party functionaries and dissatisfied intellectuals, I was overwhelmed by the evidence of China as a declining dynasty. But Boss Zhang simply did not fit into that model. Zhang doesn't think much of Communism, but for him and for the people working in his factories, the repression of dissidents matters much less than the economic opportunities that have become available. When I discussed torture or repression or even the killings at Tiananmen with people like Boss Zhang, the conversation fell flat. They didn't deny that terrible things happened; they just regarded them as remote and largely irrelevant.

Sheryl and I were increasingly struck, as we traveled around the country, by the fruits of the economic boom. The growing prosperity in the coastal areas—and, more important, the diminishing poverty everywhere else—was transforming China in fundamental ways. This economic metamorphosis seemed at least as important a fact about the country as the repression. Entrepreneurs like Boss Zhang seemed to be springing up, as the Chinese saying goes, like bamboo shoots after a spring rain. All around China, the new battle cry became *xiang qian kan*. This is a play on words, for *xiang qian kan* was a common slogan that means "Look to the Future!" But the same expression, written with a different character for *qian,* loosely translated means "March Toward Money!" And in the 1990s, you didn't need to ask which they meant.

In the bustling city of Wenzhou, along the coast south of Shanghai, I met a twenty-three-year-old named Wang Junjin, a boyish-looking fellow in a double-breasted suit. Wang used to be a traveling salesman, a Chinese Willy Loman whose second home was a creaky sardine can of a train carrying him thirty-eight hours each way to the factories that bought badges from him. Wang thought there had to be a better way. So he and his brother started an airline.

Their Sky Dragon Charter Air Company runs scheduled flights to cities around China on leased Boeing 737s and other aircraft. They had revenues in their first year of almost $2 million, some of which went to buy Wang's cellular telephone—for which he has much more need than a razor. At the airport, Wang helps check in passengers, looks after baggage, and makes sure that the flight crew is ready. He hopes that the government will allow his charter company to become a regular airline, with a network of domestic and international flights. "If the government lets us do it," he said simply, "we'll do it."

In the remote villages of the interior, life is much harsher. Western skeptics of China's boom often point out that inland economic growth rates are much lower than in coastal areas, and that as a result the income gap between the coast and the interior is getting larger. Taiwan and other economies in the region managed an economic miracle that made society more egalitarian, not less. That was also the case in China in the early 1980s, when the first round of economic reforms created a burst of rural prosperity. But this is no longer true. In the 1990s, the income gap between the coast and the interior is widening.

Yet I think the skeptics make too much of this. Even in the dry hills of Gansu and Ningxia provinces, near the Gobi Desert, it is obvious that the standard of living is rising steadily. Families that had lived on the edge of famine for thousands of generations are able to move out of their caves—or at least into nicer caves. Most can build a mud-brick home, eat meat once a month, and inoculate their children against disease.

The World Bank calculates that since the reform era began in 1978 a total of 170 million Chinese have risen from absolute poverty, defined as subsistence living with often inadequate food, clothing, and shelter. That marks a 60 percent decline in the number of the destitute in China, which is impressive by any standard. In the Philippines in 1990, the number of absolutely poor people, 13 million, was the same as in 1970. And in Thailand, the number of the absolutely poor actually rose from 8 million in 1980 to 9 million in 1990.

To be sure, about 100 million Chinese remain in absolute poverty. By any standard, they are desperately poor, for they often lack such basics as clean drinking water and adequate blankets for winter. Yet for them the change in living standards is arguably even more overwhelming than for Boss Zhang. At least their babies generally live through their first year, at least they can often eat their fill of rice, at least every family member usually has one piece of clothing to call his own. The incremental increase in a peasant's income from $50 a year to $100, so that he can feed his children enough rice that they do not cry from hunger, may mean a more fundamental improvement in the quality of life than the subsequent increase from $500 to $1,500.

Take Xing Yisheng. I met him in a village on the edge of the Gobi Desert in northwestern Gansu Province, one of the areas that is falling behind relative to coastal China. Immediately I wanted to interview him and take his photo. Seventy-four years old, Xing was a wrinkled little man with a white wispy beard, the kind of fellow who looked as if he had stepped out of an ancient Chinese painting. He was wearing a much-patched and faded Mao suit with a cap that looked about as old as he was. He was hobbling down the rutted dirty path, and he invited me into his shack a few doors away.

The shack had two rooms, each dominated by a *kang,* a platform bed with a fire underneath. The dirt floor was swept clean, and the furniture consisted of three tiny, rickety wooden chairs set around a crude wooden table. The mud walls were papered with newspapers, and pictures from old calendars provided a bit of decoration. Above one of the *kang*s was a surprising shop-purchased addition: a color wall poster, four feet tall, showing two healthy baby boys. It was a kind of icon to bring sons to younger generations who used the *kang* as a marital bed. Xing grandly commanded a daughter-in-law to bring tea, which she carefully poured into a couple of cracked cups, and he told me about his life.

"Before Liberation, I was just a farmhand, working for the landlords, because I didn't have any land," Xing recalled, tugging his beard reflectively. "I had two sons then, but I had to sell them because I didn't have any money. I was really ill with typhoid, and I was out of cash. So I sold my two boys for 400 *jin* [441 pounds] of rice each. I never saw them again.

"There's a huge difference between life now and the way it was then," Xing added, growing more and more animated. A grown son—one of four children born after 1949—sat quietly a few feet away, looking bored, as if he had heard it all before. "Our life today is better than a landlord's life in the past. But I tell this to young people and they don't want to hear. They say, Go away! They don't know about the old life."

Xing pointed reproachfully to his son, who appeared to be in his late thirties—but who was now shrinking in his chair like a disobedient five-year-old.

"Young man," Xing declared, his voice rising, "now you're living in heaven! You dress well, you eat well." Xing turned back to me and waved dismissively at his son. "Why last year, this young man wanted to buy a stereo cassette recorder for 700 yuan. I said, 'No, that's too much. We should buy a mule.' A mule can work. It's useful. A stereo isn't. And a mule is so big, while a stereo is so small."

It was clear who had won the argument. There was no mule, while a nice stereo occupied the place of honor in the middle of the room. Despite Xing's resistance, the family was learning to do more than just subsist; it was beginning to enjoy a bit of leisure. The same change is unfolding in most of the million-odd villages in China.

By 1992 and 1993, China's economy was growing 13 percent annually, faster than that of any other country in the world. Those are unsustainable figures, attributable to the boom part of a boom-bust cycle, and a slowdown is likely and will make China seem a bit less exciting. Yet even if you adjust for the cycles, China's economy has been one of the world's fastest growing ever since the late 1970s.

For all my anger at the authorities, I had to admit that the government was doing something right. I was grudgingly forced to reconsider my feelings about China. It seemed too easy, too glib, for Americans to praise the Philippines or India for their democratic systems while condemning China—even though the Chinese people were improving their standard of living much more quickly than either Filipinos or Indians.

I couldn't help thinking what would happen if a Chinese journalist roamed the United States reporting about crime. He would travel around, visiting the urban slums, entering the crack dens, interviewing the rape victims, consoling the children of the slain. No doubt he would be indignant at the senselessness of the crime, at the government's failure to control guns, at society's inability to confront the drug problem. And his passion would come through in his articles. His material would be accurate, and it would leave his Chinese readers feeling that America is a violent, dangerous, uncivilized country. Talking all the time to crime victims, he might well conclude that the United States is a society reverting to the jungle. The government would seem fundamentally immoral for looking the other way as people are gunned down in the schools and the streets.

But when this reporter dropped by ordinary middle-class homes—like those of the Kristofs in Yamhill, Oregon, or of the WuDunns in New York City—he would find conversations a bit puzzling. The Kristofs and WuDunns would certainly agree that crime is terrible, but then they would cheerfully move on to other topics. The reporter would single-mindedly bring the conversation back to crime, asking how they could live with the knowledge that they might be shot down any time they walked on a public street. The Kristofs and WuDunns would shake their heads soberly and grumble that the streets really are awful, and then they would move on to discuss the day's news or some recent book or film. The reporter would ask about rape and burglary and bank robbery, and a few awkward silences would result. If the Chinese reporter asked whether the United States government would collapse in the next few years from the crime problem, he would get funny looks. And when he left, the Kristofs and WuDunns would say to each other: "This guy may know his crime statistics, but he sure doesn't know America."

As I flew back to Beijing from my interview with Boss Zhang, I wondered if that was the kind of role I was playing. Was I so obsessed with human rights violations that I missed the rest of the tableau of China and the buds of a civil society? Was my writing so focused that, however accurate, it was misleading? Was I deceiving myself?

With those questions echoing in our heads, Sheryl and I probed the Chinese economic boom. Contrary to the conventional wisdom, the economy was not entirely a disaster during the Maoist period. The statistics are not reliable, but it appears that very high levels of forced savings and investment produced respectable economic growth for most of the Communist period, even during the Cultural Revolution. National income in 1976, at the end of the Cultural Revolution, was 60 percent higher than when the turmoil began ten years earlier. Of course, the growth would have been much higher if it had not been for the chaos, and 30 million deaths by famine might have been avoided if Mao had not launched the Great Leap Forward in 1958, but even so, the economy muddled along in the Maoist era.

After Deng Xiaoping took over in 1978, growth rose from respectable to spectacular. Since Deng launched his reform program, the Chinese economy has enjoyed an annual average growth rate of a bit more than 9 percent. That is triple the average growth rate of the United States in that period, and about 70 percent more than the growth rate in India or Indonesia.

China is now the biggest producer in the world of coal, cement, grain, cotton, meat, and fish. While it remains low on the per capita charts, overall as a nation it ranks third in steel production, after Japan and the United States. In output of crude oil, China ranks fifth, after the United States, Saudi Arabia, Russia, and Iran.

To get a sense of the giddy pace of change in China, consider the process of industrialization around the world. Britain was the first country to enjoy an industrial revolution, beginning in the late eighteenth century, and in that period it took fifty-eight years for real per capita British gross domestic product to double. The American industrial revolution was a bit faster, with per capita output doubling in just forty-seven years from 1839. Beginning in 1885, Japan doubled its per capita GDP in thirty-four years.

Now China is roaring along with its own industrial revolution, doubling its real per capita output every ten years. Its 9 percent growth rate in the reform era, or 7.5 percent on a per capita basis, compares with a per capita growth rate in nineteenth-century America of just 1.6 percent per year. The reason for the accelerated pace is simple: China can take advantage of foreign inventions and technology; it can import assembly lines instead of devising them from scratch. Yet even if it is a game of catch-up, as far as major industrial revolutions go, China's takes the prize. The "Four Dragons"—Taiwan, Hong Kong, Singapore, and South Korea—managed similar growth rates, or even slightly higher ones, in peak periods of their development, but all put together they are no more than the size of a large Chinese province. As for such growth rates in a huge country like China, there's been nothing like them in the history of the world.

It is rather fashionable these days to see the Chinese people as natural capitalists, born wheelers and dealers, and to explain the economic boom in that way. A stream of American corporate executives and investment bankers passed through Beijing, telling us in awestruck tones how brilliant the Chinese people are in business. Maybe it's in the genes, they suggested.

When I was about to be posted to Hong Kong in 1986, I met with a group of *New York Times* editors to discuss story possibilities, and one editor asked why the Philippines was always the laggard of the region. I tried to come up with a few reasons. Then one of my favorite editors burst in: "Because the Filipinos aren't Chinese."

That explanation has rattled around my mind ever since. On the one hand, it is attractive because it explains so much. The fastest-growing countries in the world in the last couple of decades have been those with large Chinese populations or else those exposed to strong Chinese influences: China, Japan, South Korea, Hong Kong, Taiwan, Singapore. And while the Philippines has trailed far behind, its Chinese minority has done extremely well and plays a huge role in the business and financial community. Ethnic Chinese account for 1.5 percent of the population of the Philippines, for example, but the companies they own generate 35 percent of sales by locally owned firms. Ethnic Chinese make up 2 percent of Indonesians and, by one count, may own as much as 70 percent of private domestic capital.

The ethnic explanation bothers me, however, because it is rather racist. If some people are credited with unusual business acumen, then what does that say about the others? Moreover, it's worth pointing out that today's conventional wisdom about the genius of the Chinese people is precisely the opposite of the previous conventional wisdom, which was that they were hopelessly muddled and could never get their act together. Lord Byron wrote that China possessed

"the miserable happiness of a stationary & unwarlike mediocrity."
Ralph Waldo Emerson was even more scathing:

> *Why does the same dull current of ignoble blood creep through a thou-*
> *sand generations in China without any provision for its own purifica-*
> *tion, without the mixture of one drop from the fountains of goodness &*
> *glory . . . ? The summit of their philosophy and science is how to make*
> *tea. . . . The closer contemplation we condescend to bestow the more*
> *disgusting is that booby nation. The Chinese Empire enjoys precisely a*
> *mummy's reputation, that of having preserved to a hair for 3 or 4,000*
> *years the ugliest features in the world. I have no gift to see a meaning*
> *in the venerable vegetation of this extraordinary people. . . . But*
> *China, reverend dulness! hoary idiot! all she can say at the convocation*
> *of nations must be—"I made the tea!"*

Yet even if Chinese entrepreneurship has impressed the world
only in the last couple of decades, even if Chinese business acumen
was well hidden for the previous few thousand years, my editor had a
point. In recent decades, Chinese societies have all sizzled, and no
region in the world has come close to matching the performance of
East Asia. In 1993, the World Bank published a major study on the
region and concluded that there was only one chance in 10,000 that
so many miracle economies would randomly be located so close to
one another.

Moreover, there was no single "East Asian Model"; national
strategies differed significantly. Hong Kong adopted a laissez-faire
approach, while Singapore and South Korea were much more inter-
ventionist. Still, there are some important common threads among
East Asia's success stories, and they may shed a bit of light on China's
prospects. The successful countries tended to promote agriculture at
an early stage in their development, and they also tended to expose
themselves to foreign technologies and markets. For example, many
of them emphasized exports, thus instilling the discipline of competition with other nations.

These countries also maintained realistic exchange rates, and they
ensured a relatively stable economic environment by avoiding long
periods of high inflation. They encouraged high savings and investment and boosted education and health care, raising the capabilities

of the labor force. They also empowered a technocratic elite within the bureaucracy, which was given some autonomy to manage the economy.

How does China do by these standards? Reasonably well, I think. As the World Bank study said, there are "striking parallels" between China and the East Asian miracle economies. Like its neighbors, China began its reform program with an effort to boost agricultural incentives. It has also opened itself up, more and more, to foreign investment and management, and the export drive in the coastal provinces has forced China to compete with other manufacturers around the world. Exchange rates have been steadily devalued and domestic prices made more rational. The government has never quite let inflation soar out of control, although it has come close, and it has promoted education and health care while giving increasing leeway to the technocratic elite within the bureaucracy. As in Japan and Singapore, some young Chinese still regard a career as a government bureaucrat as one of the most prestigious around, so smart people become economic planners and regulators.

Another partial explanation for East Asia's success, a better one than genes, may be the legacy of Confucianism. A Confucian belt runs from Japan to Singapore, encompassing the miracle economies of Taiwan, South Korea, Hong Kong, and now China. The fringe of the Confucian belt touches Thailand and the Southeast Asian countries speaking Malay-based languages: Malaysia, Indonesia, and the Philippines. These nations were influenced by Confucianism but to a lesser degree.

Ever since Max Weber argued that Protestantism is particularly suited to capitalism, there has been a fierce and somewhat inconclusive debate about the connection between culture and development. In the case of Confucianism and capitalism, any link is likely to be just as complex and ambiguous, not least because Confucianism itself looked down to some extent on business, putting entrepreneurs on the bottom of the social heap. And a Confucian background obviously can't explain why South Korea has done well and also why North Korea has done poorly. Likewise, Confucianism didn't do much for the region's economy during the last five centuries—when people were much more serious than they are today about paying homage to Confucius. It was only when they rebelled against Confucius that this heritage somehow began to play a useful role.

Still, I think that there are some features of Confucianism that prove beneficial to a market economy and rapid industrialization. For example, a Confucian sense of self-restraint—and thus a disdain among some Confucians for extravagance and conspicuous consumption—may help explain the very high savings rates in China and its neighbors in recent times. There are plenty of other factors, such as tax policy and interest rates, but the high savings rates in today's East Asia are striking—China, for example, has a personal savings rate that ranges between 35 percent and 40 percent, compared with about 5 percent in the United States. These savings generate the capital that can be invested in new factories, roads, and shops to boost economic growth. China's savings rate, among the highest in the world, helps provide the funds to finance the industrial revolution.

The other kind of capital that is necessary for sustained growth is human capital—the kind of healthy, educated labor force that can work on assembly lines and figure out how to do things better and faster. Here, too, China shares the distinct advantages of its neighbors. The Confucian emphasis on scholarship, and the tradition of examinations to recruit the civil service, led to comparatively high literacy rates throughout the countries of the region. Even today, despite the difficulty of learning Chinese characters, and despite the peasant girls who drop out of elementary school, only 27 percent of the Chinese population is illiterate. Even that is much too high a rate, and it could be lowered by more efforts to keep rural girls in school. But it holds up well against other developing countries. The illiteracy rate is 52 percent for India, 65 percent for Pakistan, and 52 percent for Egypt.

Moreover, Chinese laborers are far healthier than Bolivians or Ghanaians; Chinese can go to work without worrying about a guinea worm or other parasite inside their bellies, and they are well enough fed that they can concentrate on their work. China's life expectancy of seventy is excellent for a developing country, and malnutrition is usually a problem only in remote villages.

Confucianism has been around for 2,500 years, however, prompting the obvious question: If China looks so promising today, what held it back for so many centuries?

I found one answer when I was living in Hong Kong in 1987, while reading an obscure article published in 1886 in the *Journal of the North China Branch of the Royal Asiatic Society*. The article described Chinese guilds, trade unions, and chambers of commerce. It cited a few examples of why China was not making much progress.

Coppersmiths, for example, used to make a living by pounding thick sheets of copper or brass into thinner sheets. Then in the 1880s, a bright entrepreneur got the idea of importing sheets of brass that were already thin enough to use and making brass pots out of them. He imported some, and the coppersmiths were so outraged that they went on strike and threatened havoc. To prevent a riot, the thin brass sheets were sent back to Hong Kong, and Chinese continued to use thick sheets of brass that first had to be pounded thin.

This was not an isolated incident. The article cites a Chinese-American who returned to his homeland with some powerful sewing machines to manufacture shoes. The local shoemakers promptly destroyed the machines, and the entrepreneur gave up his idea of starting a factory in China. Another Chinese entrepreneur set up a steam-powered cotton mill, but the local people blocked this scheme by banding together and refusing to sell him any cotton.

One Chinese entrepreneur, also in the late nineteenth century, suffered a worse fate. He was a member of the goldsmiths' guild, and he earned a commission to produce a large amount of gold leaf for the emperor. The goldsmiths had a rule among themselves that they would each take on only one apprentice at a time, to keep their numbers down and prices up. But this goldsmith asked the magistrate for permission to take on several apprentices to fill his order for the emperor. The magistrate agreed, even though other goldsmiths were furious. One of them spread the word that "biting to death is not a capital offense," apparently on the theory that no single bite is the fatal one. So 123 other goldsmiths attacked the entrepreneur, each taking a bite of his flesh. No one was allowed to leave without showing bloody teeth and gums, and the entrepreneur was chewed to death.

In fact, the goldsmiths had misunderstood the law, for the one who took the first bite was arrested and beheaded. Even so, the episode understandably discouraged other craftsmen from introducing innovations at odds with guild rules.

As these incidents attest, the Middle Kingdom in those days never came close to being a market economy. Europe had some of the same problems—such as the Luddites who smashed labor-saving machinery—but in China they were all much worse. Partly because of the stern impact of Confucianism, China tended to look down on business and businessmen, just as it looked down on science. In the West, it was various technological advances—the cotton gin, the mechanical reaper, the steam engine—that provided an underpinning for the industrial revolution. In China, the intelligentsia had little interest in inventing new machines, and the emperor declared in 1793 that his country had no need to import "ingenious articles." Even if some Mr. Wu had invented a cotton gin, China did not have a modern economy in which he could have marketed it. It might simply have sat unused and rusting in Mr. Wu's cottage.

While China scorned technology and business, and operated under a stifling system of guild rules, that was not even the worst of it. One of the biggest problems was simply that China in the nineteenth century was terribly corrupt and unstable. Rebellions, famines, mass migrations, floods, and warlords swept across the country, knocking down those who tried to set up small businesses. Even trade within China was restricted by tariffs and less elegant methods, like confiscation. Our hypothetical Mr. Wu, for example, would have been foolish to set up a factory to manufacture cotton gins. Before he could recoup his investment, the factory would have been seized by some warlord.

The Communist Revolution changed everything. It ushered in a strong central government and did away with the guilds and the Confucianism that were strangling business. Instead, it allowed the commissars to strangle business, and that turned out to be a big step forward.

Mancur Olson, an American economist, outlined a theory of development in his 1982 book *The Rise and Decline of Nations*. I felt an immediate excitement as I read Professor Olson's book, because it addresses the fundamental question of what turns a nation into an economic dynamo. He asks why Germany and Japan generated economic miracles after being defeated in World War II, while other countries—China among them—go on and on without much ever happening. As Samuel Taylor Coleridge said, China represents "permanency without progression."

Professor Olson says that over time countries become sclerotic from the influence of special interests—like the goldsmiths and other craftsmen in China. Restrictions and established interests manage to block far-reaching change and dampen mobility. These special interests prevent the painful dislocations that are inherent in change and essential to progress. Innovations threaten the status quo, and labor-saving devices put people out of work. New efficiencies hurt, so special interests fight back. In some cases, it takes a war—particularly a defeat—to destroy entrenched interests, clear the slate, and start again. Their catastrophic loss in World War II, after all, cost Japan and Germany not only many of their buildings but also much of their social infrastructure. In the war's aftermath, the arteries of commerce were clear. Labor and capital flowed to their most efficient uses, until special interests gradually reemerged. Professor Olson's explanation may not be a perfect one, but it helps illuminate the process of industrialization and economic revolution.

In the case of China, the entire nation used to be nearly paralyzed by this economic sclerosis. But then the Communist Party came along with a revolution that fulfilled much the same role as war did in Japan. The revolution destroyed the old system, so that now there are no real unions and few absolute restrictions on economic activity.

To be sure, it might have been simpler if another kind of party had staged a revolution in China. The Communist Party itself is a paralyzing social force, and nothing could be more sclerotic than a huge Chinese state-owned company. But in the nonstate sector, anything can be negotiated. There are complex rules, of course, but bribes and *guanxi* are a powerful solvent that clears them away—at a price. In some ways, business is far less regulated in China than in the United States or Europe.

In early 1993 I visited the coastal boom town of Wenzhou and found it as laissez-faire as anything in Asia. Wenzhou is bustling and prosperous, with tiny winding streets full of private shops and street vendors. Fortune-tellers stand on the sidewalk, offering to read faces with their fingers and advise on matters such as marriage. Prostitutes in short skirts sit in hotel lobbies. Book vendors sell "art books" about naked women. Taxi drivers complain about the Communist Party as a "gang of bandits." Everybody's out to make money.

To be sure, I'm partial to Wenzhou for a reason that has nothing to do with its vibrancy: On three occasions during my stay there, people looked me in the eye, listened to me speak, and asked if I was

Chinese. Their own dialect is so bizarre that they mistook my American accent in Mandarin for a standard Beijing accent. This may not be a tribute to their intelligence, since I don't look remotely Chinese, but it sure endeared me to Wenzhou.

Wang Yuejin, a hearty thirty-four-year-old, almost as wide as he is tall, is typical of the Wenzhou capitalists. When we met, Wang wore a green wool suit, with the French label still attached to the sleeve—otherwise people might think it was a local suit. He was loaded down by a brick of a gold ring on his finger and a twenty-four-carat gold bracelet that could have been used for weight lifting. We lounged around his huge apartment, with its marble floors, twenty-five-inch Panasonic color television, Kenwood stereo, and Toshiba air conditioners. Wang showed off his $2,000 gold Rado watch—"My wife has one just like this; it's a set"—while workmen banged on the outside wall, where they were installing the cable from his satellite television dish. The banging rattled the bottles of Napoleon brandy in his liquor cabinet.

Wang, in short, is the kind of fellow that the Communist Party was organized to overthrow. And the people whom the party aimed to rescue were those like Zhou Sailu, a thirty-seven-year-old peasant who toils on Wang's factory floor. I found Zhou sitting on a little stool, surrounded by a mountain of shoes that she was lacing up. Beside her was her daughter, a gorgeous nineteen-year-old, hunched over the shoes in her lap, her fingers flying as she worked the laces through the sockets. The factory floor was chaotic, filthy, and noisy, yet this was their entire life. In tiny niches above the workplace, shacks had been constructed with bamboo mats for walls—rather like tree houses. These tiny rooms were the workers' dormitories.

I tried to engage the daughter, whose name was Chen Suchi, in conversation. She seemed terrified of me, and she had probably never spoken with a foreigner before. But I couldn't pass her by: She looked as if she'd been sent from central casting to fit the role of a belle working for a capitalist ogre. She reminded me of a female Oliver Twist.

"So when do you begin work each morning?" I asked her. She avoided my gaze and hunched more tightly over the shoes in her lap.

"Between seven and eight each morning," her mother answered brightly from a few feet away. I ignored the mother, trying to coax a few words from Cinderella herself.

"And when do you quit in the evening?" I quizzed the daughter.

"About eleven-thirty at night," the mother replied.

That shocked me, and I turned to the mother. "You work—let me see—fifteen or sixteen hours a day?" I asked incredulously. "What about lunch?"

"We nibble on something right here—we don't go out," the mother said indifferently. "I don't know how many hours that is."

"How many days a week do you work like that?" I asked.

"Huh?"

"You take Sundays off?"

"No. It's like that every day. But for Chinese New Year we'll go home to the village, of course. For a week or two."

I checked around with the other workers, and it was mostly the same. They worked more than twelve hours a day, every day of the week, for a month or so at a time. Then they sometimes took a day or two off. And the really hardworking ones didn't even do that.

"The workers are all paid by the piece," explained Zhen Linling, one of the floor managers. "So they want to work extra hours and earn lots of money. If they rest, they don't earn money. So they want to work. If you don't give them work, they go to another factory at night and moonlight. So you give them a task and they keep to it."

I returned to Zhou and again tried to chat up her daughter. "So how much do you make a month?" I asked.

"Six hundred yuan each," replied her mother. At that time, 600 yuan was worth a bit more than $100—more than a university professor's salary and a large sum in their home village. Still, it was a tiny amount compared with the huge profits the factory owner was earning from the sweat of her brow.

"It's kind of a tough life here, I guess," I suggested.

"Oh, it's better than the village," the mother gushed. "We earn lots of money here, and the life is pretty good."

"What about your husband?" I asked. "Is he happy about you leaving him and coming here to work?"

Zhou smiled patronizingly at me. It was clear she thought I had asked a stupid question.

"How could my husband object?" she asked. "Look at how much money I'm making!"

Whenever I poked around the factories in cities like Wenzhou, I thought about Professor Olson's theories about economic sclerosis. The Communist Party, it seemed, had cleared away some of the dead weight of Chinese special interests, had finally adopted laissez-faire as a guiding principle—at least in the nonstate sector. On a visit to Dongguan, I once asked Liu Shuji, a district party secretary, whether a minimum wage might be a good idea. He recoiled. "What's the point of a minimum wage?" he asked, scrunching up his eyebrows. "If both sides want to work for a given wage, why should we interfere?" So, paradoxically, it is the Communists who are finally making a market economy in China. A century from now, that may be remembered as the Communist movement's greatest achievement anywhere in the world.

The most important entrenched interest that the Communists cleared away was perhaps that of the landowners. The land reform that followed Liberation was one of the most important things that have happened in the Chinese countryside in the last 4,000 years. Wealthy landowners were dragged before struggle sessions, denounced, and spat upon by landless peasants, and their land was divided up along with their livestock, their clothing, even their homes. If they were lucky, the landowners were moved into tiny shacks and allowed to wade into the rice paddies and farm tiny plots. If they were not so lucky, they were beaten to death.

However brutal it was, this land reform created for the first time a moderate degree of equality, and that is another important ingredient for an economic takeoff. Japan, Taiwan, and South Korea also underwent land redistribution in the aftermath of World War II, and the relative equality of assets seems to have been a factor in their boom. This is a major advantage that China enjoys over countries in much of Latin America, where land is still concentrated in a few hands.

The Communist Party also unified the country, so that people can ship goods from one province to another without paying duties—although some illegal duties have been reimposed since the late 1980s. And after a century of convulsions in China, Deng

Xiaoping has provided a somewhat more stable political environment. Investors now know that if they start a business this year, it will probably be around for a few years at least. Stability remains one of the weak points in the Chinese equation, partly because no one knows who if anyone will be able to consolidate power as the next emperor. But at least the uncertainty about the future that exists today is better than the old certainty that things would be unstable.

Perhaps more important, the Communists built up capital. They borrowed from the Stalinist economic model in generating very high investment rates to create financial capital. Better yet, they built up human capital—although not nearly as much as they claim. The Communists launched literacy drives and public health campaigns that are still going on. After the 1949 revolution, peasant girls were encouraged to go to school for the first time, and adults went to night school to struggle to learn a few basic characters. Literacy is still far too low, but it is at least much higher than it ever was before in Chinese history.

The Communists have done best in primary education, and nearly all children get at least a few years of elementary school. Even accounting for distorted statistics and girls who are kept home, my guess is that more than 95 percent of all children start school and that more than 80 percent graduate from elementary school. That's not a bad record for a developing country.

The problem is that only about 44 percent of children in the appropriate age group are enrolled in secondary schools, a higher rate than in India but lower than in Mexico or the Philippines. And only 1.7 percent of young people attend college, an appallingly low proportion. Even Sudan (2.3 percent), Vietnam (2.3 percent), Swaziland (3.9 percent), Burma (4.8 percent), and India (6.4 percent) do better.

China desperately needs more university graduates, and it also needs to spend much more on education. Expenditures on education account for only 2.4 percent of Chinese gross national product, and the proportion has held steady or even declined slightly since the early 1980s. That proportion is higher than in Indonesia (0.9 percent) and Bangladesh (2.2 percent), but it is lower than in India (3.2 percent) and Uganda (3.4 percent). Nonetheless, China does focus its training on the specialties it needs. Every year it now manages to graduate more than 200,000 engineers, nearly twice as many as the United States.

There is another reason why human capital is growing in China: the one-child policy. Like Sheryl, I think that the policy causes enormous heartbreak in many homes, and I worry about a society where sex-selective abortion produces many more males than females. But I also have to acknowledge that declining fertility may be good for China's long-run prospects.

When parents can have only one child, they do everything they can to help that kid get ahead. They send the kid to nursery school, read aloud and help with homework during elementary school, and hire private tutors in high school. In the cities, many of our friends arranged their lives around their children, teaching them their first Chinese characters at two years of age, calligraphy at five, piano at seven, English at ten, and so on. Even in the countryside, families are less casual about their offspring when they have only one or two, and they do what they can to raise them to be healthy and educated.

To be sure, the Communist Party also squandered tremendous amounts of capital, both financial and human. The Great Leap Forward and the Cultural Revolution wasted lives and money, monumental amounts of each. Mao terrorized and imprisoned intellectuals, so China could not properly use its human resources. The Communist Party's suspicion of intellectuals is one reason why China has such a low university enrollment. Yet Mao created as well as destroyed. He created human capital in places like Tuqiao, a poor village in Anhui Province in central China.

I spent an afternoon in Tuqiao with a seventy-six-year-old illiterate named Wang Chigang. Wang is a sinewy little man with wrinkled skin the texture of a softball about to be retired. His three remaining teeth are all set at odd angles, and he speaks only the local dialect. His grandson, sitting on another stool in the living room, translated his words into Mandarin.

The home was made of mud bricks, with a pig shed behind the house, and Wang's great-grandchildren played on the dirt floor. The furniture consisted of a bed, a table, and a bureau, all dilapidated, and a few stools. Outside, on the dirt road bisecting the village, a handful of children were playing Ping-Pong on the ground, with a row of bricks serving as the net. They had homemade wooden paddles, but the ball was the genuine article. We talked to the staccato beat of the Ping-Pong game and the grunting of the pigs behind the house.

Wang grew up a landless peasant and had been a beggar in the 1940s. He never went to school, and he still cannot write his own name. "Sometimes I go to the county town by bus, with my sons," he said, sipping a cup of dark tea. "But I don't like the city. Too crowded. Nobody has time for you. And it's embarrassing when I have to go to the toilet—I don't know which is which. Since I don't know the characters for 'man' and 'woman' I have to ask for help finding the right one." Yet Wang gloated that his children and especially his grandchildren have risen to higher levels. They all went to school, and a grandson graduated from high school. "He can write really well," Wang said, beaming.

While some local governments ignore the illiteracy problem, particularly in the countryside, others are actively campaigning to teach people to read and write. In the villages of Xiping County in Henan Province in central China, students stop visitors and ask them to read a few characters on a blackboard. Any visitor who cannot read the characters is not allowed to enter the village. This means that illiterates are effectively grounded, and in frustration many have joined the special reading classes offered in each village. Now in Xiping County, according to local officials, only 1.7 percent of those between the ages of twenty and forty are still illiterate.

As an American, I was particularly struck by the government's determination to teach English to all young people in the country. In many ways it was a foolish decision, for peasants in remote villages never even see foreigners, let alone get a chance to speak to them. But I found myself awed by the audacity of the idea: Remote mountaintop village schools might lack electricity, desks, and glass windows, but they at least had an English teacher.

To be sure, the English teachers often don't speak English. In the Dabie Mountains of Hubei Province, I visited Chen Xinyu, an English teacher who has had only four months of formal training in English.

"Hello," she said awkwardly, in what was obviously a well-rehearsed spiel. "Welcome to our school."

"Thank you," I replied, speaking word by word in painfully slow English. "You speak English very well."

She scrunched her eyebrows and looked blank. "*Ni shuo shenma?*" she replied, asking me what I had said.

"Where did you learn your English?" I asked, even more slowly than before. No response but puzzlement. "Your English," I repeated. "How did you learn it?"

"*Ni shuo shenma?*" she asked again.

Then I watched her conduct class in the dilapidated school. She wrote the word *both* on the blackboard, in an elegant script, and then turned to the forty-five pupils.

"Bose!" she said.

"Bose!" the pupils repeated.

It is not Chen's fault that her English is atrocious. She used her own meager salary to buy a radio, and she wakes at 5:00 A.M. each day to listen to the English-language news from Beijing. When I left her school, my overriding impression was not so much scorn for her incompetence as admiration that such a place would even bother to try to teach a foreign language. In my high school in Yamhill, Oregon, only about one-fifth of the graduating class ever took a foreign language (Spanish), yet every Chinese school in the country made English a mandatory subject beginning in grade seven. And in some places, like Shanghai, English classes begin in the second grade.

One of my most interesting responsibilities in China was interviewing high school students applying to Harvard College. The caliber of the students, all of them from big cities, particularly Shanghai, was simply stunning. You could fill Harvard's entire freshman class with kids from Shanghai and probably raise the intellectual level of the student body. The pupils at the best Shanghai high schools are in class from 8:00 A.M. to about 4:30 P.M., sometimes with another round of evening classes. Then they do a couple of hours of homework each night. They take Saturday afternoons off, but Sundays are often devoted to "Olympic Schools"—special advanced courses in chemistry, physics, and the like. Summer and winter vacations are brief, and the students are supposed to turn in homework at the end of the vacations.

These students are, of course, wildly unrepresentative of Chinese students as a whole. Perhaps it is unfair to devote resources to the Olympic Schools instead of trying to keep more peasant girls in elementary school in the Dabie Mountains of Hubei. But whatever the inequities, an educational elite is emerging. China now has more students attending American universities than any other nation, and in the 1990s an explosion of private schools is adding to the educational infrastructure—again, alas, only in the cities. So these Harvard applicants may be the cream of the cream, but China is such a vast country that this still amounts to a huge number of people. It seems to me that one factor in China's economic miracle is this investment in human capital. I always finished the Harvard interviews feeling more optimistic about China's prospects.

The other crucial kind of human capital in which the Communists have invested is public health care. The Chinese medical system is in many ways a model for developing countries. While China spends only about 4 percent of its gross national product on medical care (compared with about 15 percent in the United States in 1994), its health statistics are comparable to those of much richer nations. And in the cities, health statistics are as good as those of American urban areas.

In Shanghai, for example, 9.9 out of every 1,000 infants die in their first year of life. In New York City, the infant mortality rate is 10.2 per 1,000. And a baby in Shanghai can expect to live 76 years, while life expectancy in New York is 73.8 years. As I wandered China's hospitals and clinics, I found it embarrassing that in a direct comparison between America's largest city and China's largest, it should be Shanghai that comes out on top in certain health statistics. Equally embarrassing, a child born in Shanghai today is more likely to grow up to learn to read than a child born in New York City.

Now, these comparisons are not entirely fair. If New Yorkers ate mostly rice and vegetables, and bicycled an hour each day to work, they would be healthier, too. In addition, New York's health statistics are affected by the urban underclass, the high proportion of teenage pregnancies, and the ubiquitousness of guns. Shanghai avoids these problems by banning handguns, compelling unwed mothers to get abortions, and forbidding members of anything resembling an underclass to move to the city. Even if a pregnant peasant does move to Shanghai and has a baby that dies, the death will not be counted in Shanghai's health statistics. Rather, it will be counted in the statistics of the woman's home province—if the authorities there even know about it.

All this said, life expectancy has approximately doubled since the Communist Revolution, and back in 1949 Chinese were also eating rice and getting lots of exercise. The Communists achieved this revolution in medical care by emphasizing preventative programs. From its first days in power, the party sent work teams to drain the swamps that bred malarial mosquitoes. Factories offered hygiene classes, teaching workers to wash their hands and brush their teeth. The state virtually wiped out the urban underclass—the homeless and penniless—and, most of the time, ensured everyone rudimentary health care and basic nutrition.

To be sure, Chinese hospitals are pretty grim places, and none of my Chinese friends could ever understand what I saw in their medical system. In the countryside, doctors have not always had a high school education, and clinics have little or no modern equipment. Hospitals are crowded and dirty, and patients usually have to pay the doctors bribes to get any attention. An old man with heart trouble will not get a coronary bypass; he will die. A young woman whose kidneys fail will probably not get dialysis; she, too, will die.

Instead of allocating resources for such complex procedures as coronary operations or dialysis, China has channeled its money to basic health care—an approach that is far more cost-effective. For example, the most basic treatment for a leukemia patient costs about $5,000 and on average adds a bit more than a month to the person's life. The same $5,000, used to buy vitamin A supplements for children, adds a total of 10,000 years of life expectancy for those kids. And $5,000 spent on measles immunization adds up to 5,000 years of life expectancy.

No wonder that China each year sends people out into the countryside, mobilizing peasants to bring their children forward for immunizations. About 85 percent of all Chinese children are inoculated against six basic ailments before their first birthday. That is a remarkable immunization record in a country where more than two-thirds of the population lives in the countryside.

For years I'd been intrigued by the "barefoot doctors" whom Mao sent out to treat the peasants. It seemed a terrific idea: Instead of training a small number of top-notch medical specialists, who don't want to get their feet muddy, give ten times as many people a basic training in health care and send them out to work among the peasants. But whenever I visited the countryside and asked about the *chi-*

jiao yisheng, or barefoot doctors, the local cadres laughed in an embarrassed way. "Oh, we don't have them anymore," they invariably replied. "That only happened in the Cultural Revolution."

Plainly, barefoot doctors were not as highly regarded within China as they were abroad. Plenty of cadres seemed to yearn for CT scanners and for the radiologists and brain surgeons who were the last thing they needed. Unfortunately, the decline of Communist Party leadership and the collapse of the communes has meant that public health work has faltered in some rural areas. At the same time, the rise of a market economy has meant that people can get health care only if they can pay for it. Likewise, as Chinese get richer they eat more pork instead of vegetables, and they take buses instead of walking or riding bicycles. The result is that in the 1990s health care is still improving, but more slowly than it might.

Finally, I did manage to track down some barefoot doctors—now typically clad in sandals—and I got to spend some time with them. First I visited some rural clinics in Fujian Province, and then I arranged to spend a day with the perpetually sorrowful Dr. Su Ke in the villages of Xishuangbanna, a tropical region in the south of China near Vietnam. A forty-six-year-old with a graying crew cut, Dr. Su works out of a rural clinic but regularly hikes with the other doctors into the mountains to see the peasants who don't believe in doctors. As we drove into the mountains in my hired car, he explained the difficulties.

"When we go out and try to inoculate babies, some of the peasants are very frightened and hide their kids," Dr. Su said. "Or they turn their dogs on us to bite us and drive us away." Even if Dr. Su manages to get his needle into the derriere of a local child—a task made easier because none of them wear pants—he is likely to get in trouble. "We give them injections against measles, and then the kid gets a cold. So the parents come and complain. They say, 'You promised that my child wouldn't get sick!'"

We stopped the car at a roadside one-room clinic operated by an eighteen-year-old peasant who had just opened up shop as a doctor. It was a good thing we came by. The peasant was trying to pull the abscessed tooth of a teenage girl, but he wasn't making much headway. Blood was all over, knives and pliers were scattered about, and both the doctor and the patient looked a bit discouraged. There was no Novocain, but the girl was using some Chinese medicine that seemed to deaden the pain pretty well. Dr. Su took over the pair of pliers, rapped away with a chisel, and after about five minutes the tooth came out. By this point I was pretty glad that I was not a Chinese peasant with a toothache.

We got back in the car and drove down a narrow dirt lane for several miles, until the road ended and we had to walk. Dr. Su packed his little black bag, and we hiked down a trail for a mile until we reached the tiny village of Manboxinzhai, a cluster of several dozen huts on stilts. By raising the houses, the villagers keep out the rats and snakes. As we entered the village, the peasants rushed out with their complaints: There was a little boy with chicken pox, a young man with a swollen leg, and an old man with chest pain.

Before treating the patients, Dr. Su rebuked the village's health officer, Sha Piao, for failing to implement a new policy for prenatal health checkups. "You're too busy getting ready to build your new house to look after the pregnant women," Dr. Su said sternly as Sha hung his head and shifted his weight from one foot to the other. The new program that Sha was supposed to implement involved charging all pregnant women an obligatory fee of ten yuan. They were then supposed to receive three prenatal checkups from gynecologists who hiked from village to village. When it was time for birth, the woman was supposed to use a midwife with government training. If she did, the authorities would pay the midwife's two-yuan fee and return eight yuan to the mother as a bonus. If she did not use the approved midwife, she lost the ten yuan.

As we hiked back to the car, Dr. Su continued to grumble about the problems that rural doctors face. "A lot of women in the villages develop urinary tract infections and various gynecological problems. They're really common in the villages. The problem is that the peasants think that women only develop these problems if they sleep around a lot. So the women are humiliated if we tell them they've got these problems. When we make our diagnosis, they're outraged and do nothing but yell at us."

I was fascinated by China's strides in promoting public health, so I arranged to look at a different kind of project: a leprosy clinic in the mountains of Guizhou in the south. The clinic had been started by Christian missionaries early in this century; then the Communists took it over in 1949. Leprosy used to be common in China—there were about 500,000 cases in 1949—and for many people the worst thing about getting it was not the fear of disfigurement but concern about how the neighbors might react.

"People were afraid of us then and looked down on us," said Du Dayi, a seventy-year-old who remembers when the peasants often burned lepers alive to try to get rid of the disease. Du is a short, soft-spoken man whose speech is distorted because he has lost his nose as well as an eye to the disease. But the change of attitudes among local citizens was startling. While I talked to Du, as he stood outside the leprosy hospital, about a hundred local peasants pressed around us, touching him and holding their children on their shoulders. Nobody seemed interested in looking at his disfigurement; they found my long Western nose far more startling than his lack of one.

China has managed to reduce leprosy to the point that it is a problem only at the fringe of society, affecting some 30,000 people. Most victims are caught in the early stages and treated, free of charge, before they are disfigured. "The biggest problem we face is that lepers don't go to the doctor soon enough," explained Liu Fang-min, the deputy director of the Salaxi Leprosy Hospital. "We tell them that the earlier they come to us, the easier it is to cure. But the biggest headache is still finding the lepers." The problem is that people continue to be rather bashful about being identified as lepers.

So the local government came up with an innovative—and characteristically authoritarian—method for finding the victims. The authorities announced that they would pay one hundred yuan, the equivalent of several months' income in such a poor area, to anyone who turned in a leper. People can turn themselves in and claim the money, or doctors can turn in their patients. Those who supply names are guaranteed secrecy, since their friends might not appreciate being fingered in this way. In any case, the method works. The easiest way to make a bundle these days is to turn in a leper, so most cases are now caught early. Leprosy is on the way out in these parts.

So China's economic boom seems to have been a chemical reaction of sorts. The first ingredient was the Confucian heritage that emphasized education and savings. Then came the Maoist revolution that unified the country, broke the entrenched interests, divided up the land, and supplied financial and human capital. Third were the quasi-capitalist policies of Deng Xiaoping. None of these factors was enough by itself; in combination they have been explosive.

For all its cruelty, the Communist Revolution laid the groundwork for the economic revolution that came later. Mao was a bit like a fellow who tries to light a fire by assembling a huge pile of tinder and firewood, carefully organizing it in just the right way. But he doesn't believe in matches, so he can't figure out how to light it.

Then Deng Xiaoping strolled by and tossed in a match. As we watched the fire grow, Sheryl and I began to feel that perhaps China wasn't such a bad place after all. Sure, we still thought that our obnoxious Foreign Ministry handler, Zhao Xingmin, could best be employed as kindling. But overall we began to feel that the Middle Kingdom had real possibilities.

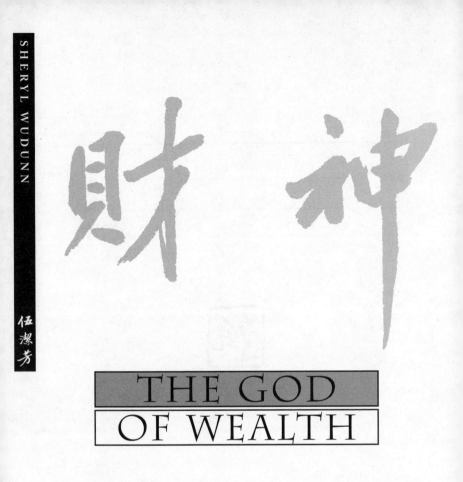

伍潔芳

THE GOD
OF WEALTH

Thank you for your shoddy pesticide; that's why my wife is still alive.

> —A Chinese villager, in a letter to a pesticide
> company. His wife had attempted suicide
> by swallowing the poison.

12

The "ding-dong" of the Avon lady (translated into Chinese as the "refined and fragrant young woman") is becoming familiar in southern China. In the Avon center in Guangzhou, new recruit Tian Ruihua (*right*) receives training on the use of the cosmetics. [Photo by Nicholas D. Kristof.]

I t took a while to get used to the sunlight, and for the first couple of years after Sunjin stepped out of prison, he couldn't stop thinking about the past, a China where political repression had become such an obsession for him that it had landed him in that damn cell in the first place. Sunjin was a dissident who had served a long prison term. After his release, he still had to report to the police, but basically they left him alone. When we arrived in China in late 1988, Sunjin was helping out at a stall in one of the free markets, and I used to visit him there every now and then to inquire about other dissidents. I would stand by his stall, pretending to browse as I fired questions in a hushed voice about politics, dissidents, and the direction of the economy. He would rearrange a sweater or a jacket as he replied to my various questions.

At times, Sunjin still seemed to be living in a world of politics. He didn't like selling. But he had nothing else to do.

Four years later, I almost didn't recognize Sunjin. He was a roly-poly millionaire, a man with puffy cheeks, an expansive stomach, a car, and virtually no interest in politics. I discovered all this one cool autumn day when he came by and asked for help getting a visa to the United States. Sunjin wanted to do business in America, and he wanted to take with him a pretty young woman whom he called a translator. We went out to lunch that day, Sunjin, I, and his translator. She didn't say much, and all I noticed was that she had wire-rim glasses, a quiet voice, and what seemed like more than a passing commercial interest in Sunjin.

"I've been exporting down jackets to Russia," Sunjin explained, as he stuffed a large morsel of lamb in his mouth. "We've been doing wholesale for a while. That's where the money is. We have a rep office in Moscow. My brother moved there with his family, and the business is much better than when we did retail. I have stalls everywhere. But I hardly ever work there myself. They're just windows onto the market. I use them to keep an eye on the market.

"Do you think the United States will give me a visa? I'm not going to stay in America. My life's here. China is where I make my money, and I'm not going to give that up."

Over the course of the conversation, it emerged that Sunjin now had more than $1 million in assets. He wouldn't say how much more. Needless to say, Sunjin picked up the tab for lunch. As he doled out his hundred-yuan notes, I mused at how our roles had reversed. When Nick and I first arrived in China, we often delighted our new friends by taking them out to dinner, shocking them by the prices we were willing to pay for food. Sunjin was scraping around for money in those days. But now, it was obvious that things had changed. Sunjin was buying me lunch. He was the sugar daddy (with a twenty-five-year-old sugar baby at his side). He hardly ever devoted a moment's thought to politics, except insofar as it affected business.

A dozen years of some of the highest economic growth rates in the world have nurtured the reemergence in China of the superrich, a class that the Chinese masses used to "struggle against" and now struggle to join.

China is entranced by money. The successes of people like Sunjin have provoked a scramble for prosperity in every hamlet in the nation. Caishen, the god of wealth, must be watching bemusedly. He was neglected in the years after 1949, but in the 1990s he is in favor again. Chinese once more buy his picture and leave him offerings of apples and cigarettes. Not everybody believes, but it can't hurt. Even middle school kids were singing the chant:

Money is the only thing worth a measure,
And kids with money are like a treasure.

With an explosion of private wealth but relatively few ways to invest it safely, China is undergoing a vast consumption boom. Yaohan, the Japanese department store company, opened its first outlet in Beijing in time for Christmas 1992, and the public went wild. On opening day, the store was packed. When the merchandiser for pens was arranging his display, he decided that a fourteen-carat gold pen would attract people. He thought it would be a nice joke to have a price tag that said 88,888 yuan, or about $11,000. Eight is a lucky number in China, because it sounds like the word for "to make money," and a string of that many eights would bring enough luck to last a lifetime. It wouldn't matter if no one bought it; the oohing and aahing would at least draw crowds. Nearby, he displayed the cheaper pens he thought would be more popular, along with some selling for up to 10,000 yuan. His display didn't last long: A Chinese promptly bought the 88,888-yuan pen.

China has entered the stage of conspicuous consumption.

In Hangzhou, two *dakuan,* or fat cats, got into a contest to display their riches by burning real paper currency. Each burned 2,000 yuan without a blink. In Beijing, a rich entrepreneur inviting some Cantonese magnates to dinner spent 20,000 yuan, or $3,500, a table on a banquet dinner. Afterward, one of the Cantonese guests returned the treat by inviting the group to a 60,000-yuan-per-table dinner. Not to be outdone, the Beijing host arranged for another round. He brought his briefcase, opened the combination lock, and pulled out 350,000 yuan, or $61,000, and said, "Today we'll be eating this amount of money!" In Guangzhou, a restaurant began offering meals dusted with gold—eating gold is supposed to be good luck. My own view is that anybody who can afford to eat gold doesn't need any more good luck.

The $20 key chain, the $17,500 imported coat, the $50 bra, the $1,000 watch—they all sold briskly. Rolls-Royce decided to open a distributorship in China after selling thirty Rolls-Royces in the country in the first eight months of 1993 alone. Three were stretch limousines for $375,000 each—before taxes and duties.

Nick dropped by Shanghai's Glorious Clock and Watch Shop, a typical storefront, but it was tough to get an interview. Shi Guanghui, the store manager, kept looking contemptuously at Nick's plastic Casio digital watch. Hard to take anyone like this seriously, he seemed to be thinking.

"With consumer standards rising, we're planning to sell Rolexes soon," he finally said, once he'd been warmed up. "A lot of other shops already have Rolexes." Shi said the shop was already doing a brisk business selling Rado watches, imported from Switzerland and priced at up to $3,000 each. The Rolexes will cost up to $20,000 each, and Shi said there would definitely be customers. One potential customer is the real estate magnate who paid $55,000 in an auction for Shanghai license plate Z0518. It is regarded as an auspicious number, because, in Chinese, it sounds vaguely like the words for "make me rich."

On that trip to Shanghai, Nick met a fellow called James Shen, a twenty-nine-year-old businessman dressed in a suit, and staying at the $105-a-night J. C. Mandarin Hotel. For the previous five years he had been living the Chinese dream: He worked abroad for an English company, earning a Western salary. But then Shen, who sells flame retardant chemicals, returned to Shanghai to visit friends and had a rude surprise. "I'd worked abroad, so I figured I was rich," he told Nick over breakfast. "But I came back and discovered that I was poor. There are so many rich people here now, so many millionaires."

I learned very quickly, however, that often the money everyone was making wasn't exactly clean.

"You know, we all have after-five jobs," said a young woman who is the secretary of a senior official. "But some people's money is a bit gray. Do you know about the three kinds of money that people are talking about these days? There's the white money. That's the clean stuff that we all get from the state, our salaries. Then there's black money. That's downright illegal. That's what the underground gangs make, and it's dangerous stuff. Then there's the gray money. Hmm, that has lots of definitions. It's money that, well, isn't quite white and isn't quite black. You know what I mean."

I got various answers when I asked about this gray money. Some people said that gray money was illegal, while others said it wasn't. "If you ask me, the people in the clothes stalls make gray money," said the Chinese secretary. "They get the clothes illegally from factories. They know someone there, and they get that person to divert some of the production to them at a cut-rate price. So isn't the money they make rather gray?"

But my entrepreneur friend Sunjin was insulted at the suggestion that his gray money was ill-gotten. "No, no, no," he insisted to me. "Gray money is, well, it's actually legal. Yes, gray money is definitely not illegal. It's just . . . it's just different from white money. It's not a salary."

After Deng Xiaoping made his imperial tour to the south in early 1992, the entire country seemed to change its personality. As if he had flicked a switch, politics was out, business was in. It seemed as though 1.2 billion people seized a new religion: *baijinzhuyi,* "money worship."

All of a sudden, making money was not a grubby occupation but a resourceful, clever way of surviving and improving one's lot in life.

Confucianism had looked down on merchants, and twentieth-century intellectuals shared that distaste. That's one reason why the first entrepreneurs in China were mostly ex-convicts and other undesirables, those who had no chance of getting any other job. They were people like Sunjin, except that most had been common criminals rather than political prisoners. During the 1980s, young people wanted to marry officials or, if none were available, at least employees of state-owned companies. Entrepreneurs were the bottom of the barrel, because they had low status and no job security. That changed very rapidly in the early 1990s.

The new slang was to *xia hai,* or jump in the sea, and it meant "to go into business." Beginning in 1992 and 1993, everybody seemed to *xia hai*: university professors, minister-level officials, political dissidents, doctors, and the children of the leaders. Especially the children of the leaders. Bo Xicheng, the head of the Beijing Tourism Bureau and the son of Bo Yibo, one of the Gang of Elders running China, quit his post to start a tourism company. Deng Zhifang, Deng Xiaoping's youngest son, became a real estate tycoon.

"Anyone who has any smarts can boost his income in China these days," said a Chinese friend of mine. "Only the dumbest bums aren't doing anything." Just about everybody we knew had *xia hai* or was at least moonlighting: waitressing at night, writing articles for popular magazines, teaching English or aerobics, consulting on computer programs, or giving seminars on stocks and bonds. And if their workload during the day was light, they could scoot out of the office and do their own thing. If they didn't already have an evening job, Chinese intellectuals and officials were taking night classes to train for a second career. This way, they were able to triple or quadruple their salaries and, at the same time, keep their "iron rice bowl" with its job security, housing, and health insurance.

When he came to power in 1978, Deng Xiaoping launched an economic revolution in the countryside. Although life changed somewhat in urban areas, with the rise of free markets and private businesses, it wasn't until Deng's imperial tour that the economic revolution finally came to the cities.

Today, foreign-owned companies and private businesses contribute nearly 10 percent to China's industrial output, and township and rural enterprises nearly 40 percent. But the most important question of the economic takeoff remains: What will be the fate of the state-owned enterprises that account for roughly half of the nation's industrial production? Most urban Chinese continue to be employed by state-owned enterprises, following the principle "You pretend to pay me, and I'll pretend to work." Unsurprisingly, these enterprises are notoriously inefficient, with only one-third of them earning any real profit, another one-third breaking even, and one-third running losses.

The problem is that no one really knows what this statistic means. Some state enterprises are transforming successfully, but as long as their prices are fixed, profitability doesn't have much to do with efficiency. A coal company, for example, will lose money since the government selling price for coal, although it is rising, is still set too low. State enterprises rarely fire workers, and they are forced to operate as small towns, running schools, hospitals, and movie theaters for their employees. It isn't even entirely accurate to think of them as just companies; they are more like social welfare agencies.

Since Deng Xiaoping's imperial tour, that state of affairs has been slowly changing. City dwellers no longer get grain coupons, and most prices have been liberalized so that profitability is more meaningful. The government is struggling to develop a new banking system, which would lend on the basis of creditworthiness rather than need. That's a revolutionary concept in China, and the implication is that many unprofitable state-owned enterprises will go bankrupt—and that billions of dollars in loans will be unrecoverable. At the same time, the government is turning to stock markets to transform state-owned enterprises into shareholder-owned companies. The word *privatization* still makes Communist officials shudder, but it denotes what is happening.

The process of ushering state industry into the market will be a painful and tortuous one, and there is a risk that layoffs and bankruptcies—which are necessary to raise efficiency—will provoke wildcat strikes and labor unrest as the state sector shrinks in proportion to the rest of the economy. One government think tank has predicted that by the year 2000, state enterprises will account for only one-quarter of industrial production, with private enterprises and foreign companies accounting for another quarter. The remaining half of production will come from rural and township enterprises.

Yet even as some state factories are floundering, another kind of state enterprise is thriving. These are the sideline enterprises run by government offices. The State Security Ministry, for example, secretly runs a dry-cleaning establishment that caters to foreigners in Beijing. At first I thought that this was a way to plant bugs in the suits of foreign diplomats and journalists. My Chinese friends laughed at my suspicions. "Of course not," one said. "State Security just wants to make money." For the same reason, State Security also runs a bakery, while the national police has gone into hotel management. The Army General Staff Department is part owner of one of China's best hotels, the Palace, and for a time a local army unit ran a travel service that operated a brothel. The army also runs scores of factories that make televisions, refrigerators, clocks, and other products. The Public Security Ministry runs a fascinating pair of shops selling nightsticks and electric cattle prods. When Nick dropped by and asked to test a cattle prod, the clerk picked one up and demonstrated, sending a shower of sparks across the counter.

What happened was that government offices began to feel that they'd been left out of the money game. With budgets tight, they didn't have enough money to do what they wanted. So they decided to go into business, often taking advantage of extra land, well-placed contacts, or special skills that they possessed. Sometimes the government offices seemed to have an unfair advantage over private businesses—particularly when the office regulated the industry in which it competed—but on other occasions the sideline companies competed equally. Even schools began to run their own factories or farmyards to raise extra money for chairs and textbooks and teacher salaries.

There's a downside to all this, of course. Many school principals seem to devote more energy to their sideline businesses than to the curriculum. And when a liquor bureau runs a bar on the side, rival taverns may have reason to complain about the fairness of the regulations. Yet there's also a benefit: These companies give the bureaucrats a stake in the market economy. Officials at every level now depend for their incomes and benefits on the progress of the reforms and the economic system. Only a thriving market can sate their greed.

China is a bit like California during the 1849 gold rush, with a twist: a lawless place motivated by a strange mix of greed and apprehension that this wonderful moneymaking opportunity could end at any moment. But there's also an analogy to nineteenth-century American and British industrial capitalism. China may not use little boys as chimney sweeps, but the textile and garment industries employ children and young adults to work fourteen hours a day, seven days a week, and sleep by their looms. If you lose your arm in the loom, you're fired.

So China is something of a cross between Dodge City and Dickensian England. That may sound grim and unappealing, but nineteenth-century capitalism is a big improvement over eighteenth-century feudalism. Marx acknowledged that fact, and most young Chinese would agree, if they could take time off from their looms to think about it. We sometimes forget that nineteenth-century America was a pretty heartless and brutal place: women and children working at piece rates in sweatshops for twelve hours a day, six days a week; robber barons, railroad magnates, and oil tycoons seizing profits any way they could; police beating and arresting labor organizers and leftists; urban political machines and wealthy tycoons manipulating the political process, to the point that the 1876 presidential election was probably stolen; blacks working as slaves in the first two-thirds of the century and as virtual serfs for the remaining one-third.

People often told me that China is not really moving toward Western-style capitalism because the capital still belongs to state-owned banks that assign it for noneconomic reasons. In other words, the price of capital in China isn't interest. It's a bribe. Or else it's the work that has gone into cultivating *guanxi* with the bankers and local officials. They are right, to some degree; the country may be practicing a form of capitalism with Chinese characteristics. But nineteenth-century capitalism in the West wasn't exactly by the book either. Some of the vast fortunes were collected through monopolies, which in turn were frequently awarded because of bribes or *guanxi* in Washington or the state capitals.

The same kind of manipulation of economics and politics is happening today in China, and there is a strong sense throughout the country that now is when the great financial empires will be made. People like Sunjin—or like Nick's friend Zhang Guoxi, the furniture maker in Jiangxi—may be the progenitors of the great new wealthy families that will dominate China for decades to come. It's hard to know who they are, but the future Rockefellers and Carnegies of

China are out there today, just beginning to amass their fortunes. This is the time to get rich, for in another decade or two the system will be more rigid and the opportunities fewer.

The analogy with the industrializing United States is also a helpful reminder that a country can endure enormous shocks and turbulence when it is enjoying economic growth. In the nineteenth century, the United States fought with both its northern and southern neighbors and endured the Civil War and dozens of Indian wars. There were huge tensions among the regions, between city and farm, resulting even in an angry populist movement that in Chinese terms would be called virtually a peasant rebellion.

The American dream was marred by appalling inequity, by gross manipulations of the political system, by lynchings, by bank collapses, by brutal repression of labor and leftist activists. Any Chinese who visited the United States in the 1800s might easily have been overwhelmed by the injustice and disorder. He could have interviewed penniless immigrants in the crime-plagued slums of Boss Tweed's New York, chatted with dispossessed farmers in the Great Plains during one of the several depressions, toured the cotton plantations of the South and the manufacturing cities of the Northeast and listened to the mutual rage. And he could well have concluded that the center would never hold, that America would be swept by revolution. Instead, the history of the United States underscores how much abuse a country can absorb when it is growing economically.

China now enjoys that kind of economic growth, and perhaps it, too, will demonstrate this kind of resiliency. But there is one difference. The United States had the basis of a civil society and a far more flexible political system, one that could respond to popular pressure—however belatedly—without exploding. A free press always flourished, and elections were always held, even if they were sometimes rigged. However inadequate the United States political and legal system was in the nineteenth century, it was far more responsive than China's is today. That responsiveness enabled it to evolve into the system we have now; in China, the question remains: Will the emperors allow their system to evolve in similar ways?

The rough-and-tumble times in China have nurtured a new breed of entrepreneurs, people who don't draw a salary from the government but instead live on their own smarts, doing deals whenever they can. One of these is Ah Chang, a man in his early thirties, five feet two with thinning hair, a wrinkling smile, and a thickening waistline that reflects his success. Nick and I met him through friends, and I looked him up whenever I visited his hometown of Guangzhou. Each time I dropped by, he was engaged in a different line of business. And each time he was richer.

Ah Chang, called by this nickname used by his Cantonese friends, never went to college. After he finished high school, he spent a year sawing boards and soldering wires in an electronics shop. From there, he was transferred to work in a coal-burning furnace, where he shoveled coal all day long, breathing the moist dust each time he inhaled. Every evening when he came home, his hair and face clouded by a veil of black soot, his mother would look at him and cry.

He made his first fortune in the late 1980s as a restaurant owner. But he worried that the environment might change after Deng Xiaoping died, so he was looking for a way to move abroad. Then the 1989 Tiananmen movement gave him a chance. Ah Chang had long regarded the government as a corrupt and bloated bureaucracy, but he was not particularly inspired by the idea of democracy. He was simply one of the millions of passive supporters of the Tiananmen movement, and he was in no danger of being arrested. Nevertheless, he heard through the grapevine that America was giving political asylum to anyone who claimed involvement in the movement, so he decided that this was his chance of a lifetime.

He sold his business and bought a false American passport for $20,000. The passport was a good forgery, with his name and photo, but even so Ah Chang was worried about being caught. Instead of flying directly to the United States, he flew throughout Asia, stopping in Hong Kong, Singapore, and Tokyo, where he stayed a few days before he made his way to San Francisco. Once he arrived in California, he thought he had made it. He destroyed his passport, because he was afraid of being caught with a forgery, and turned himself in to the immigration authorities. He claimed political asylum.

The immigration office detained him for several months and then determined that he was not a genuine political refugee. It returned him to China. Ah Chang bribed and ingratiated his way out of trouble, but his money was gone—he had spent $30,000 on his passport, air tickets, bribes, and other costs—and he had no business.

He started again from scratch, with nothing more than his *guanxi,* and opened a small restaurant and bar, paying off the authorities so that he could run a cable from a satellite dish on a nearby roof. That enabled him to show Hong Kong television in his bar, and business improved. Even so, he wasn't making as much money as he wanted. His big break came when a major foreign developer wanted to buy out his restaurant and demolish it as part of a large construction project. The foreigners handed $40,000 to Ah Chang.

"It wasn't a very good restaurant," he told me over dinner one evening. "I didn't manage it very well. I had all my friends over and they ate cheaply. But I had a good location. In a flash, I had $40,000."

Ah Chang took the money and bought an apartment, which he decorated and furnished with a stereo system, a beveled ceiling, bathroom and kitchen tiling. When I visited the half-finished apartment, in an old building whose windows and barred terraces were cluttered by clothes hanging out to dry, a dozen peasant workers were busy sawing, sanding, laying tiles, and hammering nails. Giant boxes filled with files, kitchen utensils, and clothes were stacked in the center of one bedroom. Ah Chang took me to the nearly completed kitchen and bathroom, and it struck me that when it was done, this home could be a model for a Chinese version of *Better Homes and Gardens.* Ah Chang and I sat in a corner as he told me about his new dreams.

"I have everything I need now. I have enough money. I help out my parents, and we all eat well. Look, I even get my clothes tailored. See these slacks? They're made by a tailor who caters to Westerners. This is an Italian cut. It fits much better than the Chinese-made stuff.

"Of all the kids in the family, I'm the one that made the money. My sisters, they studied. They studied English and art, and now one of them married an American and she can travel to the United States. That's my one wish, now, to go to the United States."

I soon realized that I figured into that wish. Ah Chang wants to marry a Chinese-American. I think he would prefer a genuine match based on love, but failing that, a marriage of convenience would be fine. He was even willing to pay; the market price in Guangzhou for marrying an American is about $20,000, although Ah Chang might expect a discount from me because of our friendship. Of course, Ah

Chang realized that I was already married, but he knew that I had a younger sister living in Hong Kong. Perhaps I could introduce him?

For all his scheming, I liked Ah Chang. It was exciting to watch him get rich. His total assets grew again to about 400,000 yuan, or roughly $70,000. He hardly cared about politics, but he did like his freedom and he did want to travel. He had hooked up with a Hong Kong *taipan,* or big boss, and was helping him hunt for property deals. He had also begun trading in shoes, contracting with factories and selling the shoes in other cities in China. His storerooms were filled with shoes—black patent leather with buckles, mauve suede with high heels, tall leather boots that belonged on the feet of American cowboys. Ah Chang wasn't stunningly rich, but he was very comfortable. He could set his own schedule. He could wander into a dim sum restaurant at 10:30 A.M. and eat a leisurely breakfast. He had carried a beeper for several years already, he had his eye on a car, and he had plunked down 250,000 yuan (nearly $50,000) to buy a lakeside summer home based on a sketch in an office.

Ah Chang was always devising ways of making money, like the plan he had to break into selling medicines. He happened to befriend the factory manager of a large pharmaceutical manufacturer, and the manager agreed to supply him with one of the latest kinds of intravenous solutions.

"I've known the guy for an entire year," Ah Chang explained. "He calls me practically every day, and I accompany him wherever he wants to go. I eat meals with him and run around and have fun with him. So he trusts me and I trust him.

"Then I took the purchaser at a hospital out to lunch, and he says he'll buy the medicine from me. I'll slip a little to him on the side."

"How much will you give him?" I asked curiously. "A hundred yuan each time?"

"I'll give him 50 percent."

"How much will you give the factory manager?" I asked, rather incredulous at these commissions.

"I'll give him about 20 percent."

"But then all you have left is 30 percent," I said.

"But 30 percent isn't so bad. If I get 30 percent here, 30 percent there, and 30 percent somewhere else, that's not so bad. There's really no other way. I have to give them a cut to make them happy. At least I make something. After all, the law doesn't allow individuals to trade in medicine, so I need a way to hook up with someone who has a license."

Ah Chang described his actions matter-of-factly, and he didn't seem devious. Rather he came across as a good-hearted man making a living, someone who also cared about family, reputation, even art. He liked being around educated people, and he put his sister through college. He just seemed to be an ordinary man with ordinary ambitions. That's why I was even more shocked to discover another kind of moneymaking scheme he was involved in: smuggling dogs into China.

Ah Chang was bringing in dogs as pets, not as food, which is how Cantonese traditionally viewed dogs. "In fact, this is good for society," Ah Chang told me. Chinese should stop looking at dogs as dishes, he said, and should start looking at them as companions. There was a great demand for pets, but there was a rule against importing dogs: You simply couldn't bring them in for sale.

"Everyone smuggles, and I'm just a pea in the business," Ah Chang explained to me. "It may be against the law, but the law is ridiculous. You see, I'm not cheating anyone, really. I'm cheating the government, but that's nothing. The government has cheated the ordinary people for years, and it still cheats us because it doesn't let us import many things. Anyhow, I'm not smuggling drugs."

I was always curious how these smugglers operated. Were they the Chinese Mafia? Were they an organized network of people who carried cellular phones and wore black suits? Ah Chang explained that a friend had introduced him to a maritime smuggler, a man who lives in a multistoried brick house with lots of privacy. Most farmers use their land to grow rice or dig fishponds. This man, an uneducated peasant who knew the sea but couldn't even write his name, had converted his plot of land into a nice lawn. His entire family had quit farming to work in the smuggling business. No big networks. This guy fended for himself.

His family owned two big boats that they kept hidden by the coast. Even Ah Chang didn't dare ask where the boats were; he didn't want to know.

"How does he actually smuggle the stuff into China?" I asked.

"I tell him what I want, where to get it, who to pick it up from in Hong Kong," Ah Chang said. "Then I give him a deposit, and when he brings the merchandise to me, I pay him the rest."

The whole family invited Ah Chang over to the house and treated him to a fancy meal at a dimly lit restaurant with beautiful—and available—women. "Each time we go out, he pays several thousand yuan," Ah Chang explained. "He needs to find customers, too.

"Is this the underground Mafia? Hmph! I don't know what this Mafia is that everyone refers to. You call my small-time peasant fisherman the Mafia? I don't think so. He just wants to make some money. Would you say I'm dealing with the Mafia? I don't think so. What's the Mafia, then? Maybe it's the people who smuggle heroin, maybe it's the pimps and prostitutes, the weapons dealers. Maybe that's it.

"In America, you know what's illegal. Your laws are clear. Not in China. In fact, in China, the police, they're the blackest of them all. They're linked to the smugglers, too. China is a crazy country now."

Indeed, organized crime seemed, in part, organized by the state. Everyone knew that the police and the customs officials were involved in smuggling and other illicit practices. One day, I discovered how bad it was.

Fangcheng, a small port in the Guangxi region, had suddenly become one of the most popular harbors in China. The reason was that the local customs officials were involved in small sideline broker companies that offered to handle all the paperwork for importing goods. These companies set up offices along a street near the port, and the importer simply handed shipping documents to a company, which then filled out all the customs forms, obtained the import licenses, and ushered the goods through customs. For this they took a fat commission, but the buyer didn't feel the pinch. The customs officers never assessed the true substantial duties on goods handled by the sideline companies, so importers saved large sums on duties and the brokers could then skim some for themselves.

Finally, the central government realized that something was up when cargoes destined for all parts of China lined up to use this one small port in Guangxi. There were huge delays for ships to get into the port, and hardly any duty was being paid. So the authorities investigated and temporarily closed down the port in mid-1993. A business executive was furious when the company's shipment was left sitting in the port for weeks. The company had been importing sophisticated steel products. The customs documents, however, referred to pig iron and similar materials that have much lower duties. Of course, the customs documents had been filled out by the crooked customs officials themselves. They had essentially hijacked their own agency. No wonder one of the hot slogans of the 1990s is: The cops and the crooks, they're all in the same family.

What I like about Ah Chang is that he understands what business is about: two parties coming together to build, trade, or create something. He knows that there has to be a benefit to both parties. That's more than I can say about many entrepreneurs; they believe China is such a big place that you can go on forever cheating people and never get caught. That's what Shen Taifu tried to do when he issued one billion yuan, or $175 million, in corporate bonds in Beijing at the end of 1992. Shen, a thirty-nine-year-old businessman, saw the crazy rates that many localities and state-run enterprises were offering to attract capital, and he devised an instrument of his own: an eye-popping 24 percent annual interest rate, or twice the rate the government was paying depositors on its bonds.

Shen paid news reporters to write glowing articles about his company and his bonds, and he curried favor from big guns in the government so that they would write flattering essays about him. Shen hired dance hall girls to peddle his paper and also hired salesmen to sell on commission. The money poured in, and Shen spent his evenings sitting in his expensive houses, riding in his luxury cars, or eating scrumptious meals, including one that cost $3,500. He opened up offices around the country to collect the money, but the corporate branches were no more than deposit-taking receptacles. His company was called Great Wall Machinery and Electronic High Technology Industrial Corporation, but it never produced a single product. Still, he hid his scheme for months, during which I saw a rush of public enthusiasm for Shen. I remember friends asking me if I had heard about these great high-yielding bonds. It was Beijing's biggest financial scam in recent history, and it fooled nearly 200,000 Chinese residents, including some top Chinese political officials. It collapsed, of course, when Shen couldn't make the interest payments.

The scandal caused outrage from investors who were unaware of the concept of risk. Bondholders staged a small protest to demand that the government refund their money. The authorities were sufficiently alarmed to agree immediately to pay depositors 50 percent of the value of the bonds—and to ban the Chinese press from writing much about the incident. I sneaked over to one of the stands where bondholders could go to apply for refunds. There were clumps of people crowding in the doorways of the offices, trying to figure out what forms they had to fill out, what pieces of identification they needed in order to claim refunds.

"I poured my entire life's savings, 30,000 yuan—what I was going to retire on—into these bonds," said a sixty-four-year-old plumber who had come for his money. The plumber, a father of four, said he earned the equivalent of thirty-five dollars a month. "I believed the government; I believed the government's newspapers," he said. "Now again, I have to believe in the government and wait for it to do something."

The plumber wasn't the only Chinese upset by what was going on. On March 4, 1994, the government sentenced Shen Taifu to death. Deng Xiaoping himself reportedly said, "If our society's atmosphere deteriorates, then of what significance is economic success?"

It wasn't just the occasional scandal that disturbed Deng. It was the entire social morality, the new *baijinzhuyi*, money worship, that was sweeping the nation. Even jailers participated: Some prisoners were released after they sent money or extravagant gifts to prison officials. At a time when China was caught at a junction between market and Marxism, people began cutting corners to become wealthy.

Sometimes, *baijinzhuyi* even cost lives.

I had always been concerned about hygiene at Chinese hospitals, and, when I first arrived in China in 1988, I remember going to a special clinic to have a syphilis test required of all incoming foreign residents. The nurse opened a clean package, took out a disposable hypodermic, and then drew my blood.

"Are these disposable needles?" I asked to make sure.

"Yes, yes, don't worry, we use them only once," the nurse replied, with condescension.

But after she had transferred my blood to a test tube, she put the needle into a basin of water. I looked down and saw about two dozen needles in the basin. I asked a doctor friend of mine about this soon after that, and his response was not encouraging. "Jiefang, needles are expensive in China. They wouldn't dare throw them away. They wash them and probably send them out to smaller hospitals in the countryside. But I tell you, if there is an AIDS epidemic in China, it will spread faster than you can imagine, and not through drugs, but through hospitals," he said.

I think he exaggerated a bit. But in 1993 I was staring at confirmation that hospitals actually recycled disposable needles. An outraged Chinese friend gave us confidential documents and other information about a frightening medical scandal. An entrepreneur had washed more than one million used disposable hypodermic needles and resold them as new ones. This had been going on for five years, and no one knew how many people had been infected or had died from the use of the unsterilized needles. A doctor familiar with the case told us that four people had died a few months earlier shortly after injections of blood with the unsterilized needles at the Youan Hospital in Beijing. But that was uncovered by accident; no one had any idea how many others had been infected elsewhere.

"Throughout this period, hundreds of thousands of blood donors and recipients in Beijing—including state and party leaders—have been threatened with infection," an internal government report declared. "Those who should save lives became murderers, all for the sake of cash."

The problems began when the Beijing Red Cross Blood Center, a main supplier of hypodermics to hospitals, contracted in 1988 to make disposable needles in collaboration with an entrepreneur in nearby Hebei Province. According to the internal document, the blood center lent its name to the venture and purchased the needles but provided no inspection or supervision and obtained no proper licenses or permits. The Beijing center is completely independent of the International Committee of the Red Cross.

The document says that the entrepreneur turned the courtyard of his home into a small but busy factory. He gathered used needles from hospitals and hired two dozen muddy-fingered peasants to wash the disposable hypodermics under a hand pump and lay them out in the sun to dry. Then the peasants sealed the hypodermics in plastic with the name of the Red Cross Blood Center printed on the outside. In fact, the packaging was the most sophisticated part of the operation. The newly packaged needles were then shipped to scores of hospitals across China. Traces of dried blood could occasionally be seen on the hypodermics, but in most cases doctors apparently did not examine the needles closely and were unaware that they had been used before.

Then in March 1993, the authorities received a complaint from a peasant and went to investigate. They promptly closed down the factory, confiscating 250,000 hypodermics that they found at the scene. The next day, the entrepreneur squeezed in one last sale. He sent a special truck with 5,000 of his repackaged needles to a medical institute that serves many military hospitals.

Nick called various hospitals to try to confirm the document. Naturally, officials from the Health Ministry, the Red Cross Blood Center, and several major hospitals refused to comment. Even the Sino-Japanese Friendship Hospital, where I had gone for blood tests and checkups when I was pregnant with Gregory, declined to discuss the matter, although it was clear they were aware of the problem. Some of the officials Nick contacted confirmed indirectly that the events described in the document had taken place. Beijing Hospital, for example, said that they had written a report on the case for the central authorities, but they denied that their own doctors had used contaminated needles. The Youan Hospital declined to comment on the four patients believed to have died there after contaminated needles were used during blood transfusions. "We have decided that the City Health Department will handle everything on this case," said a hospital official. When Nick called the Health Department, he could hear officials anxiously consulting in the background before one returned to the telephone to tell him, "No one here can discuss the matter."

Several days later, the Health Department called us back in alarm after several hospitals reported that Nick had been nosing around, asking questions about the scandal. A department official, Lu Peng, acknowledged that there had been problems with the rural factory as a supplier of hypodermics, but he asserted that there had never been any risk to blood donors or recipients. "We've always been extremely strict in our blood program," Lu said. "All of the paraphernalia must undergo strict sterilization."

The scandal rose to the Politburo level, partly because the Politburo members themselves were worried about infection. Yet there was never a peep about it in the Chinese press. The government simply tried to hush up the matter without investigating how many people had been killed or harmed by the contamination. A group of horrified health officials released the news quietly to a few Chinese reporters, but higher authorities found out and barred the journalists from writing about it.

A doctor told me that physicians had noted a high proportion of infection and complications after surgery and transfusions but had not known the reason. The risk of using the contaminated needles is hard to measure. The document says one study in Hebei Province found that 80 percent of those using the needles could become infected, but another survey indicated that in a Beijing hospital, with much better sanitary conditions, about 20 percent faced infection.

I felt sick after I read this, and I couldn't help wondering what Ah Chang would have done if he'd been offered a stake in the needle-recycling enterprise. Ah Chang, after all, was already in the medicine business. Not that I thought Ah Chang would want to sell dangerous products, but what if he was desperate for money?

That's why I've got some advice for visitors to China. If you anticipate any need for medical care, bring your own hypodermic.

The problems arose, of course, partly because the market economy is embracing the health-care system. Hospitals are becoming cost conscious and are willing to find the cheapest suppliers of things like needles. They also want to make sure they get paid by patients.

Wang Yingmei, a twenty-seven-year-old native of Hainan with long hair and fragile features, soon found that out. The day I talked to her, she was wearing a flowered white blouse tucked into an orange skirt, and she kept rubbing her back. That's where the tumor was. She had had an operation in May 1993 to remove the tumor, but the doctors at her local hospital couldn't get it all out. So they wrote her a letter of introduction to take to more sophisticated hospitals in Beijing. Her parents gave her train fare, plus 500 yuan for food and other expenses, and she set off to save her life.

She went to the Peking Union Medical College, one of China's best hospitals. The doctors looked at the letter and agreed to treat her—provided she put down a deposit of 10,000 yuan. Once her bill approached that sum, she would have to put down more money or else be ejected onto the street. The problem was that Wang Yingmei didn't have that much money. All she had was her 500 yuan in food money, plus 300 yuan given to her by a passerby who saw her crying on the street. So the hospital refused to take her. "I want to go home," she whimpered to me on a small alleyway in the western part of Beijing. "I don't know what's going to happen to me."

I know what's going to happen to her. She's going to die.

Wang Yingmei is not the only patient finding today's China a heartless place. These days, many big hospitals are refusing to take patients—even on an emergency basis—unless they prove at the registration desk that they can pay for treatment. One of our friends tried to commit suicide and overdosed on sleeping pills. His wife rushed him to the hospital but forgot to bring any ID certifying his high-level status. The hospital refused to treat him, leaving him in a waiting room until the wife managed to get through on the phone to a senior Central Committee member.

The official then ordered the hospital to treat our friend and said that the party would cover the expenses. The next day, someone rushed a check over. Our friend recovered, but others didn't have his *guanxi*. We heard several stories of people dying on the streets after being refused admission to hospitals in Beijing. One man who was brought in a coma to a hospital didn't have any ID and was left in a waiting room, untreated, until he died. There was an outcry only because he turned out to be a retired senior military officer.

So China was turning toward the market, toward profit incentives. Wasn't that what we all wanted?

Yes, but . . .

I never doubted that China should move in this direction, and intellectually, I know that there will be real costs. But it makes me think twice when I see people, like Wang Yingmei, who are suffering as a result of this no-holds-barred gallop toward a capitalist dream. It would be nice if China could sustain a bit of socialist compassion, helping the disadvantaged so that they don't get squashed in the economic contest, but I don't see that happening. For a time, Chinese quasi capitalism will probably resemble a Hobbesian jungle, a much more natural state of existence than China has been in for the last four decades. As Hobbes wrote, life in the state of nature has its limitations: "No arts; no letters; no society, and which is worst of all, continual fear and danger of violent death; and the life of man, solitary, poor, nasty, brutish, and short."

Most people will benefit from the free market boom, as the new incentives stimulate a surge in economic growth. But rising waters do not lift all ships; a few get swamped.

May poor Wang Yingmei rest in peace.

It wasn't just the Chinese who were trying to cash in on the big money to be made in this booming economy. Americans, Taiwanese, Japanese, and Europeans were banging at the doors leading into the country. In 1992, foreigners invested $11 billion in China. They pledged even more: $57.51 billion, or nearly four times the amount reported for 1991. In 1993, the investment shot up to $25.75 billion—nearly equal to all the foreign investment in China since it embarked on economic reform in 1978. And pledges hit $110.85 billion. To be sure, not all of this money is genuine foreign investment. A fair amount is Chinese money that is funneled through Hong Kong and then returned to China. That way the investor gets a bit more protection, as if he were a foreigner, plus the tax breaks that are given to joint ventures.

Yet there's no doubt that genuine foreign investment has soared. After years of struggling with the system, banging their heads against a Chinese wall, some Western companies are finally making piles of money. In 1992, the Guangdong market for shampoo was one of the largest in the world for Procter & Gamble. The first three outlets that McDonald's opened in China each set a new worldwide company record for opening-day sales. The country is becoming a significant market for Motorola's pagers and cellular telephones, and the number of Avon ladies in China's south soared from zero to 21,000 in just a few years. The next big "cola war" is likely to be in China, and Pepsi-Cola is already predicting that in a dozen years the country may be its biggest market outside America. In 1993 alone, foreign-funded enterprises traded $67 billion worth of goods, accounting for one-third of China's total trade volume.

I was finding it difficult not to be swept into the process. Some of my friends from Harvard Business School were now working in the China market and doing very well. Investment banks, securities firms, accounting companies, and law firms were all desperate to hire Chinese speakers who knew the Chinese market and the right people. It was comparatively easy for someone with the right skills to command compensation of many hundreds of thousands of dollars a year, and I was flattered to get some calls. At times I was tempted to abandon journalism and go into the China business, for I had started out as a banker and was still attracted to commerce. If I ever wanted to get rich, this was my chance. Some reporters actually made the jump: Jim McGregor, my colleague at *The Wall Street Journal,* crossed the wall and opened the business office for Dow Jones & Company in Beijing. Other reporters told me that when they left their posts, they might come back to China to do business. Imagine swaying a bunch of cynical journalists who had spent years writing about human rights abuses by the Chinese Communists to leave their professions and stay in China!

It was the lure of a generation. It was just infectious.

But foreigners had to be extremely careful. If Chinese could swindle one another, they could certainly trick foreigners, especially those who didn't speak Chinese or didn't know China. Everyone was trying to lasso a foreigner and squeeze him for all his money. Even in Beijing, a sophisticated metropolis where foreigners had been doing business for years, it seemed as though the entire city were on one big rampage to *zai lao wai*—"slaughter the foreigner."

One foreign businessman had the misfortune of parking his $6 million in a Nanjing bank. One day, during a credit crunch in 1993, the branch decided that it just wasn't going to give his money back to him. "Yes, you deposited the money in the bank," he was told. "But sorry, the bank is short of foreign exchange. We simply won't release the funds. Maybe later."

Meanwhile, as foreigners and their money were pouring in, the Chinese and their money were pouring out, so that the two-way flows were turning into unstoppable floods. I once found myself talking to Yu Zhian, who headed one of the largest state-run enterprises in China. He bought up failing Chinese enterprises, turned them around to make millions of dollars, and then reinvested the money elsewhere. Some of his investment went to the United States to buy a farm where he would grow ginseng to import back to China. "Land in America is so cheap these days I couldn't resist," he told me, his bald pate glistening under the sun as we stood by his headquarters' front gate in the Yangtze River port city of Wuhan.

Yu wasn't the only one investing abroad. Chinese were sending billions of dollars overseas—$27.9 billion in 1992, according to the

International Monetary Fund. Some of the money was coming back into China, disguised as foreign investment, and some was remaining in foreign bank accounts—many of them private ones. But with only $27.6 billion in capital moving in, officially China had a net capital outflow. And the unofficial outflow is probably much higher. Chinese are buying condos in Canada, restaurants in Germany, apartments in Hong Kong. One mainland investor spent $517,000 for a parking space to go along with his luxury home in Hong Kong's pricey midlevels district. For all the opportunities, it should sober foreigners to realize that the Chinese, who understand the risks and rewards better than we do, are moving some of their money out. Capital flight is difficult to measure, and there are many reasons for it, but one indication that it is substantial shows up on a tiny line in the International Monetary Fund reports. "Net errors and omissions," a partial reflection of missing funds that have shifted in and out of China, moved from a $115 million inflow in 1989 to a $3.2 billion outflow the next year. The figure surged to $6.8 billion in 1991 and reached $8.2 billion in 1992. By 1993, it had settled to about $7 billion.

The campaign to slaughter the foreigner was particularly active in the real estate industry. An investment banker friend of mine told me that when he signed a letter of intent to build an office building on prime land in the center of Beijing, his Chinese partner said that the foreign investor would have to pay $100,000 to each family living on the site for resettlement costs. Would it really cost that much to sweet-talk residents into moving? Of course not! Resettlement is where China's government is most efficient, for this is how resettlement really works: The state-run demolition company notifies the residents where and when they must relocate. If they don't move, the police will move them. The money? Part of it goes to the demolition company, part to the families, and a large part to the brokers who set up the deal on a Western fee scale.

When I accompanied a couple of American friends to look at some potential property sites, I discovered that even *laobaixing*, the ordinary Chinese, had unrealistic dreams. One of my friends was looking for a house to renovate and live in, and she heard about a place in Qianmen, a crowded, centrally located district just south of Tiananmen Square. "It's a really good location, right in the heart of

Qianmen, and very convenient because it's in the center of Beijing," her contact explained.

We were told to meet a Chinese agent, who was acting as broker, at the gate to the Yuetan Park one Saturday afternoon. We waited half an hour before he appeared, then hopped a cab with him to Qianmen. But after we got to Qianmen Street, just as I was about to open the taxi door, the cab took off for another half hour, winding down narrow lanes, swerving past bicycles and old men carting crates of soda bottles and coal briquettes on their small wagons.

"It's just up ahead," the man, a heavyset Chinese with a thick Beijing accent, echoed a few times. "We'll be there in a moment. Just a moment."

We finally arrived at Xiqiaoshu Alley, a lane so narrow we had to get out of our car to walk the rest of the way. As we neared the house, a courtyard home, I noticed a sign on a doorway just before the site. It said: police station. When we went inside the house, it was in shambles. In the middle of the courtyard was a large furnace where four families burned coal, leaving a dark shadow etched into the ground from decades of use. Each family lived in a part of the house. The doors creaked; the windows were stained with grime, soot, and the imprints of squashed flies. The steps had crumbled, and the ceilings had cobwebs. There was no heat, and the new buyer would not be allowed to renovate because this was a historic courtyard, protected from alterations. Moreover, since it was near a police station, the authorities could watch every step.

"You can't touch the beams or the walls, but you can repaint," said the seller, a short, pudgy old man. "This is my daughter's husband's family's property, and we're just helping them sell this."

There were three families who had to be evacuated, and the old man said that the resettlement fee would probably be $7,000 per family. "We haven't talked specifically to the families yet, but that money should be enough."

The land was the government's, and only the decrepit building was for sale. My friend wasn't happy with it, but if it was cheap, she might consider it. What was the price?

"There are three apartments here," the old man said, speaking in an earthy Beijing dialect. "That one is about 300,000 yuan," he said, pointing to the small set of rooms on one side. "The two-room set over there is 400,000 or 500,000 yuan, and this square one is 400,000 to 500,000 yuan."

Including the relocation expenses, that meant up to $250,000 for a run-down building on a dingy alleyway in Beijing, inaccessible by car. We laughed. My other friend explained to them that in Minnesota, where she lived, she could buy a beautiful four-bedroom house with a garden—and own the land—for the same amount of money.

I often puzzled over how things got so expensive so quickly in Beijing. Part of it was the Chinese government's fear of being ripped off by foreigners, so that it set floor prices to rip off the foreigners first. The other reason was that there truly was a dearth of Western-style offices, apartment houses, and entertainment centers. Western businesses were scrambling to open offices in China, and competition among expense accounts sent prices soaring.

If you wanted a modern apartment, you went on a waiting list of hundreds. If you were lucky, you got one—for $3,000 to $10,000 a month. Or you could buy a Western-style home for up to $1 million in parts of Beijing and Shanghai—not the best parts, but in the outskirts, where development sites were available. Office space was going for roughly the same price as in Manhattan, sometimes even higher.

China was caught up in a bubble mentality, rather like Japan in the late 1980s, before the bubble burst. A Chinese reporter called me up one evening and asked if I could introduce him to foreign companies that would be interested in a special advertising campaign in the *Beijing Daily* or the *Beijing Evening News*. Perhaps, I said, but I was curious what a sports reporter was doing selling advertising.

"Oh, I'm just helping the paper out," he told me. "This is a special campaign for Beijing's bid to get the Olympics. We think a lot of foreign companies will want to support Beijing's bid here.

"Here's the plan: We will let a foreign company, for the first time in the history of this Communist country, place a full-page ad on the front page of the *Beijing Daily* or the *Beijing Evening News*. The *Beijing Daily* has a circulation of 600,000 and the *Evening News* 900,000."

I snickered. Much of the circulation of the *Beijing Daily* was compulsory. Work units automatically subscribed to the newspaper, and most copies languished unread in the offices. The *Evening News* was better but only a tabloid. I was intrigued by his proposal, though, and decided to find out more about it.

"So, how much are you charging for this special deal?" I asked.

"Well, we already have two Japanese companies interested. It would be for only one day."

"Well, what's the price?"

"Three hundred thousand U.S. dollars."

I swallowed. "Xiao Dong," I said. "Don't you think that's a bit high? I mean, that's expensive, and it's only for one day."

"Beijing is the capital of China! And this newspaper is the flagship for Beijing. It'd be very prestigious for a company to advertise in our papers. How could we not charge a high rate? We think it's an appropriate price. And we hope that you can do us a favor and introduce us to some potential customers. Some Japanese firms have said they're interested, but we would prefer an American company."

"Well, if I hear of anything, I'll be sure to call you, Xiao Dong."

Neither of the Beijing dailies ever did end up running the ad.

NICHOLAS D. KRISTOF

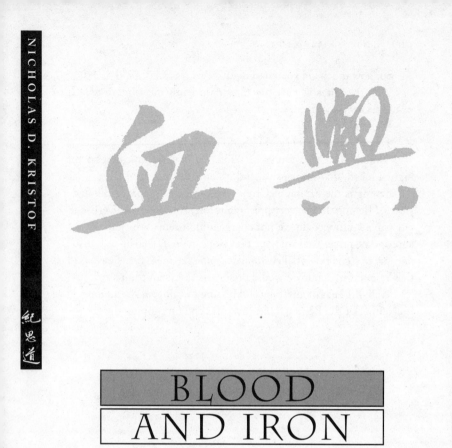

BLOOD
AND IRON

China rejuvenescent! It was but a step to China rampant.

—Jack London, in a 1908 short story

The lion and the calf shall lie down together, but the calf won't get much sleep.

—Woody Allen, *Without Feathers*

13

鐵

The People's Liberation Army Marches Forward in Huge Strides," proclaims this Beijing billboard. Photo by Fumiyo Asahi.]

Near the end of his life, Walter Lippmann was asked during a television interview what would be the worst calamity he could imagine. He thought about it, and there was a long silence. Then he answered, very deliberately, "China on the loose."

These days, some Asian countries would say, "A rich China on the loose." In their eyes, the only thing more frightening than 1.2 billion poor people in total chaos, pouring across the borders, is a rich nation of 1.2 billion highly organized people, sending tanks and fighter jets roaring across the borders. To them, China's economic miracle is not heartwarming but alarming. At China's average 9 percent annual growth rate since the late 1970s, an economy quintuples every nineteen years. And often so does its military budget.

The ramifications of China's economic boom are not just economic. The global diplomatic, political, and military balance may also have to be recalibrated, and the world has yet to focus on what the rise of China would mean.

Of course, it is perfectly possible that China will fall apart. But China is now sufficiently important and connected internationally that even its collapse could give the world a shake. Tens of millions of refugees could swarm across the seas to Japan, Indonesia, Malaysia, and other countries—even to the United States. Put another way, a dead elephant is not as imposing or alarming as a stampeding bull elephant. But the corpse still presents a monumental sanitation and disposal problem.

In any case, there is a strong chance that China will succeed over the coming decades in sustaining an economic boom. If that happens, China will demand far more of the world's energy resources. It will add substantially to the world's problems with acid rain, chlorofluorocarbons, and global warming. It may well come to dominate a number of sports and sweep the medals chart in every Olympics. Its trade accounts will be breathtaking, and its bankers will be major international players. So, perhaps, will its generals.

"The size of China's displacement of the world balance is such that the world must find a new balance in thirty to forty years," Lee Kuan Yew, the former Singaporean prime minister, said in 1993. "It's not possible to pretend that this is just another big player. This is the biggest player in the history of man."

Already, the economic revolution that Deng Xiaoping launched at the end of the 1970s is probably more important than Mao's revolution of 1949. Chinese history is littered with peasant rebellions and new dynasties. But never before in recorded history have so many people or even so large a proportion of humanity risen from poverty so quickly. And the economic rise of China may only be beginning.

One of the first economists to see China's potential was Dwight G. Perkins, a tall, lean Harvard professor. I remember his delivering a guest lecture to my introductory economics class at Harvard in 1979, but at that point he was more analytic than optimistic. The enthusiasm came in the next few years and inspired a slim volume that remains one of the best general books on the Chinese economy, *China: Asia's Next Economic Giant?* Professor Perkins's book was published in 1986, a year before a major crackdown and three years before the much more serious Tiananmen killings. After Tiananmen, Professor Perkins's enthusiasm looked a bit naive, but by the early 1990s he simply looked visionary. I called him up in 1993 and asked him, if he were redoing the book, whether he would still include the question mark at the end of the title. "I'd leave it off, I think," he said slowly. "Or at least I'd run the question mark in smaller type." China's economic boom, he insisted, is here to stay.

"I don't see what's going to stop it, unless you can tell me a story of civil war or real chaos amounting to civil war," he said.

Another economist whom I encountered at Harvard, Lawrence H. Summers, is if anything even more bullish on China. When he was chief economist of the World Bank in 1992, Summers wrote: "It may well be that when the history of the late 20th century is written 100 years from now, the most significant event will be the revolutionary changes in China, which will soon be Communist in only a rhetorical sense. . . . For more than a century, the United States has been the world's largest economy. The only nation with a chance of surpassing it in the next generation in absolute scale is China."

Chinese statistics are maddeningly unreliable, but by some measures China's economy is already the second or third biggest in the world.

And, according to these same statistics, at its present growth rates China may surpass the United States in another dozen years or more to become the biggest economy in the world.

How can this be?

It is true that official statistics show China with a per capita gross national product of only about $370, about the same as India's. Multiply this by China's population of 1.2 billion, and you get a gross national product of $444 billion. That is less than 10 percent of the American figure of $5.5 trillion.

The problem is that these official figures are pretty silly. It's meaningless to look at Chinese cash incomes without any reference to prices. While incomes are extremely low, so are costs. Take the family of Jiang Lianxiang, a forty-one-year-old teacher whom I met in the southern city of Guiyang. Jiang, a high-cheeked woman who wears her long hair in a ponytail, lives with her husband and (rather spoiled) ten-year-old son in a one-bedroom apartment. They have the basics—a television, a sofa, and a refrigerator (even if it doesn't quite fit in the kitchen and has to be placed in the living room). "We have most things we could want," Jiang told me, as she watched her son practice calligraphy on the coffee table.

Jiang formally earns a salary of $18 a month for teaching first grade. But like most workers, she gets lots of bonuses on top of that. Here is what her income looks like in a typical month:

Salary	$18.00
Seniority bonus	1.30
Intellectual bonus	1.11
Work experience bonus	2.12
Bath and haircut subsidy	2.04
Bus fare subsidy	1.30
Subsidy to buy newspapers and books	1.11
Bonus for serving as class adviser	2.04
Inflation subsidy	1.11
Food subsidy	2.78
Regular bonus	3.15
Total	$36.06

Jiang also gets special bonuses for Teacher's Day and for Chinese New Year. Her husband, Yu Qian, is a factory technician. His basic salary is $23.70 a month, but bonuses and subsidies almost double that. Then, on top of all this, the couple gets a bonus of 80 cents a month for having just one child. The result is a cash income each month of about $85.

It's not much, but neither are their expenses. Like most Chinese, Jiang and Yu pay no taxes. Their medical expenses are all covered by their *danwei*. Heat and electricity are provided free, and they pay less than $1 a month for their two-room apartment. Food takes up $37 a month, the biggest part of the family budget, but prices are still very low. A pound of spinach costs 8 cents, a pound of pork costs 60 cents, and a pound of rice is 12 cents. Even a luxury like dog meat is only $1 a pound. Cigarettes can cost as little as 7 cents a pack in rural areas.

Another $19 of the family budget goes each month to buy clothes. These, too, are much cheaper in China than abroad. A down winter jacket costs about $22, a shirt is a few dollars, and shoes for young children cost less than $1 a pair. The family spends another $19 or so on incidentals, such as the evening newspaper (2.5 cents a copy), bus fares (a penny a ride), and movies (40 cents a ticket, although the *danwei* often gives out tickets for free). The couple saves about $10 a month, adding to a bank account that already has more than $700.

One method of coming up with a more realistic figure for Chinese GNP is to calculate the value of everything produced in international prices. For example, if a bus fare in the United States typically costs a dollar and one in China costs a penny, then you might multiply the value of Chinese bus services by one hundred.

The use of international prices is called the purchasing power parity technique—PPP for short. The problem with the PPP method is that valuations are extremely difficult to adjust for quality. For example, many Chinese buses are jammed so full that passengers are sticking out the doors. And the buses are slow and uncomfortable, with noxious fumes and broken windows. Americans might not be willing to pay even a penny for such a bus ride. So valuing it at a dollar would be inappropriate.

Partly because of these quality differences, estimates of Chinese per capita GNP using the PPP method range from about $650 to $4,000. China's huge population means that at the higher levels, the total Chinese GNP would be the second highest in the world, lagging the United States's but higher than Japan's. That may be overstated, however. One distinguished economist, Nicholas R. Lardy, believes that China's per capita income is only a bit more than $1,000 and that growth rates will moderate in the coming decades. He suggests that China's economy will become the biggest in the world only around the year 2040. As for the World Bank, it offers two estimates of China's per capita GDP in international prices. Using one methodology, Chinese produced $1,680 per person in 1991; by the other, it was $2,040. Multiplied by 1.2 billion people, these numbers suggest that China's overall economy is still a bit smaller than Japan's but is catching up fast.

To be sure, we shouldn't get carried away by what this means. Chinese do not actually earn those sums. It's just that they live about as well as an American might live, in America, on $1,000 or $2,000 a year. Needless to say, that means not very well. China is still a country of poor people; it just has a lot of them.

China will become even more formidable in 1997, when it regains Hong Kong. While Hong Kong has only 5.9 million inhabitants, it has a volume of international trade equivalent to France's and a per capita income higher than England's. At midnight on June 30, 1997, when the red flag rises over Hong Kong, China will instantly gain a new financial capital.

Already, Hong Kong and southern China have become increasingly integrated. Indeed, future historians may well conclude that 1997 marked the year when Hong Kong took over China, instead of the other way around. Some 3 million laborers in Guangdong Province work for Hong Kong companies or subcontractors, because higher wage costs have forced businesses to move production into Guangdong. Hong Kong is becoming the financial center, trading center, operations center, retailing center, and the headquarters itself, while the assembly lines are across the border. Gordon Wu, a hefty, Princeton-educated *taipan,* or big boss, pored over maps on his desk and described it to me in this way: "China is the factory, and Hong Kong is the storefront."

This integration of Guangdong and Hong Kong reflects a broader phenomenon: the rise of a "Greater China" as an increasingly integrated economic entity. Greater China consists of China, Hong Kong, and Taiwan, and for all their political differences their economies are being melded into one. Taiwan manufacturers faced the same pressures as Hong Kong's *taipans*—rising wages and other costs—with the added headache of a sharply appreciating exchange rate. So Taiwan companies began moving entire assembly lines across the Taiwan Strait into southern China. Virtually all of Taiwan's shoemaking industry has already relocated to Guangdong and Fujian provinces, and much of the garment and sportswear industries have moved as well. Once Taiwan allows direct flights across the strait, that air route may well become one of the busiest in the world, the Asian equivalent of the Boston–New York–Washington corridor.

The global economy is sometimes said to be tripolar, revolving around the United States, Japan, and the European Community. But Greater China is rapidly becoming a fourth pole, a new pillar of the international economy. According to World Bank projections, Greater China's net imports in the year 2002 may be $639 billion, compared with $521 billion for Japan. Likewise, using comparable international prices, Greater China in the year 2002 is projected to have a gross domestic product of $9.8 trillion, compared with $9.7 trillion for the United States. If those forecasts hold, Greater China would not just be another economic pole; it would be the biggest of them all.

For much of recorded history, China has been more advanced than the West. Chinese philosophy, poetry, science, and government were for long periods more sophisticated than those of Europe, and China's standard of living may have been higher. China, after all, invented paper, gunpowder, the magnetic compass, the clock, the wheelbarrow, and nautical and shipbuilding innovations such as the rear rudder. Chinese technicians were casting molten iron seventeen centuries before Europeans figured out how to do it. Chinese peasants used seed drills 2,000 years ago to plant several rows of grain at a time; Europeans did not use seed drills until the seventeenth century. Chinese mathematicians calculated pi to five decimal places in the third century B.C. and used coordinate geometry more than a millennium before Europeans became skilled at it.

In other words, the world as we know it—in which the West is modern and China is backward—is a relatively recent phenomenon. For much of history, it's been the other way around. It's just that China never exploited its innovations. While Europe experienced the Renaissance and then the industrial revolution, China dozed for most of the past five centuries. Only since about the year 1500 has China lagged behind the West by most economic, cultural, and scientific yardsticks, but that was precisely the period when change was accelerating in the West.

If China can raise its standard of living and education, if it can squeeze out of its present ideological straitjacket, then—who knows? In a century or two, even if it lags significantly by per capita measures, its huge population may enable it to regain its earlier stature as number one. The world's leading historians, who would of course be Chinese, would convene conferences about the rise and decline of the West, just as we study the Mongols or the Mayas.

This is, of course, idle speculation, but the purpose is simply to remind ourselves that there is nothing fixed or inevitable about the primacy of the West. Already we are seeing some of the possibilities in a wide range of fields. The world's woman chess champion is a Chinese, Xie Jun. Chinese athletes, particularly swimmers, divers, and gymnasts, are improving dramatically, and women runners from Liaoning Province have come out of nowhere to set world records by astounding margins. In six days in September 1993, one slender twenty-year-old woman from Liaoning, Wang Junxia, single-handedly shattered assumptions about human athletic potential. First she ran the 10,000 meters in 29 minutes, 31 seconds, a new world record by 42 seconds. Then she broke the 1,500-meter world record and twice shattered the 3,000-meter record. The old 3,000-meter record had stood for nine years, but in the 1993 Chinese national games five women beat it. In the 1992 Barcelona Olympics, Chinese women won not a single medal in running events, but a year later at the world track and field championships they captured the 1,500-, 3,000-, and 10,000-meter events. In the 3,000, they won all three medals.

The Chinese authorities, deeply resentful of Western suspicions of drug use, insist that the secret of Wang's success is simply that she trains 180 miles each week and drinks a potion made from caterpillar fungus as well as a soup made from soft-shelled turtles. But whatever she drinks, China's athletic performance is likely to improve, for scouts now routinely search the elementary schools for young children whose physical builds indicate that they may be good at one sport or another. The most promising children are sent to special schools, far from their families, where they live with their coaches and train almost full-time.

Meanwhile, Chinese scholarship is still mostly second-rate, but younger scholars are impressing their colleagues abroad and Chinese students do very well in international high school competitions in math and the sciences. Chinese film is earning a reputation abroad, and more young people around the world are studying Mandarin, particularly in Southeast Asia. With its weight of population and economic strength, China may in the twenty-first century become a formidable power in a wide range of fields, even a rival for dominance of the globe.

So the question is this: Can China sustain its economic boom?

The answer will depend largely on whether it can continue to improve productivity. In the Maoist era, most of China's economic gains came from increases in investment and in the labor force. In the Deng era, China continued to enjoy those gains. But the big difference was that China benefited from a more productive workforce. Productivity will have to continue to be the engine of growth.

On the bright side, China is so inefficient that there is plenty of room for increases in productivity. Foreign skeptics often point out the absurdities of China's economic system as the basis for their pessimism, but that is wrongheaded. As long as there is reform, absurdities are a reason for optimism, simply because they provide easy room for improvement. The reforms that China is now undertaking—creating a banking system, floating the yuan, deepening the stock and bond markets, forcing state enterprises to stand or fall on their own—could provide the basis for significant increases in productivity. Moreover, China is steadily opening up its economy to the outside world, and that will hone the competitive skills of domestic companies and make them more efficient.

Another important factor in stimulating economic growth is simply investment, and there, too, China is laying a foundation for the future. China's own savings rates are very high, about 38 percent, and it is also drawing in huge sums from abroad. Most of the investment is private, in new factories, but China's leaders have invested public funds in upgrading the national infrastructure.

Already there are bottlenecks that curtail growth—freight trains are jam-packed, for example, and some factories worry that if they produce more toys and sweaters they will have trouble shipping them to markets. Entrepreneurs also worry that if they expand their factories they will not get enough electricity to run assembly lines. Still, for all the problems, China is building enough new ports, electrical plants, and highways that the country may be able to sustain its growth rates. Ironically, market economies like the Philippines' have paid much less attention to infrastructure, so that Manila has run out of electrical power and Bangkok is so jammed with traffic that it's impossible to get around. Chinese central planners did not do enough, but at least they did better than some of their neighbors.

After examining these and other factors that affect international competition, the Union Bank of Switzerland in 1993 ranked thirty-eight countries in terms of their future competitiveness. The United States ranked nineteenth, tied with Germany. China was second, behind only South Korea.

To be sure, there are plenty of hazards on the road ahead. At the extreme, there is the risk of catastrophic political instability or even civil war as the Communist dynasty collapses. If the authority of the center continues to weaken, some provinces may become increasingly assertive, squabbling with Beijing to gain autonomy. A coup d'état is also a significant possibility, and the army is said to have conducted a study on how to avoid military intervention in politics. In one sign of the high-level anxiety, when President Jiang Zemin reviewed the People's Armed Police in 1993, he did so from behind a bullet-proof screen. That was the first time a Chinese leader had felt the necessity for such protection from his own troops.

Of course, a coup d'état might not pose a problem for the economy; Thailand has thrived despite a succession of coups. But in Thailand and Italy, governments may come and go without affecting the business environment. In China, new leaders could come into office with significantly different economic policies. Stability in that sense is very fragile in China.

Another risk is a possible confrontation with Taiwan. China has repeatedly warned that it will use military force to prevent Taiwan from declaring itself an independent country. But Taiwan is wearying of the fiction that it is the "Republic of China" and a rival regime to the Communists. Already plenty of Taiwanese are impatient with the absurdity, and even President Lee Teng-hui is trying to get Taiwan back into the United Nations. Taiwan is searching for ways to gain a more international identity, and it is very unclear where that process will lead.

Any move by Taiwan to establish itself as a sovereign country, independent of China, could lead China to declare a quarantine of Taiwan. The next step could be a naval and air war. The West would have to decide whether to help Taiwan, and whether to impose economic and diplomatic sanctions against China. Even if China won a war with Taiwan, which is far from certain, it would pay a huge economic price. Trade and investment would plummet, and it could be decades before China recovered.

Then there are the less cataclysmic risks. Corruption may begin to bog down the system and impair efficiency. Infrastructure investment, while generally impressive, is still short of what is needed, and the bottlenecks will limit growth. Oil may run out, unless new supplies in the Xinjiang region of northwest China prove as promising as the government hopes. Rail and port capacity may not keep pace. As the Chinese environment deteriorates and natural resources grow more scarce, the present pace of growth may prove unsustainable.

China's education levels are good for a developing nation but not remotely good enough for an industrialized country. If China wants to graduate from assembling shoes to making cars and computers, it must have a more literate and skilled labor force. Yet the government is not spending enough on schools and universities to ensure that it will have a large supply of technicians in ten or twenty years' time. There are still far too many peasants who cannot read adequately and will not be able to integrate themselves into a modern labor force. As Sheryl rightly points out, too many girls are dropping out of elementary and middle schools.

Finally, there is simply the challenge of success: As the economy becomes more efficient, it becomes increasingly difficult to squeeze out further productivity gains. Sometime after the year 2000, economic growth rates are likely to subside as diminishing returns set in.

While no country as large as China has ever bloomed so rapidly and burst onto the international scene with such force, there is one parallel of sorts. This was a country that, like China, had a proud and ancient history and enjoyed a rich sense of national identity. Yet it had been bullied and defeated by its neighbors, and its territories had been taken. Then it managed to get its economic act together, and it began to build up its military forces as well. It even built a blue-water navy for the first time. Some neighbors were concerned, but international analysts scoffed at the alarm—there was so much economic integration, the analysts said, that it would be against each country's interests to resort to war. A few years later, that country—Germany—used its new power to become more assertive in the region. There was an assassination in a little country nearby, and the neighbors all began throwing their weight around. The result was World War I.

Obviously there are profound differences between China and Germany. It would be rash to predict some kind of Asian war, but I think it would be just as foolish to ignore the risks. China's buoyant economy is feeding its military force, and for the first time it is acquiring the power to project force beyond its borders. Despite reaching boundary agreements with half a dozen of its neighbors, China still has border disputes with Russia, India, Bhutan, and Vietnam, as well as disagreements about sea boundaries with most of the countries in the area. It would be natural for China to try to use its growing strength in military and strategic ways, and for it to attempt to resolve in its favor these territorial disputes. This is particularly true because China perceives a vacuum emerging in the Pacific, as the United States and Russia trim their forces, and it understandably aims to fill that vacuum.

Under Bismarck, nineteenth-century Germany had limited ambitions. It jockeyed for more power within the "concert of Europe" but did not seek to overturn the established order. But then Bismarck was ousted in 1890 and Kaiser Wilhelm II became more greedy and aggressive. Deng Xiaoping fundamentally resembles Bismarck in his desire to gain power for China without overturning the international order. There is a danger that Deng, too, will be succeeded by someone who is less able and more aggressive—a Chinese version of Wilhelm II.

Until the mid-1980s, China was no threat to anybody because its armed forces were so miserable. In China's last war, a 1979 attack on Vietnam to punish it for invading Cambodia, China was humiliated to discover that tiny Vietnam could absorb the attack and push the Chinese troops back to the border. Then in the early 1980s, Deng Xiaoping demobilized large numbers of troops and trimmed the army to 3 million soldiers. That is still a huge force, the world's largest army, but the recruits were poorly trained and lacked modern equipment. They could swarm across a land border, but they were not much of a concern in the region.

Mao had always emphasized a "people's army" based on huge numbers of soldiers to serve as cannon fodder and overwhelm the enemy. Even a nuclear war was winnable in this way, he said. But in the 1980s, the military became increasingly professional and less ideological. The generals realized they needed fewer troops and more training, fewer slogans and more tanks.

This became possible after the army won the leadership's gratitude in 1989 for crushing the Tiananmen democracy movement. Deng Xiaoping repaid this debt by sharply boosting military spending. Between 1988 and 1994, the military budget soared 70 percent even after adjusting for inflation, more rapid growth than in the economy as a whole. Military expenditures outstripped the budgets for education or public health, each of which is crucial to China's long-term development.

Moreover, China's military budget is highly misleading. It includes only half or even less of the money spent on the army. Funds spent on weapons acquisition, on research, and on pensions are not included. The officially disclosed military budget in 1994 was $5.9 billion, while a more realistic estimate of total military expenses may be somewhere between $12 billion and $18 billion. This sum goes much further in China than it would abroad, for a Chinese soldier earns less than $20 a month. If the $18 billion figure is adjusted to reflect equivalent purchasing power in the West, the total is much higher—perhaps as much as $90 billion. That is much too imprecise a figure for exact comparisons, but it is worth noting that it would be the third-biggest military budget in the world, behind only those of the United States and Russia.

China's military modernization covers all fronts, including such basic items as tanks. China's current tanks are virtual antiques, copies of old Soviet designs and poorly armored. They are sitting ducks, with a short range, slow speed, and a tendency to break down. The government is now benefiting from Israeli help in developing a new generation of tank that will presumably be much more sophisticated and give the army more power in any ground war with India, Vietnam, or Russia.

Still, the focus of the modernization is not the ground forces but rather the air force and navy. The air force in particular has alarmed China's neighbors with its acquisition in the early 1990s of twenty-six Russian-made SU-27 fighters. China has also been considering buying more SU-27s, as well as up to seventy-nine MiG-31 fighters.

The air force has also purchased Russian S-300 ground-to-air missiles, which are a bit like the American Patriot missiles, along with improved radar and guidance systems. With help from Pakistan and perhaps Iran, it is developing a capacity for air-to-air refueling, so that it can dramatically increase its air cover. China is already believed to have reconfigured a couple of bombers to serve as tankers, and it is working on training its pilots so that by the year 2000 it will have a significant fleet of fighter planes and bombers that can be refueled in midair.

One of China's most puzzling forays abroad is its apparent deal with Burma to develop two Burmese islands as observation posts—and perhaps eventually as bases. China has no traditional interest in the Indian Ocean, but in 1985 it sent the navy on a cruise through the area, with port calls at Pakistan, Bangladesh, and Sri Lanka. If China is really trying to play a role in the Indian Ocean, that would be a major concern for other countries in the region.

Perhaps the biggest symbol of China's new interest in projecting power beyond its land borders is its desire to have an aircraft carrier. Sheryl aroused some skepticism when she wrote in 1991 about China's efforts to buy an aircraft carrier, but a year later we found further confirmation from an impeccable source: President Yang Shangkun himself. President Yang said in an internal speech that China had already decided in principle to acquire an aircraft carrier, either by buying one from abroad or by building its own.

The aircraft carrier reflects China's aspiration to develop a blue-water navy of oceangoing vessels, rather than just coastal ships. This naval expansion has attracted less attention than the air force modernization, but it is at least as significant. The new Jiangwei class of frigates, the Luhu class of destroyers, and the newly upgraded version of the older Luda class destroyers are all formidable vessels, especially in the context of the other powers in the region. A Jiangwei frigate might not intimidate an American sailor, but it looks pretty unnerving to a Vietnamese.

China's buildup has attracted attention from its neighbors and contributed to an arms race in the Pacific. But in any kind of arms race China is the likely long-term winner, so in the early 1990s, the neighbors began grumbling openly.

"They've really got a very major buildup going on," said one senior Asian diplomat, his brow furrowed. "It could be quite dangerous. It's very destabilizing, because the balance of power seems to be shifting. We don't know what China is trying to do, why it thinks it needs all this equipment. It says it's not a threat, but then why buy all this threatening equipment if they're not planning to use it?"

Singapore's defense minister, Yeo Ning Hong, is unusual in that he voiced publicly what nearly everyone says privately. China's assertiveness, he said, "has aroused distrust and suspicion," and he cautioned that even if China's generational transition goes smoothly, "countries in the region may still be uncertain about how an economically stronger China will behave in the longer term."

In January 1993, I wrote a long front-page article about China's growing military capabilities. The Chinese government was livid. The leadership could tolerate articles about dissidents getting tortured—hey, cops get carried away all over the world—but it was outraged by the suggestion that China might threaten the neighbors. Almost immediately, the propaganda apparatus began churning out statements denouncing Western alarmists for "spreading slanderous rumors" about China's military capabilities. Such people are "simply unhappy that there is no chaos in Asia, and they are trying to drive wedges among the Asian nations," the New China News Agency fulminated. Prime Minister Li Peng also weighed in, saying, "All these fabricated rumors and absurd tales are totally ridiculous."

To be sure, China's military buildup has to be kept in perspective. It may look ominous to Vietnam or the Philippines, but it is nothing for Western countries to sweat about—at least for decades to come. China's total outlays for military spending probably account for only about 4 percent of its gross national product. By comparison, the United States spends 5 percent of GNP on the military, and the Soviet Union in the 1980s spent at least 15 percent and perhaps much more. Moreover, it is perfectly understandable for China to try to play a broader international role, for it is, after all, one of the five permanent members of the U.N. Security Council. The Perm Five are supposed to be muscular. It's just that because China traditionally was a ninety-five-pound weakling, the weight-lifting program seems a bit alarming to the diminutive neighbors.

All the new money pouring into the Chinese military will have an effect, but only gradually. Take the twenty-six SU-27 fighters purchased from Moscow. It's a nice start, but two dozen planes mean little in the context of a nation's overall military strength. And that's true even if the pilots are well trained. We heard that even after lengthy training in Russia, the Chinese preparing to take over the SU-27s were so unskilled that Russian pilots had to deliver the planes to Chinese bases.

Likewise, in-flight refueling is incredibly difficult to do. Navigating so that the tanker and fighters can find each other over midocean is a complex task, and maneuvering close enough for the fuel line to connect is even tougher. And even if the Chinese aircraft carrier dream comes true, it will be years before Chinese pilots could learn to land their planes on a heaving, moving slab of metal in the middle of the ocean. A former Chinese air force officer told me that fighter pilots in China train for only about eighty flight hours a year, less than one-quarter the level in the United States, and they tend to avoid complicated maneuvers that put the plane at any risk.

Our friend Danping, the son of a general, told us of a meeting he had with a group of senior military officers who had just reviewed films of the American air war against Iraq. The generals were horrified at the ease with which the United States bombed Iraq, for they knew that Iraq's Soviet-designed equipment was not so different from China's. "They sat around the room, moaning about China's lack of preparation, asking what we could possibly do to modernize," he recalled. "I felt like piping up and saying that there was one thing we could do: go capitalist."

The military modernization, in short, will not take place overnight. Only sometime after the year 2000, if all goes well, will China begin to have in place a world-class military force with the ability to project its power over long distances. At that point, this power may be profoundly destabilizing for the region because of the combination of three factors: China's huge population and resources, its military capability, and its territorial disputes and increasing assertiveness in solving them its own way. It's a bit like a sumo wrestler playing with the kids in the sandbox—someone's likely to get hurt. And it won't be the sumo wrestler.

In such a situation, it's natural to blame the sumo wrestler for any accidents. Likewise, there is a tendency for Westerners to accuse China of bullying its neighbors, of harboring evil designs on the region. The Chinese, naturally, view matters in a different light, as a yearning to recover territories that they believe they lost when China was weak. The more I studied the various territorial disputes, the more difficult it became to say who was "right." In most cases, China's position has some merit—which it then exaggerates, as all countries tend to do.

The underlying problem is that when a country develops extremely rapidly, it tends to channel some of its wealth into arms. And that is likely to disrupt the balance of power—particularly in Asia today, when there is something of a vacuum. China arguably is being more reasonable in its exercise of power than the United States was in the nineteenth century, when Americans seized Texas from Mexico and then concocted reasons to go to war with Spain and gain control over Cuba and the Philippines. China is claiming only those lands with which it has a historic link—albeit sometimes a very tenuous one. No "Manifest Destiny" here. Yet even so, China's growing strength is going to create an imbalance of power, and this may be increasingly disruptive.

"China is moving from a regional power to a regional superpower," says Paul Beaver, publisher of *Jane's Defense Weekly*. "That doesn't upturn the balance of power completely, but it does cause a lot of ripples."

One of the oldest problems in international relations, ever since the rise of Assyria and Sparta, has been how to accommodate the ambitions of new powers. It is rarely a question of right or wrong; rather, instability is simply inevitable as the old balance of power is readjusted. Accommodating China may be one of the biggest challenges for the international community in the twenty-first century, for there are potential flash points on almost every part of China's border. Among the possibilities:

Mongolia. Mao was forced by Stalin to give up Chinese claims to outer Mongolia, which had been a part of China under the Qing dynasty. Now some Chinese would like to recover those lands. Beijing also resents the way Mongolia allows dissidents from China's Inner Mongolia region to operate from bases just over the border. At a deeper level, the tension between Mongolia and China is the historic one between the herdsman and the planter, the nomad and the city dweller. Relations have been strained ever since the Mongol leader Genghis Khan invaded China, killing millions of Chinese; Genghis reportedly even toyed with the idea of slaughtering everyone in northern China and turning it into a giant pasture. He relented only when an adviser pointed out that the Chinese, if allowed to live, could be taxed.

Russia. The czars took advantage of Chinese weakness beginning in the nineteenth century to seize huge chunks of territory in the far northeast and northwest of the country. While not demanding the return of those territories, China has minor disputes with Russia concerning the precise demarcation of the frontier. Some Chinese believe that China now has a historic opportunity to take advantage of Russian weakness and recover those lost territories. It seems very unlikely that there will be new border clashes, as there were in 1969, but tensions and distrust remain.

Central Asia. The Xinjiang "autonomous region" in the far west of China is populated primarily by Muslims who speak Turkic languages similar to those of Kazakhstan, Kyrgyzstan, and the other new nations of Central Asia. Separatist sentiment appears to be growing in Xinjiang, and in 1990 a group of rebels launched an armed revolt and declared a "holy war" against the Chinese government. Their effort collapsed, but further turbulence could create sympathies in Central Asia and create tensions between China and its Muslim neighbors.

North Korea. Although China suffered a million casualties helping North Korea forty years ago during the Korean War, relations between the two countries are now awkward and tense. North Korean leaders were particularly incensed that China established diplomatic relations with South Korea in 1992, and by some accounts they sent commandos to try to assassinate the former South Korean president, Roh Tae Woo, when he visited Beijing that year. There have been a few mysterious incidents of North Korean soldiers firing across the border, and there is a long-standing disagreement about navigation rights on the Tumen River, which flows along the border. While Chinese leaders pretend that relations with North Korea are still close, they are also deeply concerned by North Korea's efforts to build nuclear weapons.

Japan. China, Taiwan, and Japan all claim a set of uninhabited islands in the East China Sea. China calls them the Diaoyu Islands, Taiwan calls them the Diaoyutai, and Japan calls them the Senkaku Islands. For now there is an unofficial truce, with no one country pressing its claims or trying to establish a base. But if any country becomes aggressive in asserting control over the islands, or if lucrative oil deposits are found in the area, a conflict could erupt.

India. Close friends in the 1950s, China and India fought a border war in 1962, and relations have been strained ever since. The disputed area along the border is huge but largely uninhabited, so there is little chance of clashes in the ordinary course of events. But nationalism makes it difficult to imagine the two countries reaching an agreement on a common border.

Vietnam and the South China Sea. This is one of the most likely arenas for war. China fought a border war with Vietnam in 1979, and since then there have been several clashes in the South China Sea. As China gains a blue-water navy, it is likely to increase its presence in the South China Sea, and that is already causing anxiety throughout Southeast Asia. A look at the map explains why. China claims the entire South China Sea as its own 1,000-mile-long pond. By this measure, Chinese territory extends farther south than Vietnam or the Philippines, almost to the Equator. The potential for conflict arises because parts of the South China Sea—and the Paracel and Spratly islands that lie within it—are also claimed by Vietnam, Taiwan, Malaysia, the Philippines, and Brunei. In addition, major international shipping routes pass through the South China Sea, carrying huge volumes of cargo and all the oil that Japan gets from the Persian Gulf.

The first indication of a more aggressive posture came in early 1992, when China passed a new law regulating its territorial waters.

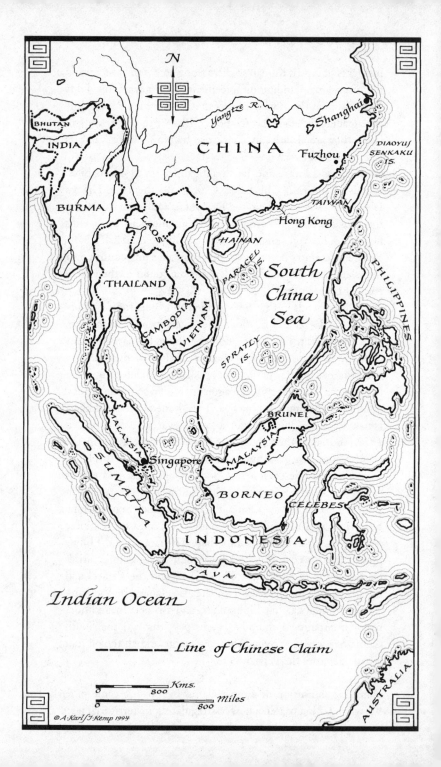

N

Yangtze R.

CHINA

Shanghai

BHUTAN

INDIA

Fuzhou

DIAOYU/
SENKAKU
IS.

BURMA

TAIWAN

Hong Kong

LAOS

HAINAN

PARACEL
IS.

South
China
Sea

THAILAND

PHILIPPINES

CAMBODIA

VIETNAM

SPRATLY
IS.

MALAYSIA

BRUNEI

SUMATRA

Singapore

MALAYSIA

BORNEO

CELEBES

INDONESIA

JAVA

Indian Ocean

——— ——— Line of Chinese Claim

0   800   Kms.

0   800   Miles

AUSTRALIA

© A·Karl/J·Kemp 1994

Chinese officials refuse to say whether the entire South China Sea is their territorial sea, or only the waters within a twelve-mile limit of each of the atolls—a lesser but still sweeping claim. Chinese government maps are less ambiguous and indicate that the entire sea is China's. In either case, the 1992 regulations do not allow innocent passage for foreign warships and require foreign submarines to surface when passing through, although this has not been enforced.

Then, in the spring of 1992, China signed a contract with an American oil company, Crestone Energy Corporation, authorizing it to explore for petroleum in 9,700 square miles of waters claimed by both China and Vietnam. I found out about the contract only because a Chinese newspaper wrote about it and happened to include a map showing where the parcel—referred to in print only by its coordinates—was located. It was immediately obvious that this was a major provocation by China, for no country had signed an exploration contract in the South China Sea since 1973. South Vietnam, then about to collapse, in that year sold a concession to American oil companies, and the result was a brief naval battle between Vietnamese and Chinese vessels.

I called up Randall C. Thompson, the head of Crestone, at his office in Denver. He knew that the waters were disputed, but he said he agreed with Beijing that the territory was really China's. And he said that Chinese officials had promised him military support. "I was assured by top Chinese officials that they will protect me with their full naval might," Thompson said. "That's what they told me in negotiations—that they'll have the entire full naval fleet out there backing me up, if necessary."

The navy knew what it was doing. With the collapse of the Soviet Union and the absence of any major threat to China, the generals of the People's Liberation Army—like their American counterparts—were looking for a new raison d'être. The one they came up with was this: safeguarding China's economic interests. In particular, they emphasized the huge petroleum potential of the South China Sea and suggested that substantial naval power was the only way to ensure that it could be exploited.

The reverberations of China's rise will not be military alone. China's awakening will "shake the world," in Napoleon's words, in other ways as well. One problem is where the energy will come from to supply China's economic revolution. China is already the world's biggest coal producer, and it appears to have become a net oil importer in 1993. Oil reserves in the Tarim Basin in the far west of China are promising, but they will be enormously expensive to exploit and transport. In the meantime, energy demand will rise not only with population growth but also with the level of industrialization. In 1991, per capita consumption of energy in China was only 602 kilograms of oil equivalent, compared with 7,681 kilograms of oil equivalent in the United States. In other words, only a modest increase in China's industrialization would place a huge new strain on global energy supplies.

China probably can manage the energy crunch, for it does have the oil and natural gas and coal, even if they are not easy to extract. It has an estimated 910 billion tons of coal in the ground, or about 900 years' supply. The danger is the environmental cost, to China and the entire world, of a vast industrial revolution. A few billion tons of coal, burned without proper pollution control devices, produce enough soot to blacken countless lungs. Even China's well-intended plans could have dire consequences. Paul Kennedy, in his book *Preparing for the Twenty-first Century,* points out that China's ambition to equip every family with a refrigerator by the year 2000 could result in a huge increase in chlorofluorocarbons, further depleting the ozone layer. The upshot is that Chinese peasants get cold drinks, and we get skin cancer.

China's environment is already a mess. The most polluted place in the country may be Benxi, a Manchurian city with air like soot. The *Economic Daily* wrote in 1992 that "Benxi has a population of 800,000 people, but they might as well be 800,000 vacuum cleaners." When a surgeon in another city glimpsed the blackness of the lungs of a patient he was operating on, he immediately guessed (correctly) that the patient was from Benxi. In fact, at times in the 1980s the city of Benxi completely disappeared from satellite photographs because of the haze.

Sheryl once went to Chongqing to write about air pollution there, and she found what she was looking for: The smog was so bad that her plane couldn't take off for her return to Beijing, and she spent a full day waiting in the Chongqing airport. In fact, the air was so polluted that Sheryl had trouble getting a photograph to go with the story. The scenes were so gray that it looked as if she had been taking photos underwater.

Think of Chongqing's fog and rain as vinegar. You can just about season your food with it, for its acidity sometimes measures nearly 3.0 on the pH scale, while Chinese vinegar is only slightly stronger (2.8 on the same scale). "The worst fog in London in the 1950s was when you couldn't see three or four meters," Wang Gang, an environmental official in Chongqing, told Sheryl. "Chongqing is about the same. Even in the summer we don't take walks."

China's air pollution problems are largely caused by the burning of coal: for heat, for cooking, and for industry. While China has huge amounts of coal, much is of poor quality and contains large amounts of sulfur. The result is that there are coal dust particles everywhere, particularly during the winter. In 1991, Chinese polluters emitted 11 trillion cubic meters of waste gases and 16 million metric tons of soot. To put that in perspective, the amount of soot produced in three years in China approximately equals the total weight of all Chinese people. The sulfur in the coal also causes acid rain, which travels across international borders to destroy forests in Siberia or Korea. Some experts believe that China will become the world's largest source of acid rain by the year 2010.

After an hour or two outside in the winter, we would come home and find our nostrils blackened from the soot. The coal dust would creep into our apartment through every cranny, and when I went on one of my six-mile jogs through Beijing, I would come back with a blackened tongue.

As we probed the environmental problems, we found that in many cities, particularly in the north, air pollution exceeds World Health Organization standards by five or six times. Respiratory disease, often a result of lungs clogged with soot, is the leading cause of death in China, accounting for 26 percent of all deaths. This mortality rate is 5.5 times the level in the United States. One careful study in 1993 found that particles in the Chinese air cause 915,000 premature deaths each year, including those of 300,000 children who die from lung infections. Another 600,000 adults die early of respiratory blockage, and 15,000 fall victim to lung cancer caused by the bad air.

Finally, I decided that running might be doing my health more harm than good. I stopped jogging in the winter.

Chinese water is no better than the air. In 1991, for example, industry poured 1,836 metric tons of heavy metals into Chinese rivers, along with 1,127 tons of arsenic and 4,666 tons of cyanides. Eighty-five percent of Chinese cities are now short of clean water, and in the countryside only one Chinese in seven has safe drinking water.

Yet perhaps the biggest worry of all is China's contributions to global warming. Burning coal releases carbon dioxide, the most important of the greenhouse gases that are suspected of trapping heat around the earth's surface. A sustained rise in the earth's temperature could have far-reaching effects on the global climate and raise sea levels enough to flood many coastal cities around the world—not to mention entire countries, like the Maldives in the Indian Ocean. At last count, China ranked third in emissions of greenhouse gases, behind the United States and the former Soviet Union. If the output of the former Soviet Union is divided up by country, then China may well exceed Russia and rank second in the world.

Is this China's fault? Not entirely. On a per capita basis, China does not even rank in the top fifty countries worldwide. Every American is responsible for nine times as much greenhouse gas as every Chinese. The crux of the matter, as in the military field, is simply that China is huge and growing very rapidly. That makes it, almost by definition, the fastest-increasing emitter of greenhouse gases. The Stockholm Environment Institute calculated that if China's economy grows 8.5 percent a year for the next three decades, by the year 2025 China will produce three times as much carbon dioxide as the United States. In one sense that is perfectly fair, since China will have far more than three times America's population. But it is discouraging for the rest of the world, for while the West is making efforts to curb greenhouse gases, China is blithely going ahead as it always has.

"China must develop, and its people must enjoy a better life, but we can't make it without energy," said Bai Xianhong, a senior government scientist. "You can't say that for the sake of lowering carbon dioxide emissions, China shouldn't burn coal anymore. This is impossible." Jing Wenyong, an environmental specialist at Qinghua University, agreed. "You can't even talk about economic sacrifice," he said. "Above all, we must have economic development."

And there goes the New Jersey shoreline.

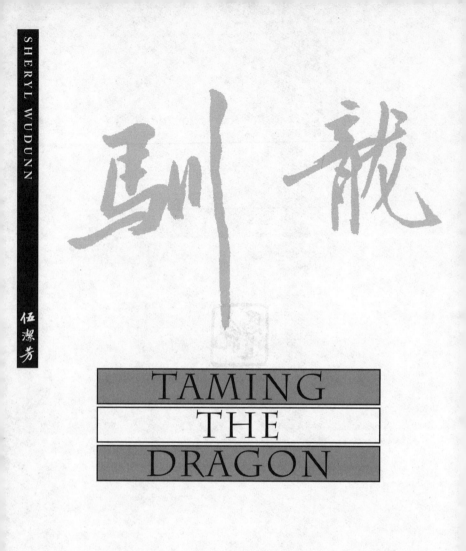

馴 龍

伍潔芳

TAMING
THE
DRAGON

They got Taiwan, We got Egg Rolls.

—U.S. headline after Nixon's 1972 visit to China

14

"旗手" · 朱根华 ·

The U.S. government is portrayed in this *People's Daily* cartoon as a Nazi-style storm trooper wielding a club with a banner labeled "Human Rights Report."

I never thought I'd be detained in China until one day I found myself caught in the middle of a huddle of hostile Chinese security officers. It was nearly sunset, with the bright sky fading into gray on an autumn day near the end of my five years in China, and I was interviewing a peasant who had journeyed to Beijing to seek assistance from a government office in a small, isolated alley in the south of the capital. He was a frail, middle-aged man whose spindly legs scarcely seemed able to support both him and the black cloth bag he had carried for hundreds of miles from his hometown in central Shaanxi Province. I was finishing up and about to turn away when suddenly a man, surly and stocky in a beige windbreaker, put his hand on my shoulder.

"You're not allowed to leave," he said sternly, his feet planted like posts in mud. "Who are you? Where do you come from? What are you doing here?"

"I'm from overseas," I replied, working up a weak smile. "I don't speak Chinese very well. Excuse me, what did you say?" I started speaking loudly in English.

"Where are you from?"

"Excuse me? I don't understand you," I replied in English.

"I know you understand!" he roared. "You were just speaking Chinese before. I heard you. You'll have to come inside and explain all this." He gestured toward the government office, now to my left.

"I am a Chinese-American, and I'm a friend of China," I said, speaking slowly in bad, broken Chinese. I figured that if I spoke slowly, like a child, I'd have more time to think of what to say. I didn't dare ask who this man was, because then he would use his official position to demand that I go inside.

"Show me your identification," he said. I didn't budge. "Come with me," he said.

I began to panic. I usually didn't carry my passport with me for fear of its being stolen or confiscated. There wasn't a foreigner in sight, and no one knew I was here. What if they took me in and never brought me out again?

"There's absolutely no need to go anywhere," I said firmly. "Why, if you have any questions, you can ask me right here and now. I'm just an ordinary person on an ordinary street."

"No, you'll have to come in," he said again, and grabbed my arm. I pulled away gently.

"There's really no need for that, and I just happen to be on my way out. Anyway, I'm just like all these other people standing around here." I took a few steps away from the building, but the crowd tightened around me, and another man, a thin, bony-faced bully, took a step forward to block my path.

"You can't escape from here," he said. "We know who you are now, and you can't run away. Do you know that this is a private street, and you're not allowed to be here? So we have to take you inside. Show me your identification."

"I'm sorry, I didn't bring it. I told you, I'm a Chinese-American—"

"Then you must come inside," he interrupted.

If I complied, perhaps they would take me in, confiscate my notebook, and question me for several hours. Maybe I'd get off easy, but maybe they'd keep me longer. On the other hand, if I didn't go with this man, maybe he'd beat me up and detain me anyway. Still, maybe he wouldn't dare strike a woman in front of the crowd. I prayed that most of the men in there were innocent bystanders, not security men, and made my decision.

"I'm sorry, but it's very late and I have to get back to my family," I said confidently, though I was shaking inside, and I started pushing my way through there down the street. I walked as fast as I could, without running, and no one grabbed me. When I got to the main road, I heard someone yelling for me. I turned around and saw that one of the peasants had followed behind, wanting to tell me his story! What guts. But I was too worried that if I stopped to hear his story, they'd come after both of us. So I ran off.

And the men never came. Paper tigers.

When it came to the Chinese authorities, I discovered that if you pushed a little, you usually got a lot. But you had to push at the right time and with the right amount of force. If you didn't push enough, you got nothing. If you pushed too hard, you got into a fistfight.

That is also a metaphor for relations between China and the West. Perhaps no country gives the West so many headaches as China. And as China continues to get stronger, the migraines will get worse. What will we do if China seizes a Western merchant ship in the South China Sea, claiming that these are Chinese waters? How will we react if China announces a naval quarantine of Taiwan? What should we do if China massacres Tibetan Buddhist monks and nuns in the central square of Lhasa?

The test of our China policy will be not only how we react to such incidents but, more important, whether we can reduce the chance of their happening in the first place. The problem is that, for most of the last two centuries, the West has pursued a misguided and ineffective China policy—when it has had one at all. The last fifteen years of the post-Mao era have been no exception. We need a new and more coherent approach.

More than 2,500 years ago, China's greatest military analyst outlined the basics of a successful strategy. Sunzi, or Sun-Tzu (as his name traditionally was spelled), wrote, "Know the enemy, know yourself; your victory will never be endangered."

It's good advice today, even though we don't necessarily regard China as an enemy with whom we will come to blows. The problem is that we do not know China; indeed, we often find it incomprehensible. Lord Macaulay offered the same complaint more than a century ago. Speaking in the British Parliament in 1840, he lamented: "What does anybody here know of China? Even those Europeans who have been in that Empire are almost as ignorant of it as the rest of us. Everything is covered by a veil, through which a glimpse of what is within may occasionally be caught, a glimpse just sufficient to set the imagination at work and more likely to mislead than to inform."

Secretary of State Warren Christopher, asked about China as he spoke to the Council on Foreign Relations in New York in 1993, offered the same complaint in more modern language. He said that he just couldn't understand why Beijing acts as it does. He found Beijing unfathomable.

That is our fault just as much as it is China's. And in understanding Beijing's actions, it helps to know that China likewise finds the United States incomprehensible. Chinese leaders just can't understand why Washington acts as it does. Step into Deng Xiaoping's shoes for a moment. The relationship with the United States got off

on a good footing when Richard Nixon arrived in 1972 for his landmark visit, laying the groundwork for a marriage of convenience
between two countries fearful of a common Soviet enemy. "The
week that changed the world," as Nixon later called it, began with
Chairman Mao's summoning the president to a meeting and
announcing that he "liked rightists." President Nixon suggested that
the United States wouldn't poke its nose into Chinese human rights
abuses. "What is important is not a nation's internal political philosophy," Nixon said. "What is important is its policy toward the rest of
the world and toward us."

But then, according to the world of Deng, the United States
reneged on that implicit promise of noninterference. Particularly
after Tiananmen, the United States decided that what was important
about China was its abuse of its own citizens. Washington inspires
"traitors" on Voice of America and supports convicted "counterrevolutionaries" who fought the People's Liberation Army during the
Tiananmen clashes. From the Politburo's point of view, the United
States even aims to carve up China. In the 1950s, America armed
Tibetan insurgents, and in the 1990s Washington opened a Tibetan-
language broadcast service on Voice of America and arranged meetings between the president and the Dalai Lama.

America's concerns about weapons proliferation sound like double-
talk when Chinese officials see Washington selling sophisticated
missiles and jets to Middle Eastern countries, even to Taiwan. And
Chinese don't see how the United States can be serious about curbing the spread of nuclear weapons when it agrees to allow shipments
of plutonium to a really dangerous country like Japan. From the perspective of leaders whose memories stretch back to the 1930s and
Japan's invasion, in which some 10 million Chinese died, no nation
is so unreliable and potentially threatening as Japan.

So in Zhongnanhai, the leadership compound, it is the United
States that looks like the thug of nations. Now, obviously we don't
agree with this perspective. We can still regard Beijing as a brutal and
self-deluded paranoiac. But paranoiacs have feelings, too, and the
first step in dealing with the Chinese government is to understand
where those feelings are coming from. The gulf between us is real, in
interests as well as perceptions.

This gulf is dominated by four specific areas of dispute between
China and the West. The first is human rights, which the Chinese

government initially did not even acknowledge as a legitimate topic of discussion. Then at the end of 1990, China agreed to discuss human rights concerns so long as there was an atmosphere of "mutual respect." The problem is that the West's goal isn't simply to talk about human rights but to see progress in human rights. China often objects that the West has no right to impose its own standards on developing countries, but I think that's a bogus argument. That's not what we're doing. We're not saying that China should have a presidential system, or a federal system, or a right to bear arms. Rather, we're trying to encourage China to adhere to its own laws— such as those that prohibit torture. The Chinese leaders themselves say that they're against beating up labor activists or raping Tibetan nuns, and there's no reason why we can't hold them to their own standards.

To be sure, we have to acknowledge that Beijing is making progress in observing human rights. Prisoners are beaten to death less often than they were in the 1970s or even in the 1980s. Chinese are now able to tell jokes about Li Peng in their homes or among friends, and it is far easier than ever before for them to travel abroad. In 1993, for example, nearly 700,000 Chinese went overseas on personal business, and only 4 percent of the aspiring Chinese travelers who applied to public security for permission to leave the country were turned down, compared with 20 percent the year before. China may get a D in human rights, but that's better than the F it used to get.

The second area of tension is the proliferation of military and nuclear technology. China insists on selling modern missiles to unstable countries and then lying about it. The last straw was its secret sale in 1992 and 1993 of components of M-11 missiles, which have a range greater than 186 miles and can be fitted with nuclear warheads, to Pakistan. China also acknowledges helping Algeria, Iran, and Pakistan in constructing nuclear power plants, arguing that these are civilian programs. While this is probably true, the technologies that those countries are gaining will also be useful in developing nuclear weapons.

Under strong pressure from the West, China is trying to improve its image in this respect. After years of opposition, China acceded to the Nuclear Nonproliferation Treaty in March 1992. A few months earlier, in November 1991, it agreed to abide by the parameters of the Missile Technology Control Regime, thus promising to curb missile sales abroad. Even so, China apparently went ahead with M-11 sales to Pakistan.

The third area of conflict is trade, for China is proving an even more unfair trader than most other countries. It relies on tariffs, secret rules, administrative fiat, and absurd requirements to keep foreign goods out. Until recently, for example, an importer of foreign cars had to buy an extra of each model and give it to the government for testing, in addition to paying import duties that ranged up to 200 percent. Such protectionism is accompanied by widespread cheating on export quotas. United States customs officials monitoring the Chinese border have seized millions of dollars worth of outgoing merchandise tagged with labels of other countries. Moreover, China is notorious for its theft of foreign copyrights and patents; President Bush's autobiography, for example, was circulated in China in three pirated translations. In many bookshops in the provinces, there is a room that foreigners are not allowed to enter, and that piqued my curiosity. What national secrets lurked within? Finally I sneaked inside such a room and found it full of nothing more secret than pirated American textbooks.

While China has a rapidly growing trade surplus with the United States—the second biggest, after Japan's—we should recognize that China does not have a trade surplus with everybody. Unlike Japan, China imports more than it exports, running trade deficits in 1993 and other years recently. Westerners also do not realize that the products displaced by imported Chinese shoes and toys are not so much domestically made items but rather the low-end penny loafers and stuffed pandas that used to come from Taiwan and Hong Kong. Nor do they realize how large the China market is for our own exports, from grain to aircraft. In the early 1990s, China was purchasing one out of every six new Boeing commercial airliners. Moreover, Beijing has signed international copyright conventions and taken other steps to protect foreign intellectual property. The computer shops of Zhongguancun in Beijing still contain pirated software—when I bought a computer in 1992, I couldn't find a legal copy of DOS and had to order one from Hong Kong—but less than they used to. When the book *Scarlett*, the sequel to *Gone with the Wind*, appeared in Chinese translation, the publisher actually said it paid royalties to the American publisher. The government is also gradually disclosing its secret regulations that interfere with trade, so that foreign businessmen are no longer stymied by laws that they can't even see. And, grudgingly, as part of its efforts to get into GATT, China is lowering its tariffs and lifting the most ludicrous and burdensome regulations.

The final dispute is one that China has with us, instead of the other way around. It concerns Western sales of weaponry to Taiwan and, more broadly, Western support for Taiwan. The United States has been "interfering" in this respect ever since 1950, when we sent the Seventh Fleet to prevent China from "liberating" Taiwan. That is a perfect example of how the United States played a constructive international role at little cost to itself. If President Truman had not sent in the Seventh Fleet, China almost certainly would have conquered Taiwan—with a considerable loss in human lives. Instead, U.S. protection meant that Taiwan has managed to grow rich, free, and democratic. The biggest beneficiary, of course, is China itself, for Taiwan is now a major investor in China.

Yet the Communist leadership is outraged that the West continues to deal with Taiwan, even after transferring its diplomatic recognition to Beijing—which in the case of the United States happened in 1979. Above all, the Chinese are offended by Western arms sales, arguing that the French sale of Mirage fighters and the United States sale of F-16 fighters to Taiwan in 1992 violated agreements with China. The Dutch and Germans have also been tempted by Taiwan's desire to buy submarines, ships, and other military equipment.

The problem is that China's paranoiacs misconstrue these actions and believe that the United States and others are trying to keep Taiwan as a quasi colony; they particularly suspect America of aiming to divide and control China itself. "The United States inevitably will try to pin us down by developing relations with Taiwan," a classified Chinese document warned in early 1993. "Because of its political, economic, and security interests, it is in America's best interest to preserve the situation in the Taiwan Strait as it is, with Taiwan remaining indefinitely as an independent entity." This may be a biased misinterpretation of reality, but that is how China sees it, and Beijing's irritation at Western dealings with Taiwan is likely to remain a significant source of tension in the coming years.

That brings us to the most irksome aspect of China's foreign policy: that it seems unpredictable, at times even irrational. The first Westerners to deal with the Qing dynasty had the same complaint. In 1793, Britain sent a mission to Beijing to open up China to trade. The mission was headed by Lord Macartney, an experienced diplomat, but the cultural gap between China and Britain was so huge that the two sides spent their time talking past each other. For all their words, they never communicated.

Lord Macartney had brought some gifts for the Qianlong emperor, but the Chinese regarded these as "tribute" and insisted that Macartney perform the ritual three kneelings and nine prostrations while presenting them. Macartney refused to kowtow, although he did manage what another member of the mission called a "profound obeisance." This was not enough. The mission was sent packing with a letter addressed to King George III advising him to swear perpetual obedience to the Son of Heaven. The Dutch sent an ambassador of their own, and he eagerly kowtowed—so deeply that his wig fell off, amusing the court. But the Chinese treated him no better, sending him away as well. And Qianlong dismissed a Russian delegation with the words "You're a daft race. Be gone!"

The Qing dynasty's obstreperousness turned out to be foolish, however, for the Europeans returned with gunboats. The Chinese emperors soon found that they had acted irrationally and against their own interests, for China was forced to fight several wars—in which it suffered humiliating defeats—and to cede trading enclaves to foreign countries. In the winter of 1911–12, partly as a result of the defeats, the Qing dynasty collapsed.

One mistake we still make today is to assume that China will act in its own best interests. Instead, as a Chinese saying goes, the leaders often lift up a rock only to drop it on their own feet. Or, more precisely, on the feet of their fellow citizens.

That distinction—on whose feet the rocks fall—is one explanation for why China sometimes seems to act against its own interests. The leaders don't act in their country's interests; they act in their personal interests. Thus army leaders regularly try to peddle weapons abroad so that they can make money for their units or for themselves, even if this risks embarrassment and economic sanctions for their country. Some hard-line military and State Security officials may also deliberately provoke disputes between Beijing and Washington, because an exchange of invective tends to strengthen the position of the hard-liners. In the early 1970s, for example, the military tried to sabotage the warming of Sino-American relations, and in 1992 there were some signs that hard-liners were again trying to cause mischief by conducting a huge underground nuclear test, antagonizing the West by undermining international efforts to halt nuclear testing. At about the same time, State Security detained my *Washington Post* colleague, Lena Sun, and searched her office and notebooks. As a way of generating anti-Chinese press in Washington, it was a brilliant maneuver: The upper-left-hand side of *The Post*'s front page the next day was filled by a photo of Lena and her first-person account of the incident. (Our foreign editor later advised Nick that to get the same treatment on *The Times*'s front page, "they'd have to hang you upside down by your toes and torture you for a bit." We hoped that our State Security eavesdroppers, listening on the phone, wouldn't get any bright ideas.)

Even when the Politburo isn't torn by factional rivalries and is inclined to act in the nation's interests, it frequently doesn't because of bad intelligence. In 1991, a scholar named David Shambaugh published a study of America watchers in China and concluded: "Chinese understanding of the United States remains shallow and seriously distorted. With a few exceptions, the vast majority of America-watchers in China do not understand the United States very well." It would be difficult to imagine a worse policy maker than a misinformed paranoiac, but China's octogenarians are often just that. Even Deng Xiaoping reportedly believed, at first, that the Tiananmen democracy movement was the result of American plotting. It sometimes seemed to us that Western governments should stop trying to uncover Chinese spies; instead we should encourage Beijing to send more. If Beijing had more moles, it might understand us better.

From time to time, Chinese friends gave us secret government documents, and often the most interesting ones were not about China but about the United States. These were the briefing papers for senior government officials, yet they reflected an appalling misunderstanding of how America works. In 1989, for example, a Chinese journalist gave us a couple of copies of an internal periodical called *Neican Xuanpian*, or *Internal Reference Articles.*

That was immediately after the Tiananmen killings, when China was an international pariah. The decline of the Soviet threat had cost China its leverage as a partner against the bear, and there was little reason for the United States to give a damn about China. Even

China's economy then seemed moribund. The only thing in China's favor was President Bush's soft spot for the country in which he had once served as de facto ambassador. Yet at that bleak time, this classified document presented an analysis of Sino-American relations in which China appeared to have all the trump cards. The article suggested that it was the United States that would be forced to modify its position so as to preserve its interests in China. After quoting the Bush administration as saying it would balance its wish to help the democracy movement with the need to protect the Chinese-American relationship, the document added:

> *However, more profound observation reveals that the Bush Administration is not putting absolutely equal weight on both stances but in fact tips toward the protection of Sino-American relations. The slant does not reflect any special affection for China; rather it is decided by the best interests of the American nation. To be specific, the United States has five fears in its relation to China:*
>
> *First, that China will be forced into isolationism and hostility toward the West. Second, that China will be pushed into the embrace of the Soviet Union, thus costing the United States the use of an important political and military power to check the Russians. Third, China might back away from its reform and open policies, thus destroying American efforts to encourage China to evolve peacefully to capitalism. Fourth, if China and the United States quarrel, then Japan, West Germany and South Korea will jump into China's huge market on an unprecedented scale and cause colossal damage to American businesses. Fifth, a divided and weak China would not have the power to check Japan economically and militarily, and that might complicate the process of maintaining peace and stability in the Asian-Pacific region.*

In 1989, this was largely fantasy. To think that the United States wanted a strong China to check Japan! That reflected Chinese angst, not American. Some of the points, such as the commercial potential of China, later became more important, but in the fall of 1989, Americans weren't thinking about China's market potential; IBM and other companies were then thinking about scaling down or pulling out, not about expansion.

Other classified documents confirmed the impression that Chinese leaders are living in a fantasy world. The documents exaggerated

China's own negotiation position and falsely portrayed an elaborate Western conspiracy to cause the collapse of the Chinese government. One explained that the downfall of Eastern Europe was entirely the result of a careful Western plot, led by the United States. In 1993, another classified analysis warned, "The United States may be running out of energy, but it has never abandoned its ambition to rule the world, and its military interventionism is becoming more open."

Coming as they do from a closed political system, Chinese leaders could never understand that, in America, public opinion and the news media often drive policy. Nor could they comprehend that, partly as a result, the United States might pursue a human rights policy simply because it thought this was the right thing to do. Chinese officials used to explain to me, painstakingly and condescendingly, that cutting off most-favored-nation trade status would hurt the United States as well as China. They thought that ended the discussion; they could not see that the United States might be willing to pay an economic price for its ideals.

Even China's embassies abroad tend to reinforce prejudices at home rather than engage in real reporting. The former Chinese ambassador to Washington, Zhu Qizhen, who retired in 1993, was inept. He had no idea how to communicate with Capitol Hill or the press, and he seemed congenitally unable to provide bad news to his bosses at home. So he sent a series of optimistic cables back to Beijing, and the State Department fretted that even when it summoned Zhu for a scolding he wouldn't relay the warnings to his bosses. (To be sure, Zhu didn't seem to know much more about China than about the United States. An American whom Zhu regarded as important wrote to ask about the status of Liu Gang, one of the most famous political prisoners in China. The government acknowledges imprisoning him, and even Chinese publications like *Beijing Review* write about him—claiming he is not tortured, as foreign reporters say. Yet Ambassador Zhu wrote back to say that he had carefully investigated and found that China had no prisoner named Liu Gang.)

Hong Kong provides a similar case study of how China can lift a rock and drop it squarely on its own feet. When I lived in Hong Kong in 1987, the conventional wisdom was that Hong Kong would do fine. "China needs Hong Kong," business executives told me. "They depend on Hong Kong for investment and trade." Others noted that if China messed up Hong Kong, it would have no hope of peacefully recovering Taiwan. All this was true. Yet in the years after Tiananmen, China repeatedly and unnecessarily pounded Hong Kong.

Why? Mostly because of bad information. Chinese officials are convinced that Britain is secretly scheming with the United States to sabotage Hong Kong. When the British government in Hong Kong proposed building a new airport for the territory, China was convinced that this was merely a plot to empty the coffers and give the money to British contractors. It refused to give its approval to the airport, which was needed both as an infrastructure project and as a boost to local confidence. When Britain proposed modest political changes in 1992, China was convinced that this was a scheme to foment rebellion after the 1997 handover, so that London could control the territory by pulling the strings from afar. In response, China announced that legal contracts would not necessarily be binding after 1997 and even threatened to invade Hong Kong. There may be no place in the world so resilient as Hong Kong, so the territory has managed to bounce back—but no thanks are due to Beijing.

How about us? How does the West do at understanding China?

I think that China watchers in the West have a rudimentary grasp of what is happening in China—except for the countryside, of which we do not know even that much. Yet even our marginal understanding of China often goes unused, because China watchers in the West don't make policy, they simply advise or inform. Western leaders neither know much about China nor care a lot about it. For all their misimpressions, Chinese leaders pay far more attention to America and Europe than American or European leaders pay to China. Often the West has neither a good China policy nor a bad one—it doesn't have any China policy at all.

In the 1990s, policy making toward China has become polarized. The business community wants better relations, without much fuss over human rights. And the human rights lobby wants the West to stand up for its values. To some extent, these are incompatible aims. But this was true in the early nineteenth century as well.

In 1821, an American seaman named Francis Terranova was accused of killing a Chinese woman who had come out on a small fishing boat to trade with the men aboard his ship, the *Emily*, which had sailed from Baltimore to Guangzhou. The Chinese authorities were outraged and demanded that the Americans turn over Terranova to be tried in a Chinese court. Naturally, the Americans were suspicious of Chinese trial practices. The *Emily*'s captain, a man named Cowpland, simply refused to turn Terranova over. Other captains of American ships sided with him.

But the American merchants vociferously objected. They feared that offending the Chinese authorities would lead to a cancellation of American trading privileges. After much debate, the Americans reached a compromise: The Chinese authorities would be allowed onboard the *Emily* to conduct their trial there.

A Chinese judge shuffled his way up the gangplank and immediately announced the verdict. Terranova was guilty and sentenced to be executed by strangling. The Americans protested that the trial was a farce, and they refused to hand Terranova over. The Chinese retaliated by suspending trade with all Americans. The Americans searched their consciences, briefly, and chose profit over principles. They turned Terranova over to the Chinese, and he was executed.

The British were appalled at what they saw as American kowtowing. The East India Company condemned the Americans for "barbarously abandoning a man serving under their Flag." But the obsequiousness of the American merchants was unfailing. They issued their own statement to the Chinese: "We consider the Terranova case prejudiced. We are bound to submit to your laws while we are in your waters, be they ever so unjust. We will not resist them. You have followed your ideas of justice, and have condemned the man unheard. But the flag of our country has never been disgraced. It now waves over you. It is no disgrace to submit to your power, surrounded as you are by overwhelming force, backed up by a great Empire. You have the power to compel us."

More than a century and a half later, it seems that the West is still caught up in the same dilemma over its relationship with China: business versus politics. There are too many zeros at stake in the amounts of money involved for commercial interests to be ignored. In some ways, when less money was at stake, when China seemed a less appealing market, it was easier to invoke principles.

The Chinese love numerical phrases: the "Four Modernizations," the "Six Evils," and so on. So I would like to outline the "Three

Headaches" that roil Sino-Western relations. In pressing China in pursuit of our interests and our ideals, we should do what we can to alleviate these migraines.

The first headache is the psychological roller coaster in perceptions of China. We must remember that China is never as good or as bad as it looks at any one moment. China and the West are a bit like some couples I know, embracing each other one moment and shrieking at each other the next. Since Deng Xiaoping came to power, the cycles have become more frequent. One moment we think China is the most fascinating and economically vibrant country in the world; the next moment, we see it as a vicious police state that is likely to collapse at any time; and then back again. The result is the same kind of zigzag policy making that we decry in China itself. So as a starting point, we should recognize that the mood of the moment—be it euphoria or outrage—will probably pass and should not be the basis of our policy.

The second headache is our erroneous assumption that we can change China. We can't, and any attempt to do so is likely to backfire. In fact, we must recognize that we can play only a marginal role in modifying China's internal behavior. We can exert considerable influence over its foreign and trade policies, but very little over its internal human rights situation. Ultimately, the will to improve human rights will have to come from within. This is not to say that we shouldn't try, but we must be realistic about what can be achieved. The leaders' first priority is to stay in power, not to have good relations with the United States. If they see their power threatened by the democracy movement, they will continue to suppress it, however much we holler. Our complaints are likely to be effective only in encouraging China to be repressive in a slightly nicer way, to use less torture, to release some prisoners early, to allow them medical treatment.

The third headache in Chinese-Western relations is the importance of saving face. Everybody knows intellectually that face is very important in Chinese culture, but we often forget this in practice. It's not that we should kowtow to China but rather that its leaders' concern with face gives us another lever over them. In making demands of the leaders, for example, it is crucial that we give them some face-saving way of meeting the demands—rather than force them to be seen as caving in to us. If, for example, we openly and angrily demand the immediate release of Ren Wanding from prison, the one thing that we can bet on is that Ren doesn't have a prayer of getting out. We're more likely to achieve Ren's release if our ambassador secretly asks the Chinese to look into Ren's reported ailments and see if a medical release is possible, politely reminding them that if nothing happens there will be a State Department human rights report and congressional hearings to deal with in a few months. The idea is to structure pressure so that the Chinese leaders gain face by doing what we want and lose it by resisting.

As Sunzi said, "Leave a way of escape to a surrounded enemy, and do not press a desperate enemy too hard."

One example of how this works in practice involved the hearty astrophysicist Fang Lizhi, who in 1989 was at the top of Deng Xiaoping's enemies list. Fang realized immediately after the Tiananmen crackdown that his freedom and perhaps his life were in jeopardy. A mutual friend called us to see if we could use our car to ferry Fang across town; fortunately we were out, and by the time we returned the call, another car had been found. We were extremely relieved, for we didn't want to have to make a choice of whether to lend the car or not. It wouldn't have been appropriate to use a *New York Times* car to smuggle the regime's most important opponent to safety. On the other hand, since it then looked as if Fang might be executed or sent to prison for twenty years, could we have possibly refused to help?

In any case, Fang—pressured by his wife, also a distinguished and thoughtful physicist—asked for asylum in the United States Embassy. The embassy checked with Washington and agreed, and Fang and his wife were hidden in a room in the embassy's clinic. But then the State Department made the colossal error of announcing to the world that the embassy had given Fang refuge. Until then, there was hope of reaching some secret agreement to get Fang out of the country; once it was public, the Chinese felt that they could not afford to back down. They launched blistering attacks on the United States and even hinted that they might invade the embassy grounds to seize Fang. Since it wasn't clear that State Security knew where Fang was hiding, this meant a risk that the Chinese would raid the wrong compound, perhaps storm the main office building, with its windowless CIA station and communications center behind it. The embassy was sufficiently alarmed that it destroyed classified files so that they would not fall into Chinese hands. American Embassy personnel for a time also slept outside Fang's room to prevent any kidnapping by the Chinese at night.

Tempers were so high on both sides that it was difficult to see how the crisis could be resolved. Some Chinese speculated that Fang would have to stay in the embassy for twenty or thirty years. But the following spring, Ambassador Jim Lilley maneuvered brilliantly and achieved Fang's release. Lilley told the Chinese that Fang had had a heart attack and asked them to allow him to go abroad to a third country for medical treatment. In fact, Lilley exaggerated a bit: Fang had an irregular heartbeat, but he had not suffered a heart attack. Still, the Chinese feared the consequences if Fang died, untreated, in the American Embassy. And the heart condition gave them an excuse, a face-saving way to release him. So just one year after Fang entered the embassy, an American military transport flew into Beijing and Fang and his wife were whisked aboard and rushed to England.

Americans and Chinese alike often assumed that we had many close contacts at the U.S. Embassy, but in fact we didn't. We found the diplomatic cocktail circuit for the most part both tedious and fruitless, and it was almost always more helpful to talk to Chinese than to talk to diplomats about China. The U.S. Embassy had some first-rate diplomats, and we had strong professional and personal relationships with a few people there. But they came and went so frequently—a two-year posting is standard for a junior diplomat—that they had little time to build *guanxi* with Chinese. Moreover, the embassy emphasized official meetings and contacts with Chinese, instead of going to the homes of Chinese friends and chatting informally over tea and watermelon seeds. In some cases, that made me skeptical of their judgments.

To be sure, I don't want to paint with too broad a brush. It was extremely difficult for many diplomats and journalists to make contacts and develop sources, particularly in the few years after the Tiananmen crackdown. Chinese were explicitly told to stay away from us, and the guards at the gates of our compound harassed those Chinese who dared to come. Moreover, some American diplomats, a small minority, did frequently go to the homes of Chinese friends—even though that meant writing contact reports for their superiors. But the embassy was so preoccupied with security and official contacts that it sometimes seemed it might as well have been situated in Hong Kong. A generation of diplomats cut their teeth as China watchers by analyzing the *People's Daily,* and that is essentially how they operate today. They neglect another possibility that we pursued: making friends with the *People's Daily* journalists and asking them, over a beer, what the articles mean.

Of course, the security concerns are legitimate. When we arrived in Beijing, one American diplomat was breaking the embassy rules by having an affair with a young Chinese woman. Then one day State Security burst in on them, in flagrante delicto, and asked him to help them out by providing some information from the embassy. Instead, he immediately reported the incident to his security officer, and the embassy quietly flew him back to the States the next day.

In any case, most journalists found meetings with diplomats— above all, American diplomats—pretty uninformative. We always assumed that they knew considerably more than they indicated. At least we hoped so. But occasionally, there were disturbing signs that this was not so. One time, for example, we were at a dreary dinner party and the topic of Deng Xiaoping's home came up. A senior American diplomat asked us, with a puzzled look, where that was. He really seemed to have no clue.

Then there was the time that the armed forces decided to cut off the telephone linkage between all the military exchanges and the 532 exchange that served foreign diplomats and reporters. One by one, the compounds in which our military friends lived or worked were cut off from us. If we tried to dial their numbers, we got a recording that the number was unavailable. When they tried our numbers, the same thing happened. It was a common topic of conversation among the Chinese, and I decided to write about it. So I went and saw a military attaché, a China watcher who was both intelligent and con- genial, but he had never heard a word about this. "Let's try it," he offered, and he called the official Defense Ministry Foreign Affairs Office. "You see?" he said patronizingly. "It works. There's been no change in the telephone system."

What he didn't realize was that all the numbers in the armed forces, with the sole exception of that one for official inquiries, had been cut off from the telephone exchanges used by foreigners. He apparently never called army friends.

The upshot was that foreign reporters found other Westerners much more helpful than the U.S. diplomats. Foreign scholars were enormously helpful, and so were resident Westerners such as lawyers, business executives, and the local officers of the Ford Foundation. Relations with the American Embassy and reporters were also complicated by a growing mutual antagonism in the early 1990s. The embassy, under Ambassador J. Stapleton Roy, felt that reporters were too critical of China, unfairly emphasizing its shortcomings. Ambassador Roy is a smart and shrewd observer of China, and he may have had a point. But the result was that the embassy became increasingly isolated from the press. "They've got a bunker mentality," one of my American colleagues complained in frustration. "It's just like the old U.S. Embassy in South Vietnam."

The embassy often refused to make anybody available to discuss issues, and diplomats sometimes even worried about meeting us privately, without going through proper channels. We were good friends with one senior American diplomat who used to go to great lengths to deny that he even knew us. Once his wife called to offer some newly baked banana bread, and Nick arranged to drive over and pick it up. Then another American diplomat dropped by their home, and the wife called up frantically to warn us not to go to their door. Instead, Nick went to the main gate of the compound, and the wife furtively met him and passed him the banana bread.

Reporters have sharp tongues, and among them the embassy came to be something of a joke. It constantly displayed a rosy optimism about the future that was proven wrong time after time, yet the diplomats did not stay in China long enough to notice. On certain occasions, the embassy briefings turned into public relations exercises for China, and embassy officers occasionally called us up to scold us about articles that portrayed China in a bad light. When I was writing about China's interest in obtaining an aircraft carrier, the embassy refused to discuss the topic with me. Immediately after the article appeared, an embassy press officer telephoned me and asked, "Why are you bullying China like that? If India were getting a new aircraft carrier, you wouldn't write about it, would you? Why pick on China?"

The result of this growing mutual distrust was that American journalists worked more with diplomats from other countries. The Japanese and Australians often were particularly well informed, and there were some very good French and Germans. While the Americans were careful to avoid any indiscretion, European diplomats went to the other extreme: They sometimes seemed to conduct their foreign policy by sleeping with local Chinese. It was a security nightmare. But pillow talk can be a million times more insightful than official discussions, and I think that the philanderers often had a far richer understanding of China than the American straight arrows.

Sex, of course, is not the only kind of intercourse between two peoples. The best kind, for national leaders at least, is conversation. But American officials have been reluctant to visit Beijing, partly because the talks don't usually go well. During the four years of George Bush's presidency, Secretary of State James A. Baker III made only one trip on his own to China, and it was a bit of a debacle. Two dissidents were detained during his stay, and he got few assurances from the Chinese. President Bush visited China early in his presidency, as part of a stopover after a trip to Japan, and the result was nearly a fiasco. Bush had invited Fang Lizhi, the dissident astrophysicist, but the police blocked Fang from entering the banquet hall.

President Clinton started off very critical of China, with the president himself lambasting Bush for "coddling dictators from Baghdad to Beijing." But his administration initially failed to articulate a new China policy; it essentially maintained the policy that it had inherited. Then, in the fall of 1993, Clinton finally focused on China and began to promote a strategy of "engagement," a dialogue with Beijing. He sent officials to China, starting with Agriculture Secretary Mike Espy and Treasury Secretary Lloyd Bentsen. Clinton also allowed the sale of a supercomputer to China, supposedly for weather forecasting. He expanded cooperation and contacts between the Chinese and American armed services, and, most important, he invited President Jiang Zemin to a meeting of Pacific Rim leaders in Seattle. That was the first meeting between Chinese and American presidents since Tiananmen.

Then, in March 1994, Clinton sent Secretary of State Warren Christopher on a Beijing mission that disappointed everyone. Christopher unfortunately made his visit during the annual session of the National People's Congress, when the security authorities annually praise democracy and arrest democrats. The Chinese leaders made no substantial concessions and instead reacted to American calls for improving human rights conditions by detaining a string of dissidents in Beijing and Shanghai. The visit was a humiliation for Christopher, and he was roundly criticized for making it at all.

Yet it's very important to have a dialogue. We may not get our way, but at least we should talk—or even yell—to try to engage China. We should try to bring the Chinese leaders into the international community and not isolate them, for, as its economy continues to develop, China is likely to become even more prickly and less compromising as a negotiator. As Singapore's patriarch, Lee Kuan Yew, suggested, "Why not hoist this fellow on board? He needs you at this moment. In ten years he might not." Indeed, one Chinese friend, the son of a cabinet member, told me that China's recent economic successes were already beginning to transform attitudes among the leaders. "China is very self-confident," he said a few days before I left Beijing. "They won't compromise. They say, 'We can't collapse. Look at us. Look at Russia.' China is very very confident."

Of course, dialogue is not an end in itself. Some people think that if they build a rapport with Chinese leaders, they will get favors in exchange. Afraid of ignoring Chinese "face," they neglect to apply pressure. That's a mistake. The Chinese leaders act out of their interests, not their friendships. We needn't try to appeal to the Politburo's humanitarian side, for there isn't one. When Wei Jingsheng got out of prison after fourteen and a half years, he warned American leaders not to be taken in by the Chinese Politburo. China's leaders are realists, he said, and he cited the fable of the lamb that tries to talk reason to the wolf. The wolf accuses the lamb of having urinated in the wolf's drinking water, and the lamb points out that this was impossible—the lamb was downstream. The wolf eats the lamb anyway.

In the late 1980s, the way to get the Chinese leaders to budge was to threaten to cut off most-favored-nation trade benefits. During the Bush administration, Congress tried to condition MFN for China, and Bush warned he would veto the attempt. In the end the result was always that MFN was preserved, but the process so frightened the Chinese leaders that they agreed to important concessions: releasing prisoners, signing the Nuclear Non-Proliferation Treaty, permitting dissidents to travel abroad, and so on.

When Chinese think of sanctions, they automatically think of America—not Germany, not Japan, not Britain, not France. In

1989, after the military crackdown, there was unanimous outrage in the West over the killings in Beijing, but by the early 1990s the harmony had broken down and the United States had become almost the lone voice on human rights. Sure, the European countries talked a good game, but except for Sweden and Norway there seemed to be an implicit wink: "Look, I've got to say this stuff about human rights, but it'll only take a moment and then we can get on with business." The United States is the only country in recent years that has seriously considered imposing economic sanctions against China, and the leaders in Beijing have pointed out that if Uncle Sam walks away—well, there are other dance partners around the world.

What happened? After Tiananmen, Japan was the first country to break ranks. Tokyo never seemed to think that human rights should play a role in its relations with China, and it went so far as to hand back to the Chinese government at least one dissident who had sought refuge in Japan. As soon as it was polite to do so, Japan returned to business as usual, extending huge loans to China and sending officials to shake hands with Li Peng. In part, this reflects the Japanese tendency in recent times to cave in whenever China makes a demand. China has generally insisted, for example, that Japanese banks and news organizations stay out of Taiwan. So while all other international banks have offices in Taipei, hardly any Japanese banks do. Likewise, most Japanese newspapers do not base correspondents in Taiwan, for fear of antagonizing China. With a few exceptions, the Japanese reporting about China was also pretty mushy, because the newspaper editors were reluctant to offend Beijing. When it comes to China, we still haven't seen the Japan that can say no.

One might think that this would please the Chinese, but it doesn't work that way, for Chinese leaders haven't forgotten their friends and relatives killed during the Japanese invasion in the 1930s. Just as Americans can't understand why China can trust Iran, Chinese think that the United States is being terribly naive about Japan. Ask a Chinese, particularly an older one, about Japan, and you get a spurt of scarcely printable invective. In fact, if you ask a Chinese about the character *hen*, meaning "hate," he will often define it as what Chinese people feel for the Japanese. Many Chinese still believe that Japan should pay billions of dollars in war reparations, even though that issue appeared to have been settled when relations between the two countries were normalized in 1972. Even among university students, there is considerable resentment against Japan, and in the 1980s there were brief protests against what the students called "Japan's economic invasion" of Panasonic and Hitachi stereos and televisions. Much of the bitterness that Chinese feel for Japanese seems to border on racism, and Chinese often use vicious epithets—dwarfs, turnip-heads, bandits—to describe Japanese. I was often horrified when I heard intellectuals snarl about the *wokou*, an ugly term roughly equivalent to "Jap bandits."

Considering this legacy of hostility, it is a tribute to Japanese companies that they have done so well in China. Far more than American or European companies, Japanese concerns have set up networks of offices throughout the country, even in remote cities like Urumqi in the Xinjiang region. And while American companies often post an expatriate in China for just a couple of years, without language training, the Japanese train their salespeople in Chinese and then post them in China for four or five years at a time. The result is that they often make the initial sales of equipment to a Chinese factory, ensuring that as the Chinese client's business grows it will continue to purchase machinery from the Japanese seller. Americans sometimes say that the Japanese have done better in China because they are fellow Asians and have some advantage. That's not true—in fact, most Chinese companies would prefer to buy American. The reason Japanese companies have done better is that they have been smarter and more energetic than the Americans and Europeans.

European countries, in contrast to Japan, seem to care about human rights but feel that those concerns are outweighed by the commercial potential of China. Another distinction is that, unlike Japan, European nations are willing to antagonize China, not over human rights issues but for commercial reasons—such as sales of military equipment to Taiwan. France outraged the Chinese in 1992 by announcing the sale of Mirage fighters to Taiwan. Commercial concerns are dominant, and while delegations from France, Germany, and other European countries still call for the release of political prisoners, the main purpose of the visits is to do business. Germany's chancellor, Helmut Kohl, no doubt cares about human rights, but he cares more about jobs and exports, so he takes business leaders in tow and visits Beijing to plead for contracts.

In May 1994 President Clinton ended one chapter in relations with China by cutting the link between human rights and MFN. He acknowledged that Beijing's human rights performance was disappointing, but he renewed MFN anyway. More important, the renewal was unconditional, so that the MFN threat no longer hangs over everyone's heads.

Business whooped with joy and editorial writers called foul, but I think Clinton made the right call. It was not really a matter of placing commerce over human rights, for withdrawing MFN from China would have been the worst possible move for human rights in China. The Communist Party would immediately have retaliated by tossing even more human rights campaigners in prison. More worrisome, the confrontation would have been an enormous political boost for Beijing's hard-liners, whose campaign platform (within the Politburo) is more torture and repression. We could have tipped the balance in favor of the hard-liners for years to come. We also would have enabled them to blame the United States—rather than their own policies—for their economic difficulties.

Many Chinese want the United States to pressure their government on human rights, but hardly any—even the dissidents in Beijing and Shanghai—wanted MFN taken away. They wanted us to use MFN as a bluff, but not to follow through on the threat. While Nick and I talked to scores of Chinese about their views on sanctions, a few comments reflect the general mood. First, a pro-democracy university student: "We're very torn inside. We want pressure on our government to change its policies. We want our government to eat bitterness. But on the other hand, we're afraid that sanctions would simply hurt ordinary people like us. So we want America to threaten sanctions, to pressure China to change. But we don't want sanctions themselves."

A young female government official: "Sanctions wouldn't hurt Li Peng. They would hurt people like me. They would make it harder for me to find a way abroad. So I don't want to see any sanctions."

A private businessman: "Chinese don't want sanctions. We figure if the United States imposes sanctions, we won't be able to smoke Marlboros anymore."

The problem is that the MFN threat has lost all credibility to the Chinese leaders. It worked well in the early years, but by the summer

of 1993 the Communist Party bosses realized that we weren't prepared to pull the trigger, so they didn't care if we aimed the gun at
them. Renewing MFN with more human rights conditions would
have been an empty gesture, for it would have been clear, once again,
that we wouldn't shoot.

Although MFN lost its credibility as a weapon, we still have plenty
of tools available for putting pressure on Beijing. These other weapons
are much more frightening to the Chinese leaders because they know
that we really might use them. Instead of all-or-nothing atomic
bombs, these are tactical devices that we can set off in a calibrated
way—always reserving a little more firepower for the next occasion.

For starters, we can turn the Chinese leaders' obsession with Taiwan on themselves. We can send emissaries to Beijing warning that if
they continue to sell M-11 missiles to Pakistan or if they fail to improve
their human rights record, we will invite Taiwan's president, Lee
Teng-hui, to the White House for an exchange of views. The Politburo
fears such a warming of ties between Taiwan and the United States as
much as it fears the loss of MFN, and it will try just as hard to avoid it.

The State Department has always fretted about offending
Beijing, so we do not allow senior American officials to have contact
with Taiwan counterparts. President Lee was banned from the
United States until June 1995, when the White House caved in to
Congressional pressure and allowed Lee to attend his class reunion at
Cornell University. It was a major reversal in United States policy,
but we got nothing for it. Instead of using the Taiwan card as a sign
of strength, the White House appeared weak and vulnerable to
intimidation—the worst signal to send to Beijing. In contrast, other
countries have been far more willing to stand up to China; Singapore, the Philippines, Indonesia, Thailand and South Africa have all
hosted President Lee in recent years, yet the United States is still too
timid to let Lee set foot in New York City or Washington.

The Taiwan card is a useful one for the United States because
unlike MFN we can play it without harming ourselves. Indeed, closer
ties with Taipei would help American businesses in Taiwan, which for
now still buys more American exports than China does. Moreover,
Chinese hard-liners would not gain politically if we improved relations with Taiwan; ordinary Chinese citizens don't want trade, but
they don't really care what the United States does with Taiwan.

By the same token, we can make it clear to China's leaders that if they crack down harshly in Tibet, the Dalai Lama will be invited to give a joint press conference with the president in the Rose Garden. That is such a horrifying spectacle for the Chinese leaders that they will do whatever they can to avoid it.

Obviously, the Chinese leaders will be apoplectic if we improve relations with Taiwan or with the Dalai Lama. China will test our resolve, and we will have to call its bluff and follow through on our threats. In the end, I think that China will react in the same way it did after we sold fighters to Taiwan: ranting, threatening, and eventually acquiescing.

There are other sticks to use, such as targeted sanctions. China is hungry for American high technology, especially the kind of products, like supercomputers, that European countries can't offer. When China breaks its promises, we should come down hard and fast, for example, by slapping sanctions on a state-run company that violates a missile agreement. The key is to make the punishment as painful as possible but to target it directly at the offender.

Another stick is the bully pulpit. Some China experts argue that the Chinese obsession with "face" means that we should avoid lecturing them. Instead, I think that their concern about embarrassment gives us a useful tool. The Chinese leaders yearn to be accepted as part of the international community. They fear humiliation even more than they fear sanctions. If they know that they will be denounced as rogues for selling nuclear technology to Iran, if they anticipate that a crackdown in Tibet will mean a United Nations investigation into their conduct there, they will be a bit more careful. As with everything else, the threat of humiliation works better than the humiliation itself. But it is a mistake to think that we shouldn't complain publicly about torture and repression in China. We should meet with Chinese leaders, but we needn't keep our voices down.

In looking for tools to moderate the regime in Beijing, it's also worth considering one thing that the Chinese leaders dread more than sanctions: *heping yanbian,* "peaceful evolution." Chinese say that the term comes from a secret plot that the United States developed in the 1950s to overthrow Chinese Communism, not by armed forces but by cultural and political subversion. Hard-liners worry that the spread of American ideas, movies, novels, music, and even dance styles is all part of a broad conspiracy to undermine Communist rule. Of course, they give us too much credit. But what a great idea!

Peaceful evolution, in the sense of exposure to Western ideas, helped bring democracy to Spain in the 1970s, and peaceful evolution has helped bring freedom to Taiwan in the 1990s. China is a Communist dictatorship, which differentiates it from Spain or Taiwan, but peaceful evolution in China will at least get the country going in the right direction. To get peaceful evolution, we need more contact rather than less. We need more trade, more cultural exchanges, more engagement. So if we're serious about trying to make China a more open place, we should be threatening not a cut-off of trade but an expansion.

To bring China into the international community, we can encourage more dialogue; we can promote multilateral regimes like the Asia-Pacific Economic Cooperation forum; we can do more to help bring China into GATT, the international trade organization, instead of holding out indefinitely for more trade concessions; and we can also invite Beijing to become a member of the Missile Technology Control Regime, instead of simply asking Beijing to adhere to the regime's restrictions on missile sales. Integrating China further into the international community will work only very slowly, on a zigzag path, to ease the repression there. The pace will be unsatisfying and frustrating, but I don't see any better alternative.

Obviously we can't expect too much of an American policy toward China. No method will be very effective in moderating China's conduct. It is perfectly possible that peaceful evolution will mean that for some years torture chambers will simply be equipped with MTV, and that the torturers will tap their feet to the beat as they break the fingers of dissidents. But already Western values have had a modest influence on Chinese repression, and I think they will continue to do so. If the Chinese Communists are so afraid of it, it must be worth a chance.

It's difficult to discuss Sino-Western relations in the abstract, but one conflict offers a first-rate example of how to push China to just the right degree. It was also a case that mattered immensely to me.

It began in the spring of 1990, when my press pass expired. I was in Taiwan and had forgotten to renew it. After I returned, it was a couple of months before I noticed that it had expired, and I called up Wan Jisong, my liaison at the Foreign Ministry, to explain and apologize. In fact, I had been writing on an invalid pass, and Wan hadn't noticed either. He said no problem, just bring it in. I did, but a few days later he called up to say that my press pass could not be renewed. I was supposed to stop writing.

"Well, what can I do to get my credentials back?" I asked.

"There is nothing you can do," he replied tersely. Several weeks later, our foreign editor, Bernie Gwertzman, came to Beijing on a tour of Asia and tried to raise the matter with the Foreign Ministry. But the head of the information department refused to see Bernie, and his deputy reiterated that there was no way to renew the credentials. We asked if we could reapply, and he shrugged that we could, but he did not seem encouraging. So I applied for new credentials, a process that takes two months, and in the meantime I didn't write about China. Instead, I traveled to Hong Kong, Taiwan, Burma, Australia, and the Philippines, reporting from there.

Two months passed, and the Foreign Ministry still refused to act on my request. It looked as if the government would not let me write again. At that point, we asked the American Embassy to help. Ambassador Lilley planned the strategy, and again, he was masterful.

The embassy made a representation to the Foreign Ministry about my case, but more important, it quietly stopped giving American visas to Chinese journalists. The embassy didn't formally refuse the visas; it simply delayed any decision on granting them. Several Chinese journalists were on hold, including one from the *People's Daily,* but for a long time they couldn't figure out what the problem was. Finally, frustrated that the Chinese couldn't make the connection for themselves, the embassy gave them a hint. "There is a bit of a problem," an American diplomat explained to the Chinese news organizations. "You might want to check with the Foreign Ministry."

Twenty minutes later, they erupted in fury. How could the United States possibly make such a linkage? It was outrageous to refuse to give visas to Chinese journalists simply because the Foreign Ministry was still considering Ms. WuDunn's application! At that point, the Chinese were so choleric that there was a risk that American pressure might backfire, so Lilley quickly ordered the visa office to give

American visas to two of the waiting Chinese reporters. It was the perfect move, for it showed the United States trying to be conciliatory and attempting to break the logjam, yet it left open the threat that other Chinese journalists would not be accredited unless the Foreign Ministry came through with my credentials.

A couple of days later, when I was still out of the country, the Foreign Ministry summoned Nick. "We have good news," Wan Jisong explained impassively. "We have decided, as a special favor, to grant Ms. WuDunn's application for press credentials. Of course, we have acted reasonably all along in this matter, and we are doing this solely to be helpful to you and your wife."

Then Wan shifted in his chair and glowered. "It has come to our attention that you contacted the American Embassy and sought its help, so that the embassy unreasonably refused to give visas to some Chinese journalists. This was a foolish and arrogant action. It is absolutely not the reason why we are granting you the credentials. There is no connection whatsoever."

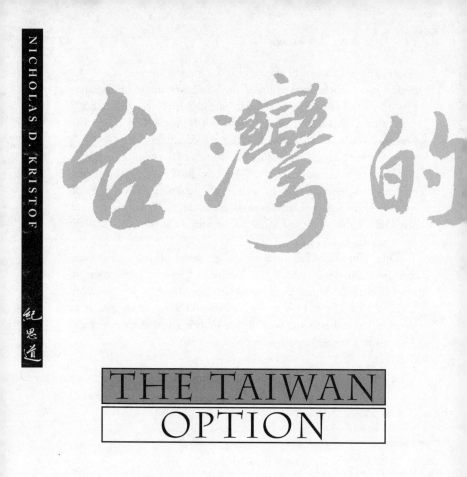

NICHOLAS D. KRISTOF

紀思道

台灣的

THE TAIWAN
OPTION

We must make Taiwan the base for national recovery, a vanguard
for the struggle of the free peoples of Asia.

—Chiang Kai-shek, July 22, 1950

15

道路

Wang Junjin, the twenty-three-year-old head of a charter airline company, stands on the tarmac in Wenzhou, in the swath of coastal China that is increasingly under the influence of Taiwan. [Photo by Nicholas D. Kristof.]

Lin Yi-hsiung's wife wasn't home when the murderers came. She was off at prison, visiting her husband, consoling him for the beatings he was receiving during interrogation. As circulation manager for an opposition magazine in Taiwan, Lin was a key figure in the antigovernment movement—and thus a natural candidate for beatings.

So at noon on February 28, 1980, she was at the prison seeing her husband, instead of in her apartment on the bottom two floors of a six-story apartment building. The apartment should have been well protected, for it was located on a small lane and the police were obligingly bugging the phones and maintaining twenty-four-hour surveillance. The police did not bother, however, to stop the men who apparently knocked on the door—there was later no sign of forced entry. Nor did the police intervene when the men stabbed Lin's mother and his twin seven-year-old daughters. The mother and one daughter died; the other daughter survived.

Officially, the case was never solved. Unofficially, it's pretty clear who did it: thugs hired by the Taiwan government. Slaughtering a woman in her seventies and stabbing her two little grandchildren— that's the way Taiwan sometimes did things back then.

What does this have to do with mainland China in the 1990s? Plenty, I hope. The point is that Taiwan not so long ago was in some ways as repressive and brutal a place as the mainland. Taiwan was the same kind of jumble of contradictions that the mainland is today, a peculiar blend of economic takeoff and dynastic disintegration. Taiwan in 1980 faced many of the challenges that China does today: rampant corruption, an alienated youth, a Leninist political system, widespread repression, ostracism in the West, and a leadership clinging reflexively to an irrelevant ideology. Yet Taiwan, perhaps more than any other place in the world, underwent a transformation that ended up enriching its people as well as freeing them.

I'll never forget my first glimpse of Taiwan as a journalist. It was late November 1986, and I had just arrived from Hong Kong to cover the legislative elections. I stepped off the plane and saw hundreds of riot policemen in the immigration area. They wore helmets with visors down, and they carried truncheons in their fists. Some also carried guns. They were lined up in rows, looking like Nazis, and periodically a row trotted forward in perfect unison. Hundreds more of them were waiting in the baggage area, and the arrival hall looked like an armed camp: Riot police and army troops were lined up and down inside, and through the window thousands more were visible in the parking lot beyond, surrounded by military vehicles and coils of barbed wire.

As a perceptive journalist, trained to pick up the most delicate signals, I concluded that something might be up. I left my suitcase with the representative of the Lai-Lai Sheraton Hotel and stepped out into what seemed to be a war zone. Thousands of demonstrators were battling the troops, heaving bricks and bottles back and forth. The protesters managed to push the troops back briefly and seize a row of empty police cars. The crowd turned the cars over—all twenty-one of them—and smashed the windows and the police lights. Meanwhile, the troops were charging where they could and smashing heads with their nightsticks. Several times, four or five of the soldiers managed to knock down a few protesters and club them on the ground for several minutes as blood stained the pavement.

It turned out that the reason for the uproar was the anticipated arrival of an exiled opposition leader, Hsu Hsin-liang. Hsu, a thin man with a shiny pate and an eager smile, had been living in the United States for seven years but had decided that it was time to return. Although Hsu was wanted by the police, the Taiwan government decided it didn't want the embarrassment of a political trial. It simply turned Hsu away and put him on the next plane out of the country. As for the clashes between the troops and the protesters, well, that was a Chinese-style political debate.

Now, whenever I go to Taiwan I drop by and see Hsu Hsin-liang. He entered the country in 1989 and served eight months in prison for sedition. Today he is one of the leaders of Taiwan's opposition political party, the Democratic Progressive Party. Someday, he says, it will be the ruling party. It could be. I always leave Hsu's office agog at the pace of the political liberalization in Taiwan, and profoundly cheered about the prospects for repressive Chinese regimes.

There are lessons in Taiwan's experience for other developing countries, including China. Above all, Taiwan shows that a collapsing dynasty can lead to a prosperous and vibrant democracy. Obviously there are huge differences, not least of them differences of scale, and it would be foolish to think that the transition in a behemoth like China could be as smooth or as rapid as in Taiwan. But Taiwan at least shows that there is a *chulu*, a way out, for brutal Chinese autocracies. I take the elevator down from Hsu Hsin-liang's office feeling better not only about Taiwan but about China as well. Sheryl and I are never so optimistic about the future of mainland China as when we stroll the bustling streets of Taipei.

The island of Taiwan, one hundred miles off the coast of southeastern China, is still haunted by memories of misrule as brutal as the mainland's. In 1947 the Nationalists presided over a massacre far larger than Tiananmen. It began when a policeman pistol-whipped a forty-year-old widow suspected of selling smuggled cigarettes. An angry crowd gathered, and a frightened investigator fired his pistol and killed a bystander. That incident provoked an islandwide uprising, which the Nationalist troops were called in to suppress. One distinguished political scientist gives this account:

> As the Nationalist troops came ashore, they moved out quickly through Keelung streets, shooting and bayoneting men and boys, raping women and looting homes and shops. Some Formosans were seized and stuffed alive into burlap bags found piled up at the sugar warehouse and were then simply tossed into the harbor. Others were merely tied up or chained before being thrown from the piers.

Estimates of the fatalities range from 1,000 to 100,000, with the most careful scholarly study suggesting about 8,000 deaths in the crackdown. In any case, that was merely the prelude to a prolonged period of political terror. When Generalissimo Chiang Kai-shek fled the Chinese mainland for Taiwan in 1949, he ruthlessly liquidated his opponents, real or imagined. In 1950, for example, a fellow named Hsieh Jui-jen made the mistake of defeating a Nationalist-endorsed candidate in an election to head a local agricultural association. The security authorities arrested Hsieh, suspended him by his thumbs, and forced wire into his penis. At this point, Hsu agreed to confess to having joined a Communist conspiracy. So the authorities executed him.

The repression continued for decades, but the Stalinist approach—the midnight knock on the door followed by a secret execution—gradually went out of style. Torture and imprisonment remained common, however, and in 1979 a harsh crackdown shook the entire island. Two years later, a professor from Carnegie-Mellon University was found dead after having been interrogated for thirteen hours by Taiwan security officials. The professor, a Taiwanese with an American green card, had criticized the Nationalists while in the United States. The government claimed he had committed suicide; few believed that.

In 1984, the authorities went further. They assassinated an American citizen in California because he had written a book critical of President Chiang Ching-kuo. The government acknowledged that the killing of Henry Liu had been ordered by the head of the intelligence bureau of the Ministry of National Defense. Not even mainland China had ever killed a foreign citizen on foreign soil, and the incident underscored the ruthlessness of the Taiwan security services.

"When I was in prison, I decided that the Nationalists and the Communists were basically the same," said Bo Yang, one of my oldest friends in Taipei. Now in his seventies, a solid man with a jutting chin and craggy features, Bo Yang has been through it all. Born on the Chinese mainland sometime in 1920—he doesn't know his birth date—he fled the Communist Revolution in 1949 and became a writer in Taiwan. He used his acid pen to write books and essays criticizing torture, corruption, and other social problems, and this offended Chiang Kai-shek. The authorities arrested Bo Yang in 1968 and accused him of spreading Communist propaganda.

"Here, look," Bo said one afternoon as we sat in the bar of the Lai-Lai Hotel. He rolled up his right pant leg, ignoring the stares of the other people in the bar, and pointed to a scar on the knee. "They broke my leg to get me to confess to being a Communist. When it gets cold quickly, my leg really aches. Then I can't walk very well and need to bandage it up."

The prosecutor asked for the death sentence, but because of American pressure Bo Yang was sentenced to only twelve years in prison. He served eight years, plus another year under house arrest, before being released in 1977. He subsequently produced some of his finest writings, including *The Ugly Chinaman,* a withering attack on Chinese culture. Bo complained that Chinese are rude, loud, contentious, uncaring, dogmatic, unthoughtful, and blindly proud and protective of a historical legacy that in fact needs an infusion of Western ideas. *The Ugly Chinaman* became hugely popular on the Chinese mainland, even though it was banned, and it helped inspire a profound and anxiety-ridden search among Chinese intellectuals for a new basis for a more democratic society. Chinese have always been taught that theirs is the greatest race, the greatest civilization, and then Bo Yang came along and ridiculed Chinese ways as contemptible. He forced people to think again about their society.

I always thought of Bo Yang as the ultimate dissident, someone who dissented not only from the political system but also from his entire civilization. So I remember my shock when Sheryl and I visited him one evening at the end of 1987, shortly after we had moved to Taipei to study Chinese. That was a time when Taiwan was beginning to blossom: Martial law had ended, travel restrictions were being lifted, the opposition was being allowed to form a political party, and the press was enjoying growing freedom. I expected Bo to complain that this was not enough, but instead he took a longer view. He described Taiwan as a golden age of Chinese civilization.

"China has 4,000, maybe 5,000, years of history, but it has never had an era like Taiwan today," Bo explained to me later. "There has never been a time when people were so wealthy or so free. Living conditions are so great! I'm just glad my wife and I have lived to see this period. It's a golden age."

Bo has a point. The liberalization has continued, and Taiwan now is pretty much a democracy. All political prisoners have been released, the press is essentially free, and elections are vigorously contested. A blue-ribbon panel investigated the 1947 massacre and released conclusions offensive to the government. The first direct presidential election is expected by 1996, and it is remotely possible that the opposition might win. To be sure, the Nationalists still have a huge advantage in resources and in the way they tilt the playing field, but all the taboos have been shattered. There is even an Amnesty International chapter active in Taiwan; one of its members is Bo Yang.

Taiwan is simply one of a group of nations in Asia that have transformed themselves from impoverished dictatorships to rich quasi-democracies. Japan was the first, but it had the help of an American occupying army. South Korea pursued the same path as Taiwan, with an economic boom in the 1960s turning into a political liberalization in the 1980s and 1990s. Thailand now appears to be traveling down this same road, although it is not so far along as the others. Indonesia is still further behind.

The political strides in Asia are particularly remarkable because the region has relatively little tradition of democracy and few mechanisms like labor movements that bring citizens into the political system. The Chinese language didn't even have a word for democracy until the existing political and economic vocabulary was imported from Japan a hundred years ago. Among these relatively new words are such essential terms as *zhengzhi,* politics; *jingji,* economy; *minzhu,* democracy; and *ziyou,* freedom.

Elsewhere around the globe, in areas that traditionally had more exposure to labor movements, parliaments, and elections, economic growth and rising levels of education have also stimulated political development. Spain is a shining example, for it was an underdeveloped dictatorship in the 1950s; the late 1940s are remembered as the *años de hambre,* the "years of hunger." Generalissimo Francisco Franco, the dictator who ruled from the end of the civil war in 1939 until his death in 1975, was brutal and authoritarian, but he presided over an economic boom that changed Spain. By the time he died, Spain had the nucleus of a middle class as well as a yearning to be more like the rest of Europe. Despite social polarization and regional separatist movements, Spain has held together and flourished. Now it is both prosperous and democratic.

More recently, Chile appears to have taken a similar route. General Augusto Pinochet was a brutal and ruthless dictator, and more than 2,000 leftists were murdered under his seventeen-year rule. But in addition to torture and murder, Pinochet brought stability and economic growth to his country. By the time he retired as the national leader in 1990, Chile was a far more mature country, and for now it seems to be headed along the same path as Taiwan and Spain. Of course, Spain and Chile both have had far more experience with democratic institutions than China ever did; if the wheels eventually slipped into the democratic tracks, that is partly because there were already democratic ruts in the national consciousness.

There are, it seems, two kinds of roads that China might take. The first is that of the rest of the Communist Bloc: revolution, overthrow of the leadership, and national upheaval. This might well involve national fragmentation or even civil war. The other scenario is of an evolution similar to that which has taken place in authoritarian economic dynamos like Spain and Taiwan. Naturally, China might carve out some middle path, but broadly speaking, those scenarios represent the range of possibilities for China in the coming decades.

So far, of course, Communist countries have been unable to take the Taiwan road. But then again, it's a mistake to think of China as a Communist country. It's really a fascist country led by a Communist Party.

China is fascist in roughly the way that Spain was fascist under Franco. There are also strong parallels with Taiwan, South Korea, and Chile, which were all fascist in some respects. Of course, the word *fascist* has picked up a lot of pejorative connotations over the years, and I didn't bother to mention to Chinese officials that I thought they were fascists. They might not have understood. Political scientists sometimes use more polite terms, such as *bureaucratic authoritarianism*.

When I say that China is fascist, I mean that it is a one-party dictatorship with a market economy and a large number of state-controlled corporations. The regime shrouds itself in nationalism and places a strong premium on order and stability. Chinese trains may not run on time, as Mussolini's did, but Chinese leaders suggest that in the chaos of Western-style democracy they would not run at all. As in other fascist countries, this orderliness is achieved through strong participation of the army and paramilitary organizations. As in Mussolini's Italy or Chiang's Taiwan, state-controlled corporations play a major role in the economy, yet there is also economic pluralism. Contacts are permitted with the outside world, a professional bureaucracy is cultivated, and the state generally limits its repression to the domain of politics.

Obviously no label fits China perfectly, and I don't want to stretch the fascism analogy too far. But whatever China is, at this moment it is not a Communist country. No Communist country has ever owed so much to capitalism, or ever reduced central planning to such a marginal role, as China has in the 1990s. No Communist country has ever enjoyed such a profusion of photocopiers, satellite dishes, private schools, talk shows, karaoke bars, hula hoops, and sex shops. No Communist country has ever opened itself up so much to trade and foreign investment, given out passports to its citizens so easily, or so gleefully sent tens of thousands of its students to the West. No Soviet Politburo member ever sent his children to study in America; nearly all Chinese Politburo members do so. Deng Xiaoping's own grandchild was born in the United States and is eligible for American citizenship. In other words, it is not just in its allegiance to a market economy that China is coming to look like Taiwan; gradually the entire character of the nation is changing. If this continues, China will slip off the Communist track and into the tradition of East Asian market authoritarianism.

It was Mao himself who was the first to foresee the risk of Communist China's evolving into fascist China. In 1963, he said, "We are very disturbed when we talk to our children and grandchildren and we find that they don't understand the bitterness, the hardships of the revolution, and what sacrifices it took to get where we are today. We are disturbed that they don't feel the need to keep the revolution going. We are afraid that we will stop being a revolutionary country and will become a revisionist one. When that happens in a socialist country, it becomes worse than a capitalist country. A Communist Party can turn into a fascist party."

Mao also warned about Deng Xiaoping's lack of interest in Marxism. When Deng was purged in 1976, the *People's Daily* quoted Mao as saying of Deng: "He knows nothing of Marxism-Leninism." In retrospect, I think Mao was half right. Deng cares little for Marxism itself, and in the late 1980s he even told visiting African leaders not to bother with socialism. Yet Deng is a Leninist through and through. He believes in central authority, suppression of dissident "troublemakers," and a one-party hierarchical state.

So I offer a new expression to characterize China today: *Market-Leninism.* The substitution in China of Market-Leninism for Marxism-Leninism is surely one of the most important transformations in the world today. Yet this allegiance to both market economics and Leninist political principles is not as unusual as it sounds. Taiwan also pursued Market-Leninism for decades; the Nationalist Party was itself consciously organized along Leninist lines in the 1920s, when the Nationalists admired Russia. In those days, Chiang Kai-shek even sent his son, Chiang Ching-kuo, to study in Russia, and the Nationalist Party—with its centralization, political repression, and hierarchical rule—for decades looked much like the Soviet or Chinese Communist Party.

Market-Leninism on the mainland, in other words, is not a serious impediment to pursuing the Taiwan model. In fact, it is the Taiwan model. There are differences and obstacles, but ideology is not one of them.

So how did Taiwan do it? There is no clear formula for democracy, but several factors seem important—and all are increasingly apparent on the Chinese mainland. The first is simply wealth. Most of Taiwan's people were poor peasants a few decades ago; today the per capita income is about $11,000, making them wealthier than Spaniards or Greeks. The flowering of the private economy has created an independent power base outside the ruling party and fostered a middle class that insists on participating in the decision-making process. Wealth also leads to mobility and ease of communications, so that people can travel abroad, tune to foreign radio and television, and spread the word when there is trouble.

A second factor is pressure from abroad. Taiwan in the 1970s and early 1980s faced the same kinds of criticisms for human rights abuses that China faces today. Taiwan then responded the same way that China does now—by insisting that this is unwarranted foreign interference in the country's internal affairs. To be sure, the pressure on Taiwan was much greater than on China, simply because the authorities in Taipei were so dependent on the United States. Yet in the end, both Taiwan and China grudgingly responded to foreign pressure by releasing dissidents, curbing torture, and easing the system of terror.

The third factor, perhaps the most important, is rising educational levels. In the early 1950s, only 34 percent of Taiwan's children went to high school; now all do. There are now more than forty times as many university students in Taiwan as there were then. The leadership is particularly well educated, largely because of the Confucian tradition that values scholarship. President Lee Teng-hui, with a Ph.D. from Cornell, sets the pace, and typically more than half of the cabinet members in Taiwan hold doctorates from American universities—a far higher proportion than in the American cabinet. These government ministers may not be more moral people than those who are less educated, but they seem to be more squeamish about torturing dissidents. And when they go back to their class reunions at Harvard or Yale, they want to be treated as philosopher-kings, not as tyrants.

The longer Sheryl and I lived in Beijing, the more we became tantalized by the Taiwan option. If China could take this road, then one-fifth of humanity could be ushered into the democratic community, probably reducing the risk of military confrontation with the remaining four-fifths. If China could reach the per capita income level of Taiwan today, then China's economic output would be greater than that of the rest of the industrialized world put together. A new superpower would be born, but it would resemble the Germany of Helmut Kohl rather than that of Wilhelm II.

I asked friends in Taiwan whether they thought their experience could be replicated on the mainland. Replies were mixed, but many were cautiously optimistic. Many said that China today reminded them of Taiwan in the 1960s or 1970s. I particularly respected the views of Antonio Chiang, a prominent Taiwan journalist and social critic, now publisher of Taiwan's foremost newsmagazine. A casual man, allergic to neckties in a nation where dark suits are virtually the uniform, Antonio has a mop of thick black hair hanging over an angular face with high cheekbones jutting beneath the skin. He constantly wears a mischievous grin, like a schoolboy caught in some prank just as the teacher enters the classroom.

Born in 1944 in a village in central Taiwan, to parents who were farmers, Antonio grew up speaking only the Taiwanese dialect. He first learned Mandarin at the age of seven, when he entered elementary school, and like most Taiwanese he still speaks Mandarin with a thick accent. One remote relative was arrested and executed during the 1947 crackdown, but otherwise his family was unaffected. And as a boy he believed in the system. "I was indoctrinated," he remembers. "Education was all about patriotism. I thought Chiang Kai-shek was a great leader. In high school, you were always taking tests, always getting this official ideology, and you couldn't have different thoughts. Only in university, or afterward, did we liberate our minds."

It was after Antonio graduated from university in Taiwan, when he began working for *China Times,* one of Taiwan's establishment newspapers, that he began to have doubts. He was assigned to cover the national legislature, and it just didn't match up with the expectations that his education had cultivated.

"We used to joke that the best place to turn someone into a democracy activist was the legislature. After two or three months, a journalist covering the legislature would be turned into a radical. It was just so vastly removed from what we learned about 'democracy' in class."

The upshot was that the *China Times* asked Antonio to leave. He started an opposition magazine, playing a cat-and-mouse game with the authorities—who often banned and confiscated such publications as soon as they hit the streets. He became increasingly intertwined with the democracy movement, and when Lin Yi-hsiung's mother and daughters were stabbed in 1980, Antonio was one of the first called to the scene.

On one of Antonio's trips to Beijing, I bicycled over to his hotel, the Beijing International, and sat down with him in the coffee shop. We ordered a couple of coffees, and I asked him whether the mainland in the 1990s is on the road that Taiwan pioneered a few decades ago.

"Economically, the mainland is vibrant and bubbling away uncontrollably, and that's like Taiwan in the sixties," he reflected. "There begins to be wealth, people begin to travel abroad, students go overseas and don't want to come back—that's similar to Taiwan. And people want a voice in their affairs. Gradually education, experience, and confidence build, so that people begin to disrespect authority. They stop being afraid of police, and then they're no longer afraid of the party. They realize there's nothing special about the party.

"This public confidence is very important. It means that people on the mainland are starting to challenge authority, so that the party loses prestige, loses control. This cultural change, this economic base, is very important. It's because of these transformations, and because of the rise of the middle class, that pressure groups emerge. People want to participate in the system. They want a voice. The authoritarianism gradually rots, from the inside out. It erodes. It's not an explosion, it just melts down. It melts like ice cream in the sun."

Antonio paused and looked around the coffee shop. It was filled with a mixture of local and Hong Kong Chinese, mostly dressed competitively to impress their business partners, girlfriends, or hookers. Cellular telephones were ostentatiously laid on the tables, and beepers went off constantly.

"Yet Taiwan wasn't quite the same as the mainland is now," he said. The biggest difference, he explained, is that Taiwan had more of an independent economy and civil society. The Taiwan authorities banned opposition periodicals, for example, yet underground printing factories could always be found to publish them. Even in the 1970s, Taiwan's leaders could never control information or ideas as well as China's leaders are still able to. Moreover, Taiwan's citizens had much more exposure in their educational system to at least the idea of democracy than mainlanders have, and Taiwanese also had extensive experience with elections—local elections, often meaningless ones, but still elections. Finally, Antonio noted the difference in size: Taiwan is an island with just 20 million people, and thus it is far more manageable than an empire like mainland China.

"In the long term, I'm rather optimistic that China can take Taiwan's path rather than Eastern Europe's," Antonio said. "China has so many people, so much talent, that it should be able to find a way out. But in the short term, it'll be difficult.

"This process, this transition to a normal country, is a bit magical. It's always precarious and dangerous."

It is encouraging that China's leaders themselves want to take the Taiwan road. In the 1950s, Mao used to say that "the Soviet Union's today is China's tomorrow." Now it would be a counterrevolutionary offense to say that. But in the early 1990s, Deng Xiaoping seemed to settle on another model that is just as counter to China's original revolutionary principles. It is Singapore.

During Deng's famous "imperial tour" to Guangdong in 1992, mapping China's new directions, he mentioned only four places by name: Hong Kong, Japan, Singapore, and South Korea. He called on Guangdong to establish several Hong Kongs, for example. But he reserved special praise for Singapore: "Singapore's social order is rather good. Its leaders exercise strict management. We should learn from their experience, and we should do a better job than they do."

On the surface, it seems odd that China's Communist Party should take a capitalist bastion as its model. Singapore, after all, is an island state with just 2.7 million people, and until recently Communists there faced imprisonment. But the attraction of Singapore is understandable. "Of course Old Deng likes Singapore," a young Chinese government official explained. "It's run by Chinese, it's efficient, it's rich, and no one jabbers about human rights." An influential Chinese economist put it a bit differently: "The talk about Singapore says a lot about what Deng wants. He would like to free up the economy, but he wants tight political control."

The advantage of Singapore is in part that it is a brilliantly managed—and in some ways centrally planned—market economy, one of the best performers in the world. Singapore now has the highest per capita income in Asia outside Japan, and it is also appealing to the Communists because it satisfies their desire for order and stability. There is no pornography, extreme poverty, or even jaywalking. Bubble gum is banned, along with some critical foreign magazines. People not only have the vote but are legally obliged to go to the polls during elections. The government harasses its critics, manipulates the legal system, and steamrolls the opposition, yet people use their ballots to return their leaders to power. Singapore, in other words, has achieved Western living standards without being infected by Western political standards. It is a paramount leader's dream, for it is populated by clean-cut, law-abiding citizens who obligingly use their ballots to sustain one-party rule.

Perhaps one lesson of Singapore's experience—and Taiwan's—is how much voters are prepared to forgive when they are enjoying rapid economic growth. Taiwan, for example, faced the same "ghosts" problem as China: The regime had slaughtered so many people that liberalization of history would be profoundly unsettling. People would learn that all the old propaganda had been a lie, and the government would lose credibility. Yet Taiwan weathered this crisis of the soul, and in the end the Nationalist Party continued to win elections. It may eventually fall from power, but what is most striking today is that liberalization has not destroyed the ruling party's mandate and in some ways has broadened it—a very reassuring lesson for the Chinese Communist Party. In Eastern Europe, all the Communist Party leaders knew that if they held free elections they would lose, and that was naturally one reason why they did not want to hold elections. But in China, the leaders could probably hold quasi-free elections and win them, manipulating the news media and relying on the peasant vote to pull them through. This makes it much easier for the Communist Party in China to move toward democracy than it ever was for the Polish or Czech Communist Party.

In the West, we tend to presume that democracy is good for economic growth. By contrast, we associate repression with the stagnation and poverty of Eastern Europe and the third world. In Asia, however, many people see an inverse relationship between democracy and prosperity. They complain that democracies are so hobbled by special interests that they cannot accept austerity or make hard choices. Chinese sometimes say contemptuously that democratic leaders *dunzhe maokeng bu la shi,* that they squat in the outhouse but never produce anything.

Aside from Japan, the Asian countries that in recent times have enjoyed the longest periods of democracy are India and, since 1986, the Philippines—and they are the laggards of the region. Other countries with on-and-off democracy, like Pakistan, Bangladesh, and Sri Lanka, have done no better. South Korea fell into chaos during its brief experiment with democracy in 1960 and 1961 but then enjoyed an economic boom beginning under strongman Park Chung Hee.

So, all things considered, many Asians believe that authoritarian governments are most likely to put food on the table. They see China's experience over the last fifteen years as the great proof of this proposition. Authoritarian China is enjoying a tremendous economic flowering, while democratic India limps along and democratic Russia stagnates. Already some Russians are arguing that they should be pursuing the China model: perestroika without glasnost.

Over the course of the last dozen years, the democratic ideal made tremendous progress around the world, with military governments giving way to democracies throughout Latin America, in parts of Africa, and in countries like South Korea, Taiwan, and the Philippines. Democracy triumphed in those countries in part because it offered people hope for better lives, for more wealth as well as more dignity. But the democratic tide could reverse. If China manages to sustain its economic boom, the lesson that many people in developing countries will draw is that autocracy offers the best hope for an economic miracle.

I find this view deeply troubling. There is something in us that wants to see democracy rewarded and despotism punished. We expect to see a moral pattern in the quilt of history. We think, perhaps only subconsciously, that tolerant democracies should prosper while corrupt autocracies should pay a price for their sins. That's what offends me about China. Where's the economic price that the regime is paying for its oppression? How can corrupt Communist gerontocrats preside over such an economic boom? Where's the justice in the world?

This view that democracy can be an obstacle to economic growth is a heresy in the West. And yet, unwillingly, I'm drawn to the conclusion that in some circumstances there is a bit of truth to it—just a little bit, though.

Among poor countries without much of an educational foundation, particularly those nations torn by ethnic or religious strife, it probably is true that dictators can assure more order and stability than elected presidents. This is crucial because economic growth requires stability. Without stability, individuals and businesses dare not invest their savings and expand their factories or stores.

In addition, in nations where people do not yet accept the rights of others to express opposing viewpoints, election campaigns can easily disintegrate into violence, reinforcing ethnic and religious cleavages instead of alleviating them. Moreover, dictators worry less about public opinion and so perhaps are somewhat more likely to introduce unpopular but necessary economic measures. They can, for example, raise bread prices to rational levels because citizens dare not demonstrate against the generals. If a democratic president tried the same thing, the public would be in the streets. For the same reason, democratic governments are sometimes unable to resist inflationary demands for pay increases from labor unions.

Yet I think the criticisms of democracy are often taken much too far. Some democracies have performed poorly in Asia, at least in economic terms, but they are at least doing better than dictatorships like Burma and North Korea. And it is difficult to know ahead of time whether an aspiring autocrat will be a benevolent despot like Lee Kuan Yew in Singapore or a malevolent one like Kim Il Sung in North Korea. If Filipinos don't like Fidel Ramos, they can vote him out of office, which is not an option they had with Ferdinand Marcos.

It also seems to me that even if dictatorships have a mild edge in promoting stability, this is so only when countries are poor, backward, and uneducated. As nations grow wealthier and better educated, dictatorship becomes a source of instability. The emerging middle class yearns for more of a voice, and students take to the streets. If the dictator tries to hang on, the result is chaos. At that juncture, democracy can provide a better environment for economic growth. And at that point, an elected leader probably will have more legitimacy than a military leader and so may be better able to raise the price of bread and introduce other economic reforms. In Poland, for example, Lech Walesa could introduce austerity measures that his immediate Communist predecessors never could have gotten away with.

So even if dictatorship has economic advantages at the bottom of the socioeconomic staircase, China may be above that level. The Tiananmen movement made it clear that Chinese, at least in the cities, want more democracy and will take to the streets to get it. By the time a nation has an emerging middle class, democracy usually makes good political and economic sense, to say nothing of the intrinsic value that democracy brings by allocating power more fairly than dictatorships. Communist officials often asked me derisively how democracy could possibly function in a peasant country like China, but I think that the question is a red herring. Chinese democracy would obviously not be as sophisticated as American democracy, and it would probably look more like Mexican democracy. At its absolute best, it would look like a past version of Japanese democracy. It would, in short, be manipulated by the ruling party and be marred by corruption and cheating. Yet this would at least provide some kind of a mandate for the rulers, and it would create a base on which further democracy could gradually grow. Moreover, economic growth is not the sole value we have in mind. Even an imperfect democracy is less likely to torture dissidents than a dictatorship is, and that is an important difference.

I don't think, therefore, that dictatorship is good for China. But I also doubt that democracy offers much economic benefit to poor countries. I wish it did, for we all feel in our souls some idealistic yearning to see right make might. But unfortunately I don't see it. And I fear that if China continues to be the world's fastest-growing economy, then more people will conclude that autocracy makes economic sense. Other countries, in Central Asia and farther afield, will look on enviously. They may decide to pursue the "Chinese model" by junking their ballot boxes and hiring more police. China's experience is giving new luster to fascism.

When we called China a fascist regime in the presence of Chinese friends, their faces sometimes fell. But in fact China is far better off with fascism than it was with Communism. Fascist countries like Spain managed to evolve into democracies, after all, while the Communist world simply collapsed. Moreover, this evolution in Spain and Taiwan was not an accident.

One of the lessons of Market-Leninism is that it is an inherently dynamic, unstable combination. As the market grows, it tends to nibble away at the Leninism. This process is beginning in China. It is simply an open question whether the Communist Party will allow the process to work, if that means the party presiding over its own demise.

Even if China falls short of the Taiwan or Singapore model, it could evolve into another Indonesia. Like China, Indonesia is a huge, multiethnic country that relies on Market-Leninism to combine one-party rule with vibrant industrial growth. It is marred by graft, nepotism, repression, and the likelihood of a succession crisis in coming years, but it still is enjoying extremely rapid increases in living standards and modest gains in political tolerance. When pressed, Indonesia may still massacre pro-independence protesters in East Timor, as China may continue to massacre Tibetans, but there is no doubt that Indonesia is making great progress.

During the Cold War, one of the longest-running arguments among students of the Soviet Union was between those who foresaw the state's collapse and those who predicted convergence with the non-Communist world. In the end, those who took the bleakest view were proven right. Now the same argument is raging about China. One of the most talked about books in China in recent years was a prediction of the collapse of the Communist world, written by Zbigniew Brzezinski in the 1980s and published in Chinese in a pirated edition for senior officials.

Immediately after the 1989 Tiananmen crackdown, I thought that China might be on the same road as Eastern Europe. Gradually, Sheryl and I changed our minds. While collapse is still a significant possibility, I now think that the more likely scenario is the kind of gradual "peaceful evolution" that the Chinese leadership warns against. There is a real chance that China will be able to sustain its economic miracle and create a political one as well.

KRISTOF/WUDUNN

紀思道　伍潔芳

下一個

THE NEXT
DYNASTY

*China is the theatre of the greatest movement now taking place on
the face of the globe. In comparison with it, the agitation in Russia
shrinks into insignificance. . . . It promises nothing short of the
complete renovation of the oldest, most populous and most conservative of empires.*

—W. A. P. Martin, *The Awakening of China*, 1907

16

Perhaps the richest man in China, Zhang Guoxi stands outside his corporate headquarters in Jiangxi Province, looking forward to the future. [Photo by Nicholas D. Kristof.]

I t was sobering, as we were finishing work on this manuscript, to browse through old books about China. We came across turn-of-the-century works like *The Awakening of China*, all predicting the same kind of resurgence for China that optimists now foresee. Another book, *China in Transformation*, declared in 1912 that the outcome of the overthrow of the Qing dynasty "will be a remodeled China, as efficient in her way as the new Japan, and more wealthy—perhaps more powerful."

Such books underscore the dangers of optimism, and even today we frequently encounter starry-eyed optimists who think that China is run by enlightened managers and is a sure bet for the future. We want to tie those people down so that they don't float away with their own enthusiasm. It's worth remembering that no country ever managed a "peaceful evolution" to freedom and prosperity while under Communist Party rule. At various times Czechoslovakia, Yugoslavia, and Hungary seemed to come close, but eventually they and other Communist-led countries proved unable to switch tracks. Instead, they just derailed.

Still, there has never been a Communist country like China. Anyone basing judgments only on Communist precedent would have denied the possibility of the bloom of talk radio, joint ventures, stock markets, and private schools in China. So gradually we, like the turn-of-the-century optimists, came to believe that China will succeed in its goals for development—in the long run. We came to this conclusion grudgingly, after having been kicked by Chinese soldiers, berated by an inane official press, and tailed by leechlike agents of a vicious security apparatus. Some of the Chinese leaders hate us, and, well, we've never had any soft spot for despots either. But for all our animosities, we see that China has come a long way, and we believe it has a fighting chance to go the rest of the distance.

Heraclitus, the ancient Greek philosopher, said that you can never step into the same river twice. The water flows, so the river is always different.

We felt the same way about China. We arrived in one China in 1988, and we left a very different China in late 1993. It was richer, healthier, and more self-confident, ornamented with glass buildings and neon lights. Jailers still torture political prisoners, but now the family members complain and sometimes hold press conferences.

Above all, many Chinese live far better than they did when we arrived. In the cities, people can now buy their vegetables and pork in fifteen minutes instead of lining up for an hour. Sales clerks are not polite, but they no longer regard courtesy as a sign of weakness. As the quality of merchandise improves, Chinese no longer have to put up with the indignity of zippers that burst or seams that split. In poor villages, peasants can now frequently afford coarse toilet paper instead of relying on leaves and grass. In some cities, women now can obtain sanitary napkins and tampons instead of making do with rags or paper. Leprosy has been virtually eradicated, and most peasants can be reasonably confident that their newborn babies will survive into adulthood.

China is far from a free country. But for the first time since the Communist Revolution, many people can leave their employers and strike out on their own as entrepreneurs. If a party secretary writes something nasty in a personnel file, or *dangan*, it won't necessarily matter. Chinese can travel freely around the country and, to a degree, around the world.

Fear is diminishing, and that, too, makes a huge difference in a nation's well-being. Chinese are still afraid of the government, but not as much as they used to be. For years after the Tiananmen Square crackdown in 1989, we tried to get an interview with one prominent government institute, but we were always turned down. We asked friends to help arrange a meeting, but they said it was impossible. Then, shortly before we left China, Sheryl succeeded in setting up an appointment with the head of the institute. The official sat stiffly and nervously in a green, soft-cushioned chair, but he spoke freely even when the conversation touched on sensitive political issues. At the end of the discussion, he explained why he had never met with us before: "We aren't supposed to meet foreign journalists. That's an explicit rule. And when we turn down your requests for interviews, we're not supposed to tell you that there is this rule. We're supposed to say that we're sick or that we're busy at a conference. But I think the atmosphere in China is changing, and I want to get my views across. So I decided to see you today."

It was the same story with others. For several years after Tiananmen, almost no one called except on official business. Then gradually, as Chinese became bolder, our phone started ringing again. Scholars called to offer us anti-Communist tracts they had written. Dissidents from the provinces telephoned to tell us what was happening in their areas. Family members of political prisoners called to let us know about prison abuses. Peasants complained about their land being taken away. Workers protested that their homes had been confiscated.

One day Nick conducted an official interview with a hard-liner in a Central Committee department. The official, in his gray Mao suit and stubby black shoes, was boring and useless, as such officials almost always were. Then the next day the phone rang. It was the official's seventeen-year-old daughter. She wanted to meet, and Nick suggested a nearby coffee shop.

"Dad brought your business card home and said you'd interviewed him," she explained over a pot of tea. "I copied down your number, but of course Dad doesn't know that I called you. He'd be horrified."

The girl wanted advice on applying to American universities, and Nick offered a little. After that, we met with her from time to time, and she passed on news about what was really happening in her father's organization. She was much more informative than he was.

There is an ancient legend that helps illuminate the intellectual question of how to regard the changes under way in China. Confucius and his disciples once passed through the forests of Mt. Tai and came across a woman weeping bitterly by an open grave. One of Confucius's disciples asked the woman why she was crying.

"First, my father-in-law was killed by a tiger," she explained. "And then later the tigers got my husband. And now the tigers have eaten my son as well."

"But why don't you leave this place?" Confucius asked.

"Because at least there is no oppressive government in these parts," the woman replied.

Confucius turned to his disciples and said, "Remember this, my students. Oppressive government is more terrible than tigers."

We think that the woman would have been well-advised to move to a city. Confucius spoke too rashly, for tigers and autocrats alike come in all degrees of ferocity. If the tiger is a small one and fond only of rabbits, then it make sense to live in the woods. But if the tiger has a taste for human flesh, then the city may be a safer bet.

Our point is that there are worse things than today's political repression, and China has endured many of them: famine, utter poverty, and the straitjacket of totalitarianism. Friends sometimes protest that it is insidious to draw distinctions among nasty regimes, but it really does matter: Dissidents do care whether they are simply imprisoned or also tortured. There is a significant difference between a regime that locks up its critics and one that *mie jiuzu*—wipes out the critic's entire family, slaughtering even distant cousins, neighbors, and acquaintances.

We in the West may wish that China's citizens had ballots as well as bank accounts, but it would be wrong to dismiss the progress as meaningless because it is unbalanced. In impoverished hillside villages, a new factory to make hoes or hats may be as important in fostering dignity among the local peasants as a bill of rights would be. A few hundred more yuan a year means that poor families can go to clinics and count on mothers and infants alike surviving childbirth, can then inoculate the babies against polio, and finally can put behind them the trauma of hearing a child cry from hunger and have nothing to offer.

Consider China's infant mortality figures. In 1980, 56 of every 1,000 babies died in their first year of life. These days, fewer than 38 of those babies die in their first year. On a Chinese scale, that amounts to a savings of 378,000 lives a year. Nobody pays attention to that, however. It's a statistic. And no statistic can compete with an anecdote, particularly one about a brave young dissident who is battered by the regime.

That raises a fundamental question of moral equivalency that nagged at us for much of the time we were in Beijing. Is it true, as Adolf Hitler wrote in *Mein Kampf*, that "success is the sole earthly judge of right and wrong"? Do rising living standards make up for political repression?

For starters, we don't give the government full credit for the rising living standards. The economy is booming not because of Communism but because of the collapse of Communism. The boom is a tribute not to the brilliance of the Central Committee but to the hard work of hundreds of millions of peasants and workers. The policies of the reform era succeeded so well partly because the policies of the Maoist era were so foolish. The regime should not get bonus points for breaking up the communes when it was silly enough to have established them two decades earlier.

Even to the limited extent that the Communist Party gets the credit for improving living conditions, we don't think that saving a baby makes up for torturing a dissident. Our courts don't excuse child molesters from prosecution if they give generously to charity. Someone who saves a busload of passengers from being struck by a train doesn't then get the right to knock off a few of his enemies. Likewise, we shouldn't forgive the Communist Party for killing students because it saves more people than it kills.

We could never devise a formula of moral equivalency that says that if a regime enriches its citizens it can also torture them. We wish we could balance good against evil on a single scale and come up with a net positive or negative reading, but life isn't so simple. Making moral judgments requires more than the use of adding machines. Forgiving China its torture instruments because of its economic statistics would be like mixing apples and orangutans; it's meaningless to measure them on the same scale. At the same time, however, our irritation at the regime's brutality should not blind us to its accomplishments. Childhood inoculation programs do not compensate for the rape of Tibetan women separatists, but neither do torture and autocracy negate the party's genuine achievements.

As living standards soar, it becomes increasingly dizzying to try to reconcile the two faces of China. Westerners often make the mistake of seeing China in stark, almost Manichaean terms: Human rights campaigners focus on the horrific treatment of political prisoners, while business executives regale their home offices with stories about new millionaires. The important thing is to recognize the reality of both dimensions of China, to acknowledge that the government represses the people at the same time that it allows them to emerge from polio and poverty. To Western eyes, there is a tension between these two realities, and it was hard for us when we were being denounced to acknowledge the promise of the economic revolution. Likewise, it is difficult for some business executives to recognize the extent of the corruption and the potential for upheaval.

Ultimately we simply have to accept that there are two sides to China and that they can't be measured on the same scale. They are the yin and yang of China, both genuine, both relevant, both crucial to understanding the whole.

In the West, we tend not to like contradictions, for it seems tidier intellectually to point to a single overarching force. We incline toward monotheism, in social science as well as in faith. But the Chinese embrace polytheism, and Chinese philosophy has always been rooted in the idea of finding a balance between competing forces. The Middle Kingdom is huge enough to accommodate two versions of reality. Walt Whitman could have been describing China when he wrote:

Do I contradict myself?
Very well then I contradict myself.
(I am large. I contain multitudes.)

As China's citizens get bolder, as reforms cut deeper and people get laid off, there will be confrontations and there may even be more massacres ahead. China in the coming years faces many other challenges as well. Energy shortages will constrain growth. Environmental damage will harm public health and perhaps slow the economy. Reform of state-owned enterprises will lead to unemployment and strikes. Peasants will become more mobile and perhaps more embittered. Crises of legitimacy and succession in the central government probably will worsen in the coming years, and jockeying for power could lead to serious battles among factions.

Yet it would be wrong to focus only on the dangers. Anyone with a crystal ball in 1978 would have foreseen chaos and convulsions ahead. He could have painted a grim picture of rising corruption, of periodic peasant revolts, of successive party leaders being ousted by an aging tyrant, of a huge antigovernment movement that would be bloodily suppressed by the army. All of that happened. Yet China flourished, and more important than any of those predictions was the explosion of wealth that has given new opportunities to 21 percent of the world's population. For all the drama of Tiananmen, perhaps nothing was so significant in the reform era as the lifting up from absolute poverty of 170 million people in China since 1978. Whatever doubts remain about the future, there is one certainty: China has already enjoyed the most rapid rise in living standards in human history for such a large share of the world's population.

Moreover, while China resembles a disintegrating dynasty, Taiwan shows that a Chinese dynasty can collapse without chaos, without even an interruption of economic growth. The old dynasty can be replaced by a civil society, the autocratic emperors by elected presidents, *renzhi* by *fazhi*. Our greatest hope is that this transition will take place in China.

It is of course valid to question whether China can continue its economic boom. But we should keep poking ourselves to avoid concluding that because the regime is offensive it cannot sustain its economic growth. We may think that bad people and bad countries should come to a bad end, but moralism makes bad economics. Ruthless individuals often climb to the top of their fields, sometimes over the backs of their nicer competitors, and the same is true of nations. China may be a gerontocracy, a kleptocracy, and a thugocracy all folded into one, but it could scarcely have done better for the living standards of its people in the last fifteen years.

Whether China can sustain its economic miracle probably has less to do with authoritarianism and more to do with savings rates and productivity. For now, the signs look reasonably promising. China's savings rate ranges between 35 and 40 percent, one of the highest in the world, and it is pursuing sensible pro-growth policies such as opening up its economy to foreign trade and investment. China is still inefficient, but that simply creates major new opportunities for further growth as productivity improves. Of course, all kinds of things can still go wrong, just as the international debt crisis came out of nowhere in 1982 to sideswipe the rise of Brazil. The downside in the case of China is particularly bleak, for the risk is not just of stagnation but even of civil war. Our point is that it would be presumptuous to assume that there is any foregone conclusion. China can still go either way.

Sometimes the very act of reporting creates problems: The process of selecting and organizing material can lead to misperceptions. So we want to emphasize that the stories we have told are the most vivid ones we know of, drawn from myriad interviews over five years, and they are mostly not representative of day-to-day life. Wang Chaoru, for example, lived for thousands of perfectly ordinary days in which he didn't suffer any harassment at all. We just happened to write, in Chapter 4, about the day when the police beat him to death for the sake of the Olympics. That incident still gives us chills, and it illustrates better than any other how *renzhi,* rule by individuals, chokes and brutalizes Chinese society. But such episodes do not represent typical days in typical lives. This is also true of the successes; we write in Chapter 11 about Zhang Guoxi, the millionaire, but most Chinese are still poor peasants.

Our aim is not really to portray daily life, for a *typical* slice of a *typical* peasant's life would be an uneventful morning wading barefoot in the muck of the rice paddy. Rather, our aim is to employ the most striking stories we know of as a way of underscoring and clarifying the principal themes of life in China in the 1990s.

A second concern is that readers may leave with the impression that we're absolutely confident that we know what we're talking about. On the contrary, China is such a vast and confusing subject that it is difficult to be sure of either the facts or the conclusions. Winston Lord, the former U.S. ambassador to China, likes to say that "a 'China expert' is an oxymoron." During our first summer in Beijing, Nick wrote a long political analysis for *The Times* and got back a plaintive note from an editor: "You use 'appears' or 'apparently' or 'seems' in every paragraph. Can't you say anything without hedging?" In the interest of readability, we now fight back the temptation to toss such qualifications into every paragraph. But in a larger sense qualifiers belong in every sentence that anyone writes about China.

We deeply respect many China experts who have come to conclusions different from ours. Some are much more pessimistic, believing that China's economy and political system will collapse within a few years. Others are far more optimistic, anticipating that China will follow a relatively smooth road to becoming a new superpower. There are similar disagreements about almost every topic that we've written on, from family planning to Sino-American relations. The worst danger for China watchers is to be dogmatic. So we've formed our own ideas on these topics, and we offer them in this book. But readers should know that there are many experts, both Chinese and foreigners, who will look at what we've written and raise their eyebrows—or simply guffaw.

China watching, simply put, is an exercise in humiliation. Whenever we felt we had a handle on some aspect of China, whenever we felt pretty sure of ourselves, we forced ourselves to contemplate China in the time of its great famine of 1958–1961. It was a desperate time, when peasants tried to stay alive by eating leaves and grass and even sawdust. Mothers tried to nurse their babies with withered breasts, and the infants soon died along with the old people. At first the corpses were buried in shallow graves; then in some areas the peasants began to eat the flesh of those who had died.

It was the worst famine ever not only in China but in the world. The 30 million deaths far exceeded the death toll that any country had ever endured from any natural disaster, or perhaps any war, in recorded history. It was, in other words, one of the most important events of the latter part of the twentieth century.

As luck would have it, the greatest of the China correspondents was on hand to cover the tragedy. Edgar Snow, the author of *Red Star over China,* spent five months wandering through China in 1960. He was a perfect candidate to bring back the story, for he spoke Chinese and had lived in China for many years. He knew China's leaders from Mao Zedong down and was regarded by them as a friend; this meant that he was allowed considerable freedom to travel as he wished. Almost never has there been such a perfect match between a great correspondent and a great story.

Here is what Snow had to say: "While I was in China *Look* kept sending me queries about 'the famine' and I diligently searched, without success, for starving people or beggars to photograph. (Nor did anyone else succeed.) . . . I must assert that I saw no starving people in China, nothing that looked like old-time famine, and only one beggar. . . . I do not believe there is famine in China at this writing."

What of other visitors to China? Gilbert Étienne, a Swiss economist, wrote in *Le Monde*: "It may be said at the outset—and it is one of the rare points where we have the pretension to be categorical—that it is false to speak of 'general famine.' The dolorous times of the Kuomintang, when millions of human lives were eliminated for want of minimum subsistence, have not reappeared." Likewise, the *New York World-Telegram and Sun* reported in 1962, "There is not one shred of evidence known to the West that famine threatens Communist China." *The Times* of London warned in a 1962 editorial against exaggerating China's problems and added that "the sufferings of the ordinary peasant from war, disorder, and famine have been immeasurably less in the last decade than in any other decade in the century." Lord Boyd-Orr, the former head of the U.N. Food and Agriculture Organization, visited China and announced that Chinese peasants had raised their crop yields to British levels and ended the traditional famine cycle. Speaking in 1959, he concluded, "China has one-quarter of the world's population but seems capable of feeding it well."

It is easy to poke fun at Snow and the others, but frankly that kind of fumble is one of our worst nightmares. China is more open now than it was in 1960, but we in the China-watching business are still capable of colossal idiocy. As we've pointed out, for example, in 1991 China substantially tightened its family planning policy—thereby affecting more people in a more intimate way than any other policy in the world. It took us two years to notice.

So it's only right to tell you, in the interest of fair labeling of our product, that we and others in our field have an appalling record. China watching is the only profession that makes meteorology look accurate and precise.

Yet for all the caveats, for all the misgivings, the breadth of change that we witnessed for five years still leads us to believe that China will flourish and evolve. The distance China has come can be measured in the outcome of a contest of wills that was taking place as we were preparing to end our tour in Beijing. This tiny battle illuminates the problems that China faces in the 1990s—and also how far the nation has already traveled.

An Italian businessman, a member of our health club in Beijing, was trying to set up an $18 million Sino-Italian joint venture factory in Henan Province in central China. The factory would manufacture disposable syringes—really manufacture them, not just wash out old ones—and 85 percent of the financing would come from a loan by an Italian bank.

As a sweetener, the Italians agreed to pay for all the Chinese officials involved in the deal to go to Italy to sign the loan agreement. The Italians paid $80,000 for plane fares, hotels, and food so that the Chinese officials could visit Venice, Milan, and Bologna before arriving in Rome for the signing. Among the Chinese officials were two from a Henan Province government-owned bank, which was guaranteeing the loan. One was a director, in his late thirties, and married. The other was an employee of his, a woman in her late twenties, also married, with a son.

Throughout this all-expense-paid vacation, the Chinese director kept ordering his female employee to sleep with him. She kept refusing. Once they were put in adjoining hotel rooms, and he tried to force himself on her. She ran crying to the joint venture officers, saying that he was trying to rape her.

Despite this unpleasantness, the Italian bank officials flew to Rome, and everything was ready for the signing. But two days before the date, the Chinese director announced that he wouldn't sign anything. It turned out that he was trying to blackmail his female employee, by saying that they wouldn't complete the deal—and return to China—unless she slept with him. The Italians, who were spending thousands of dollars each day in hotel bills, began to get nervous that the standoff could continue indefinitely in the luxury hotel.

The Italians applied some pressure. They suggested to the man that Italy had some fine women, professionals, whom he might want to sample instead. No! The director was adamant. Only his employee could satisfy him. The Italians sent their wives to cozy up to the woman, suggesting that since she was in a foreign country she might want to let her hair down. No! She would not yield.

"Here we are, close to signing an $18 million deal, and he's chasing her," the Italian businessman said. "It's absurd!"

At the last minute, the Chinese director agreed to go ahead with the signing, without getting what he wanted from the woman. Presumably one motivation was that the Italians had already agreed to pay him a personal commission of one percent—$180,000—just for signing the loan agreement.

The tale illustrates the corruption in China today, the way officials abuse their positions, the degree to which men regard women as toys. Yet it also underscores the strides that China is making. In the old *renzhi* system, the woman probably would have yielded. She would have had no way of fighting back, for if she had resisted he could have destroyed her career.

So what was reassuring was that she did fight back. She resisted every step of the way, even reporting his misconduct to the joint venture partners. And she won. In fact, she managed to get compensation—from the foreigners, for this is China—for her "emotional trauma."

The situation is not ideal, for he is still her boss and he has not been punished. He may not have worked his way into her bed, but he did pocket $180,000. Yet at least Chinese now dare to stand up for themselves. And at least, in a pluralistic economy, they can now defend themselves and even switch jobs to escape their bosses if it is necessary. At least the system has opened up so that people are not prisoners and playthings of their bosses. That is the first step on the road to a civil society.

During the American civil rights struggle, the Reverend Martin Luther King, Jr., used to tell of the prayer of an old black woman. "Lord, I ain't what I want to be," Dr. King quoted her as saying. "I ain't what I ought to be. But thank God Almighty, I ain't what I was." That prayer could be echoed by nearly every Chinese alive today.

We have a Chinese friend in the chemical industry who puts it a different way. Our friend, a man who grew up barefoot in the countryside, now wears a necktie and lives the good life as head of the representative office of an American company. We would occasionally drop by his office and relate the latest little tidbit we'd heard: some new sexual harassment case, a corruption scandal, a peasant rebellion, a soccer riot. And he would invariably shrug and say, "China's a normal country now."

His point was that most countries around the world have corruption scandals, peasant rebellions, and soccer riots. It was only in the artificial environment of Maoism, when there was no oxygen to sustain life, that such things did not happen. In the regular hurly-burly of China, there will be such upheavals: There will be village riots, labor clashes, and political demonstrations. Tear gas will waft through Beijing and Chengdu and Changchun.

Those kinds of things happen in normal countries, particularly in developing countries, but they do not mean that the system will collapse. Instead, as our friend sees it, such disturbances can even be seen as a measure of normality. We're not sure he's right, but we hope so.

We also hope that an increasingly normal China will be able to withstand the perils of the dynastic cycle. Perhaps the best idea for overcoming the dynamic of dynastic disintegration was put forward by Mao Zedong, himself an avid reader of history. In July 1946, when Mao was still a gaunt guerrilla leader living in the earthen caves of Yanan, he received a visit from a prominent scholar named Huang Yanpei. According to Communist records, Huang asked Mao what would happen if the Red Army succeeded in staging a revolution.

"Dynasties begin with a surge of vigor, and then decay and disintegrate," Huang Yanpei noted. "Has the Communist Party found a way to break this vicious cycle?"

"We've found a way!" Mao beamed. "It's called democracy!"

It's a pity that Mao didn't try it, for his idea might have worked. The founders of China's next dynasty might bear Mao's words in mind. Both of us came to be convinced, while living in China, that Churchill was generally right: Democracy is the worst form of government, except for all the rest. It is not that democratic decision making is necessarily better. Rather, it's that democracy provides a correcting mechanism to keep a regime from veering too far off course. China's problem has been that it steers like a drunken driver, careering this way and that, dynasty after dynasty. Perhaps a civil and democratic society could change that. If a middle class gains power, if peasants become citizens and not just subjects, China will be better able to hold its course. Mao may have been called the Great Helmsman, but an informed public is an even greater helmsman.

What will China's next dynasty be like? Obviously we don't know, but there is an intriguing historical parallel. The dynasty most like the present one is the Qin, which was founded in 221 B.C. by the great Qin emperor Qinshihuangdi. A brilliant military leader and cruel tyrant, he was in many ways like Mao Zedong—a similarity that Mao himself noted and accepted. The Qin emperor defeated an array of local warlords to unite China, and he became one of China's greatest nation builders. He linked existing fortifications to make the Great Wall of China. He established national standards for weights and measures. He ensured order and built a great national capital near the present city of Xian.

The Qin emperor was also a brutal man. Thousands died building the Great Wall. He attacked Confucian intellectuals, burning their books and burying them alive. And he ordered that those who built his tomb should be executed so that they could not reveal the location of the secret entrances. The famous terra-cotta warriors of Xian were made to protect the burial area, but the Qin emperor's tomb itself still has not been excavated. Located under a hill a few hundred yards from the terra-cotta warriors, it may well be the most fabulous tomb of ancient times—historical writings suggest that it is at least as spectacular as the burial chambers of the Egyptian pharaohs.

Partly because the Qin emperor was so fierce, his dynasty lasted just three years after his death. His heirs proved unable to support the crushing weight of his vast regime, and it suffered a crisis of legitimacy once he was gone. Yet the Qin emperor, for all his cruelty, had laid a foundation that served China well. The next dynasty was the Han, which lasted more than four centuries and was a golden era of Chinese history, a flourishing age for the arts and scholarship and the economy as well.

We like to think that the Communist dynasty, like the Qin, has inadvertently laid a foundation for the next dynasty. For all the tragedies of their rule, the Communists united China, redistributed land and wealth, and destroyed the special interests that were asphyxiating economic growth. China now has a chance, the first it has had in several hundred years, to grow and prosper and become a major international power, perhaps eventually a superpower such as the world has never known.

The Foreign Ministry customarily holds a farewell banquet for departing foreign correspondents. We wondered whether the culinary courtesy would be extended to us, when the phone rang one day, and our "handler," Zhao Xingmin, instructed us to appear at the Restaurant for Diplomatic Missions for our dinner. We happily agreed, for we wanted to end our China posting on a nice note, and a scrumptious ten-course banquet would do just that.

On the appointed afternoon, we put on our suits and prepared for a light and cheerful evening of good-byes. The Foreign Ministry sent only Zhao and another low-ranking diplomat, but the evening started off cordially. We sipped *laoshan* mineral water in a private dining room and chatted amiably in Chinese about our children and the weather. Then, just before the meal began, Zhao gave us the standard farewell gift, a Foreign Ministry plate with a colored Great Wall painted on it, and we oohed and aahed and said that it was beautiful.

"You foreigners may not always understand these things," Zhao said in an avuncular tone. "Other countries don't have the same emphasis on politeness as China does, so it must be difficult for foreigners to understand how to be as courteous as Chinese are."

"Customs are different, but we're very grateful for your help in trying to bridge the gap," Sheryl said. "We'll always look at this plate and remember with great fondness our time in Beijing."

We sat down at the table, and the waiter brought out a giant plate of jellyfish and barbecued pork. Zhao commented on the dishes, and we traded stories about some of the delicacies eaten in China: scorpions, snakes, fish eyes, field rats, bear paws, and the fried feet of live ducks. Then, Zhao cleared his throat.

"Well, at this farewell banquet, I wish I could say something nice," he said. "But the fact is that you have both been harmful to Sino-U.S. relations. Instead of reporting fairly, you both fabricated facts and distorted events."

We were stunned that Zhao should raise this at our farewell banquet. All of a sudden, the butterfly shrimps tasted like dry fish balls, the chicken like greasy eel. Everyone had stopped eating by now. Zhao's colleague had bowed her head and was staring down at her plate.

We sat quietly for a few moments before Nick responded: "I'm sorry you feel that way, Mr. Zhao. But maybe it's best to agree to disagree. And we both appreciate the Foreign Ministry's help over the years in facilitating our work."

"The problem is that you break our rules and write false things in your articles. Ji Sidao, you went to Xinjiang without permission! You can't hide these things from us!"

"Nick went to Xinjiang on a tourist trip, which is legal under the rules," Sheryl said, speaking softly to defuse a rising tension in the air. "As for our articles, I'm sorry you didn't like them, but that's over now."

"We cannot forget the way you fabricated articles for ulterior purposes," Zhao retorted, his strong voice and swift hand gestures suggesting that he relished the exchange. "You lie about our family planning policy and say that it operates by coercion, but what would the United States do if it had 1.2 billion people?"

Did we want to open Pandora's box? We exchanged quizzical looks across the table.

"Mr. Zhao," Nick said steadily. "You pointed out that Americans don't have as sophisticated an understanding of courtesy as Chinese do. One of our crude conventions is that we don't yell at each other over meals, so I hope you don't mind if we don't argue back."

Zhao hesitated for only a moment. "I'm just pointing out that you should not have lied and fabricated facts in your articles," he said. "The Chinese people will not forget that."

We changed the topic and also switched to English, in the hope that Zhao felt less comfortable with the language—although he spoke it fluently—and would be a bit more restrained. Sheryl asked questions about the food, and a cease-fire developed that held until the end of the meal. As soon as it was polite to do so, we warmly thanked Zhao for the meal—and fled.

People often ask us whether we enjoyed our time in China. Enjoyed? Given the atmosphere at dinners like that, *enjoyed* is not quite the right word. If we hadn't been tailed by State Security goons, if we hadn't been subjected to Foreign Ministry charmers like Zhao, if we hadn't seen friends like Zhang Weiguo and Ren Wanding imprisoned, then perhaps we would have enjoyed our stay in Beijing.

No, Beijing wasn't a fun fest. But it was fascinating. It was enormously exciting for us to watch close up as a huge nation like China awakens from its slumber and searches for its future. Communism has been discredited, and thoughtful Chinese are now scouting for a new path. There is a range of ideas, from fascism to market democracy, with the leadership apparently determined to try Market-Leninism.

We'll remember the deaths we saw: the corpses around Tiananmen Square, and even more than that the stench of death as the dynasty decays. But there's also the excitement of birth in the air. Chinese are experimenting with new ideas, new ways of running factories, new concepts for a hard currency, new schemes to get rich. The outlines of the next dynasty are already visible in the satellite dishes sprouting from rooftops, in the cacophonous rock music that fills the darkened dance halls, in the new private schools that are proudly opening their doors. There's a revolution going on out there.

AFTERWORD

As Deng Xiaoping's ashes were scattered across the sea after his death in February 1997, the Communist Dynasty seemed to flutter along with them, wandering, devoid of purpose, destined for oblivion.

Paradoxically, one of Deng's greatest accomplishments was that he changed China so much that most people did not weep for him. He had removed the Communist Party from the center of daily life, making it seem irrelevant to many Chinese, and the result was that there was none of the torrent of grief that had followed Emperor Mao's death in 1976. After Deng's death, Chinese simply went about their business, and they were now too sophisticated and too worldly to be distraught at the death of an old dictator. A few hours after Deng's death was announced, we got a call from a friend in Beijing, whose matter-of-fact attitude was typical. "Deng Xiaoping has died," she announced calmly. "They say it's Parkinson's Disease. By the way, did you get the fax I sent you earlier?"

The Communist Dynasty is ending. The question is simply how long it will stagger on, and how it will end—with a bang, in a coup d'état, or with a whimper as it fades away more gradually. Deng's own death has generated new instability in China that will hasten the collapse of the regime, for China is now faced not only with installing a new emperor, but also perhaps with launching a new dynasty as well. This does not mean that anything will happen immediately. When Brezhnev and Tito died, for a few years there were no dramatic changes. But in hindsight we can see that Tito's and Brezhnev's deaths, in each case, marked the end of the old order and the beginning of a process that ended with the extinction of their respective countries in their original form. Deng's death, too, has set in motion a new dynamic that will end, perhaps years from now, with the formal collapse of the Communist Dynasty.

Look at the potential new emperor: President Jiang Zemin is not, of course, a committed Communist. His bottom line is: I'll stay in power, and everything else is negotiable. He is a classic late-dynasty emperor, the kind who typically rules weakly and briefly before the mandate of heaven passes on. This is not to say that he is stupid; on the contrary, he is a bright and cosmopolitan man, genial, gracious, and sensitive, and he certainly is the first Chinese emperor ever to have gone to college. He had the good sense to send his children to study in America, and he has a flair for putting people at ease. When he meets democrats he can quote Lincoln in English ("Government of the people, by the people, for the people") and he startles Romanian visitors by quoting a nineteenth-century Romanian poet, Mihai Eminescu, in the original Romanian. Yet Jiang, unlike Deng, commands neither fear nor respect. The jokes have been swirling for years about Jiang; while he is justly proud of his ability with foreign languages, the daughter of one top official jokes that Jiang is fluent in four languages: pomposity, exaggeration, nonsense, and lies.

So what will happen to the Communist Dynasty in its endgame?

The most dire risk is national disintegration and civil war. There has sometimes been a tendency in Chinese history for the country to fall apart after the collapse of a dynasty, but now this seems to us unlikely. In Tibet and Xinjiang, rebellions may well grow more bloody, but in the Chinese heartland there simply is no hint of a popular yearning for political independence. As they chew on snake meat or chicken's feet, their cell phones ringing amid the cacophony of lively discussion, the Cantonese may grumble about the nincompoops in Beijing. But it is difficult to imagine a Cantonese willing to die for the Republic of Canton. Cantonese are too busy eating, decorating their homes, singing karaoke, scheming about their next business deal, and above all making money, to risk all this for some ideal of independence. The only way the heartland might split, as we see it, is from a coup d'état that was only partly successful. If a commander in Beijing were to seize control of the capital and Jiang were to flee to Shanghai, then it would be possible to imagine national division and fierce fighting between rival units. So civil war is conceivable, but very unlikely.

Much more likely is a successful military coup. Since Deng's death, the People's Liberation Army has emerged as the most powerful force in China, and its generals may prefer to be kings rather than king-makers. Jiang himself has fretted about this risk and has commissioned studies on how to avoid a coup. In any case, whether or not a coup takes place, the military will have greater say in national decision-making, and China may become more aggressive toward its neighbors. Just about every other great nation, from America to Germany, from ancient Athens to modern Russia, has tried to expand abroad, and there is no reason to think China is an exception. An assault on Taiwan is the most horrifying possibility, for it could set back all of East Asia by a decade or more. Yet even short of that option, the People's Liberation Army may also choose to be more assertive vis-à-vis Japan in maritime boundary disputes between the two countries, and there is even a possibility that the United States might be dragged in. Moreover, as China spreads its wings, there is also a growing risk of a serious miscalculation. In the fall of 1994, the American aircraft carrier Kitty Hawk was in the Yellow Sea when it detected a Chinese submarine and sent an American submarine to shadow it. An American S-3 anti-submarine plane also dropped sonar buoys to locate the Chinese submarine, and the Chinese commanders were furious when they discovered what was going on. Although the incident took place in international waters and the Americans were clearly within their rights, two Chinese fighters scrambled and attempted to intercept the American anti-submarine plane. A Chinese general later told an American military attaché in Beijing that "the next time, we'll shoot to kill."

The most likely scenario for China's future, and the fondest hope of many Chinese, is continued evolution along the path that China is already taking, rather like the trajectory of other quasi-fascist countries—South Korea, Taiwan, Chile, and Spain. China moved from being an ultra-leftist country under Mao to being an ultra-rightist country under Deng, and so the challenge will be to evolve as Spain or South Korea did in recent decades. The pressures for economic and political liberalization are the same in Beijing today as they were in Madrid several decades ago: an economic transformation that is creating a middle class is also nurturing a yearning for political participation, raising education levels, and leaving dictators embarrassed at being seen around the world as bloody tyrants. Whether China is ruled by Jiang or by the generals, the forces pushing China toward greater tolerance and liberalization will be the same, and this is the direction that it is most likely to take. It will be a long and unstable road, and there may be massacres along the way, especially in places like Tibet and Xinjiang, but the fruit of this evolution will be a flourishing middle class and greater pluralism, and eventually some form of greater democracy. In other words, a new dynasty.

The coming end of the Communist Dynasty worries some people and naturally provokes fears of instability. But the end of the dynasty is not only inevitable but also a good thing for China. It is time to move on. The tragedy of the Communist Dynasty is that its extraordinary achievement, an economic boom that has transformed China, is spawning yearnings for political participation that the party has always attempted to crush. Deng Xiaoping was like a gardener who planted all varieties of seeds and then delighted in the plants' luxuriant growth—but who then refused to move the plants as they grew to bigger pots to accommodate their larger roots. The Communist pot that they are in now simply won't work for China. It is too confining, too stifling, and if the plants are given no outlet they will wither and die. More likely, some new emperor will provide a larger pot, or else the plants themselves will use their roots to press against the cracks in the pot and break free.

The greatest crack in the pot is the Tiananmen massacre. Before Deng died, his children would sometimes meet over lunch in fancy restaurants with other *taizi*, or princelings. If the topic of the Tiananmen crackdown came up, Deng's children were always anxious to let people know that Papa had nothing to do with it. "He didn't give the order to open fire," his youngest daughter told a friend. "He was as surprised as anyone else when he found out."

That is implausible. But it illustrates how Deng's own children see the future. Tiananmen remains an open wound screaming for attention, and it refuses to heal. After seizing power in 1978, Deng tried to distance himself from the hated policies of the past by putting the Gang of Four on trial and making them scapegoats for the Cultural Revolution. It was of course ludicrous to think that those four people alone had been responsible, and indeed Deng himself had participated in the Cultural Revolution at times. But as a political gesture, condemning the Cultural Revolution and blaming it on the Gang of Four worked beautifully, bolstering Deng's own legitimacy while discrediting his rivals. In the same way, Jiang or some other Chinese leader may see the political benefit of choosing a scapegoat for Tiananmen (the obvious one is Li Peng) and putting him on trial. Such a gesture would be poor history, but it might be a shrewd political move for a would-be dynastic founder.

Ultimately, people will look back on today's China the way we look back on Franco's Spain, Park Chung Hee's South Korea, or Pinochet's Chile—as periods of economic dynamism and political repression, transitional phases that laid a base for later political liberalization. China is very early on this road, and it will be a sign of progress when there are elections to rig, when there are independent labor union organizers to club in the streets. But ultimately China in the post–Deng Xiaoping era will be a freer and a richer country. Jiang may even realize that he has everything to gain from a move toward a slightly more democratic state, one a bit like traditional Mexico, where unfair elections are held, so that the voting provides a bit of legitimacy. Indeed, Jiang might even be able to rely on the peasant vote, easily manipulated, and win a free election. That would provide him and his successors with a new mandate of heaven and could be the beginnings of a grand new dynasty.

Nicholas D. Kristof and Sheryl WuDunn
March 1997

NOTES

The sources for most information and quotations were simply interviews with the person cited. In the case of long interviews, where extensive quotations are recorded, the transcription is generally based upon tape recordings of the interview. In other cases, particularly for quotations of just a sentence or two, we took notes on the scene. When that was impossible, we sat down immediately thereafter and wrote down those direct quotations that we remembered clearly. So the quotations in this book are not simply reconstructed later as a literary device; they are as accurate as a translation can be.

In those cases where we did not rely on personal interviews and observation, we have cited books or articles that were useful to us.

One of the headaches in writing about Chinese names is how to romanize them. Sheryl's Chinese surname, for example, is variously spelled in English as *Wu, Woo* (both Mandarin pronunciations), *Ng,* or *Eng* (both Cantonese pronunciations). Throughout this book we have relied primarily on the mainland pinyin system of transcribing Chinese sounds roughly according to the Mandarin pronunciation. However, we use a few traditional names, such as Hong Kong instead of Xiang Gang and Tibet instead of Xizang. For people from Taiwan and Hong Kong, we use whatever romanization they prefer. Two usages tend to stump English speakers: the *q* and the *x*. The *q* should be pronounced as *ch;* for example, *Qing dynasty* is pronounced "Ching." And *x* is pronounced *sh,* so that Mr. Xu is pronounced "Shoo."

OPENING EPIGRAPH

P. iii The epigraph at the beginning of the book has long been attributed to Napoleon but apparently does not appear in any of his collected writings. Napoleon is said to have made the comment in 1816 or perhaps 1817 after reading accounts of Lord Macartney's trip to Beijing in the 1790s. It is known that Napoleon did make a number of comments about China (though less eloquent ones) and that he was very interested in the experiences of Lord Amherst, a British envoy to China. In a visit to St. Helena, Lord Amherst met for two hours with Napoleon in July 1817.

Napoleon thought that the British made a mistake in refusing to kowtow to the Chinese emperor, and the record shows that he had considerable respect for China's potential. Told that Britain did not need to kowtow because it could use gunboats to force China to comply with its demands, Napoleon responded, "This idea is madness. You would be very badly advised indeed if you were to call to arms a nation of two hundred millions of inhabitants, and to compel them in their own defense to build ships against yours." See Barry E. O'Meara, *Napoleon in Exile* (New York: AMS, 1969), reprint of edition published in 1853, esp. vol. 1, pp. 288 et seq., and vol. 2, pp. 100–101 (from which the preceding quotation is taken). O'Meara was Napoleon's surgeon and recorded his comments in exile. Incidentally, Napoleon's population figure was off; China's population then was about 340 million.

While on St. Helena, Napoleon had a number of Chinese servants, and for a time he even had a Chinese cook. Napoleon apparently was more used to cream sauces than to stir-fry, for he soon replaced the cook. Still, Napoleon treated his Chinese servants politely and scolded his assistants for being rude to them. On his deathbed, Napoleon said, "Who will look after my poor Chinese now?" See Gilbert Martineau, *Napoleon's St. Helena,* Frances Partridge, trans. (Chicago: Rand McNally, 1969), esp. pp. 179–182.

1. FLYING PIGEON

P. 2 The source for the chapter epigraph is Alain Peyrefitte, *The Immobile Empire,* Jon Rothschild, trans. (New York: Alfred A. Knopf, 1992), p. 314.

P. 8 Zhang Weiguo was released, after twenty months, without trial. He was not beaten, apparently because he is an intellectual; at one point the guards excused him from his cell before beating up everyone else. Our contacts with him apparently were not a major factor in his arrest.

P. 11 Wenchangtai is a Tibetan name, so it is written as one word. It is his real name; he defended the government instead of criticizing it, and I have already complained to the authorities about their mistreatment of him.

P. 17 The Tang Boqiao statement comes from "Anthems of Defeat: Crackdown in Hunan Province, 1989–1992," a report from Asia Watch published in 1992. Professor Peng Yuzhang's plight is described in that report, and further information about his apparent release comes from the subsequent Asia Watch report, "Detained in China and Tibet," published in 1994.

P. 19 Of course, even if someone had sent us information, it probably wouldn't have arrived. State Security agents checked our mail before allowing the post office to deliver it. However, spooks sometimes are not the brightest people. One State Security spy (working in our house while pretending to be a maid) triumphantly seized a list of radio frequencies in my possession; she presumably thought that this was my frequency list for transmitting cables to the CIA. In fact, it was simply my BBC and Voice of America broadcast schedule.

P. 23 The Qianlong quotation about bringing Guo to Beijing comes from Peyrefitte, *The Immobile Empire,* p. 314.

P. 24 Reporters in Beijing may be a cynical and embittered lot, but one reason we become paranoid is that sometimes our wildest suspicions turn out to be justified. The cars of several reporters were stolen, some from our guarded compound, so there were mutterings that only the authorities could have done it. Suspicions grew when the Jeep of one reporter, Seth Faison, who was then working for the *South China Morning Post,* disappeared from in front of the Palace Hotel. Seth went to the nearest police station to report the theft—and found his Jeep parked in front.

Our suspicions were confirmed when Jan Wong, a Chinese-Canadian journalist for the Toronto *Globe and Mail,* found her car on the street eleven months after it had been stolen. When she spotted it, her car had police license plates and a flashing light on top. Wong used the serial number to prove to the police that it was her car, and the authorities returned it a month later. The police said that they had found it on the street. "We didn't want it to go to waste," a policeman explained.

2. WHAT KIND OF CHINESE ARE YOU, ANYWAY?

P. 32 The Hu Shih epigraph is from Wm. Theodore de Bary, *Sources of Chinese Tradition* (New York: Columbia University Press, 1960), p. 853.

P. 37 In the end, Li Zhaoxing was never able to arrange a visit to Mao's old home, even for me.

P. 45 There are various estimates for how many overseas Chinese there are in the world, depending principally on who counts as a Chinese. If residents of Taiwan, Hong Kong, and Macao are considered overseas Chinese, then the worldwide figure is about 50 million. While China still argues that Taiwan is part of China, the 20 million Chinese on Taiwan clearly do not belong to the Communist system, and they have been instrumental, as overseas Chinese, in investing and contributing to the recent economic growth in China.

3. GHOSTS

P. 58 The Li Si epigraph is from Derk Bodde, *China's First Unifier: A Study of the Ch'in Dynasty as Seen in the Life of Li Ssu* (Hong Kong: Hong Kong University Press, 1967), p. 83.

P. 60 The best English-language source of information on the Wang Shiwei incident is Dai Qing, *Wang Shiwei and "Wild Lilies": Rectification and Purges in the Chinese Communist Party, 1942–1944* (Armonk, NY: M. E. Sharpe, 1994). The case is also discussed in Simon Leys, *Chinese Shadows* (Penguin Books, 1974), pp. 123–127; in Wen Bi, *Zhongguo Zuo Huo* (Beijing: Chao Hua Publishing House, 1993); and in Geremie Barmé,

"Using the Past to Save the Present: Dai Qing's Historiographical Dissent," *East Asian History,* June 1991.

On February 7, 1991, nearly half a century after he had been arrested, Wang Shiwei was rehabilitated. The Public Security Ministry sent two officials to the home of his widow, eighty-five-year-old Liu Ying. Tears ran down her cheeks as she read the official announcement clearing his name—and once more using the word *comrade* to describe him. An account of the rehabilitation is in Dai Qing's book.

P. 61 Zhu Xi's proposal is cited in Wm. Theodore de Bary, *The Trouble with Confucianism* (Cambridge, MA: Harvard University Press, 1991).

P. 63 The rediscovery of Soviet history is powerfully described in David Remnick, *Lenin's Tomb* (New York: Random House, 1993). *Lenin's Tomb* is also the source of the quotation in this chapter from Milan Kundera.

P. 65 Zhou Enlai's role in slaughtering Gu Shunzhang's family is acknowledged even by biographers friendly to Zhou, but estimates of the number killed vary widely. The figure of thirty, representing the high end of the estimates, comes from Tsai Meng-chien, *Cai Mengjian Chuan Zhen Ji* (Taipei: Biographical Publishing Studies Publishing House, 1981), pp. 10–12. Tsai says that about thirty were killed in all, including thirteen of Gu's family members.

P. 65 The 1957 speech by Mao is "On the Correct Handling of Contradictions Among the People," delivered on February 27, 1957. This is one of Mao's most famous speeches, but the official version is heavily censored. The full version, apparently based on a tape recording, is published in Roderick MacFarquhar, Timothy Cheek, and Eugene Wu, eds., *The Secret Speeches of Chairman Mao* (Cambridge, MA: Harvard University Press, 1989), p. 142. The reference to Luo Ruiqing's estimate of 4 million killed is on p. 142, n. 12.

P. 66 Estimates vary considerably for the number of dead in the famine that followed the Great Leap Forward. Judith Banister, a specialist on the Chinese population at the U.S. Bureau of the Census, estimates that in the period 1958–1961 there were 30 million excess deaths, meaning those on top of normal mortality rates. See Judith Banister, *China's Changing Population* (Stanford, CA: Stanford University Press, 1987), p. 85. Another study also calculated about 30 million excess deaths from the famine: Basil Ashton, Kenneth Hill, Alan Piazza, and Robin Zeitz, "Famine in China, 1958–61," *Population and Development Review,* December 1984, p. 613. The Ashton study cites 9.5 to 13 million deaths in the 1876–1879 North China famine and describes that as the worst one in world history until the one in 1958–1961. Xizhe Peng estimates excess deaths in the 1958–1961 famine may have been 23 million in "Demographic Consequences of the Great Leap Forward in China's Provinces," *Population and Development Review,* December 1987, p. 639. See also Penny Kane, *Famine in China 1959–61: Demographic and Social Implications* (London: Macmillan Press, 1988). These estimates refer only to the number of excess deaths; in addition, some 30 million were not born who would have been expected to be born. So the total "population deficit" resulting from the famine was around 60 million.

P. 70 Zhou Enlai is said to have argued behind the scenes that it was a mistake to instruct drivers to go forward at red lights and halt at green lights. He noted that the entire world went the other way and that changing the system could wreak havoc. After a few pileups, his view prevailed.

P. 76 Fang Lizhi's comments are in his book *Bringing Down the Great Wall* (New York: Alfred A. Knopf, 1991), pp. 267–275.

P. 77 In Chinese, *The Catastrophes of Chinese Leftism* is called *Zhongguo Zuo Huo*. It was written by Wen Bi (a pen name) and was published in 1993 in China by the Chao Hua Publishing House.

P. 86 The descriptions of the 1989 student movement come from assorted interviews at the time and afterward with many of the players or their family members. The quotation by the military officer comes from *Tong Su Wen Xue Xuan Kan*, November 1989.

P. 87 When the authorities reopened the Avenue of Eternal Peace a few weeks after the Tiananmen crackdown, I saw a tank parked at precisely the spot where I had left my bicycle. I livened up my expense account with the following claim: "$81, to purchase new Forever-brand bicycle to replace one possibly crushed by tank."

In fact, hundreds of other Chinese had also abandoned their bicycles at Tiananmen Square or elsewhere along the Avenue of Eternal Peace. A couple of months later, the city of Beijing announced that the owners could reclaim them, but naturally people worried that they would have to explain what they were doing in the area. So while swarms of people went to reclaim their bikes, they all insisted that they had been stolen by "hoodlums" a few days before June 4.

4. RED EMPERORS

P. 95 While handicapped people are often treated badly in China, it is worth noting that they are still frequently better off there than in other developing countries. This is largely the result of the campaigns of Deng Pufang, Deng Xiaoping's eldest son, who is paralyzed and confined to a wheelchair. Deng Pufang is the head of the association for the handicapped in China and has done a great deal to raise money for the disabled and to raise the leadership's consciousness about them.

P. 107 Wei Jingsheng described his encounter with the woman at the train station in an essay published as "A Dissenter's Odyssey Through Mao's China," *The New York Times Magazine*, November 16, 1980.

P. 109 The Chinese language actually has several expressions referring to what happens when the authorities punish someone by exterminating his clan. The one I cite is *mie jiuzu*, but in the historical literature *zhu jiuzu* is perhaps more common. The word *zu* (the latter part of *jiuzu*), now a noun meaning "clan," originally was also a verb meaning "to wipe out a clan." A similar expression is *manmen chaozhan,* meaning "to kill and confiscate the property of an entire extended family."

P. 110 Information on Yu Zuomin comes from the *Wen Wei Po,* a Hong Kong daily, the New China News Agency, local Chinese press accounts, interviews with Chinese journalists, and visits to the village of Daqiuzhuang.

P. 113 The statistic on the number of lawyers in China before 1949 was published in the *Far Eastern Economic Review,* January 20, 1994, p. 39. The number of law offices, which was 4,900 at the end of 1993, along with the number of lawyers, was reported in the *China Daily,* January 5, 1994.

P. 113 The account of the lawyers being jailed for trying to defend their client comes from a *People's Daily* article in April 1989.

P. 121 The Shanghai entrepreneur says he received a "fair price" for his land, but he admits that he wouldn't have sold if he hadn't been pressured.

P. 122 Larry Yung's real estate purchase was first reported in the *South China Morning Post,* and we subsequently confirmed it by contacting real estate brokers in Hong Kong and Britain.

P. 123 Zhang Yufeng, Wang Hairong, and Nancy Tang (Tang Wensheng) all still live in Beijing. Tang, who now is head of the Railway Ministry's Foreign Affairs Office, never married and shares an apartment with Wang. Zhang lives quietly with her family.

5. THE DYNASTIC CYCLE

P. 129 The only political thinker anywhere in the world who arguably preceded the Duke of Zhou is Hammurabi, the great king of Babylon in the eighteenth or nineteenth century B.C. Hammurabi did not articulate a broad philosophy, but he laid down a sophisticated legal code with some 300 provisions, based on the principle that "the strong shall not injure the weak."

P. 129 The Duke of Zhou quotation is from the *Book of History,* "Prince Shih." The translation here is slightly modified from the one in Clae Waltham, *Shu Ching* (Chicago: Henry Regnery), pp. 183–184; and the one in James Legge, *The Chinese Classics,* vol. 3, pp. 476–477.

P. 129 As for Li Peng's playing the role of the evil eunuch, it is intriguing that Li had a vasectomy so that he could be a model husband and encourage other Chinese men to do the same. At least, that presumably was the intention. But the Chinese press and family planning authorities never publicized the vasectomy, so it was a pointless gesture (Li Peng's wife, Zhu Lin, is in her sixties and clearly not fertile). I wondered sometimes if Li, after getting the vasectomy, hadn't worried that news about the operation would encourage more jokes about him and harm his public position.

P. 132 There are many other parallels with the late Qing dynasty. The central government today, for example, is facing the same struggle as it did under the Qing to keep the provinces in line and to control the military. The

Communist emperors face the same problem of *renzhi* as their predecessors, for power still resides in individuals rather than in institutions. And since individuals have the handicap of dying, the central leadership still faces succession crises and power struggles. The Chinese government today also faces the traditional problem of how to ensure adequate revenue to sustain itself. It confronts the same threats as the Qing did from Christianity, narcotics, cults, and other quarters. Today, as a century ago, the court is frustrated by the difficulties of presenting an appropriate image in the West, and in particular of negotiating with Britain over Hong Kong. The emperor must battle to prevent himself from being deceived and outwitted by flatterers around him, and he must establish secret channels of communication so that he can find out what is really happening beyond the palace walls. *Plus ça change, plus c'est la même chose.*

The secret channels of communication today come in the form of a system of *neibu,* or internal publications, that report on sensitive information or trends as one way of informing the leaders about things that no one dares tell them directly. The *People's Daily,* for example, gets its correspondents to produce a daily *Dongtai Qingyang* for minister-level officials, with unvarnished news and analyses. The New China News Agency produces about a dozen such internal newsletters, and other newspapers and organizations also produce such reports and newsletters, with bad news as well as the standard good news. But even these publications cannot be fully frank. They report that crime is rising, or that peasants are annoyed at corruption, but they never hint that citizens do not like Li Peng. There is even an expression in Chinese, *bao xi, bu bao you,* for the common practice of telling superiors good news but not the bad.

P. 133 The account of Zhang Jingui and his severed penis appeared in *Heilongjiang Legal Daily* and is cited in "Soothsayer's Painful Advice," *South China Morning Post International Weekly,* January 22, 1994, p. 6.

P. 134 The best introduction to Islamic China is Dru C. Gladney, *Muslim Chinese* (Cambridge, MA: Harvard University Press, 1991). A shorter and more recent version is Dru C. Gladney, "The Muslim Face of China," *Current History,* September 1993, pp. 275–280.

P. 138 The figure for narcotics addicts comes from "New Drug to Help Addicts Recover," *China Daily,* October 21, 1993, p. 3.

P. 138 I conducted the interviews with heroin addicts at a rehabilitation center in Yunnan in 1991.

P. 139 To be sure, even in the Communist movement's early days, expressions of ideology were often no more than play-acting. Back in the pre-1949 days when the Communist guerrillas were based in Yanan, the propaganda apparatus once broadcast a speech by Mao in which he used a slogan meaning "From the masses win respect." A party unit in Shanxi Province received a garbled version in which the slogan was rendered "From fog win treasure." Instead of asking for clarification, the editors of the local Communist newspaper wrote an editorial on the profound importance of winning treasure from fog. Michael Lindsay, "The Ideology of Chinese Communism: Causes and Effects," in George Hicks, ed., *The Broken Mirror: China After Tiananmen* (Harlow, U.K.: Longman Group, 1990), pp. 220–221.

P. 142 Deng's trip around Beijing was reported in *Ta Kung Pao*, a Hong Kong newspaper controlled by China. Agence France-Presse dispatch, December 2, 1993.

P. 144 Ma Yuzhen's speech, "China in a Changing World," was delivered on December 17, 1992, at the European-Atlantic Group in England. Text supplied by the Chinese Embassy in London.

P. 146 The best introduction to Tibet is Melvyn C. Goldstein, "The Dragon and the Snow Lion: The Tibet Question," *China Briefing 1990* (New York: Asia Society, 1990), pp. 129–167.

P. 149 The ethnic picture is a bit more complicated than it appears at first. China's fifty-five officially recognized minorities account for just 9 percent of the population. Still, the problem in China is that the government arguably defines ethnicity so as to avoid recognizing some of the biggest minorities. The 91 percent of the population that is nominally Han Chinese—what is normally described as the dominant ethnic group—includes what could be regarded as separate ethnic groups elsewhere.

Cantonese, for example, make up about 5 percent of the population and speak a language that is virtually unintelligible to Mandarin speakers. Cantonese tend to be physically smaller, so that one can often tell a group of Cantonese apart from a group of northerners. Cantonese have a considerable sense of self-identity, in that they complain about northerners and prefer that their children marry other Cantonese. Southerners have also been ruled separately from northerners on and off for much of China's history. The difference between Cantonese and northerners, all told, may be greater than that between Russians and Ukrainians.

The same can be said of other peoples in China, like the Hakka, accounting for 4 percent of the population, and the Hokkienese of southern Fujian, totaling another 4 percent. So we should not necessarily buy the government line that the ethnic minorities live only in remote border areas. The Cantonese may eventually want more autonomy for themselves, just as the Tibetans do now.

It is true, however, that for now the Cantonese and Hakka and Hokkienese fundamentally see themselves as Han. So while the Cantonese or Hokkienese may become more assertive and demand more autonomy from the central government, I doubt that they will seek independence; that will be the demand of the peoples of Xinjiang and Tibet.

The argument that Han nationality embraces several distinct peoples that would normally be called ethnic groups is made in Dru C. Gladney, "Representing Nationality in China: Unveiling Minority/Majority Identities," *Journal of Asian Studies*, forthcoming.

The proportions of the population made up by Cantonese, Hakka, and Hokkienese come from C. Fred Blake, *Ethnic Groups and Social Change in a Chinese Market Town* (Honolulu: University Press of Hawaii, 1981). Blake studied a town in Hong Kong, so he referred to these peoples as "ethnic groups"; the same references within China's borders would be much more striking, since the PRC regards them all as members of the Han ethnic group.

6. THE GOOD EARTH

P. 162 The effort in Henan Province to overthrow the Communists and set up a new dynasty was described in *Democracy and Law,* a Chinese monthly, December 1992. See also *South China Morning Post,* December 27, 1992, p. 1.

P. 168 See Felix Greene, *Awakened China* (Garden City, NY: Doubleday, 1961), esp. pp. 145–153.

P. 171 The figures for the number of people coming out of poverty are in World Bank, "East Asia & Pacific Region Country Briefing Note, China," September 1993.

P. 172 The statistics on rural output come from the *China State Statistical Yearbook.* The figure for the number of farmers employed by rural enterprises was for 1993 and was reported in *China Daily,* January 7, 1994.

P. 172 The New China News Agency reported that in 1993, the average per capita net income for China's 900 million peasants was 880 yuan, about a 2 percent real increase over the previous year, according to the *South China Morning Post International Weekly,* January 15–16, 1994, p. 7. The *Post* added that the statistics, including the average peasant income growth figures of 2.2 percent since 1985, were released by Chen Junsheng, a state councillor. By comparison, during those years the overall economy was growing at about 10 percent per year.

P. 174 The Cai Yutang story was reported in an article in the *Peasants' Daily* on January 31, 1993. Peasants were supposed to cremate their dead, but they often tried to bury them in coffins. In 1993, the official Chinese newspapers began reporting a number of suicides by peasants, which indicated how severe the problem must have been. Usually such reports would not be released without high-level approval, which would be given only if the situation was fairly grave.

P. 176 The government probably can continue to count on peasant soldiers' being willing to fire their machine guns at protesting students. Peasants are particularly good at obeying orders from commanding officers, and even after the Tiananmen crackdown they seemed eager to oblige the generals.

In 1990, for example, Nick went to a village in Henan Province and interviewed an eighteen-year-old peasant named Gao Lu, whose dream was to join the army. He said that if his military unit were summoned to Beijing and ordered to fire on demonstrators, he would pull the trigger.

"We didn't support the rioters," he explained, referring to the Tiananmen demonstrators. "If Beijing is in chaos, then the whole country collapses. The leadership had to stop it. Besides, you have to obey your orders from one notch above. That's your role."

P. 182 The account of the Xiaogan clan battles appeared in the *China Women's News*, July 28, 1993.

P. 182 The Hunan clan clash was reported in *Yangcheng Wan Bao* and in the *South China Morning Post*, September 20, 1993, p. 1.

P. 182 A series of independent articles on clan warfare appeared in the summer and fall of 1993. The *Yangcheng Wan Bao* carried both accounts of the battles in Xiaogan and in Hunan in the summer of 1993.

P. 183 The story about Wu Guang and Chen Sheng is related in Dun J. Li, *The Ageless Chinese: A History* (New York: Charles Scribner's Sons, 1965), p. 103.

P. 183 Wan Li's comments were quoted in the Hong Kong magazine *Contemporary*, April 15, 1993, pp. 13–14.

7. THE ROTTING STATE

P. 184 The Abbé Huc epigraph is from M. Huc, *L'Empire Chinois* (Paris: Librarie de Gaume Frères, 1854), p. 113. The translation is mine.

P. 188 The $10 billion fraud was reported in *China Daily*, June 19, 1993.

P. 189 The best two reports on Wang Zhiqiang were in *People's Daily*, March 11, 1993, and *Xin Wen Zhou Kan*, March 16, 1993. Eight local officials were later arrested for allowing Wang to conduct his fraudulent business; see *China Daily*, September 16, 1993. His conviction was reported in *China Daily*, October 18, 1993.

P. 191 The big rat song is from Wm. Theodore de Bary, *Sources of Chinese Tradition* (New York: Columbia University Press, 1960), p. 15.

P. 197 The Pan Qinghai story was reported by the New China News Agency, January 15, 1993.

P. 201 As for restaurants lacing food with opium poppies, there have been several reports in the official Chinese press. In particular, see *China Daily*, August 7, 1993.

P. 201 The prostitution in Haotou was reported in *Yangcheng Wan Bao*, July 20 and July 21, 1993.

P. 202 Aside from Liu Xiang, the Hong Kong government returned to China at least two other pro-democracy activists who had escaped and sought political asylum. They are Xu Yiruo, whom I describe in Chapter 9, and Yao Kaiwen, a high school teacher from Shanghai. Both were imprisoned after their repatriation. Yao's case is cited in the *South China Morning Post*, October 18, 1993, p. 1.

P. 208 Of the hundreds of Chinese dissidents who escaped after Tiananmen on a modern version of the Underground Railroad, one of the last to get out was a famous writer named Zheng Yi. He fled to the United States with his wife in January 1993, after three and a half years on the run. Zheng, who had been a leader of the Tiananmen demonstrations and was on a most-wanted list, wandered through cities and villages in half a dozen provinces, even though the police were desperately trying to find him.

"Lots of people helped, and I didn't even know many of them beforehand," Zheng, a balding man with immense energy, told me in an interview at a secret location before he reached the United States. His wife, Bei Ming, a writer who had shared his journey and was then sharing his couch, interjected, "People from all walks of life helped us. There were intellectuals, workers, peasants, private businessmen, soldiers, police, journalists, officials, even prostitutes."

Zheng added, "It's a fundamental difference from earlier times. There were about a hundred people who knew my identity—knew my name and knew about the arrest warrant—and yet they helped us."

8. WHERE HAVE ALL THE BABIES GONE?

P. 212 The story about the retarded woman who was sold appeared in *China Youth News* on September 19, 1993. The woman's name was not given. The New China News Agency said on April 14, 1991, that mentally retarded women top the shopping list for rural brides in China. "They are honest, don't run away, and can live in peace with their husbands and yet still give birth to babies," the report said. Prices go as high as 3,000 yuan. The Ministry of Public Health said China had 560,000 mentally retarded women of childbearing age.

P. 218 The 10,000 abductions figure was reported in the *People's Daily*, December 30, 1990.

P. 222 The *Workers' Daily* published a report on February 12, 1993, that said that 60 percent of workers dismissed from 1,175 enterprises surveyed by the All-China Federation of Trade Unions were women.

P. 222 The proportion of full Central Committee members in 1978 who were women was 6.3 percent, precisely the same proportion as were chosen for five-year terms at the Fourteenth Party Congress in the fall of 1992.

P. 222 In 1993 a hard-nosed female negotiator, Wu Yi, was named the head of the Ministry of Foreign Trade and Economic Cooperation, one of the most powerful ministries. While this was a real step ahead for women, the former minister, Li Lanqing, was elevated to oversee the ministry, and he retains an enormous amount of influence.

P. 222 China does not release national statistics on the number of women who are party members, probably because the figure is embarrassingly low. However, some counties have published gender breakdowns of local party members. In a number of these counties, the percentage of women who are local party members is less than 10 percent, and in some cases it has even declined over the past few years.

P. 224 The work on excess female mortality comes from a brilliant article by Sten Johansson, Zhao Xuan, and Ola Nygren, "The Missing Girls of China," *Population and Development Review,* March 1991. For comparison, see an interesting study on female mortality and infanticide in India: Katherine L. Bourne and George M. Walker, Jr., "The Differential Effect of Mothers' Education on Mortality of Boys and Girls in India," *Population Studies,* 1991, pp. 203–219.

P. 227 The history of female infanticide is recounted in Lillian M. Li, "Life and Death in a Chinese Famine," *Comparative Studies in Society and History,* July 1991, esp. pp. 503–504. Li cited historical records indicating that female infanticide was widespread in the aftermath of a devastating flood of the Yellow River in 1935.

P. 227 The popular moral text equating killing infants with urinating while facing the north is in the forthcoming revised edition of *Sources of Chinese Tradition,* by Wm. Theodore de Bary. See also de Bary's *Self and Society in Ming Thought* (New York: Columbia University Press, 1970), p. 347.

P. 229 The sex ratio of 118.5 in 1992 is based on a relatively small data pool and so has a wide margin of error. But the data for 1992 and 1993 combined are much more comprehensive, resulting in a two-year average sex ratio of 116.5 boys to 100 girls. That has a much narrower margin of error. Some of the most sophisticated work on sex ratios in populations has been done by Amartya Sen of Harvard University and separately by Ansley J. Coale of Princeton University. Dr. Coale calculated that 5.2 percent of Chinese females are missing, along with 5.6 percent in India and 7.8 percent in Pakistan. These figures suggest that 30 million Chinese females are missing, along with 22.8 million Indians. Two interesting studies in India found that mortality rates among very young infants were approximately what they should be, but that at later ages girls were more likely to die than they should be. This may be because infants are fed at the breast, which is gender blind, but later they are fed by parents, who favor boys. See Nick's article "Stark Data on Women: 100 Million Are Missing," *The New York Times,* November 5, 1991, sec. C, p. 1.

P. 229 Among the useful articles on missing girls in China are these: Tu Ping, "Sex Ratios and Differential Mortality at Young Ages in China," paper, 1993; Zeng Yi, "An Analysis of the Causes and Implications of the Recent Increases in the Sex Ratio at Birth in China," paper, 1993; Tu Ping, "The Sex Ratios at Birth in China: Results from the 1990 Census," paper, 1992; Ansley J. Coale, "Excess Ratios of Males to Females by Birth Cohort in the Censuses of China, 1953 to 1990, and in Births Reported in the Fertility Surveys, 1982 and 1988," undated mimeo; and the article by Sten Johansson et al. cited earlier.

P. 237 In the summer of 1993, Peng Peiyun reportedly criticized the practice of knocking down homes—after it had been going on for several years. Still, local officials say they have no other means.

P. 238 Nick's story on Li Qiuliang was in *The New York Times,* April 25, 1993, p. 1. The rebuttal was in *China Daily,* June 15, 1993, p. 4.

9. CASTRATING THE THINKERS

P. 242 The poem from Su Dongpo is entitled "On the Birth of His Son." It appears in Arthur Waley, *Translations from the Chinese* (New York: Alfred A. Knopf, 1941).

P. 248 There are a variety of accounts of Fang Xiaoru (in English, most spell his name the old way: Fang Hsiao-ju). The best English-language biography of him is in L. Carrington Goodrich, ed., *Dictionary of Ming Biography, 1368–1644* (New York: Columbia University Press, 1976). In Chinese, the best source is Fang's own writings: *Hsun Chi Chai Chi* (*Xun Zhi Zhai Ji*), an eight-volume collection available in a 1935 printing.

P. 252 When I saw Zhang Wei, we compared notes, and I discovered that I had inadvertently caused him trouble. It happened this way:

At the end of 1990, I was writing a story that mentioned Zhang by name, but he was under house arrest and I knew I could never interview him. Still, I wanted to be able to put a line in my story saying that the authorities refused to allow an interview. So I called up the Tianjin government and requested a meeting with Zhang Wei. As I expected, the authorities responded a couple of days later by saying that Zhang was too busy to see me. I had the line in my story that I needed, showing that I had at least tried to contact him. But meanwhile, Zhang Wei's home telephone suddenly went dead for six weeks. He knew nothing of my request to see him, so he had no idea why this had happened. In retrospect, we figured that the authorities had worried that I might try to call Zhang Wei directly, so they simply cut off his telephone service.

P. 252 The best source on Sima Qian is Burton Watson, *Ssu-Ma Ch'ien: Grand Historian of China* (New York: Columbia University Press, 1958). The quotations come from Sima Qian's letter to his friend Ren Shaoqing, pp. 57–67.

The general whom Sima Qian defended was Li Ling, who lost 4,600 of his 5,000 soldiers while fighting the Xiongnu, a hostile tribe to the north of China. General Li surrendered to the Xiongnu and then worked for them, teaching them something of military science. Hearing this, Emperor Wu executed all members of General Li's family. Li was understandably furious at this action and later refused all invitations to return to China. See Watson, *Ssu-Ma Ch'ien*, p. 217.

P. 255 We were sometimes amazed at how old-time Communists could still believe in the party even when they saw how nasty it could be— even when they themselves were the victims of its cruelty. Officials who had been imprisoned and tortured under Mao sometimes emerged from prison dizzy with gratitude at the party for releasing them. Confronted with the horrors of the Cultural Revolution, they argued that the party's willingness to acknowledge error and change its course was a tribute to its greatness.

Such attitudes are difficult for Westerners to understand, but it may help to draw a parallel with religion. It is a fair comparison because in a country like China, the Communist Party is more like a state church than like a Western political party.

Fervent Christians may be anguished and angry when their children die, but such tragedies do not necessarily destroy their faith. "How can you do this?" they may ask God, just as fervent Communists may wonder in their hearts how the party can be so cruel. Yet ultimately Christians and Communists alike accept that there are some things in life that they cannot understand, and they may emerge from their trials with a faith that is stronger than ever.

P. 264 The woman who divorced Deng was his second wife. His first died in childbirth; his third is Zhuo Lin, his present wife and the mother of all his children.

P. 266 Fei Yuan is discussed in a number of places in an excellent book by George Black and Robin Munro, *Black Hands of Beijing* (New York: John Wiley & Sons, 1993), esp. pp. 111–112 and 272–276.

P. 273 The notion of family members turning each other in for breaking the law is more Communist than Chinese. Confucius himself denounced the practice as antithetical to the family trust and harmony he believed in. By contrast, the Soviet Union made a national hero of Pavel Morozov, a fourteen-year-old boy who in 1932 denounced his father for hiding grain from the state.

10. A ROOM OF ONE'S OWN

P. 276 The Duke of Shao epigraph is cited in Burton Watson, trans., *The Tso Chuan* (New York: Columbia University Press, 1989), p. xvii. In fact the original source is not the *Tso Chuan* itself but the *Guo Yu*.

P. 278 The translation from *Fei Du*, or *A City in Ruins*, is a loose one. For example, to avoid cluttering it with names, I have rendered Tang Wan'r simply as "the mistress." The 518-page *A City in Ruins* was published by Beijing Publishing House in 1993.

P. 281 James Madison's views on the clash of factions are best explained in *The Federalist*, no. 10. For a brilliant analysis of the factors that can help create a civil society, see Gabriel A. Almond and Sidney Verba, *The Civic Culture* (Boston: Little, Brown, 1965).

P. 281 Mussolini's quotation is from Joel Krieger, ed., *The Oxford Companion to Politics of the World* (New York: Oxford University Press, 1993), p. 295.

P. 281 The Tocqueville quotation on associations is from the George Lawrence translation, J. P. Mayer, ed. (Garden City, NY: Doubleday, Anchor Books, 1969), p. 192.

P. 282 For a scholarly look at China's political culture, and the degree to which it could support a democracy, see Andrew J. Nathan and Tianjian Shi, "Cultural Requisites for Democracy in China: Findings from a Survey," *Daedalus*, Spring 1993, pp. 95–123.

P. 282 On education, it is true that most of China's current technocrat leaders were trained in the Soviet Union, so that they were not exposed to the philosophy of democracy. But Mikhail Gorbachev and Boris Yeltsin also emerged from that educational system to encourage a civil society in Russia. These days, many of the children of China's senior leaders are being educated in the West, and they tend to exert some influence on their parents.

P. 284 The translation of an excerpt from Wang Shuo's novel *Hot and Cold, Measure for Measure* comes from Geremie Barmé and Linda Jaivin, *New Ghosts, Old Dreams: Chinese Rebel Voices* (New York: Times Books, 1992), p. 231.

P. 289 Wu Shishen's case may be different from others like it. The government says that the Hong Kong reporter paid him for the text of the speech. It's unclear if that is true.

P. 291 The Chinese expression goes like this: *Shang you zhengce, xia you duice.*

P. 292 Local authorities sometimes are brutal in their efforts to crush the underground Christian church in peasant areas. In March 1993, for example, police attacked a religious meeting in Taoyuan village in Shaanxi Province's Xunyang County. The police focused on five Christians, three men and two women, who were visiting from another county and who were therefore seen as religious provocateurs. The police stripped the three men to the waist and beat them while also forcing all twenty-six parishioners to beat each of them a hundred times as well. By this time the three men were unconscious, and so the police turned to the two women. They were beaten, stripped, and sexually molested. All five were taken to a police station, but it soon became apparent that one of them, a twenty-two-year-old man named Lai Manping, was near death. Afraid that he would die while in custody, the police released him and forced him to leave. Lai struggled along for about six miles before he collapsed and died. This account was smuggled out (and subsequently corroborated after a fashion by the authorities) by a woman named Xu Fang, who was then arrested for informing outsiders about the incident. Xu remains in prison in Shaanxi Province. See *Detained in China and Tibet* (New York: Asia Watch, 1994), pp. 2–3.

P. 294 Lincoln Kaye wrote a terrific article about Zhang Baosheng in *Far Eastern Economic Review*, June 17, 1993, p. 74.

P. 295 On the birth of democracy, Tocqueville said, "Nothing is harder than freedom's apprenticeship. The same is not true of despotism. Despotism often presents itself as the repairer of all the ills suffered, the support of the just rights, defender of the oppressed, and founder of order. Peoples are lulled to sleep by the temporary prosperity it engenders, and when they do wake up, they are wretched." (p. 240).

P. 297 The buggery quotation is from Alexander Hamilton, *A New Account of the East Indies*, 1727, as found in *A Travellers' Dictionary of Quotation*.

P. 298 The Chinese language also has developed similar words about virginity for men. One example is *tongnan*, "child-male," but they are usually used in a joking way.

P. 298 The account of the couple engaging unwittingly in anal sex comes from "Doctor Xiong: A Pioneer in Sexual Problems of Men," *China Daily*, September 3, 1990.

11. MARCHING TOWARD MONEY

This chapter draws generally from several works, including Dwight H. Perkins, *China: Asia's Next Economic Giant?* (Seattle: University of Washington Press, 1986); Nicholas R. Lardy, *China in the World Economy* (Washington, DC: Institute for International Economics, 1994); Mancur Olson, *The Rise and Decline of Nations* (New Haven: Yale University Press, 1982); and *The East Asian Miracle* (Washington, DC: World Bank, 1993). The last is the study mentioned in the chapter. Some of the same themes are discussed in Guy P. Pfeffermann and Andrea Madarassy, "Trends in Private Investment in Developing Countries 1993," International Finance Corporation, 1992.

Foreigners often ask us whether China's economic growth statistics are to be believed. The answer is: for the most part. However, as in many developing countries, there are enormous technical problems in gathering the data. In particular, the value of the output from rural enterprises is often not adjusted downward for the effects of inflation—for example, if a factory produced 1 million yuan worth of sweaters last year and 1.2 million yuan worth this year, that may count as a 20 percent increase in production. In fact, half the increase may be just a function of rising prices. The result is that in periods of high inflation, growth rates may be modestly exaggerated. On the other hand, the underground economy is large and growing rapidly, yet it is not included in the statistics at all. Nobody knows how these competing factors balance out, but the upshot is that official growth figures are probably in the ballpark.

P. 313 The figures for poverty reduction come from a World Bank Study, "East Asia & Pacific Region Country Briefing Note: China," September 1993, pp. 1–2.

P. 316 The figures for China's production of cement, cotton, and other commodities are from *China Daily*, September 30, 1993, p. 1.

P. 316 The figures for the length of time industrializing countries took to double per capita gross domestic product come from *The Economist*, October 16, 1993, p. 84.

P. 317 The figures for the wealth of Chinese in the Philippines and Indonesia come from *The Economist*, November 27, 1993, p. 33.

P. 318 The Lord Byron quotation comes from Lord Byron, *Selected Letters and Journals*, Leslie A. Marchand, ed. (Cambridge, MA: Harvard University Press, Belknap Press, 1982), p. 271.

P. 319 Max Weber made another link between culture and capitalism: He predicted that China would not industrialize because of its Confucian heritage.

P. 320 One reason why the savings rate is high is that it is forced. Chinese are often required to buy government bonds, for example. Another reason why the savings rate is high in China is simply that there traditionally hasn't been much else to do with money. Until very recently, it was difficult to use it to buy real estate or stocks, and also until recently there wasn't much in the stores worth buying.

P. 321 The article on guilds is D. J. MacGowan, M.D., "Chinese Guilds or Chambers of Commerce and Trades Unions," *Journal of the North China Branch of the Royal Asiatic Society*, vol. 21, 1886, article 8. I discovered this article through a reference in Olson, *The Rise and Decline of Nations*.

P. 323 The lack of regulation in China is in some respects an advantage for business. But it also creates uncertainty and adds to the corruption, since officials—in the absence of a clear rule—can demand a payoff for approving something that is neither allowed nor disallowed. This uncertainty and the consequent need to negotiate and make payoffs raise the costs of transactions, so that sometimes they are greater than they might be if there were more regulations.

P. 327 The education enrollment and expenditure figures come from the UNESCO *1991 Statistical Yearbook*.

P. 331 The Shanghai life expectancy and infant mortality figures are for 1993 and come from a June 1994 telephone interview with the Shanghai Foreign Affairs Office. The New York City statistics are for 1992, the latest year available, and come from telephone interviews in June 1994 with the New York City and New York State Health Departments. The point that a Shanghai baby is more likely to become literate than a New York City baby is made by Lawrence H. Summers and Vinod Thomas, "Recent Lessons of Development," *The World Bank Research Observer*, July 1993, p. 241. However, it is worth pointing out that there are difficulties with direct comparisons.

Literacy is so difficult to measure in any society, and there are millions of Chinese who are nominally literate but who cannot read a newspaper. The same is true of the United States, but it is not clear to me that literacy rates are exaggerated to the same degree in both countries. This makes cross-cultural comparisons risky.

P. 332 The figures for cost-effectiveness of various medical treatments come from the World Bank's *World Development Report 1993* (New York: Oxford University Press, 1993), pp. 60–65.

P. 335 It is an open question how much Confucianism lingers in China. The leadership itself now purports to respect Confucius, but Maoism did enormous damage to Confucianism and other traditions, and it is clear that Confucianism is far more feeble in mainland China than in Taiwan or Hong Kong.

12. THE GOD OF WEALTH

P. 338 The epigraph was reported by *Far Eastern Economic Review,* November 4, 1993, p. 11.

P. 342 The contest of riches was described in two articles in *Beijing Evening News,* May 8 and May 9, 1993.

P. 342 The figures for Rolls-Royce sales are from "China Business Review," *South China Morning Post,* August 29, 1993, p. 3.

P. 345 The contribution to industrial output by the *xiangzhen qiye,* or township and village enterprises, is somewhat distorted in the official statistics because those enterprises record production in current prices, while contributions from other sectors are recorded in constant prices. The distortions, however, are only modest.

P. 345 The government officially says that only one-third of state-owned enterprises are profitable, while another third are losing money and the final third breaking even. But enterprises often have poor accounting methods, and they often play games with their profit-and-loss figures to pay as few taxes as possible, so true estimates of how many enterprises make money are difficult.

P. 355 We heard of several cases in which criminals bought their way out of prison. Even the official press described the phenomenon, in an account written by a *People's Court News* reporter in the *Beijing Youth Daily,* July 27, 1993.

P. 360 Foreign investment and trade figures for 1993 were published in *Asian Wall Street Journal Weekly,* February 7, 1994, p. 8. Statistics from 1992 came directly from the Ministry of Foreign Economic Relations, now called the Ministry of Foreign Trade and Economic Cooperation. In fact, foreign joint ventures helped contribute in 1993 to China's trade surplus with the United States of nearly $23 billion.

P. 360 The number of Avon ladies stood at 21,000 as of December 1993, according to a telephone interview by me.

P. 360 Pepsi-Cola's prediction was reported in *The Economist,* January 29, 1994, p. 67.

P. 361 The figures for the total capital inflows and outflows include foreign borrowings.

P. 362 The investment in the Hong Kong parking space was paid as 4 million Hong Kong dollars, as reported in "Government's Pledge to Lower Prices Seems to Damp Property Market Slightly," *Asian Wall Street Journal Weekly*, April 25, 1994, p. 2.

P. 362 The figures on net errors and omissions come from *International Financial Statistics*, published by the International Monetary Fund, IMF, vol. 46, no. 11, November 1993. The estimate for 1993 comes from the World Bank.

Underinvoicing is also a popular method by which Chinese can transfer their money illegally out of the country. To do this, a Chinese exporter simply writes an invoice for a lesser amount, while the importer pays the difference between the invoice amount and the real agreed-upon price to a bank account overseas. It is very difficult to estimate how much money leaks out this way, but it is probably in the billions of U.S. dollars.

13. BLOOD AND IRON

P. 366 The Jack London epigraph comes from a short story, "The Unparalleled Invasion," in *The Strength of the Strong* (New York: Leslie-Judge Company, 1908). The story is set in the 1970s and 1980s, and it describes a Chinese attempt to take over the world by virtue of sheer population growth. Millions spill over the borders in every direction, sweeping aside foreign armies. London tried to shock readers by suggesting that China's population would be greater than the sum of the populations of Caucasian countries, but his estimate—500 million—is still less than half of what China's population has turned out to be.

P. 368 The Lee Kuan Yew quotation is from *International Herald Tribune*, May 20, 1993.

P. 370 The interview with Jiang and Yu was conducted at the end of 1991. Since then both incomes and prices have risen, particularly in yuan terms. The figures I cite, in U.S. dollars, would be a bit higher now.

P. 371 See Lardy, *China and the World Economy*, especially pp. 14–28.

P. 372 The World Bank estimates of Chinese per capita gross domestic product in international prices are in *World Development Report 1993* (New York: Oxford University Press, 1993), p. 296 and technical notes.

P. 373 The World Bank projections for Greater China in the year 2002 are from *International Economic Insights*, May–June 1993, pp. 2–7 and 50.

P. 376 The Union Bank of Switzerland study is cited in *Korea Update*, October 25, 1993, p. 1.

P. 379 The figure of $90 billion for military expenditures was derived as follows. The World Bank's official figure for per capita gross domestic product is $370 in 1991, while its purchasing power parity estimates are $1,680 and $2,040. The average of these is $1,860, which is 5.03 times the official figure. If that multiplier is used with the $18 billion figure for military expenditures, one gets a total of just over $90 billion, in terms of how far the Chinese military budget would go with international dollars. But this calculation may overstate the case. The multiplier for GDP as a whole may be higher than for the military budget in particular. The point is that we have no idea how to measure Chinese military spending. We should, however, and this is an important field for future research.

The officially reported Chinese defense budget, translated into U.S. dollar terms at official exchange rates, dropped in 1994 to $5.9 billion from $7.5 billion in 1993. But the reason for the drop is simply that the Chinese government devalued the yuan. In yuan terms, the military budget rose 22.4 percent in 1994, the biggest increase in any recent year.

P. 380 The report about the MiG-31's is in *Asia Pacific Defence Review,* July 1993, p. 53.

P. 380 An article in an official Beijing newspaper says that in 1987 Chinese naval officers first called for construction of an aircraft carrier "to strengthen China, to develop China's maritime areas, and to achieve the several-decade-long dream of building a Chinese aircraft carrier." "China's Aircraft Carrier Dream," *Beijing Qingnian Bao,* May 6, 1993.

P. 384 Genghis Khan's consideration of wiping out northern China is discussed in David Morgan, *The Mongols* (Oxford: Basil Blackwell, 1986), p. 74. Morgan says the story is "oft-repeated if possibly apocryphal."

P. 385 The Tumen River would have to be dredged to be useful for navigation.

P. 387 The Crestone contract was also troubling because it suggested that China regards the entire South China Sea, not just those areas within twelve miles of each of the islands, as its territorial waters. The contract area is not close to an island, and China does not claim an exclusive economic zone beyond its territorial waters. So the only basis for the contract appears to be that China considers the entire South China Sea its own pond.

For a discussion of the South China Sea, see John W. Garver, "China's Push Through the South China Sea," *China Quarterly,* December 1992, p. 999; *Far Eastern Economic Review,* August 13, 1992, pp. 14 et seq.; Mark J. Valencia, "The Spratly Imbroglio: Context, Complications and a Cooperative Solution," draft manuscript, December 1993.

P. 388 One careful academic study suggests that energy consumption will not soar in the 1990s as much as one might expect, in part because of the effects of conservation and more energy-efficient technologies. The study estimates that the income elasticity of energy consumption in China is approximately 1, substantially less than in other developing countries. That means that as Chinese incomes rise 25 percent, they will use one-quarter more energy—instead of at least 34 percent more energy, which would be the case in developing countries on average. Of course, Chinese energy consumption will still rise with increasing incomes and population; the question is how much. See Chuanlong Tang and Sumner J. La Croix,

"Energy Consumption and Economic Activity in China," *Energy Journal*, vol. 14, no. 4, 1993, pp. 21–36.

P. 388 See Paul M. Kennedy, *Preparing for the Twenty-first Century* (New York: Random House, 1993), pp. 191–192.

P. 389 The figures for amounts of pollutants are from the China National Environmental Protection Agency, "Report on the State of the Environment in China, 1991," pp. 1 and 6. Note that the figures I cite are the sums of the data for regular industry and for township enterprises, which are listed separately.

P. 389 Acid rain is discussed in Michael Richardson, "The Spoils of Growth: Asia Outpaces North America on CO_2," *International Herald Tribune*, June 3, 1992, p. 2.

P. 389 An excellent study of air pollution, and the source of my figures for respiratory disease mortality rates and premature death, is H. Keith Florig, "The Benefits of Air Pollution Reduction in China," draft paper, November 1993. Florig is a fellow at Resources for the Future, Center for Risk Management, in Washington, DC.

P. 390 For global warming, see Philip M. Boffey, "Editorial Notebook: China and Global Warming," *New York Times*, December 8, 1993, p. A16.

P. 390 The best work on China's environment is Vaclav Smil, *China's Environmental Crisis* (Armonk, NY: M. E. Sharpe, 1993). Smil, a professor at the University of Manitoba, has written extensively and engagingly about China's environment and various development issues.

14. TAMING THE DRAGON

P. 392 The egg rolls epigraph is from Harry Harding, *A Fragile Relationship* (Washington, DC: Brookings Institution, 1992), p. 62.

P. 396 The Sunzi quotation is from *Sun Tzu's Art of War*, Tao Hanzhang, ed. (New York: Sterling Publishing, 1987), p. 118.

P. 396 The quotation from Thomas Babington Macaulay comes from Christopher Hibbert, *The Dragon Wakes: China and the West, 1793–1911* (New York: Harper & Row, 1970), p. 142.

P. 397 The Nixon quotations are from *RN, The Memoirs of Richard Nixon* (New York: Grosset & Dunlap, 1978). "The week that changed the world" is from p. 580. The quotation on political philosophy is from p. 562.

P. 397 The Mao quotation on rightists is from Harding, *A Fragile Relationship*, p. 3. Harding's book offers an excellent analysis of Sino-American relations from 1972 to 1992.

P. 398 The statistic on the number of Chinese going abroad in 1993 comes from *China Daily* and was reported in *The Economist*, February 5, 1994, p. 32.

P. 400 The internal document that talks about Taiwan is *Neican Xuanpian,* no. 5, 1993, pp. 18–20.

P. 401 The best account of the Macartney mission and those that followed it is in Alain Peyrefitte, *The Immobile Empire,* Jon Rothschild, trans. (New York: Alfred A. Knopf, 1992). The pronouncement that Russians are a daft race is on p. 503.

P. 401 The Chinese saying "to lift up a rock only to drop it on one's own feet" is the following: *Banqi shitou, za zijide jiao.*

P. 402 The Shambaugh quotation comes from David Shambaugh, *Beautiful Imperialist* (Princeton, NJ: Princeton University Press, 1991), p. 41.

P. 403 The internal document that is quoted on Sino-U.S. relations is *Neican Xuanpian,* no. 36, 1989, pp. 27–29.

P. 405 The Francis Terranova case is discussed in Richard O'Connor, *Pacific Destiny* (Boston: Little, Brown, 1969), p. 54.

P. 408 The Sunzi quotation is from *Sun Tzu's Art of War,* p. 110.

P. 413 The Lee Kuan Yew quotation is from *Far Eastern Economic Review,* November 18, 1993, p. 18.

15. THE TAIWAN OPTION

P. 422 The Chiang Kai-shek epigraph comes from Brian Crozier, *The Man Who Lost China* (New York: Charles Scribner's Sons, 1976), p. 353.

P. 424 The account of the murder of Lin Yi-hsiung's mother and daughter comes largely from an interview with Antonio Chiang, the journalist, who was one of the first people on the scene. Marc J. Cohen, in his book *Taiwan at the Crossroads* (Washington, DC: Asia Resource Center, 1988), says that Lin's mother had tried to report her son's beatings to Amnesty International and hints that this may have been the reason for the murder. Chiang does not believe that the mother tried to contact Amnesty.

P. 426 For a discussion of the 1947 massacre, see Lai Tse-han, Ramon H. Myers, and Wei Wou, *A Tragic Beginning: The Taiwan Uprising of February 28, 1947* (Stanford, CA: Stanford University Press, 1991). The quotation is from Peng Ming-min and appears on pp. 155–156.

P. 426 The case of Hsieh Jui-jen is recounted in Cohen, *Taiwan at the Crossroads,* p. 316.

P. 427 While China has apparently never killed a foreign citizen on foreign soil, and perhaps never killed one of its own citizens on foreign soil, it has kidnapped a few of its own citizens abroad and smuggled them back into China. This is an old tradition, for the Qing dynasty leaders kidnapped Sun Yat-sen in London and hid him in their embassy in preparation for smuggling him back to China. Word got out, and the government was forced to release him.

P. 431 The Mao quotation about fascism comes from Sidney Rittenberg and Amanda Bennett, *The Man Who Stayed Behind* (New York: Simon & Schuster, 1993), p. 272.

P. 431 I first used the phrase *Market-Leninism* in an article in *The New York Times,* September 6, 1993, and since then it has caught on and been used rather frequently.

16. THE NEXT DYNASTY

P. 442 The epigraph comes from W. A. P. Martin, *The Awakening of China* (New York: Doubleday, Page, 1907), p. v.

P. 444 The quotation about a revolution in China comes from Archibald R. Colquhoun, *China in Transformation* (New York: Harper & Brothers, 1912), p. 279.

P. 446 The tale of Confucius and the tigers is found in *Li Ji,* the Book of Rites, one of the Chinese classics. The translation here is very slightly modified from that in *Li Chi: Book of Rites,* James Legge, trans.; Ch'u Chai and Winberg Chai, eds. (New Hyde Park, NY: University Books, 1967), pp. 190–191. The story has given rise to a saying in Chinese—*Ke zheng meng yu hu ye*—meaning that oppressive government is worse than tigers.

P. 447 The infant mortality figures come from the World Bank. The figure of 38 deaths per 1,000 is from 1991, the latest year for which data are available. Such statistics are not entirely reliable, however, in part because peasants who give birth at home often do not report a death if the baby dies within the first few days. Instead they report a stillbirth. The reporting has improved over the last decade, in part because more babies are born in the hospitals, where better records are kept. So in fact the decline in infant mortality may be even greater than the statistics show, simply because a decade ago there were more deaths that were never reported.

P. 447 The government does, of course, get some of the credit for the economic boom. The leaders engineered an agricultural boom in the early 1980s by allowing peasants to divide up the communes. They also raised prices paid to farmers by 25 percent. The authorities sensibly devalued exchange rates, encouraged foreign investment, weaned city dwellers of subsidies, and set up markets for stocks, bonds, and foreign exchange. The leaders invested in physical infrastructure and human capital, promoted rural enterprises, and poked state enterprises to make them a bit more efficient.

P. 452 The Edgar Snow quotation is from Edgar Snow, *The Other Side of the River: Red China Today* (New York: Random House, 1961), p. 619. Snow offered a withering criticism of Joseph Alsop, the columnist, for stating that "the population of China is starving." In retrospect, Alsop clearly was right.

Even many years later, foreign apologists for China showed an astonishing capacity to overlook that tragedy. A particularly inane book, *China as a Model of Development,* by Al Imfeld (New York: Orbis Books, 1977, p. 151), claimed fifteen years after the fact that despite bad crops "during these upheavals China did not suffer any famine."

P. 452 The Étienne quotation comes from Snow, *The Other Side of the River*, pp. 782–783, which cites *Le Monde*, December 12, 1961. The *World-Telegram* article, also cited by Snow, appeared on July 31, 1962. The *Times* quotation appeared April 18, 1962, in an editorial entitled "China's New Priorities."

P. 453 The Lord Boyd-Orr quotation comes from *Facts on File*, vol. 19, no. 968, May 14–20, 1959, p. 162. Contrary to *Facts on File* usage, the name should be hyphenated.

P. 453 Chris Billing, a Voice of America reporter in Beijing, pointed us toward the story of the loan signing in Rome.

P. 455 Martin Luther King, Jr., apparently used the old woman's prayer in a number of speeches and sermons. Archivists at the King Center in Atlanta said that they were familiar with the prayer and that they believed Dr. King may have used it on many occasions with slightly different wording. They were, however, unable to locate it in the text of any major address by Dr. King.

P. 456 The Huang Yanpei conversation is from official Communist Party records, as recounted in a 1991 television documentary on the twentieth century and later published in the *People's Daily*. Mao, to be sure, was not talking about Western-style democracy as the solution to the problem of the dynastic cycle. Rather, he meant the "people's democratic dictatorship," or Leninist democratic centralism. He thought of democracy not as a system based on competitive elections but rather as one in which officials cultivated close ties with the masses and held meetings in which they invited colleagues to criticize them. Even that limited vision of democracy was never implemented.

ACKNOWLEDGMENTS

Before we set off for China, Abe Rosenthal gave us these words of advice: "Don't pay attention to what has been written before you. Just go out there and write what you see and hear." This book is a product of what we saw and heard for five years in China. It is informed by the voices of anger, frustration, optimism, and delight of thousands of Chinese with whom we talked—in movie theaters, restaurants, parks, offices, and homes. Without them, and the courage they showed in meeting us, this book could never have been written.

This book came to fruition, however, only because of the opportunities we received from our editors at *The New York Times*. They hired us, sent us to Beijing, and then gave us a leave of absence so we could complete this work. Abe Rosenthal and John Lee hired Nick, and then Max Frankel and Joe Lelyveld took the rare—and much appreciated—step of hiring Sheryl abroad without first bringing her back to work for a stint in New York. Newspapers and other businesses often agonize about transfers for career couples, and we were a bit of an experiment when *The Times* hired us both as full-time correspondents. Despite occasional threats to send one of us to West Africa and the other to Latin America, our editors have been enormously supportive of our efforts to maintain what the Chinese call a *fuqi dian,* a mom-and-pop shop.

Joe Lelyveld and other editors have also been a constant source of excellent, and often unexpected, advice. During the Tiananmen period, when we were working almost around the clock and other editors were demanding all kinds of stories, we planned to stay up during May and June and then sleep through July. Joe shepherded us through the crisis and offered this recommendation: "Go get some sleep." He kept insisting, "You can't work properly if you haven't had any rest." It was the best advice of all. A warm and special thanks also to Bernie Gwertzman, and others on the *Times* Foreign Desk, for providing counsel, friendship, and a bit of adult supervision. Aside from Bernie, those who rescued us from our own errors are Steve Weisman, Kevin McKenna, Tom Feyer, Jeanne Pinder, Ed Marks, Tom Kuntz, Dean Toda, and many editors, copy editors, and clerks. No one could be woken up at 4:00 A.M. by wiser or more wonderful people. Tom Feyer also read the entire manuscript and offered many useful suggestions of substance and style; he was the only person who noticed that we had misspelled Kyrgyzstan. On the picture desk, Paula Giannini and Nancy Buirski led the archeological explorations of *The Times*'s filing system to uncover most of the photographs in this book.

We also appreciated the support of Arthur and Punch Sulzberger of *The Times*. When China refused to accredit both of us as *Times* reporters, it was Punch who came up with the idea of getting Sheryl nominal accreditation for a *Times*-owned entity such as the New York Times News Service. It worked beautifully.

In China we benefited from an extremely helpful office staff in *The Times* bureau. At various times, those people included Eleanor Laquian, Catherine Hoy, and Y. W. Wang; they maintained our files and sustained our sanity. Xu Pei, Jane Zha, Henry Ho, C. L. Duan, and others were also of enormous help. Our last two interns in the bureau, Ben Read and June Shih, assisted us as the book got under way. Xu Pei, now living in the United States, read the entire manuscript and offered excellent suggestions.

We owe a special debt to Richard Halloran and Mike Oksenberg of the East-West Center in Hawaii for providing each of us with a visiting fellowship that allowed us to spend a month in Beijing and almost two months at the center. We couldn't have found a warmer, friendlier place to work, and Richard—along with his wife, Fumiko Mori Halloran—read our entire manuscript and offered many valuable suggestions. Another visiting fellow, Rick Hornik of *Time* magazine, also read an early draft and gave us a very useful critique. Chris Millward, a talented and dedicated graduate student, provided us with invaluable research assistance while we were at the center.

The Ford Foundation provided a grant that enabled us to stay in Beijing for two additional months, a period when we gathered some of our best research material. We're very grateful to Peter Harris and the other Ford Foundation officers, whose programs do a tremendous amount of good in China. During some of that time in Beijing, we house-sat for John Kohut of the *South China Morning Post* and Jake Haselkorn of ABC News. Without their apartments we wouldn't have been able to get nearly so much done, and we—especially Gregory—thank them for their hospitality.

It's a bit more delicate to thank the innumerable Chinese who helped us in one way or another, partly because we don't want to reward them by getting them in trouble. Our Chinese friends ran the gamut from young peasants with callused hands to the family members of three present or past Politburo members, and everybody in between. It was these friends, hundreds of them, who taught us what we know about China. They took all the risks and got none of the credit, and we will always cherish and respect them. It is impossible to begin to thank those who deserve it, but we would especially like to tip our hats to Gao Xiqing and Wang Boming, who pioneered the establishment of China's stock market; Zhang Weiguo, one of China's best journalists; Amy, James, and Rose, who dared see us even when the going was rough; P. S. Tang and Colombo, fine teachers and warm friends; and the late Xu Yaoping, 1959–1993. Several others deserve to be on this list but asked not to be named for fear of getting into trouble.

The foreign community in Beijing was a constant source of information and insight, and we learned a great deal from our fellow reporters. Kazuyoshi Nishikura from Kyodo and Kathy Wilhelm and her colleagues at the Associated Press were particularly helpful, but we benefited from contact with nearly all the correspondents in Beijing. Special thanks go to Manuel Ceneta, a first-rate Agence France-Presse photographer, who took time out from his busy schedule to shoot nine rolls of pictures of us for use in this book. Another photographer, Fumiyo Asahi, generously gave us pictures for a couple of chapters, while Adam Stoltman provided the photo of Liu Xiang.

We owe thanks to the many foreign diplomats who shared their thoughts with us, particularly those from Japan and the United States. For all our criticisms of the United States Embassy, we encountered many exceptionally talented and helpful American diplomats. Ambassador Jim Lilley was superb, and so was the press officer in our first few years, Sheridan Bell. They helped Sheryl get her credentials restored in 1990, and so did Bernie Gwertzman and Bill Safire from *The Times* during their trips to Beijing. Later, we benefited from the comments and criticisms of two former Beijing-based American diplomats, Lauren and Jim Moriarty, who read drafts of parts of this book, particularly those relating to the Chinese economy.

Taiwan is a journalist's dream, in that access to senior officials is relatively easy. We owe a special thanks to Marvin Ho, the head of the Taipei Language Institute, who not only helped us learn Chinese but also introduced us to many people throughout Taiwan. One of them was Zhang Xueliang, the "Young Marshal" who kidnapped Chiang Kai-shek in 1936 to force the Nationalists to cooperate with the Communists in fighting the Japanese, and who then spent nearly half a century under house arrest. Zhang kindly lent his nonagenarian fingers to write the characters for each of our Chinese names. Because Zhang is a hero to many on both sides of the Taiwan Strait, we used his calligraphy on our name cards; it was a great conversation piece, and the only problem was that Chinese sometimes wanted to spend an entire interview asking about Zhang instead of letting us get in a few questions.

There are many other Americans, particularly scholars, who helped us while we were in China or afterward as we wrote this book. Among those who helped with the book are Christine Wong of the University of California at Santa Cruz, Ted de Bary of Columbia University, Kwang-ching Liu of the University of California at Davis, Daniel Kwok of the University of Hawaii, and Yasheng Huang of the University of Michigan. Christine and Yasheng kindly read and commented on several chapters.

The Chinese calligraphy in this book was written with the deft brush-strokes of Chingan Tang. Among those who helped with the calligraphy and translations are Bo Yang, Fei Wang, and especially Michael Tang, who read the entire manuscript and gave us very good suggestions.

Mort Janklow and Anne Sibbald, of Janklow & Nesbit Associates, are wonderful agents and advisers. Times Books, with Peter Osnos as its head, has been a home as well as a house. At Times Books, we are especially grateful to Paul Golob, whose guidance, vision, and sharp pen have helped shape this book.

We owe the biggest debt of all to our families: Ladis and Jane Kristof of Yamhill, Oregon, and David, Alice, Darrell, and Sondra WuDunn in New York City. They read the manuscript and offered substantive and stylistic suggestions, as well as general advice, moral support, and pots of coffee. And thanks to Gregory, when you can read this, for continually running up to us as we were at our computers and reminding us of the joy and wonder that is life.

After all these thanks, it may seem as if we didn't do anything ourselves. We did: The oversimplifications and absurd misinterpretations are our own. The outright mistakes and distortions, however, are not ours. They are our spouse's.

INDEX